UNIDIR
United Nations Institute for Disarmament Research
Geneva

Disarmament and
Conflict Resolution Project

Managing Arms in Peace Processes:
Croatia and Bosnia-Herzegovina

Paper: *Barbara Ekwall-Uebelhart* and *Andrei Raevsky*
Questionnaire Analysis: *LTCol J.W. Potgieter*,
Military Expert DCR Project

Project funded by: the Ford Foundation, the United States Institute of Peace, the Winston Foundation, the Ploughshares Fund, the John D. and Catherine T. MacArthur Foundation; and the governments of Germany, the Netherlands, Norway, the United Kingdom, the United States of America, Finland, France, Austria, the Federal Republic of Brazil, the Republic of Malta, the Republic of Argentina, and the Republic of South Africa.

D0862562

UNITED NATIONS
New York and Geneva, 1996

NOTE

The designations employed and the presentation of the material in this publication do not imply the expression of any opinion whatsoever on the part of the Secretariat of the United Nations concerning the legal status of any country, territory, city or area, or of its authorities, or concerning the delimitation of its frontiers or boundaries.

*
* *

The views expressed in this paper are those of the authors and do not necessarily reflect the views of the United Nations Secretariat.

UNIDIR/96/7

UNITED NATIONS PUBLICATION
Sales No. GV.E.96.0.6
ISBN 92-9045-110-6

Table of Contents

Previous DCR Project Publications

Managing Arms in Peace Processes: Somalia

Managing Arms in Peace Processes: Rhodesia/Zimbabwe

Preface

Under the headline of Collective Security, UNIDIR is conducting a major project on Disarmament and Conflict Resolution (DCR). The project examines the utility and modalities of disarming warring parties as an element of efforts to resolve intra-state conflicts. It collects field experiences regarding the demobilization and disarmament of warring factions; reviews 11 collective security actions where disarmament has been attempted; and examines the role that disarmament of belligerents can play in the management and resolution of internal conflicts. The 11 cases are UNPROFOR (Yugoslavia), UNOSOM and UNITAF (Somalia), UNAVEM (Angola), UNTAC (Cambodia), ONUSAL (El Salvador), ONUCA (Central America), UNTAG (Namibia), UNOMOZ (Mozambique), Liberia, Haiti and the 1979 Commonwealth operation in Rhodesia.

Being an autonomous institute charged with the task of undertaking independent, applied research, UNIDIR keeps a certain distance from political actors of all kinds. The impact of our publications is predicated on the independence with which we are seen to conduct our research. At the same time, being a research institute within the framework of the United Nations, UNIDIR naturally relates its work to the needs of the Organization. Inspired by the Secretary General's report on "New Dimensions of Arms Regulation and Disarmament in the Post-Cold War Era",[1] the DCR Project also relates to a great many governments involved in peace operations through the UN or under regional auspices. Last but not least, comprehensive networks of communication and co-operation have been developed with UN personnel having field experience.

Weapons-wise, the disarmament of warring parties is mostly a matter of light weapons. These weapons account for as much as 90% of the casualties in many armed conflicts. UNIDIR recently published a paper on this subject (Small Arms and Intra-State Conflicts, UNIDIR Paper No 34, 1995). The Secretary General's appeal for stronger efforts to control small arms - to promote "micro disarmament"[2] - is one which UNIDIR will continue to attend to in the framework of the DCR Project.

This report on the United Nations Protection Force in former Yugoslavia (UNPROFOR) deals with one of the most controversial and complex peace

---

[1] Document A/C.1/47/7, No 31, 23 October 1992.
[2] Document 50/60-S/1995/1, 3 January 1995.

operations in the 1990's. No peace operation has been covered by the media and discussed in public as much as this one. Still, the complexities on the ground and the great variety of interests and perceptions at play have left confusion as much as clarity. The report does not try to simplify things. Thus, it does not make for easy reading. It is thoroughly researched, and hopefully, the interested reader will be left with a clear, albeit complex, picture of what UNPROFOR was and was not about.

The report focuses on the demilitarization components of the UNPROFOR peace mission in Croatia and Bosnia-Herzegovina between 1992 and 1995. Special attention is given to three specific areas of UNPROFOR operations: Sector West in Croatia and Sarajevo and Srebrenica in Bosnia. The analysis was written by Barbara Ekwall-Uebelhart and Andrei Raevsky while staying at UNIDIR in the winter and spring of 1995. The text has been reviewed by James Schear from the Carnegie Endowment for Democracy, Gerard Fischer from UNCTAD, General Carlos Zabala, Argentine Military Attaché to the United States and Canada, and by the Project staff. The analysis also benefited from the visiting experts lecture series which included, in this case, General Jean Cot, General Satish Nambiar, Captain Gilles Casalta and Ms. Svetlana Jovic. This report is the third in a series of UNIDIR publications on the disarmament dimension of peace operations. There will be a Report on each of the cases mentioned above.

The authors of the case studies have drawn on the professional advice and assistance of military officers intimately acquainted with peace operations. They were Col. Roberto Bendini (Argentina), Lt. Col. Ilkka Tiihonen (Finland) and Lt. Col. Jakkie Potgieter (South Africa). UNIDIR is grateful to all of them for their invaluable contributions to clarifying and solving the multitude of questions and problems we put before them.

Since October 1994, the DCR Project has developed under the guidance of Virginia Gamba. Under her able leadership, the project has not only become the largest in UNIDIR history: its evolution has been a source of inspiration for the entire Institute.

UNIDIR takes no position on the views or conclusions expressed in this report. They are Ms. Ekwall-Uebelhart's and Mr. Raevsky's. My final word of thanks goes to them: UNIDIR has been happy to have such resourceful and dedicated collaborators.

Sverre Lodgaard
Director, UNIDIR

Acknowledgements

The DCR Project takes this opportunity to thank the many foundations and governments who have contributed with finance and personnel to the setting up and evolution of the research associated with the Project. Among our contributors the following deserve a special mention and our deep appreciation: the Ford Foundation, the United States Institute of Peace, the Winston Foundation, the Ploughshares Fund, the John D. and Catherine T. MacArthur Foundation, and the governments of Germany, the Netherlands, Norway, the United Kingdom, the United States of America, Finland, France, Austria, the Federal Republic of Brazil, the Republic of Malta, the Republic of Argentina, and the Republic of South Africa.

Project Introduction

Disarmament and Conflict Resolution

The global arena's main preoccupation during the Cold War centered on the maintenance of international peace and stability between states. The vast network of alliances, obligations and agreements which bound nuclear superpowers to the global system, and the memory of the rapid internationalization of disputes into world wars, favored the formulation of national and multinational deterrent policies designed to maintain a stability which was often confused with immobility. In these circumstances, the ability of groups within states to engage in protest and to challenge recognized authority was limited.

The end of the Cold War in 1989, however, led to a relaxing of this pattern, generating profound mobility within the global system. The ensuing break-up of alliances, partnerships, and regional support systems brought new and often weak states into the international arena. Since weak states are susceptible to ethnic tensions, secession, and outright criminality, many regions are now afflicted by situations of violent intra-state conflict.

Intra-state conflict occurs at immense humanitarian cost. The massive movement of people, their desperate condition, and the direct and indirect tolls on human life have, in turn, generated pressure for international action.

Before and since the Cold War, the main objective of the international community when taking action has been the maintenance and/or recovery of stability. The main difference between then and now, however, is that then, the main objective of global action was to maintain stability in the *international* arena, whereas now it is to stabilize *domestic* situations. The international community assists in stabilizing domestic situations in five different ways: by facilitating dialogue between warring parties, by preventing a renewal of internal armed conflict, by strengthening infrastructure, by improving local security, and by facilitating an electoral process intended to lead to political stability.[1]

The United Nations is by no means the only organization that has been requested by governments to undertake these tasks. However, the reputation of the

---

[1] James S. Sutterlin, "Military Force in the Service of Peace", *Aurora Papers*, No 18, Ottawa, Canada: Canadian Centre for Global Security, 1993, p.13.

United Nations as being representative of all states and thus as being objective and trustworthy has been especially valued, as indicated by the greater number of peace operations in which it is currently engaged. Before 1991, the UN peace operations' presence enhanced not only peace but also the strengthening of democratic processes, conciliation among population groups, the encouragement of respect for human rights, and the alleviation of humanitarian problems. These achievements are exemplified by the role of the UN in Congo, southern Lebanon, Nicaragua, Namibia, El Salvador, and to a lesser extent in Haiti.

Nevertheless, since 1991 the United Nations has been engaged in a number of simultaneous, larger, and more ambitious peace operations such as those in Angola, Bosnia and Herzegovina, Croatia, Mozambique and Somalia. It has also been increasingly pressured to act on quick-flaring and horrendously costly explosions of violence, such as the one in Rwanda in 1994. The financial, personnel, and timing pressure on the United Nations to undertake these massive short-term stabilizing actions has seriously impaired the UN's ability to ensure long-term national and regional stability. The UN has necessarily shifted its focus from a supporting role, in which it could ensure long-term national and international stability, to a role which involves obtaining quick peace and easing humanitarian pressures immediately. But without a focus on peace defined as longer-term stability, the overall success of efforts to mediate and resolve intra-state conflict will remain in question.

This problem is beginning to be recognized and acted upon by the international community. More and more organizations and governments are linking success to the ability to offer non-violent alternatives to a post-conflict society. These alternatives are mostly of a socio-political/economic nature, and are national rather than regional in character. As important as these linkages are to the final resolution of conflict, they tend to overlook a major source of instability: the existence of vast amounts of weapons widely distributed among combatant and non-combatant elements in societies which are emerging from long periods of internal conflict. The reason why weapons themselves are not the primary focus of attention in the reconstruction of post-conflict societies is because they are viewed from a political perspective. Action which does not award importance to disarmament processes is justified by invoking the political value of a weapon as well as the way the weapon is used by a warring party, rather than its mere existence and availability. For proponents of this action, peace takes away the reason for using the weapon and, therefore, renders it harmless for the post-conflict reconstruction process. And yet, easy availability of weapons can, and does, militarize societies in general. It also destabilizes regions that are affected by unrestricted trade of light weapons between borders.

There are two problems, therefore, with the international community's approach to post-conflict reconstruction processes: on the one hand, the international community, under pressure to react to increasingly violent internal conflict, has put a higher value on peace in the short-term than on development and stability in the long-term; and, on the other hand, those who *do* focus on long-term stability have put a higher value on the societal and economic elements of development than on the management of the primary tools of violence, i.e., weapons.

UNIDIR's DCR Project and the Management of Arms during Peace Processes (MAPP)

The DCR Project aims to explore the predicament posed by UN peace operations which have recently focused on short-term needs rather than long-term stability. The Project is based on the premise that the control and reduction of weapons during peace operations can be a tool for ensuring stability. Perhaps more than ever before, the effective control of weapons has the capacity to influence far-reaching events in national and international activities. In this light, the management and control of arms could become an important component for the settlement of conflicts, a fundamental aid to diplomacy in the prevention and deflation of conflict, and a critical component of the reconstruction process in post-conflict societies.

Various instruments can be used to implement weapons control. For example, instruments which may be used to support preventive diplomacy in times of crisis include confidence-building measures, weapons control agreements, and the control of illegal weapons transfers across borders.[2] Likewise, during conflict situations, and particularly in the early phases of a peace operation, negotiations conducive to lasting peace can be brought about by effective monitoring and the establishment of safe havens, humanitarian corridors, and disengagement sectors. Finally, after the termination of armed conflict, a situation of stability is required for post-conflict reconstruction processes to be successful. Such stability can be

---

[2] Fred Tanner, "Arms Control in Times of Conflict", Project on Rethinking Arms Control, Center for International and Security Studies at Maryland, PRAC Paper 7, October 1993.

facilitated by troop withdrawals, the demilitarization of border zones, and effective disarmament, demobilization and demining.

Nevertheless, problems within the process of controlling weapons have cropped up at every stage of peace operations, for a variety of reasons. In most cases, initial control of arms upon the commencement of peace operations has not generally been achieved. This may be due to the fact that political negotiations necessary to generate mandates and missions permitting international action are often not specific enough on their disarmament implementation component. It could also be that the various actors involved interpret mandates in totally different ways. Conversely, in the specific cases in which peace operations have attained positive political outcomes, initial efforts to reduce weapons to manageable levels - even if achieved - tend to be soon devalued, since most of the ensuing activities center on the consolidation of post-conflict reconstruction processes. This shift in priorities from conflict resolution to reconstruction makes for sloppy follow-up of arms management operations. Follow-up problems, in turn, can result in future threats to internal stability. They also have the potential to destabilize neighboring states due to the uncontrolled and unaccounted-for mass movement of weapons that are no longer of political or military value to the former warring parties.

The combination of internal conflicts with the proliferation of light weapons has marked peace operations since 1990. This combination poses new challenges to the international community and highlights the fact that a lack of consistent strategies for the management of arms during peace processes (MAPP) reduces the effectiveness of ongoing missions and diminishes the chances of long-term national and regional stability once peace is agreed upon.

The case studies undertaken by the DCR Project highlight a number of recurrent problems that have impinged on the control and reduction of weapons during peace operations. Foremost among these are problems associated with the establishment and maintenance of a secure environment early in the mission, and problems concerned with the lack of coordination of efforts among the various groups involved in the mission. Many secondary complications would be alleviated if these two problems areas were understood differently. The establishment of a secure environment, for example, would make the warring parties more likely to agree on consensual disarmament initiatives. Likewise, a concerted effort at weapons control early in the mission would demonstrate the international community's determination to hold the parties to their original peace agreements and cease-fire arrangements. Such a demonstration of resolve would make it more difficult for these agreements to be broken once the peace operation was underway.

The coordination problem applies both to international interactions and to the components of the peace operation. A peace process will be more likely to succeed if there is co-operation and coordination between the international effort and the nations which immediately neighbor the stricken country. But coordination must not simply be present at the international level; it must permeate the entire peace operation as well. To obtain maximum effect, relations must be coordinated among and within the civil affairs, military, and humanitarian groups which comprise a peace operation. A minimum of coordination must also be achieved between intra- and inter-state mission commands, the civil and military components at strategic, operational and tactical levels, and the humanitarian aid organizations working in the field; these components must cooperate with each other if the mission is to reach its desired outcome. If problems with mission coordination are overcome, many secondary difficulties could also be avoided, including lack of joint management, lack of unity of effort, and lack of mission and population protection mechanisms.

Given these considerations, the Project believes that the way to implement peace, defined in terms of long-term stability, is to focus not just on the sources of violence (such as social and political development issues) but also on the material vehicles for violence (such as weapons and munitions). Likewise, the implementation of peace must take into account *both* the future needs of a society and the elimination of its excess weapons, *and also* the broader international and regional context in which the society is situated. This is because weapons that are not managed and controlled in the field will invariably flow over into neighboring countries, becoming a problem in themselves. Thus, *the establishment of viable stability requires that three primary aspects be included in every approach to intra-state conflict resolution: (1) the implementation of a comprehensive, systematic disarmament program as soon as a peace operation is set-up; (2) the establishment of an arms management program that continues into national post-conflict reconstruction processes; and (3) the encouragement of close cooperation on weapons control and management programs between countries in the region where the peace operation is being implemented.*

In order to fulfill its research mission, the DCR Project has been divided into four phases. These are as follows: (1) the development, distribution, and interpretation of a *Practitioners' Questionnaire on Weapons Control, Disarmament and Demobilization during Peacekeeping Operations*; (2) the development and publication of case studies on peace operations in which disarmament tasks constituted an important aspect of the wider mission; (3) the organization of a series of workshops on policy issues; and (4) the publication of policy papers on substantive issues related to the linkages between the management of arms during peace processes (MAPP) and the settlement of conflict.

Between September 1995 and March 1996, the Project foresees four sets of publications. The first of these will involve eleven case studies, covering peace operations in Somalia, Rhodesia/Zimbabwe, Bosnia/Croatia, Central America (ONUCA and ONUSAL), Cambodia, Angola, Namibia, Mozambique, Liberia and Haiti. The second set of publications will include nine policy papers, addressing topics such as Security Council Procedures, Mandate Specificity, Doctrine, Rules of Engagement, Coercive versus Consensual Arms Control and Demobilization Processes, Consensus, Intelligence and Media, and Training. A third set of publications will involve three papers on the relationship between arms and conflict in the region of Southern Africa. The last of the Project's published works will be an overarching policy paper summarizing the conclusions of the research and delineating recommendations based on the Project's findings.

Taking into account the existing material on some of the case studies, the DCR project has purposefully concentrated on providing more information on the disarmament and arms control components of the relevant international peace operations than on providing a comprehensive political and diplomatic account of each case.

The first volume published by the DCR Project examined the way in which three international peace processes (UNOSOM, UNITAF, and UNOSOM II) struggled with the issue of controlling and managing light weapons in Somalia. The second volume focused on the Commonwealth Monitoring Force (CMF) in Rhodesia. This volume examines the way the UN mission in Croatia and Bosnia-Herzegovina (UNPROFOR) dealt with problems of arms control and disarmament in three specific instances: Sector West (Croatia), Sarajevo and Srebrenica from April 1992 to February 1995. The volume is divided into three sections. The first section analyzes the evolution of the situation in the three areas with specific reference to arms control and disarmament needs and actions. The second section presents a full bibliography of primary and secondary material used in the making of this study. Finally, the third section provides a summary of the responses regarding this mission which were obtained through the Project's own *Practitioners' Questionnaire on Weapons Control, Disarmament and Demobilization during Peacekeeping Operations.*

My special thanks go to the researchers for this case study, Barbara Ekwall-Uebelhart and Andrei Raevsky, the compiler of the questionnaire responses, Col. Roberto Bendini, and the analyst that interpreted the responses and wrote the commentaries, Lt Col Jan Willem Potgieter. I also want to thank the project staff at UNIDIR, especially our Information Officer, Kent Highnam; our Specialized Publications Editor, Cara Cantarella; our Assistant Editor, Lara Bernini; and the interns who helped compile and edit the Questionnaire Analysis Report of this publication: Mira Berglund, Véronique Christory, Mike MacKinnon, Madhukar Murthi, Albena Petrova, Glen Rangwala, and Elisabeth Sancery. We would also like to thank Ms. Claudia Querner, UNIDIR Junior Professional Officer, for her assistance to the editors.

Virginia Gamba
Project Director
Geneva, August 1995

Disarmament and Conflict Resolution Project

Project Staff

Project Director
Virginia Gamba

Primary Project Researcher
Andrei Raevsky

Information Officer
Kent Highnam

Specialized Publications Editor
Cara Cantarella

Assistant Editor
Lara Bernini

Former Yugoslavia Production Assistance

Camera-Ready Production
Anita Blétry, Specialized Secretary (Publications)

Publication Consultant
Claudia Querner, Junior Professional Officer

French-English Translation
Véronique Christory, Intern

Editorial Assistance
Kent Highnam, Information Officer
Mira Berglund, Intern
Mike MacKinnon, Intern
Madhukar Murthi, Intern
Albena Petrova, Intern
Glen Rangwala, Intern
Elisabeth Sancery, Intern

List of Acronyms

APC	Armored Personnel Carrier
BiH	Bosnian Muslim Army
CSCE	Conference on Security and Cooperation in Europe, now the Organization on Security and Cooperation in Europe
EC	European Community
EU	European Union
ECCY	European Community Conference on Yugoslavia
ECMM	European Community Monitoring Mission
FAE	Fuel-Air Explosives
FRY	Federal Republic of Yugoslavia (Serbia and Montenegro)
HDZ	Hrvatska Demokratska Zajednica (Croatian Democratic Union)
HQ	Headquarters
HV	Hrvatska Vojska (Croatian Army)
HVO	Hrvatsko Vijece Odbrane (Bosnian Croat Army)
ICFY	International Conference on the Former Yugoslavia
ICRC	International Committee of the Red Cross
JNA	Jugoslovenska Narodna Armija (Yugoslav People's Army)
NATO	North Atlantic Treaty Organization
PDWB	Popular Defense of Western Bosnia (Abdic Forces)
ROE	Rules of Engagement
RSK	Republika Srpske Krajine (Republic of Serbian Krajina)
SRY	Socialist Republic of Yugoslavia
TDF	Territorial Defense Forces
TOW	Tube-launched, Optically-tracked, Wire-guided
UN	United Nations
UNCIVPOL	United Nations Civilian Police
UNHCR	United Nations High Commissioner for Refugees
UNMO	United Nations Military Observer
UNPA	United Nations Protected Area
UNPROFOR	United Nations Protection Force
VRS	Bosnian Serb Army
VSK	Krajina Serb Army
YA	Yugoslav Army

Part I:

Case Study

Chapter 1
Introduction

1.1. Background to the Conflict

A product of the First World War, Yugoslavia broke up as a result of the end of the Cold War. The Constitution of 1974, combining elements of federalism and confederalism, proved to be devastating for the country.[1] Tito's death in 1980 and the power vacuum it created marked the beginning of a decade of deterioration for Yugoslavia. Mutually reinforcing economic and institutional crises were accompanied by the emergence of nationalist and separatist movements. During the 1980's, the relatively successful Yugoslav economy came under increasing strain, in part, as a result of mismanagement. Nationalist movements gained strength throughout the country. In 1986, a group of intellectuals at the Academy of Arts and Sciences in Belgrade published a memorandum calling for a Serbian nationalist awakening. Partly in response to growing Serbian nationalism and fueled by growing anticommunist sentiment, nationalist independence movements began to gain momentum in Slovenia and Croatia.

In January 1990, the Communist party, a key institution for the preservation of Yugoslavian unity, collapsed when the Slovene delegation walked out of a party congress. The multiparty elections that took place a few months later brought nationalist hardliners to power in all republics, "snuffing out the very flame of democracy that the elections had kindled".[2] At this time, Slovenia and Croatia began to pursue parallel foreign and economic policies, and referenda in favor of independence were held in Slovenia (December 1990) and in Croatia (May 1991).

A constitutional crisis precipitated the final break. According to the system of rotating presidency instituted after Tito's death, Stipe Mesic, a Croat, was due to become president on 15 May 1991. Serbia, supported by Montenegro, blocked this appointment. Slovenia then took the lead in the dissolution of the Federation. Its declaration of independence on 25 June 1991 was followed by a short and

---

[1] For a more detailed account see John Zametica, "The Yugoslav Conflict", *Adelphi Paper*, No 270, London: International Institute for Strategic Studies, Summer 1992.
[2] Warren Zimmermann, "The Last Ambassador - A Memoir of the Collapse of Yugoslavia", *Foreign Affairs*, March/April 1995, p. 7.

limited conflict without ethnic connotations. This was a war of independence, not a clash between two cultures.

Croatia's battle for independence was more complex. When Franjo Tudjman's nationalist Croatian Democratic Union (Hrvatska Demokratska Zajednica - HDZ) party won the elections in May 1990, it alienated the large Serb minority with statements and acts reminiscent of the fascist Ustasha state that had emerged during World War II. Following the promulgation of a draft of the constitution which contained no mention of protection for the Serb minority or their cultural rights, the Serbs in the area around Knin launched an uprising in August 1990 demanding autonomy for Serbian-dominated areas. Croatia's declaration of independence on 25 June 1991 prompted wider-spread combat. The fighting which erupted between ethnic groups soon overshadowed the struggle of the Croat Republic for independence from the Federation.

In the case of Bosnia-Herzegovina, independence was reached before large-scale conflict erupted. This conflict was dominated by inter-ethnic fighting for territorial control.

1.2. Objectives of the Study

The UN peace operation Croatia and Bosnia-Herzegovina represents the largest and most complex operation ever undertaken by the United Nations. Generally seen as a failure by international public opinion, the United Nations Protection Force (UNPROFOR) mission has probably done most towards eroding the credibility of the UN as a peacekeeping force. It is too often forgotten that UNPROFOR's mission in Croatia was to keep peace -- often extremely fragile and at times non-existent -- and that its primary mission in Bosnia-Herzegovina was to assist in the delivery of humanitarian aid. The UN was there to help keep people alive and to alleviate their suffering until the warring parties themselves could draft an agreement that would allow the population to resume lives of dignity and security. UNPROFOR also tried to mitigate the conflict through negotiated arrangements between the parties; it played an essential role in the implementation of these agreements and in confidence building. Based on these agreements, the UN was called to carry out disarmament and management of arms within certain areas or along cease-fire lines. This aspect will be the focus of this study. Finally, UNPROFOR's most difficult mission on the ground was to ensure the protection of the civilian population and to deter attacks on certain protected or safe areas.

Difficulties during the mission related not only to the complexity of the local situation: the necessary resources for implementing the security tasks were never fully supplied; deterrence failed; and *realpolitik* finally triumphed over moral principles such as reversing ethnic cleansing and refuting territorial gains achieved through the use of force. There was often tremendous divergence between the ambition of the UN Security Council's decisions in New York which formulated UNPROFOR's mandate and the lack of political will to implement effectively these decisions on the ground.

Failures in the former Yugoslavia are leading the UN to scale back drastically its peacekeeping role. Is cutting back the only solution? What lessons have been learned as a result of the problems encountered in Croatia and Bosnia-Herzegovina? How can peacekeeping be carried out more effectively? By concentrating on the disarmament aspects of the peacekeeping mission, this paper proposes to review the problems that UNPROFOR encountered in carrying out its mandate, to analyze the failures and successes of its disarmament operations and to assess the contribution of disarmament towards confidence building and conflict resolution. It is hoped that the background information regarding the events that shaped the outcome of this peace operation in general, and its disarmament components in particular, will stimulate and enlighten debate on how to bring future political decisions on peacekeeping closer into line with the realities encountered by such operations. Based on the results of the present analysis, an attempt will be made to devise guidelines for improving peacekeeping operations rather than simply withdrawing from them.

The main finding of the study is that disarmament was a critical factor in the success of the peacekeeping operation. This is particularly true for operations aimed at the protection of civilians against military attacks or the separation of the warring parties along cease-fire lines. Where disarmament was conducted effectively, peacekeeping succeed in achieving its localized goals; where it was not effective, peacekeeping failed. Effective peacekeeping requires effectively-implemented disarmament.

It must also be recognized, however, that disarmament can only be implemented successfully if the resources and the design of the peacekeeping operation are adequate, taking into account the realities on the ground and the objectives to be attained. In any event, disarmament requires more than Security Council resolutions and moralizing rhetoric. It can only be effectively implemented if the following two conditions are present: (1) agreement between the parties; and (2) credible enforcement by the multilateral force.

An agreement between the parties is necessary for conducting disarmament operations in a conflict situation where there is no clear victor. Such agreements are the result of overlapping interests and are generally formalized in writing. Other agreements are oral arrangements or "mutual understandings". A formal agreement by the parties is required for sending UN peacekeepers into the conflict situation.

Disarmament is closely linked to the notion of security. For it to be successful in the context of an ongoing conflict, disarmament operations must neither adversely affect the security of the population nor deteriorate the strategic position of the warring parties. One way to achieve this is to disarm equally on both sides, such as along cease-fire lines. Where reciprocal disarmament is not possible, the UN may be called to meet and guarantee the security requirements of the population to be disarmed, as was the case in the United Nations Protection Areas (UNPA's) and some Safe Areas. In this context credibility is essential. To be credible, implementation of disarmament must have an element of imposition. It requires that forces be deployed with adequate strength and resources, that the operation be administered in a timely manner, and that the rules of engagement (ROE) be effective in deterring military attacks.

1.3. Outline of the Study

Based on these considerations, the main thesis of this paper maintains that overlapping interests and credible implementation are necessary factors for conducting a successful disarmament operation. The purpose of the present analysis of UNPROFOR's disarmament mission in Croatia and Bosnia-Herzegovina is to demonstrate the validity of this thesis. It will do so by addressing the disarmament operations conducted by United Nations peace forces from the date of their deployment in April 1992 until February 1995. The study consists of two main parts: the first is a chronological account of the UN mission in Croatia (Chapter II) and in Bosnia-Herzegovina (Chapter III), and the second is a more detailed account of three disarmament operations. In the chronological account, an attempt will be made to show the relationship between, and the evolution of, the events, the mandate, and the implementation of the mandate with particular emphasis on its disarmament components. Different phases have been identified for the conflicts in Croatia and in Bosnia-Herzegovina. Each phase is characterized by a certain set of factors concerning the international political framework as reflected in: the Security Council resolutions; the mandate guiding the UN operation; and the political, military and strategic situation on the ground. Each phase ends with a crisis which triggered major changes in the factual and political frameworks in which the UN forces operated.

For Croatia, three phases have been identified in the disarmament operations conducted by UNPROFOR. During the first phase, from January 1992 to January 1993, disarmament and demilitarization based on the Vance Plan were carried out in parallel to the establishment of UNPA's. The second phase, from January 1993 to December 1993, was characterized by a reversal of the disarmament accomplished in the first phase, and by periodic eruptions of localized military confrontations. The Christmas Truce of December 1993 marked the beginning of a relatively long period of eased relations between the Croats and Krajina Serbs, resulting in a widely-respected cease-fire agreement on 29 March 1994 and an economic agreement on 2 December 1994. During the third phase, UNPROFOR assumed an interposition role, carrying out disarmament and weapons monitoring missions in the zone of separation between the two parties. This phase ended in January 1995 with increased tensions resulting from uncertainties about UNPROFOR's mandate and strength in Croatia.

UNPROFOR's disarmament operations in Bosnia-Herzegovina can also be divided into three phases. During the first phase, from April 1992 to June 1993, UNPROFOR had an exclusively humanitarian mandate; and activities concerning the monitoring or use of weapons were aimed at assisting the distribution of humanitarian aid. The second phase, from June 1993 to February 1994, saw the enlargement of UNPROFOR's mandate to protect the Safe Areas and to conduct weapons withdrawal and control functions based on local cease-fire agreements reached for some of these areas. Finally, during the third phase from February 1994 to January 1995, UNPROFOR's mandate was enlarged to include the monitoring of cease-fire agreements. It also assumed an important interposition role along the lines of confrontation. [3]

The second part of this case study will address in more detail three specific disarmament operations with a view toward identifying commonalities and the pertinence of the UNPROFOR model for other disarmament operations. The operations chosen for this more detailed study concern the UN activities in Sector West, especially an enforcement operation conducted in September 1993 (Chapter VI); the demilitarization and disarmament of Srebrenica in April 1993 (Chapter

---

[3] A similar planning was used by James A. Schear, Carnegie Endowment for International Peace, in a presentation on "International Intervention into Civil Conflict: The Case of Bosnia and Herzegovina", at the United States Institute of Peace, 1 December 1994.

V); and the establishment of a heavy weapons exclusion zone in Sarajevo in February 1994 (Chapter VI). Each case will show the background leading to this particular disarmament operation and framework in terms of Security Council Resolutions and local agreements. It will describe and analyze the difficulties encountered when implementing the disarmament components of these agreements. Finally, the study will draw some conclusions on these events and will address the question of the relevance of the UNPROFOR mission as a model for future operations.

1.4. Conflict in Yugoslavia: The Factions

Political Characteristics

Of all peacekeeping operations, the operation in the former Yugoslavia is probably the most bewilderingly complex. Of the many factors which contribute to this complexity, one which is often overlooked is the number of actors involved in the conflict. Indeed, it is all too often assumed that there are three parties to this war: the Muslims, the Serbs and the Croats. This classification is, in fact, quite misleading, as is the term "Bosnian". The Serb and Croat communities of Bosnia-Herzegovina both view themselves as "Bosnians"; however, the government in Sarajevo prefers to call them Serbs and Croats because of their ties to the governments in Zagreb and Belgrade. The importance of understanding this issue cannot be exaggerated, and much confusion remains. To illustrate this, one could use a recent example from the British newspaper *The Sunday Times* which, quoting a western intelligence official, described "everyone" (involved in the conflict) as "Croats, Bosnians, Muslims and Christians".[4] Four years after the beginning of the conflict, such misclassifications (i.e., confusion of both ethnic and religious entities and omission of the Serbs), especially on the part of presumably knowledgeable intelligence officials, illustrate the persistent disorientation of many political analysts.

One way to classify the different parties would be by their allegiances to specific individuals such as Fikret Abdic or Radovan Karadjic. However, in many cases, such allegiances are hard to demonstrate. For example, while some observers believe that Radovan Karadjic and Slobodan Milosevic are coordinating

---

[4] "Turks Accused of Secret Flights to Arm Bosnia", *The Sunday Times*, 5 March 1995.

every action, others believe that they are fighting each other for influence. Moreover, allegiances have changed numerous times during this conflict. Despite this complexity, it is important to outline the terminology used in this research. The following terminology was chosen for classification purposes only and is not meant to indicate recognition of the legitimacy of any of the parties involved.

For the purpose of this study, the main cultural groups will be classified according to the following criteria: cultural background, party/faction designation, location of the party's capital or headquarters (HQ), and the designation of their army or armed force. The general cultural designation will be used in reference to several parties of one cultural background taken together or to matters preceding the breakup of Yugoslavia (as in "Croat officers of the Yugoslav People's Army"). The party/faction designation will be employed in reference to one specific party only (as in "the Bosnian Serb negotiators"), and the abbreviated designation of the armed components of these parties will be used when referring directly to military issues.

Parties to the Conflict in the Krajina and Bosnia

Cultural Group	Party/Faction	Capital/ Headquarters	Army/Forces
Serbs	Yugoslavs	Belgrade	YA
	Bosnian Serbs	Pale	VRS
	Krajina Serbs	Knin	VSK
Croats	Croats	Zagreb	HV
	Bosnian Croat	Mostar	HVO
Muslims	Bosnian Muslim	Sarajevo	BiH
	Abdic party	Velika Kladusa	PDWB

Three points should be kept in mind when using the above terminology. First, in the context of the former Yugoslavia, the term "Muslim" does not necessarily reflect the religious belief of the individual but is rather a cultural identification.

In ethnic/racial terms, Croats, Muslims and Serbs are all Slavs albeit with different religions; in fact, they speak the same language, and it would be wrong to equate Bosnian Muslims with Albanians or Turks. The term "Muslim" originally was used in the sense of "Slav of Muslim faith". The Muslims of Bosnia-Herzegovina should not be confused with Hezbollah or Islamic Jihad fighters. For these reasons, we have chosen to speak of "cultural groups" rather than of ethnic or religious groups. Second, the term "Abdic Forces" is used to describe the culturally Muslim faction which rejected the government in Sarajevo and turned to the Serb forces in the Krajina and in Bosnia-Herzegovina for support. Finally, when speaking of "Serbs", "Croats" or "Muslims", one should read **predominantly** Serb, Croat or Muslim (if only because many individuals have parents of different cultural origins).

Our list of seven main factions is by no means exhaustive. For example, other sources have reported 17 factions in Bosnia-Herzegovina and another 12 in Croatia.[5] This could be interpreted to mean that a total of 29 factions are struggling in Croatia and Bosnia-Herzegovina. Actually, the figure is lower because many factions operate in both republics; also, these are 1992 estimates, and since then, certain factions have either disappeared or have been incorporated into the seven parties indicated above.

The clashes which took place in December 1994 and Spring 1995 around Bihac illustrate the impact that these numerous factions might have on any settlement of the conflict. While confined to one small region, the conflict around Bihac soon involved at least five of the seven parties listed above. Fikret Abdic, a wealthy local businessman from the city of Velika Kladusa with the support of a part of the local population, refused to recognize the authority of the government of Sarajevo. His faction took up arms, proclaimed the "Autonomous Region of Western Bosnia", and made ready to fight against the government's forces. Meanwhile, a cease-fire had been negotiated only between the major parties to the conflict by the Secretary-General's Special Representative, Yasushi Akashi; the Bosnian Muslim and Bosnian Croat forces had agreed to a US proposal to form a federation with confederal ties to Zagreb. Therefore, the Abdic Forces found themselves isolated when the government's forces concentrated their efforts on taking control of the secessionist region. Indeed, the government's 5th Corps successfully attacked the Abdic forces and took control of the area. This attack

---

[5] C.J. Dick, *Serbian Responses to Western Intervention in Bosnia-Herzegovina*, SSRC Occasional Brief, RMA Sandhurst, 24 August 1992; and James Gow, *Military Political Affiliations in the Yugoslav Conflict*, RFE/RL Research Report No 20, Vol. 1, 15 May 1992.

triggered a flow of about 25,000 refugees who fled to the Krajina Serb controlled Krajina region.[6]

This development, while not unnoticed, did not draw much interest from the international community This attitude changed dramatically, however, when the 5th Corps suddenly and successfully attacked the Bosnian Serb forces along northeast and southeast lines. Initially the operation went very well and the Bosnian Serbs had to cede ground rapidly. However, when the counterattack came from three different directions, the results were devastating. Bosnian Serb forces attacked from the east, Krajina Serb forces attacked from the west (across the international border between Croatia and Bosnia-Herzegovina), and re-armed and re-organized Abdic forces attacked from the northwest. While some movements of Krajina Serb elements in Bosnia-Herzegovina had been regularly reported, this was the first time that a major Krajina Serb force had actually joined the fighting in Bosnia-Herzegovina. This intervention culminated in an air strike against the headquarters of the 5th Corps in Bihac by Krajina Serb attack aircraft from the Ubdina airport. Croatia officially declared that it would not allow Bihac to fall under Serbian control and threatened to intervene. Meanwhile, on another front in the Kupres region, a joint attack of Bosnian Muslim, Bosnian Croat and Croat forces had successfully pushed back the Bosnian Serb forces.

One of the many lessons which can be drawn from these events is that overlooking even a small faction during negotiations can lead to a much larger escalation in the fighting. Official documents can refer to factions as "self-declared", "self-styled", "so-called" or by any other disclaimer of their legitimacy; however, it is dangerous either to forget about their relevance to the conflict or to hope that because they are not recognized internationally such factions will disappear.

Military Characteristics

In addition to being differentiated by their affiliations, the factions should also be distinguished by the readiness of their military components. Indeed, when speaking of Serb, Croat, Muslim or any other force, it is sometimes overlooked that their combat potential widely varies; it can range from elite special operation forces to local militia. In military terms this means that if a "regular" unit of, for example, the former Yugoslav People's Army (Jugoslavenska Narodna Armija --

---

[6] Report of the Secretary-General Pursuant to the Security Council Resolution 959, Document S/1994/1389 (1994).

JNA) is given a combat potential value of 1, then less well-prepared forces could be rated at 0.4-0.5 and hastily formed local militia at 0.1-0.2.[7] The overall combat effectiveness of any given unit is determined by many factors, including training, organization, equipment, and the quality of cadre command. On the tactical-operational and operational levels, the capability of coordinating actions with larger units and formations becomes crucial. In this context, the different forces operating in Croatia and Bosnia-Herzegovina should not be considered of equal military value.

While not directly involved in combat operations, the Yugoslav Federal Army remains the single most powerful force in the region. Because of its size and power, as well as its alleged covert support of other Serb forces, the Yugoslav Army exercises an important influence on the conflict in Croatia and in Bosnia. The Yugoslav Army has retained the best and largest arsenals of the former Yugoslav People's Army as well as most of its best officers.

The Bosnian Serb and the Krajina Serb armies have been formed mainly from JNA units composed of residents of the Krajina and Bosnia and are largely equipped with JNA equipment left behind after the army's withdrawal to Yugoslavia. The main advantage of these Serbian forces is their comparatively larger stock of heavy weapons (particularly in the early stages of the conflict), and the quality of their officers. Indeed, trained on the basis of JNA personnel, the Serbian forces have more experienced commanding officers and their units are generally better trained and commanded than their Bosnian Muslim or Croat counterparts, particularly at the tactical-operational and operational levels. These Serb forces have less infantry, however, than their opponents. This shortage of men was exacerbated by the fact that the Serb forces controlled about one-quarter of Croatia and two-thirds of Bosnia; they were overextended on very long front lines which exposed their flanks.

The Croat forces are split between the Croat armed forces (from Croatia proper but often operating in Bosnia) and the Bosnian Croat HVO forces. While not as large as the Bosnian Muslim forces, the Croat forces are better equipped. They also benefitted from a safe haven in Croatia which allowed them greater freedom of movement and redeployment. It should be noted here that the Croats have put a great deal of effort into reorganizing and equipping their forces and that

---

[7]   Major-General I.N. Vorob'ev, "Taktika v lokal'nykh voiinakh i vooruzhonnykh konfliktakh" (Tactics in Local Wars and Armed Conflicts), *Voennaia Mysl'* (Military Thought), No 1, 1995, p. 42.

they have succeeded in fielding a force far superior to the one which existed at the beginning of the conflict.

The situation of the Bosnian Muslim forces at the outset of the conflict was in many ways the poorest. Bosnian Muslims were primarily city dwellers and therefore were concentrated in small areas. Furthermore, since they represented only a minor part of the former JNA (the JNA was mainly Serbian and Croat), they had few cadre or trained soldiers. Their lack of ties to the JNA also explained their difficulty in acquiring weapons. Finally, while Serbian and Croat factions had safe havens in Croatia and Yugoslavia, the Bosnian Muslims began the war nearly surrounded and without safe territory.

In spite of all this, the Bosnian Muslims also had a number of advantages. First, they were the most numerous community and, therefore, had the largest force. Furthermore, the fact that they were mainly located in cities gave them access to key industrial sites (including quite a few defense-related plants) and partial control of a number of airfields (the use of which they could deny to the other parties). Finally, the Bosnian Muslims had the tragic advantage that, being located in the cities, they could not be attacked without a large number of civilian casualties. The Bosnian Muslim combatants were, in fact, very often protected by the civilian populations surrounding them. This situation, coupled with the fact that the Bosnian Muslims had much better access to the media (particularly in Sarajevo), allowed them to make the military success of their opponents a political victory for themselves.

Types of Units and Their Capabilities

To varying degrees, all parties involved in the conflict based the organization of their forces on former Yugoslav-type structures. The Yugoslav armed forces have also strongly influenced the strategy and tactics of the different warring factions. The JNA's doctrine of conflict, called *Opstenarodna Obrana* or "Total National Defense", envisioned a two tiered defense system based on the armed forces proper (the JNA) and the Territorial Defense Forces (TDF). Another powerful force was the Interior Militia which was equipped with light armored force vehicles, armored personnel carriers (APC's) and helicopters. All of these forces had an extensive network of training centers, arms caches, supply dumps, etc., throughout the country.[8] It was precisely the decentralized structure of the armed forces, coupled with a universal conscription system, which made it possible for all of the republics of the former Yugoslavia, and for numerous factions, to be relatively well-prepared for armed conflict. In this context, it is important to state that the absence of sophisticated weapons was not a major liability for the warring factions, particularly considering the fact that most infantry weapons of the JNA were hidden in Bosnia in preparation for a lengthy guerilla war against an aggressor who would have rapidly taken the Yugoslav flatlands (see below).

Most weapons employed in this conflict were simple, cheap, and ubiquitous infantry weapons such as assault rifles, sniper rifles, hand grenades, mortars and anti-aircraft guns used in direct fire against ground targets. Heavier weapons were also used, but they did not represent an overwhelming advantage as can be seen in the inability of Serb forces to defeat decisively their opponents. Other weapons used in this conflict include: mines, booby traps, so-called "Livno Bombs" where oil drums or tractor tires which are filled with explosives and rolled downhill (Bosnian Muslim),[9] improvised rocket systems capable of delivering 275 kg bombs, and even fuel-air explosives (FAE) capable of destroying an entire block of flats at a distance of 10 kilometers (Bosnian Serb).[10] Many units, particularly TDF or partisan units, were strongly supported by local municipal authorities and used civilian vehicles (cars and trucks) and other logistics for their forces. For air-defense purposes, both anti-aircraft artillery and portable surface-to-air missiles (usually Russian "strela" and "igla" weapons) were utilized by all sides. Besides TDF and other partisan-based forces, there were special operations forces, military "advisors" and mercenaries on all sides.

It is difficult to assess the size and quality of the different forces, and estimates vary widely. Command and control was usually poor, but rough approximations, unfortunately made at different times, can give an estimate of the balance in manpower:

---

[8] David C. Isby, "Yugoslavia 1991 - Armed Forces in Conflict", *Jane's Intelligence Review*, September 1991, pp. 394-403.

[9] Christopher Collinson, "Bosnian Army Tactics", *Jane's Intelligence Review*, January 1994, p. 11.

[10] "Improvised Rocket Used by Bihac's Besiegers", *Jane's Intelligence Review Pointer*, April 1995, p. 5; and "More Light Shed on Serb Rocket", *Jane's Intelligence Review Pointer*, June 1995, p. 6.

Ground Forces of the Warring Parties: Infantry

Army/Force[11]	Active	Reserves
YA (January 1995)	130,000	400,000 (?)
VRS (May 1994)	33,000 (regular)	63,000 (conscripts)
VSK (October 1993)	20,000-40,000	15,000
HV (January 1995)	80,000	unknown
HVO (March 1993)	41,000-45,000	unknown
PDWB (December 1994)	5,000	unknown
BiH (January 1995)	80,000-120,000	120,000-200,000

A useful evaluation of the equipment holdings of the different factions is even harder to make for a number of reasons:

1. It is very difficult to evaluate the exact amount of equipment left to the Serb forces in Croatia and Bosnia by the JNA.
2. It is also difficult to evaluate how much equipment was seized by Croat and Bosnian Muslim forces around the time of the declarations of independence of the two republics.
3. According to numerous reports, much of the military equipment in the region was in very bad condition and might not be usable.
4. Stocks of equipment were hidden by all parties.
5. All parties had some type of military production capability and produced some amount of weapons.
6. In spite of the arms embargo, all parties received supplies from abroad, probably in very large quantities. For example, multiple rocket launchers were seen on *Euro News* TV footage of the Bosnian Muslim 5th Corps

---

[11] YA= Yugoslav Army, VRS= Bosnian Serb Army, VSK= Krajina Serb Army, HV= Croatian Army (Hrvatska Vojska), HVO= Bosnian Croat Army (Hrvatsko Vijece Odbrane), PDWB= Popular Defense of Western Bosnia (Abdic Forces), BiH (Bosnian Muslim Army).

offensive in Bihac. Clearly the Bosnian Muslim forces had heavy weapons despite their claims to the contrary.

It is generally agreed, however, that the Serb factions did have larger stocks of armor and artillery. They also had a number of medium-range air defense systems and tactical surface-to-surface missiles (FROG-7/Luna 9P113M).

Terrain and Situation of the Factions

Terrain played a crucial role in this conflict. With the exception of Sector East and part of Sector North, most of the conflict area was in militarily difficult terrain. A recent US study divided the terrain in the region into three basic categories whose characteristics are given below:[12]

I. Region A: lowlands bordering Romania, Hungary and Austria

This region included most of Sectors West and East. This is a fairly flat region, crossed by a number of major streams; it features a well developed network of all-weather roads and railroads, and is well suited to mobile armored warfare as well as air strikes and airborne operations.

II. Region B1: interior highlands stretching from Austria to Greece

Many mountains here are higher than 5,000 feet and hills are deeply gorged. Flash floods after heavy rain are common; low clouds often obscure peaks and fog limits visibility. All land traffic, except on foot, is limited to scarce narrow roads and single track railroads which cross hundreds of bridges and tunnels as, for example, on the 50 kilometer-long road between Gorazde and Sarajevo which runs across 44 bridges. This region is almost entirely unsuited for conventional offensive military operations.

---

[12] John M. Collins, *Balkan Battlegrounds: US Military Alternatives*, Congressional Research Service Report to Congress, No 92-679S (2 September 1992).

III. Region B2: mountain chains which parallel the Dalmatian coast

This region is characterized by sharp ridges, canyons, gorges, nearly vertical ravines, shallow sinkholes, caverns, rocky outcroppings, cliffs and extensive depressions that have flat floors and steep walls but no surface drainage. Low-capacity bridges, narrow vertical and horizontal clearance tunnels, narrow roads, and villages with narrow streets are typical of this region. As in region B1, multilayered clouds, low cloud ceilings, winter fog and high winds make low-level air strikes dangerous and high-altitude air strikes difficult to execute.

It is important to remember that 80 percent of former the Yugoslavia is located in regions B1 and B2. Keeping these figures in mind, the situation of the parties can be summarized as follows:

SERB FORCES (Krajina and Bosnia):

Bosnian Serb and Krajina Serb forces probably were the best-equipped and best- trained; however, they suffered from a comparative lack of manpower. This deficiency was aggravated by the fact that the combined Serb forces of the Krajina and Bosnia had to defend a very long front which includes the border between Sector East and Croatia, the border between the Serb-controlled areas of Bosnia and Croatia, the border between the Krajina and Croatia, and the border between the Serb-controlled and the Croat- and Bosnian Muslim-controlled areas of Bosnia. Furthermore, the Krajina and Bosnian Serbs were threatened by the Bosnian Muslim 5th Corps in Bihac and the Bosnian Muslim forces in the UN safe-heavens of eastern Bosnia (as seen in the Bosnian Muslim attack from Gorazde). Finally, the Bosnian Serbs were also threatened along the narrow and vulnerable Brcko corridor.

Besides being the best-equipped and best-trained forces, the greatest potential advantage of the Serb forces were found in two elements: (1) in both the Krajina and Bosnia, Serbs were mainly rural people who had the advantage of fighting on a terrain they knew well and which they could exploit to its fullest; and (2) the Serb forces could, at least potentially, greatly benefit from support from Yugoslavia, be it in military support or in manpower.

BOSNIAN CROAT AND BOSNIAN MUSLIM FORCES:

When acting in support of each other rather than in opposition, the Bosnian Croat and Bosnian Muslim forces benefitted from a number of advantages: they were more numerous, had access to external channels of supplies (particularly the Croats), and could control a significant number of weapons. For example, according to certain reports, the BiH operated 85 tanks and 300 heavy guns while the HVO had 250-500 tanks and 2,000 artillery pieces including a possible 500 heavy guns.

In this context, Croatia played an absolutely central role: when Croatia supported the BiH and HVO forces, the Krajina and Bosnian Serbs found themselves surrounded by hostile forces; however, when Croatia failed to support these forces, the Bosnian Croats and Muslims found themselves surrounded by overall superior Serb forces. The Croat forces also suffer from their own vulnerable choke point, Maslenica, which links Dalmatia to the rest of Croatia. Finally, without the support of Croatia, the Bosnian Muslims would find themselves in the most difficult position. Left without HV and HVO support, the BiH was surrounded by Bosnian Serb forces in many cities. It lacks communications with the rest of the world, was comparatively short on heavy weapons, and suffered from a shortage of experienced officers.

In summary it can be said that, as of early 1995, the war reached stalemate. Under these conditions, tactical attacks and successes were clearly possible, but it was still unlikely that these would have led to operational successes.

1.5. International Peace Negotiations
Prior to United Nations (UN) Intervention

The initial attempts at conciliation centered on the primarily political effort to preserve the unity of Yugoslavia following the collapse of the Yugoslav Communist Party in January 1990. The international community hoped that negotiations leading to a revision of the constitutional structures and balance between the central government and the republics would allow Yugoslavia to remain intact. The fear of ethnic conflict over borders and minority rights following a disintegration of the country was widespread. The mediating efforts of the European Community (EC) were accompanied by economic incentives to keep the Federation together. This approach was shared by the United States. Some days before Slovenia and Croatia declared independence, US Secretary of

State James Baker announced, in Belgrade, his country's support for "democratization, protection of human rights, territorial integrity and preservation of the unity of Yugoslavia".[13] This was a clear signal that western countries were opposed to independence for the Yugoslav republics, and that the emerging conflict was regarded as an internal affair of the Socialist Republic of Yugoslavia (SRY).[14] It was also an indication to the JNA, the only federal structure still functioning, that it would be responsible for maintaining the unity of the Federation.

The outbreak of fighting after Slovenia and Croatia's declarations of independence and the pictures of devastation and human suffering changed international public opinion. The Conference on Security and Cooperation in Europe (CSCE) became involved by virtue of a newly adopted crisis "emergency" mechanism. However, hampered by the requirement of consensus decisions, the CSCE soon diminished as a locus of efforts to resolve the crisis and the European Community started to play a more active role. The intervention of three successive EC troika[15] missions at the foreign minister level resulted in an agreement in Brioni on 7 July 1991. This agreement established a cease-fire, a three-month moratorium on implementing the declarations of independence, and a commitment to begin political negotiations within the European Community Conference on Yugoslavia (ECCY), chaired by Lord Carrington.

After it had become clear that the European Community's mediation efforts could not solve the escalating Yugoslav crisis, the issue was put on the agenda of the Security Council on 25 September 1991 at the initiative of Belgium, France and Great Britain. Since then, the Security Council has, on a number of occasions, considered various aspects of the Yugoslav crisis and has made corresponding decisions based on Chapters VI, VII and VIII of the UN Charter. UN Secretary-Generals Perez de Cuellar and Boutros-Ghali were actively involved in the

---

[13] Interview with H.E. Sune Danielsson, Ambassador of Sweden, Zagreb, 15 April 1995. See also James B. Steinberg, "International Involvement in the Yugoslavia Conflict", in *Enforcing Restraint -Collective Intervention in Internal Conflicts*, New York: Council on Foreign Relations Press, 1993, p. 34.

[14] As late as 24 June 1992, the day before the Slovene and Croatian declarations were due, the Commission of the European Community signed a financial protocol with Belgrade, in a deal described as a gesture of solidarity towards the Yugoslav government, signalling the European countries' wish to keep the unity of the Federation.

[15] The troika consists of the representative of the European Community nation currently holding the presidency of the Council of Ministers, together with the immediate preceding and successor presidency holders.

preparation of sessions of the Security Council and the implementation of its decisions relating to the conflict. To a lesser extent, the case of Yugoslavia has also been dealt with by the UN General Assembly, in particular when admitting new states emerging from the former Yugoslavia to membership in the world organization and when deciding to bar the participation of representatives of the Federal Republic of Yugoslavia (FRY) both in its work and in the activities of several other agencies and bodies of the United Nations.

Initially, the UN Secretariat was reluctant to support UN involvement in the conflict. After the outbreak of fighting in Slovenia, Secretary-General Perez de Cuellar rejected UN intervention in what was perceived to be a country's internal matter, and noted that Slovenia was not a member of the UN. But with the continued failure of EC-led efforts, attention increasingly focused on the UN as an alternative forum. The UN became actively involved in the situation in Yugoslavia on 25 September 1991, when the Security Council concluded that the development of the situation in Yugoslavia constituted a threat to international peace and security and adopted Resolution 713. Invoking Chapter VII of the UN Charter, the Security Council decided "that all states shall, for the purposes of establishing peace and stability in Yugoslavia, immediately implement a general and complete embargo on all deliveries of weapons and military equipment to Yugoslavia". The Resolution invited the Secretary-General to offer his assistance in consultation with the Government of Yugoslavia and all those promoting the peace efforts, namely the EC and the CSCE.

Former US Secretary of State Cyrus Vance was appointed Secretary-General Personal Envoy for Yugoslavia and, serving as UN mediator for the conflict, he negotiated a series of short-lived cease-fires. On 23 November 1991, Vance convened a meeting in Geneva, which was attended by President Milosevic of the SRY, President Tudjman of Croatia, the Secretary of State for National Defense of Yugoslavia, and Lord Carrington, then Chairman of the European Community's Conference on Yugoslavia. During the meeting, the Yugoslav parties agreed on an immediate cease-fire and on a number of other issues, and requested the establishment of a United Nations peacekeeping operation.

Based on this understanding, the Security Council, in Resolution 721 of 27 November 1991, agreed in principle to send a UN peacekeeping force to the war-torn region once fighting truly stopped and all parties fully complied with the cease-fire agreement signed in Geneva on 23 November 1991. Subsequent negotiations focused on the implementation of the Geneva agreement and the general principles for a UN peacekeeping operation. On 11 December 1991, the Secretary-General presented a report to the Security Council outlining a plan, contingent on a cease-fire, for a peacekeeping force in Croatia.[16] The Security Council endorsed this plan, also known as the Vance Plan, in Resolution 724 of 15 December 1991. While recognizing that the conditions for establishing a peacekeeping operation in Yugoslavia still did not exist, the Security Council endorsed the Secretary-General's offer to send to Yugoslavia a small group of personnel to prepare for possible deployment of a peacekeeping operation. It also decided to set up a Committee to ensure that the general and complete embargo imposed by Resolution 713 was effectively applied.

The Vance Plan called for the complete withdrawal of the JNA and other Serb military units from Croatia. It also provided for the establishment of three UNPA's in regions with large Serb populations which had come under the effective control of the JNA or Serb militias: eastern and western Slavonia, and the Krajina.[17] Within the UNPA's, the plan required the complete withdrawal or demobilization of all military units, including the Croatian national guard and army, as well as all territorial paramilitary forces. Only lightly-armed police forces could remain in the Protected Areas to maintain order, and these were subject to supervision by UN forces to assure non-discrimination and the protection of human rights. The UN forces had the authority to control access to the Protected Areas to assure that no new military forces or equipment be introduced.

Despite continuous fighting, on 2 January 1992 the warring parties signed the Implementing Accord on the unconditional cease-fire negotiated by Cyrus Vance. Thereby, they agreed in principle to the Vance Plan which was elaborated by the UN, and which differed from the plans previously presented by the European Union. The European approach had been based on mediation, stabilization and the preservation of Yugoslavia's integrity. The new plan, however, rested on a peace operation conducted by the UN that aimed primarily at halting inter-ethnic fighting and stabilizing the situation in Croatia.

On 8 January 1992 -- one day after helicopters of the European Community Monitoring Mission (ECMM) in Yugoslavia had been shot down by a JNA aircraft, killing four Italian members and one French member of the Monitoring Mission -- the Security Council adopted Resolution 727 and decided to send a group of 50 liaison officers to Yugoslavia immediately to help maintain the cease-fire. These officers arrived in Zagreb and Belgrade on 14 January. Their number was raised to 75 by Resolution 740 of 7 February 1992.

---

[16] UN Document S/23280 of 11 December 1991.

[17] These UNPA's were subsequently been divided into four Sectors: East, West, North and South.

On 15 February 1992, notwithstanding the fact that certain political groups in Yugoslavia were still expressing objections to the Vance Plan, the Secretary-General recommended to the Security Council the establishment of the United Nations Protection Force.[18] He stressed that "the danger that a United Nations peacekeeping operation will fail because of lack of cooperation from the parties is less grievous than the danger that delay in its dispatch will lead to a breakdown of the cease-fire and to a new conflagration in Yugoslavia".[19] Resolution 743 of 21 February 1992 endorsed the Secretary-General's recommendation and, finally, authorized an initial deployment of troops. In a departure from normal procedure, it provided an initial mandate for one year instead of the usual six months, to give both Serbs and Croats in Croatia greater assurance that their interests would be protected. Resolution 743, while noting that the Government of Yugoslavia had requested a peacekeeping force, left the legal basis of the UNPROFOR deployment vague, and did not make explicit reference to Chapters VI or VII of the UN Charter.[20] UNPROFOR's purpose was to create the conditions of peace and security required for the negotiation of an overall settlement of the Yugoslav crisis, and the implementation of the Vance Plan was in no way intended to prejudge the terms of a political settlement.

On 26 February 1992, the Security Council appointed General Satish Nambiar from India as UNPROFOR commander and Cedric Thornbery as head of the civilian affairs of the peace operation. A budget of $250 million (instead of the $600 million estimated by the Secretary-General) was approved to finance the initial phase of the peace operation. Deployment of UNPROFOR began on 8 March 1992.

---

[18] UN Document S/23592 of 15 February 1992.

[19] *Ibid.*, p. 7.

[20] It stated, however, that "the situation in Yugoslavia continues to constitute a threat to international peace and security", and referred to Resolution 713 based on Chapter VII. On the other hand, UNPROFOR's deployment was understood by a number of DCR questionnaire respondents as a Chapter VI operation. This conclusion rested on the argument that UNPROFOR's mission was based on an agreement between the parties. See, for example, United Nations Institute for Disarmament Research (UNIDIR), *Practitioners' Questionnaire on Weapons Control, Disarmament, and Demobilization During Peacekeeping Operations*, Geneva: UNIDIR, unpublished survey responses, No. Y-060, and interview with Victor Andreew, Senior Advisor, UNHCR, Geneva, 9 June 1995.

Chapter 2
Disarmament Operations in Croatia

2.1. Introduction

Croatia's declaration of independence marked the beginning of large-scale inter-ethnic fighting. The Serb population in Croatia was significant, accounting for 12 percent of the total population according to the 1991 census. It was concentrated geographically, constituting a majority in the Krajina and parts of western Slavonia, and a significant minority in parts of eastern Slavonia. The Serbs in Croatia were well-armed and organized politically, and were backed by the JNA forces stationed there. Croatia entered the war with a less well-equipped, trained and organized military force than the Serbs had. In less than two months, the JNA and local Serb militias had gained control of almost one-third of the Croatian territory and had the ability to block vital Croat rail and road connections throughout the country.

For an example of the kind of destruction that resulted from this Serb-Croat war, one may look to the city of Vukovar. This town in the east of Croatia was shelled by the JNA for three months. It has been calculated that some 5,000 shells landed there each day. By the end of the campaign it was leveled, and its destruction was far more severe than that of Sarajevo or Dubrovnik. Tragically, its fate has been overshadowed by the continuing strife in the region, and Vukovar is all too often forgotten.[1]

In order to find a solution to the conflict in Croatia, the EC followed a two-part strategy: the establishment of a cease-fire coupled with political negotiations. The cease-fire was enforced by EC monitors while the political negotiations were conducted by the ECCY, chaired by Lord Carrington. As the fighting continued unabated, and negotiations dragged on, some European states abandoned their hope for a united Yugoslavia and began to push for formal recognition of Slovenia and Croatia.

While pursuing political negotiations, the EC sought to broker a durable cease-fire to aid in the peace process. As the EC remained largely unsuccessful in

---

[1] Speech by Lord Owen to the Foreign Press Association, 27 March 1995.

its efforts, several European states turned to the UN for assistance. Initially, the UN Secretariat was reluctant to support UN involvement in the conflict. But UN peacekeepers were requested by the presidents of Serbia and Croatia and the Yugoslav State Secretary for National Defense, in an agreement reached in Geneva on 23 November 1991 at a meeting with Cyrus Vance, the Secretary-General's personal envoy to Yugoslavia. On the basis of this request and Security Council Resolution 721, the Secretary-General prepared a report outlining a plan, contingent on a cease-fire, for a peacekeeping force in Croatia.[2] This plan, known as the Vance Plan, was endorsed by Resolution 724 of 15 December 1991 and constituted the basis for the disarmament operations undertaken by the UN forces in Croatia.

The UN disarmament mission in Croatia can be divided into three phases. During the first phase, from January 1992 to January 1993, disarmament and demilitarization based on the Vance Plan were carried out parallel to the establishment of the UNPA's. The second phase, from January 1993 to December 1993, was marked by periodic eruptions of localized military confrontations. The beginning of this phase saw a reversal in the disarmament process: Croat incursions into Protected Areas led the Krajina Serbs to reclaim their weapons from UN storage sites. Events during this phase revealed the limitations of the UN forces and their mandate. Finally, the Christmas Truce of December 1993 marked the beginning of a relatively long period of eased relations between the Croats and Krajina Serbs; a widely respected cease-fire agreement was signed on 29 March 1994 and an economic agreement on 2 December 1994. During this third phase, UNPROFOR assumed an interpositional role, carrying out disarmament and weapons monitoring missions in the zone between the two parties. This phase ended in January 1995 with increased tensions resulting from uncertainties about the UN's mandate and its strength in Croatia.

---

[2] UN Document S/23280 of 11 December 1991.

2.2. Phase I: Disarmament Operations According to the Vance Plan and the Establishment of the United Nations Protection Areas (UNPA's)

Introduction

The first phase of UNPROFOR's activities in Croatia extended from the deployment of forces in March 1992 to the resumption of hostilities following the Croatian incursion into the UNPA's in January 1993. The phase was marked by discussions concerning the interpretation of the Vance Plan and the modalities of its implementation. Problems arose due to disagreements among the parties over the exact delimitation of the areas to be protected, and new realities on the ground required several enlargements of the mandate.

Following the Security Council's decision to proceed according to the Secretary-General's recommendations,[3] UNPROFOR began to deploy on 8 March 1992 under the command of General Satish Nambiar of India. The deployment was scheduled to be completed by the end of April but was delayed because of continued disagreements between the parties over UNPROFOR's role, as well as failures to comply with the agreed provisions on disarming militias in the Protected Areas. As with most peacekeeping operations, UNPROFOR's mission was put together from scratch, under extreme restraints in terms of time, personnel and material resources. Lieutenant General Nambiar had only four days in New York for briefings and gathering documents.[4] On 3 March 1992, he met the senior staff members of the mission; they left for Belgrade on 7 March, arriving there the following day. The preparation time was very short and this had, according to General Nambiar, a severely limiting effect on the implementation of the mission.[5]

Although UNPROFOR succeeded in calming the conflict in the UNPA's to some degree, tensions remained high particularly in Sectors East and South. Problems also arose in the areas adjacent to the UNPA's (the "pink zones") as well as on the subject of the demilitarization of the Prevlaka Peninsula. These problems led to a series of enlargements of UNPROFOR's mandate.

---

[3] Recommendations of 15 February 1992, UN Document S/23592.

[4] These documents consisted of: (1) the relevant resolutions and Secretary-General reports; (2) a background note; and (3) a brief on the political aspects of Yugoslavia. The Rules of Engagement (ROE) were made in the field when the mission started. See interview with Lt. General Satish Nambiar, former UNPROFOR Commander, Geneva, 8 March 1995.

[5] *Ibid.*

Disarmament Components of the Vance Plan

The acceptance of the Vance Plan and the subsequent cease-fire agreement between Croats and Serbs on 2 January 1992 were the formal prerequisites for a UN intervention and for further negotiation efforts. Nevertheless, there were problems with these agreements. On the one hand, the cease-fire was consistently violated along the whole front from Dubrovnik to Osijek. On the other hand, a number of fundamental issues were not addressed, particularly concerning the return of refugees, the control of border crossings, and the political status of the Croat territories under Serb control. The purpose of the Vance Plan -- and UNPROFOR's presence -- was to create the conditions of peace and security in the areas occupied by Serb forces so that an overall political settlement on the status of these territories could be reached. It was not a peace plan in the strict sense of the term, but rather a plan aimed at stabilizing a potentially explosive situation, and its interim character never ceased to be stressed.

According to the Vance Plan, UNPROFOR was to deploy in particular areas of Croatia, designated United Nations Protection Areas, in which the UN Security Council judged that special interim arrangements were required to ensure that a lasting cease-fire be maintained. For the most part, the boundaries of these areas followed the administrative boundaries of the *opstine* (districts) as they existed before the conflict. In these areas, Serbs constituted the majority or a substantial minority of the population and inter-communal tensions had led to armed conflict in the recent past. The core of the Vance Plan focused on the disarmament and demilitarization of the UNPA's. This program involved the following phases:

1. the withdrawal of the JNA and the Croatian National Guard, as well as the TDF units from the UNPA's;
2. the disbanding and demobilization of TDF units and their command structures in the UNPA's;
3. the handing-over of TDF weapons to JNA units or the Croatian National Guard before their withdrawal from the UNPA's or the handing-over of these weapons to UNPROFOR for safe keeping during the "interim period";
4. either the disbanding and demobilization or withdrawal of all paramilitary, irregular, or volunteer units from the UNPA's; and,
5. the return of displaced persons to their homes in the UNPA's.

The original Vance Plan rested on two central elements: (1) the withdrawal of the JNA from all of Croatia and the demilitarization of the UNPA's; and (2) the continued functioning of the existing local authorities and police under UN supervision, pending the achievement of an overall political solution to the crisis.[6] This arrangement was controversial: it deferred the settlement of the status of the UNPA's and provided no guidance for their disposition after the implementation of the plan. This open-ended arrangement allowed each of the parties to interpret the plan to its advantage and, as a consequence, to pursue divergent objectives. The original agreement which ended hostilities in January 1992 was, in fact, understood by each side as a confirmation of its demands. Consequently, the Croatian Government expected UNPROFOR to return the UNPA's to Croatian authority while the local Serb authorities expected protection while they engaged in creating the Republic of Serbian Krajina.

The Mandate

Set out in four reports by the Secretary-General,[7] UNPROFOR's mandate was *to ensure that the United Nations Protection Areas were demilitarized (through the withdrawal or disbandment of all armed forces in them) and that all persons residing in them were protected from armed attack.* To these ends, UNPROFOR was authorized to control access to the UNPA's and to monitor the local police within them. Outside the UNPA's, UNPROFOR's military observers were to verify the withdrawal of all JNA and irregular forces from Croatia, other than those already disbanded and demobilized there. In support of the work of the UN humanitarian agencies, UNPROFOR was also to facilitate the return of civilian displaced persons to their homes in the UNPA's and to ensure non-discrimination and the protection of human rights in these areas. The use of force was authorized in self-defense only.

The mandate was formulated in very broad terms at the end of 1991, and it reflected the situation as it prevailed at that time. Unfortunately, by the time forces

---

[6] The fact that local police forces continued to function in the Protected Areas has been considered a complicating factor by peacekeepers trying to pursue the objectives of the Vance Plan. One of the DCR Project Questionnaires, for instance, states that the local police forces are a party to the conflict and "keep on acting in support of army action". It is suggested that the local police should act as liaisons integrated in an all UN police organization (see UNIDIR, *Practitioners' Questionnaire*, No. Y094).

[7] Annex III of UN Document S/23280 of 11 December 1991, and UN Documents S/23592 of 15 February 1992, S/23777 of 2 April 1992, and S/23844 of 24 April 1992.

were deployed in March 1992, considerable changes had occurred; the lines of confrontation had moved and Croatia had been recognized as an independent state. The Vance Plan, accepted by both the Zagreb and Belgrade authorities, was now expected to solve a conflict between Zagreb and Knin, between the internationally-recognized government of Croatia and the representatives of the Serb populations in the Krajinas, a task to which it may not have been entirely suited. The Secretary-General was aware of difficulties in connection with this plan. However, he came to the conclusion that the danger of a UN peacekeeping operation failing because of a lack of cooperation from the parties was less grievous than the danger of a breakdown of the cease-fire and a new conflagration in Yugoslavia due to a delay in the UN force's dispatch.[8]

UNPROFOR's Organization

UNPROFOR initially established its headquarters in Sarajevo, the capital of Bosnia-Herzegovina, with sub-offices in Belgrade and Zagreb and a logistics base at Banja Luka. It was deployed in the three UNPA's which, for UN purposes, were divided into four sectors: Sector East (eastern Slavonia, which includes the areas known as Baranja and western Srem), Sector North (the northern part of the Krajina UNPA), Sector South (the southern part of the Krajina UNPA) and Sector West (western Slavonia).

UNPROFOR included military, police and civilian components. The overall command in the field was exercised by the Force Commander, appointed by, and serving under, the command of the Secretary-General, who in turn reported to the Security Council.

The *military* component consisted of 12 enlarged infantry battalions (10,400 troops, all ranks); headquarters, logistics and other support elements totalling about 2,840 personnel; and 100 military observers. The units deployed throughout the UNPA's were lightly armed but used APC's and helicopters. To ensure that the Protected Areas remained demilitarized, these military forces could control access to the UNPA's by establishing check-points on all roads leading into them and at important junctions inside them. Vehicles and individuals would be stopped and if necessary searched at these check-points to ensure that no military formations or armed groups or weapons, ammunition, explosives or other military equipment entered the UNPA's. If serious tension developed between different groups in an

---

[8] UN Document S/23592 of 15 February 1992.

UNPA, the UN force would interpose itself between the two sides to prevent hostilities.[9]

The 100 United Nations unarmed military observers (UNMO's) were deployed in the UNPA's to verify their demilitarization. It was initially planned that as soon as demilitarization was accomplished, these observers would be transferred to parts of Bosnia-Herzegovina adjacent to Croatia.

UNPROFOR's *police* component consisted of approximately 530 police personnel, and their task was to monitor the local police forces. They were unarmed and deployed throughout the UNPA's. In performing their duties, they were assigned to police headquarters in each region and *opstina* (district), and they accompanied the local police on patrols and in the performance of other duties. They also carried out investigations of discrimination or other abuses of human rights and had free and immediate access to all local police facilities. The police monitors were commanded by a Police Commissioner, who reported to the Force Commander through the Director of Civil Affairs.

Finally, the *civilian* component consisted largely of existing staff members of the UN and performed a range of political, legal, informational and administrative functions. In each of the four sectors, the Director of Civil Affairs established an office whose head worked in close coordination with the military commander of the sector. His main task was to identify the existing arrangements for local administration and the maintenance of public order in the UNPA's. He was also to ensure that any changes to other aspects of local administration were consistent with the spirit of the plan and posed no threat to public order.

Implementation of the Mandate

The first tasks of UNPROFOR were to stabilize the situation, to start the demilitarization and demobilization process, and to work out acceptable means of implementing the mandate. Deployment of UNPROFOR in the UNPA's proved difficult for several reasons. Not only was deployment delayed by on-going fighting in Croatia, but the mandate and its interpretation were questioned by both sides. Also, hostilities broke out in Bosnia-Herzegovina which made the political environment more complex and severely strained communications with UNPROFOR's headquarters in Sarajevo. Furthermore, deployment was delayed due to the complexity of transporting infantry battalions and their equipment from

---

[9] UN Documents S/23280 of 11 December 1991 and S/23592 of 15 February 1992.

distant countries at short notice and to difficulties in assigning civilian staff and procuring required equipment.

Prior to UNPROFOR's assumption of responsibility in the UNPA's, it had become apparent that the JNA was transferring many of its heavy weapons to local TDF units and para-military militias established in these areas.[10] All TDF units in Sectors East and West handed over their heavy weapons, which included tanks, artillery, mortars and anti-aircraft weapon systems. These were stored in a number of locations under UNPROFOR's control with a "double lock" system. By July 1992, similar action was in progress in Sectors North and South, including the "pink zones".

UNPROFOR assumed its full responsibilities in Sector East on 15 May 1992 and in Sector West on 20 June 1992.[11] Heavy weapons were removed from the front lines in Sectors East and West according to separate agreements reached between the parties. The disarmament of Serbian paramilitary units began, and their weapons were stored in magazines with two locks: one controlled by the UN and the other by a local authority.

Deployment in Sector South proved more difficult. Certain areas of Croatia, controlled by the JNA, and populated largely by Serbs lay outside the agreed boundaries of the UNPA's. The Belgrade authorities had pressed strongly for these regions to be included in the Protected Areas, and the Serb residents were prepared to resist the restoration of Croatian authority. Such resistance would have led to the resumption of widespread fighting in the neighboring UNPA's, but the Croatian authorities refused any changes in the boundaries of the UNPA's. This dispute seriously threatened the viability of the mandate.

On 1 June 1992, with the agreement of both parties, the Force Commander directed UNPROFOR military and police teams to begin moving into the "pink zones" to commence preliminary reconnaissance and patrol activities, pending a final agreement. On 21 June, the Croatian Army attacked positions of the Serb TDF near Drnis in the "pink zone" south of Sector South and advanced several kilometers. This led to a retaliatory Serb bombardment of the town of Sibenik, and, on 22 June, to a reciprocal Croatian bombardment of Knin, within Sector South. Tension was growing, with general mobilization on the Serb side and an increasing intensity of shelling by both sides. The risk of the conflict spreading to the whole of the "pink zone" was imminent. This series of attacks constituted a

---

[10] See UN Document S/23844 of 24 April 1992.

[11] UN Document S/24188 of 26 June 1992, p. 2.

serious set-back to UNPROFOR's endeavors, and it also increased fears of Croatian rule among the inhabitants of the zones. It was necessary to start afresh the process of building confidence among the parties.

UNPROFOR's objective was to demilitarize and to disband paramilitary and irregular forces. According to the Secretary-General, to attempt to do so in a region where general mobilization was underway would severely erode UNPROFOR's credibility.[12] As a peacekeeping operation, UNPROFOR depended upon the cooperation of the authorities in Sectors North and South, and this cooperation would not be forthcoming if the "pink zones" were in turmoil. On 26 June 1992, the Secretary-General outlined a course of action to stabilize the situation. This led to the first enlargement of UNPROFOR's mandate in Security Council Resolution 762 of 30 June 1992. This resolution urged the Government of Croatia "to withdraw its army to the positions held before the offensive of 21 June 1992 and to cease hostile military activities within or adjacent to the United Nations Protected Areas". The resolution put an end to the disagreement over this specific "pink zone", and allowed for the deployment of UNPROFOR forces into the Protected Area.

After assuming responsibility in the sectors, UNPROFOR's principle achievement was the elimination of cease-fire violations involving the use of heavy weapons such as artillery and tanks. By the beginning of July 1992, UNPROFOR had taken control of the four UNPA's; however, only in Sector West had demilitarization been achieved.[13] Therefore, UNPROFOR implemented the simultaneous withdrawal by both sides of heavy weapons to a distance of 30 kilometers from the lines of confrontation. As a result, there was a considerable lessening of tension in all UNPA's although occasional cease-fire violations, mostly involving small-arms fire, continued to occur, and nowhere did conditions exist to allow for the return of displaced persons. Another major achievement was the withdrawal of the JNA from all sectors, as called for in the plan, and of the HV from the front line.[14]

It should be stressed that the cultural background of the population, as well as the political and strategic situation, differed considerably from sector to sector. Consequently, so did the problems associated with the implementation of the disarmament components of the Vance Plan. In Sector West, the disarmament

---

[12] *Ibid.*, p. 4.

[13] Gustav E. Gustenau, "Die Neuordnung des Südslawischen Raumes", *Oesterreichische Militärische Zeitung*, No 5, 1992, p. 411.

[14] UN Document S/24353 of 27 July 1992.

process went furthest and occurred more rapidly; at one point, the authority and speed with which the UN forces were implementing the Vance Plan became a concern for UNPROFOR's headquarters in Zagreb. In July 1992, the Sector West Commander was asked to slow down the disarmament of the local police forces in the Sector. Discussions with UN officials suggest that, had the sectors been dealt with separately, the disarmament process could have been carried out more efficiently. A different problem affected the Krajina sectors. Probably because of the scarcity of personnel at its headquarters, UNPROFOR dealt exclusively with Knin. Unfortunately, this decision only helped to centralize the most unconciliatory forces of the Krajina Serbs and slowed any progress towards achieving the Vance Plan.[15]

After November 1992, the security situation consistently improved. Among other things, the carrying of rifles had diminished considerably, and by January 1993, these arms were only carried by elements of the "border militia".[16] The next step in the demilitarization process was the withdrawal of the infantry, either for demobilization in the case of the TDF, or to specified distances outside the UNPA boundaries in the case of the JNA and HV. This was achieved in Sector West by July 1992. There, complete withdrawal was followed by the lifting of mines by unarmed parties of the HV and the JNA (or TDF) under UNPROFOR protection.

The demobilization of the TDF in the sectors was complicated by the simultaneous emergence of strengthened police and militia organizations. These groups, operating under different names, were equipped with automatic rifles and, in some cases, machine-guns, in violation of the provisions of the plan which required that the police be equipped only with side-arms. According to Mischa Glenny, 90 percent of the JNA forces in the Krajina were members of the local population, and they remained in the UNPA's.[17] In many cases they had taken over the JNA or Serb TDF's responsibility for manning the front lines and had to be withdrawn and disbanded. The demobilization was not accompanied by any re-integration of the forces into civilian life. The Vance Plan did not include any

---

[15] Briefing with Gerard Fischer, Senior Economist, UNCTAD, former Chief of Civilian Affairs in Sector West, Geneva, March-June 1995.

[16] UN Document S/25264 of 10 February 1993.

[17] Mischa Glenny, *The Fall of Yugoslavia*, London: Penguin, 1992, p. 29.

program for ex-combatants, and no national or international organization addressed the issue.[18]

The disarmament and demilitarization tasks were very important for the success of the mission.[19] They were the precondition for implementing the subsequent steps of the Vance Plan. As the presence of weapons ensured that isolated attacks between warring factions and against UN personnel would continue, disarmament was the only way to establish a secure environment. The Vance Plan contained no strict time-table for demilitarization; it only stated that this should be done "as soon as possible". However, disarmament was not achievable as long as distrust persisted. Perhaps it could have been accomplished when the parties adopted the Vance Plan at the end of 1991, but by the time UNPROFOR deployed, all sides had been arming in anticipation of further conflict.[20] The lack of agreement and cooperation between the warring parties severely hampered the UN forces' disarmament mission in Croatia.[21]

In implementing the disarmament mandate, peacekeepers also encountered a number of problems associated with the structure of UN peacekeeping operations. The existence of different chains of command resulted in a lack of coordination between the civil affairs, the administrative and the military components of the mission.[22] Furthermore, communication problems with headquarters,[23] especially during the vital period of initial deployment, severely delayed and restricted the UN personnel's ability to fulfill their disarming tasks.[24] In Sector West, success was largely attributed to the cooperation between the Civil Affairs Representative and the Sector Commander, to the involvement of the parties in these efforts, and to the "show of force" which gained UNPROFOR respect from the parties.[25]

---

[18] This fact was confirmed by all questionnaire responses addressing UNPROFOR's operations in Croatia. See United Nations Institute for Disarmament Research (UNIDIR), *Preliminary Analysis of Practitioners' Questionnaires on Weapons Control, Disarmament, and Demobilization During Peacekeeping Operations: Former Yugoslavia,* Geneva: UNIDIR, internal memo.

[19] *Ibid.*

[20] Interview with Lieutenant General Satish Nambiar.

[21] UNIDIR, *Preliminary Analysis of Practitioners' Questionnaires: Former Yugoslavia,* internal memo.

[22] *Ibid.*

[23] UNPROFOR's headquarters were first located in Sarajevo, then in Belgrade and finally in Zagreb.

[24] Interview with Lieutenant General Satish Nambiar.

[25] UNIDIR, *Preliminary Analysis of Practitioners' Questionnaires: Former Yugoslavia,* internal memo.

Evolution of the Mandate

After its establishment, UNPROFOR's mandate in Croatia was enlarged in several areas. These included: the monitoring of the "pink zones", the control of borders, and the inclusion of the Prevlaka peninsula.

"Pink Zones"

On 30 June 1992, the Security Council (Resolution 762) authorized UNPROFOR to undertake monitoring functions in the so-called "pink zones". These areas in Croatia were controlled by the JNA and populated largely by Serbs but were outside the agreed UNPA boundaries. In order to oversee the restoration of the Croatian Government's authority in the "pink zones", the resolution recommended the establishment of a Joint Commission chaired by UNPROFOR and consisting of representatives of the Government of Croatia and the local authorities in the region. The Joint Commission was also to include the participation of the ECMM.

The resolution requested the immediate withdrawal from the "pink zones" of the Croatian Army, the TDF, and any irregular units. This included withdrawal from the area of the incursion that occurred on 21 June 1992. Furthermore, none of these forces would be allowed to re-enter the "pink zones" once their withdrawal was verified by UNMO's (with the exception of those disbanded and demobilized within the zones). Any remaining JNA elements would also be withdrawn.

United Nations Civilian Police (UNCIVPOL) were deployed throughout the "pink zones" to monitor the existing police forces' maintenance of law and order, with particular regard to the well-being of any minority groups in the areas. ECMM personnel were deployed on both sides of the lines of confrontation outside UNPA's. This was done on the basis of a division of labor between the ECMM and UNPROFOR, agreed to within the Joint Commission. UNPROFOR itself was to be strengthened by the addition of up to 60 military observers and 120 civilian police to function in the "pink zones" with the agreement of the Government of Croatia and others concerned.

Border Control

The issue of the control of the UNPA boundaries, at those points where they coincided with what had become international borders, had been raised repeatedly by Croatian authorities. However, since the Vance Plan excluded the restoration of Croatian laws and institutions in the UNPA's until the achievement of an overall political settlement, the Croatian government was not allowed to take control of international border points, and it was suggested that UNPROFOR perform immigration and customs functions there.[26] On 7 August 1992, the Security Council adopted Resolution 769 which authorized the enlargement of UNPROFOR's strength and mandate to enable the force to control the entry of civilians into the UNPA's and to perform immigration and customs functions at those UNPA boundaries which coincided with international borders.[27] This was in addition to the authority given to UNPROFOR to prevent the movement of arms, ammunition and other war-like material into the UNPA's.

Prevlaka Peninsula

In accordance with the Vance Plan, most JNA forces withdrew from Croatian territory following UNPROFOR's arrival. However, they remained in the region of Dubrovnik and on the adjacent Prevlaka Peninsula, an uninhabited area of about 93 acres located east of Dubrovnik and controlling the entrance to the Gulf of Kotor. The JNA agreed to withdraw from this strategically important area contingent on the demilitarization of the peninsula and on a guarantee that Croatian heavy weapons would not be located in proximity to it. Discussions with a view to resolving this issue were conducted by Lt. General Nambiar and led to an agreement between the parties which entailed additional tasks being entrusted to UNPROFOR.

The third enlargement of UNPROFOR's mandate in Croatia came about on 6 October 1992 when the Security Council adopted Resolution 779, authorizing UNPROFOR "to assume responsibility for monitoring the arrangements agreed for the complete withdrawal of the Yugoslav Army from Croatia, the demilitarization of the Prevlaka peninsula and the removal of heavy weapons from neighboring areas of Croatia and Montenegro".[28]

---

[26] UN Document S/24353 of 27 July 1992.

[27] The UNPA boundaries which coincided with international borders were: Sector East's shared borders with Hungary and Serbia; and Sectors West, South and North's shared borders with Bosnia-Herzegovina.

[28] Resolution 779 of 6 October 1992.

Implementing the New Elements

UNPROFOR was unable either to control the entry of civilians into the UNPA's or to perform immigration and customs functions because of the refusal by the local Serb authorities to allow the setting up of checkpoints at the UNPA's borders. The Krajina Serbs maintained that, since the Republic of Serbian Krajina (RSK) was a "sovereign state", they had the right to carry out these functions themselves. Later, they objected to the *de facto* sanctions contained in Security Council Resolution 820 of 17 April 1993, which submitted their external trade to Croatian government approval. Border control was interpreted as being intended to subjugate them through economic pressure. The border control issue was still a matter of dispute in April 1995, when the new mandate for UNPROFOR was to be elaborated.

Conclusions

During the first phase of its operations in Croatia, UNPROFOR's major concerns were the implementation of the Vance Plan (specifically of its disarmament components) as well as the interpretation of the mandate. Changes in the situation on the ground led to some mandate enlargements concerning the "pink zones", border issues, and the demilitarization of the Prevlaka Peninsula. This period was marked, in Croatia, by a relative de-escalation of the conflicts between the Croat and Serb populations, and internationally, by a shift of focus from the conflict in Croatia to the dangers in Bosnia-Herzegovina. This shift in political attention and media coverage resulted in efforts to reach a political agreement in Croatia coming to a stand-still. In the view of Lt. General Nambiar, the political settlements could have been negotiated while the process of disarmament was being carried out in the UNPA's.[29] Disarmament could then have assisted the political settlement. But disarmament did not, in itself, constitute a solution to the entire conflict.

In this initial phase, the parties had partially overlapping interests in seeing the deployment of UNPROFOR. Disarmament had been successful in the sector where parties on both sides of the confrontation line were affected in a comparable manner and where the Sector Commander showed a determination to carry out the

---

[29] Interview with Lieutenant General Satish Nambiar.

mission's mandate. The weakness of the UN force had not yet been revealed and UNPROFOR's credibility remained intact.

During this first phase, following international recognition, one of the primary goals of the Republic of Croatia was to control its territory. The deployment of UNPROFOR in the UNPA's, which brought about cease-fire and disengagement, was a step in that direction. However, as a political settlement of the conflict was not forthcoming and UNPROFOR was not able to establish Croatian control over the protected zones, the only way to achieve the Croatian goal seemed to be through the reconquest of these areas by force. This option was chosen in January 1993, and marked the beginning of a new phase in UNPROFOR's activities in Croatia.

2.3. Phase II: Reversal of Disarmament Following Croat Incursion into the United Nations Protection Areas Reveals Weaknesses of UNPROFOR's Mission

Introduction

In the absence of a comprehensive political settlement, both sides sought to use UNPROFOR to achieve their own political goals. The Serb side took advantage of UNPROFOR's presence in its efforts to freeze the *status quo* while establishing a self-proclaimed state of the "Republic of Serbian Krajina" in UNPROFOR's area of responsibility. The government of Croatia had in turn insisted on the reintegration of the UNPA's into Croatia and demanded that refugees and displaced persons be returned to their homes in these areas. On several occasions, it had launched military incursions in pursuit of these goals, further intensifying Serb hostility.[30]

Phase II began with the decision by the Croat government to take military action to recover control of the UNPA's. Hostilities then flared up around the Maslenica area and in the Medak pocket. In the words of Lt. General Nambiar, "the Croat attack put everything back to zero".[31] In January 1993, the Krajina Serbs removed their weapons from the UN storage sites and mobilized a counterattack in all sectors except Sector West. The Croat attack also forced

---

[30] UN Document S/1994/300 of 16 March 1994.
[31] Interview with Lieutenant Satish General Nambiar.

UNPROFOR to abandon the disarmament measures contained in its mandate.[32] The progress that had been made in disarming and demobilizing the warring parties during the first phase was reversed. In this situation of prevailing conflict and mistrust, UNPROFOR's major preoccupation was the mediation of a number of cease-fire agreements which allowed the use of weapons to be monitored and scaled down, but no real disarmament was possible.

Croat Incursion into Sector South

On 22 January 1993, Croatian forces penetrated UN peacekeeping lines in the "Republic of Serbian Krajina" within Croatia. Their goals were to establish a new cease-fire line before the expiration of UNPROFOR's mandate on 21 February 1993 and to recover Croatian territory from the Serbs. These operations took place in the disputed "pink zone" outside the UNPA but occupied by Serb forces. They were restricted to certain areas in Dalmatia, namely around the bridge of Maslenica -- which constitutes the only road connection between central Croatia and Dalmatia -- and the Peruca power station. The Serbian defense of the area was immediate. The Serbs mobilized on the day of the Croat incursion, managed to seize the heavy weapons and tanks stored in the approximately 200 UNPROFOR depots,[33] and registered their first success in defending the Krajinas on 27 January 1992. Nevertheless, the Croatian offensive pushed the front 20 kilometers to the southeast into the "pink zone", and reached the Peruca dam on 28 January 1993. Following the Croat offensive, heavy fighting took place along the whole front. While the Croats had taken the Maslenica bridge and the Peruca dam, these areas continued to be exposed to Krajina Serb shelling, and the important line of communication from Dalmatia to Central Croatia was cut off.

Maslenica

On 6 July 1993, new tensions arose following the decision of the Croatian government to take unilateral actions aimed at rebuilding and reopening the Maslenica bridge and the Zadar airport. Claiming that these were Serb territories, the Serbian forces mobilized, shelled neighboring Croat towns (Glina, Karlovac, Gospic and Zadar), and threatened to resume full-scale fighting. On 15 July 1993,

---

[32] UNIDIR, *Practitioners' Questionnaire*, No. Y-060.
[33] Gustenau, "Die Neuordnung des Südslawischen Raumes", No 2, 1993, p. 129.

the president of the Security Council made a statement reiterating the earlier demand (contained in Resolution 802 of 25 January 1993) that the Croatian armed forces withdraw from the areas in question.[34] He further insisted that unilateral action to reopen the Maslenica bridge and Zadar airport, in the absence of agreement between the parties, would jeopardize UN efforts to arrive at a negotiated settlement of the conflict. Following negotiations under the auspices of the UN and with strong pressure on the Croatian government, an agreement was concluded in Erdut on 15 and 16 July 1993.

Croatia failed to withdraw from the areas, and on 2 August 1993, following the Serb shelling Maslenica bridge, one of the bridge's pontoons sank. Nevertheless, negotiations resumed in Geneva for a cease-fire which included elements of the original Erdut/Zagreb agreement. Despite intensive discussions in Geneva, Zagreb, and Knin, an overall cease-fire agreement was not achieved.

Medak Offensive

Shelling intensified on both sides of the confrontation lines, and there were several grave incidents in the UNPA's and in the "pink zones". Then, on 9 September 1993, the Croatian Army carried out another military incursion in the area of Medak and seized three Serb villages. The hostilities worsened on 10 and 11 September with a serious escalation in the military means employed; the Croatian Government used aircraft to bomb Serb positions, and the Serbs fired rockets and heavy missiles at Croatian population centers along almost the entire front. On 11 September, a ground-to-ground rocket, probably a Frog-7, hit a suburb of Zagreb.[35] The Krajina Serbs took comprehensive mobilization measures (even taking areas of eastern Slavonia into account) and requested assistance from the Federal Republic of Yugoslavia.

The parties were finally led to sign a cease-fire agreement on 15 September 1993. This came as a result of mediation by UNPROFOR, a call from the Security Council,[36] and intervention by the Secretary-General's Special Representative. UNPROFOR moved some 500 to 600 troops into the area to replace the Croatian armed forces, which withdrew to positions occupied before the incursion. When

---

[34] Statement by the President of the Security Council, 15 July 1993, in United Nations, *The United Nations and the Situation in the Former Yugoslavia*, Reference Paper, January 1995, New York, p. 143.

[35] Gustenau, "Die Neuordnung des Südslawischen Raumes", No 6, 1993, p. 552.

[36] UN Document S/26436.

UNPROFOR gained access to the area, it found that most houses had been deliberately destroyed during the withdrawal and that atrocities had been committed on the civilian population.[37] These crimes further aggravated the Serb population's fears and mistrust, and despite the cease-fire agreement, artillery fighting continued around the towns of Zadar, Split, Biograd and Vodice.

Mandate Enlargements: Chapter VII of the UN Charter

During the second phase, besides a number of prolongations of UNPROFOR's mandate in Croatia and its extension to Bosnia-Herzegovina, the most important enlargement was the formal authorization of UNPROFOR to take whatever measures necessary, including the use of force, to ensure its security and its freedom of movement.

On 19 February 1993, the Security Council adopted the first resolution (Resolution 807) concerning the conflict in Croatia which was explicitly based on Chapter VII of the UN Charter, allowing for enforcement measures against the will of the conflicting parties.[38] This legal addition had been implemented previously within UNPROFOR's mandate in Bosnia-Herzegovina. However, for its activities in Croatia, Resolution 807 represented an enlargement. It called for UNPROFOR troops in the former Yugoslavia to be armed for their protection and to "take all appropriate measures to strengthen [their] security...". It urged that UNPROFOR be provided with "the necessary defensive means", and recommended that the troops "study the possibility of carrying out such local redeployment of military units as is required to ensure their protection".

Implementation of the Disarmament Components of the Mandate: Starting from Scratch

UNPROFOR's initial success in placing TDF heavy weapons in storage depots under a "double-lock" system was reversed following the 22 January 1993

---

[37] See United Nations, *The United Nations and the Situation in the Former Yugoslavia*, Reference Paper, 15 March 1994, p. 13.

[38] It should be noted that uncertainties concerning interpretation of the UNPROFOR mandate, particularly in reference to the right of the Forces to use force, existed from the outset of the operation. Divergent views were also expressed in the answers to the UNIDIR Questionnaire. See UNIDIR, *Preliminary Analysis of Practitioners' Questionnaires: Former Yugoslavia*, internal memo.

offensive by the Croatian Army in Sector South and the adjacent "pink zones". UNPROFOR's inability to shield the local Serb population from such an attack led the Serb forces to mobilize and break into a number of storage areas to remove their weapons, including heavy weapons, ostensibly to protect themselves. It should be noted, however, that such developments were successfully prevented in Sector West, due to the firm commitment of the UNPROFOR Sector Commander to keep the sector demilitarized and to protect the populations on both sides of the confrontation lines.

On 25 January 1993, the Security Council, in Resolution 802, called on Croatia to withdraw its forces behind the original cease-fire line and demanded that the Serb authorities in the Krajina return the heavy weapons which had been seized from UN depots. Intensive efforts were also made by UNPROFOR and by the International Conference on the Former Yugoslavia (ICFY) to conclude a cease-fire and to restore the prior status in accordance with Security Council Resolution 802.

An agreement was signed on 6 April 1993 between representatives of the Government of Croatia and the Serb local authorities. This agreement stipulated: the withdrawal of the Croatian forces behind the cease-fire line of January 1993; the submission of Serb heavy weapons; the withdrawal of Serb units from the "pink zones"; and the control of these zones by UNPROFOR forces. The agreement also called for the deployment of an additional 2,000 UN forces to monitor its implementation. However, the reinforcement was not forthcoming, and fighting continued in the three strategic zones around the Maslenica bridge, the airfield of Zadar, and the Peruca power station.

In a report to the Security Council on 24 June 1993, the Secretary-General drew attention to the failure of the parties to permit implementation of the UN plan.[39] He noted, however, that the presence of UNPROFOR was indispensable for controlling the conflict because it fostered a climate in which negotiations between the parties could be promoted. Its presence also helped to prevent the resumption or escalation of conflict, to provide a breathing-space for the continued efforts of the peacemakers, and to support the provision of essential humanitarian assistance. Subsequently, UNPROFOR's mandate was extended until 30 September 1993.

The Erdut agreement, signed on 15 and 16 July 1993, was intended to put an end to hostilities at the Maslenica bridge, the Zadar airport and the Peruca Dam

---

[39] UN Document S/25993 of 14 June 1993.

regions. It required the withdrawal of Croatian armed forces and police from the these areas, which would be put under UNPROFOR's control. UNPROFOR moved 2,000 troops into the areas adjacent to those from which the Croatian forces were to withdraw, but could not deploy in these areas because the Croatian military authorities would not allow UNPROFOR full access to them. As each party made the keeping of its engagement contingent on the other's compliance, the Erdut agreement was, as many others before, short-lived.

Following the Medak offensive and the cease-fire of 15 September 1993, UNPROFOR moved some 500 to 600 troops into the area to replace the Croatian armed forces which withdrew to positions occupied before the incursion began. However, the Croatian destruction of three Serb villages in the Medak pocket further increased the Serbs' mistrust of both the Croats and UNPROFOR and strengthened their determination not to disarm. This refusal, in turn, prevented UNPROFOR from implementing other essential elements of the Vance Plan, particularly facilitating the return of refugees and displaced persons to their places of origin in secure conditions. As a result, UNPROFOR found itself administering a stalemate in the UNPA's while being criticized by both sides.

In a report dealing primarily with Croatia, dated 20 September 1993, the Secretary-General recommended the renewal of UNPROFOR's mandate for a period of six months.[40] He declared that he had been "sorely tempted" to recommend the withdrawal of the Force altogether because of the criticism of UNPROFOR by both sides and the dangers and abuse to which its personnel were exposed. However, such a step, he believed, could only result in further conflict. He stressed that the solution to the problem had to be sought through political dialogue and that the parties themselves had to seek reconciliation. In this process, UNPROFOR's principal objective could only be to keep the peace, thereby permitting negotiations to take place on an overall political settlement.

UNPROFOR continued its two-track approach of providing support for the talks sponsored by the ICFY and promoting step-by-step action in the UNPA's. According to the report by the Secretary-General of 1 December 1993, there had been movement in all the UNPA's towards achieving local cease-fires. These ranged from a signed, formal cease-fire agreement in Sector East to "gentlemen's agreements" -- oral and unsigned, but implemented -- in the other three sectors. In each of the latter, discussions were continuing towards formal agreements.

---

[40] UN Document S/26470, and Add. 1 of 20 September 1993.

Sector East exemplified the step-by-step approach; a local cease-fire was first signed and implemented and was then followed by the establishment of local joint commissions to investigate violations. With these first steps in place, the Sector Commander proposed to each side the creation of zones of separation between their forces. Such local cease-fires had been supported in each sector by the establishment of new observation posts, additional patrols by UN military observers, and the installation of hot lines with, and between, the two sides. The consequence of these measures was a discernible reduction in tension and violations throughout the UNPA's.

In accordance with the Force Commander's directions, Sector Commanders took a number of other steps on the military side to enhance cooperation and reduce tensions, including the opening of several new crossing-points and the enhancement of UNPROFOR's border-monitoring capability. They managed to initiate and maintain face-to-face meetings between the two sides' military commanders in, and adjacent to, all sectors, and they pursued every opportunity to persuade the two sides to move toward greater cooperation.

On 17 December 1993, Croat representatives and local Serb authorities in Croatia signed the Christmas Truce Agreement, mediated by UNPROFOR, which initiated a new phase marked by closer cooperation and a reduction of tensions.

Conclusions

In the words of General Jean Cot, the 22 January 1993 offensive was a "Trafalgar"[41] for UNPROFOR; the Serbs removed their arms from the storage sites, and the Vance Plan was put aside. Because of resumption of hostilities and periodic flare-ups at strategic points on the confrontation line, disarmament operations became impossible. UNPROFOR took up the role of negotiator and brokered a number of local cease-fire agreements. On the ground, its tasks were reduced to bringing food and supplies to areas in need of humanitarian aid.[42]

During this phase, the main difficulty encountered by UNPROFOR in implementing its disarmament mandate was the total absence of consensus among the parties. This phase also revealed that UNPROFOR was neither able to offer effective protection of the populations in the UNPA's nor to carry out its own mission in a conflictual environment. Towards the end of the second phase, it

---

[41] Interview with General Jean Cot, former UNPROFOR Force Commander, at UNIDIR, Geneva, 12 April 1995.
[42] *Ibid.*

became obvious that none of the parties could attain its objectives by military means. The Krajina Serbs would not surrender their arms or allow the UN to control their territory; the Croats would not allow the Krajina to secede; and the UN would not mount a force to impose the original Vance Plan. In the end, the only solution was to focus on the actual lines of confrontation and to defuse as many incidents as possible in order to maintain some sort of calm in the region.

In the absence of an overall political agreement, Croat representatives and local Serb authorities in Croatia signed the Christmas Truce Agreement mediated by UNPROFOR. The two parties undertook to cease armed hostilities along all existing confrontation lines from midnight on 23 December until midnight on 15 January 1994. They also agreed to implement certain confidence-building measures and to open negotiations on a "general and lasting" cease-fire. Subsequently, the truce was extended beyond 15 January 1994, marking the beginning of a new phase in both the Croat and Serb relationship and UNPROFOR's activities in Croatia.

2.4. Phase III: Cease-Fire Agreement Gives UNPROFOR an Interposition Role Combined with Disarmament, Demilitarization and Control of Weapons Functions Within the Zone of Separation

Introduction

Most of 1994 saw closer ties between Croatia and the FRY as well as with Bosnia-Herzegovina. In the Krajinas, the relations between Zagreb and Belgrade led to an ambiguous political situation, and with the general uncertainty in the region, the tendency was to adhere to the status quo. Furthermore, as the conflict in Bosnia-Herzegovina overwhelmed international negotiators, little effort was made to achieve a settlement in Croatia.

Stabilization of the situation in Croatia was achieved through the successfully-implemented cease-fire of 29 March 1994, followed by an agreement on economic issues on 2 December 1994. The cease-fire agreement involved, *inter alia*, the interpositioning of UNPROFOR forces in a zone of separation of varying width; the establishment of additional control points, observation posts and patrols; and the monitoring of the withdrawal of heavy weapons out of range of the contact line. UNPROFOR carried out demilitarization, disarmament and weapons monitoring operations within certain areas along the former confrontation lines. The resulting reduced hostilities paved the way for economic confidence-building measures and a certain degree of normalization of economic relations.

Early 1994

Based on the need of the two countries to develop a closer relationship, Croatia and the FRY reached an agreement to normalize bilateral relations in Geneva on 19 January 1994. The agreement came as a surprise to most international observers. It failed, however, to address the main source of conflict between the two countries, namely the status of the Serb-controlled territories in Croatia.

At the same time, the Croatian leadership was seeking an arrangement with the Bosnian Muslims, proposing the creation of an economic, customs and monetary union. Negotiations resulted in the Camp Pleso cease-fire agreement signed on 23 February 1994 in Zagreb. Two further agreements were signed in Washington on 1 March 1994: the Framework Agreement, establishing a federation in Bosnia-Herzegovina; and the outline of a Preliminary Agreement for a confederation between the Republic of Croatia and the Federation. As a result, new avenues for a political settlement were opened.

Negotiations were also made possible between the Zagreb and Knin authorities. This occurred against the background of increasing internal pressure on Croatia and a change in the leadership of the Republic of Serbian Krajina. The Krajinian presidency was won by Milan Martic on 23 January 1994. His predecessors, Presidents Milan Babic and Goran Hadzic, had both believed firmly that the Krajina's independence could be guaranteed only by force and the maintenance of a hard-line against Zagreb. While pursuing the same ultimate objective of Serbian Krajina independence, Martic chose to tone down his predecessors' confrontational rhetoric and did not insist on *de jure* recognition of the Krajina as a *sine qua non* for establishing a dialogue with Zagreb.

The Cease-Fire Agreement of 29 March 1994

On 29 March 1994, representatives from Croatia and the Republic of Serbian Krajina met in the Russian Embassy in Zagreb to sign a cease-fire agreement aimed at achieving a lasting cessation of hostilities.[43] The document addressed an agreed-upon line of contact between the opposing forces and established lines of separation at a distance of one kilometer on either side of the contact line. It stated that:

1. All hostilities were to end immediately and a cease-fire on the contact line would start on 4 April 1994;
2. The forces deployed on the contact line and within 10 kilometers of that line in either direction were to be frozen, and no movement of units was to take place within that area;
3. By 5 April 1994, all indirect-fire weapons were to be deployed out of range of the lines of separation: mortars and anti-aircraft guns were to be deployed at least 10 kilometers beyond the contact line and artillery and tanks at least 20 kilometers beyond this line. As an exception to this rule, some indirect-fire weapons from both parties could be stored inside the 20-kilometer line, according to the "Rules of Disengagement"; and
4. By 8 April 1994, all units on the contact line were to be separated. The separation was to be based on a mutual withdrawal of units of not less than 1 kilometer from the contact line to their respective lines of separation. These separation lines were to be drawn on maps and accepted by the parties. All units were to withdraw to a distance from which they could not target each other with direct-fire weapons.

The area between the lines of separation would be under the exclusive control of UNPROFOR, and would admit no military, paramilitary, militia or police personnel from either of the parties. The parties were obliged, however, to assist UNPROFOR with the maintenance of law and order in this area.

Implementation of the Cease-Fire Agreement's Disarmament Components

According to the cease-fire agreement, UNPROFOR military observers were to verify that all weapons systems were deployed beyond the minimum distances from the lines of separation. They had full freedom of movement on both sides of these lines, including the right to visit military and paramilitary units and facilities

---

[43] This agreement is reproduced in UN Document S/1994/367 of 30 March 1994.

with four hours' advanced notice. Joint commissions, chaired by a representative of UNPROFOR, were to be established to determine the lines of separation on the ground. Later, the main mission of the joint commissions would be to investigate immediately any violation of the cease-fire. The agreement also listed a number of crossing points along the contact line which were to be manned by UNPROFOR. Checkpoints or other positions of the two sides had to be established as far away as needed to ensure that small arms and heavy machine-gun fire could not target the UNPROFOR checkpoint.

UNPROFOR's main tasks were to monitor and verify the cease-fire. These tasks were essential steps towards reducing tensions, allowing normal life to begin in previously insecure areas, and establishing the conditions for economic confidence-building measures which might lead to political dialogue. The agreement significantly reduced active hostilities between the conflicting sides in Croatia. By the end of May, compliance was almost total; hostilities had ceased, forces were withdrawn beyond the fixed lines of separation, and heavy weapons had been placed in agreed-upon storage sites. UNPROFOR had assumed control of the zone of separation, which covered an area of over 1,300 square kilometers.

The creation this zone of separation did not pose any particular implementation problems, nor did the creation of the 10 kilometer zone of withdrawal for light mortars and anti-aircraft guns. However, the situation was different for the withdrawal of artillery and tanks behind the 20 km line. In many cases, particularly inside Sectors East and West, it was impossible to achieve the required distances because of the size of the sectors. Therefore, weapons storage sites were established to "house" weapons systems. This arrangement was also required on the Croatian side in the area between Sector South and the Adriatic Coast.

The storage sites were located in "built-up areas" usually near a military installation and always in buildings. The warring factions maintained the weapons in the sites, and kept them in a high state of readiness. Due to the circumstances, the sites were all close to the zone of separation and within 20 km of the contact line. According to information obtained from UNPROFOR Headquarters in Zagreb, there were 185 weapons storage sites in total, of which 136 were located on the Serb Krajina side and 49 on the Croatian side.

In some locations, UN soldiers were permanently stationed at the sites. They controlled access to the site along with the warring parties. In most cases, however, the sites were only visited on a routine basis and did not have a permanent UN presence.[44] In some areas of Sector East, none of the weapons storage sites were guarded by UNPROFOR. As a result, in the mobilization following the attack on Ubdina airport, most of the heavy weapons in Sector East were redeployed in war position.[45]

A number of factors influenced UN access to the weapons storage sites. Normally, access could be achieved on short notice. Access was sometimes complicated, however, by the prevailing military situation in the area, by exercises being conducted by the warring factions, by the personalities of the local commanders, or by the types of weapons contained in the storage site. If clearance to visit the site was denied, it could be assumed that some or all the weapons had been removed. This fact was often confirmed by sightings of weapons that had been withdrawn and redeployed.

The UN maintained detailed lists of the weapons contained in each of the weapons storage sites. These lists were prepared in conjunction with the party concerned, but due to a number of factors, the inventories needed to be updated regularly. Weapons were sometimes moved from one storage site to another, previously undeclared weapons were brought in, and new weapons could be brought into the area. This last option was not very likely, according to information obtained from UNPROFOR Headquarters in Zagreb, because new weapons would be spotted by UN observation or control posts and were rarely given over to a weapons storage site.

While the establishment of weapons storage sites certainly facilitated the implementation of the cease-fire agreement, it by no means affected the operational capabilities of the warring factions. Weapons were routinely removed from storage sites for training and maintenance, and if either warring party decided to remove the weapons from any or all storage sites, they could do so quickly and easily.[46]

As reported by the Secretary-General on 17 September 1994, UNPROFOR faced several setbacks in its efforts to implement the cease-fire agreement.[47] In Sector West, it proved impossible to define the different lines of separation and withdrawal on the Croatian side because the Croats claimed that, since they were located within the UNPA, the area was by definition demilitarized and there was

---

[44] Correspondence exchanged with UNPROFOR in Zagreb.

[45] Interview with Mr Bent Jensen, ECMM, Zagreb, 24 and 25 April 1995.

[46] UNPROFOR Headquarters in Zagreb, correspondence exchanged with HQ Croatia Command.

[47] UN Document S/1994/1067 of 17 September 1994.

no confrontation line.[48] In this sector, Croatia maintained between 300 and 500 "special police" in positions close to the former contact line, and incursions by local Serb forces across the contact line had led to the death of two Croatian soldiers and one civilian. The Krajina Serbs in Sector West, after having initially withdrawn to the lines foreseen in the cease-fire agreement, came forward again when they realized that the Croatian side had not drawn back. According to an interview at UNMO headquarters in Zagreb, UNPROFOR performed its tasks in the whole area of separation as foreseen in the cease-fire agreement and as if the separation lines existed.[49] They monitored the 1,000 meters on each side of the confrontation line, even though at some places the warring parties were as close as 50 meters from each other.

Another problem related to the status of the local police forces, including the "special police". They were the responsibility of the UNCIVPOL branch of UNPROFOR, and neither the military branch of UNPROFOR nor the UNMO's could check police stations or trucks belonging to the police.[50] There were also a number of small setbacks in Sector South. The Croatian side expected water facilities on the Serb side to come under UNPROFOR control and management, without the need for Serb agreement. There was also a series of violent incidents, including the explosion of an UNCIVPOL station and an incursion into the zone of separation by 100 Serb soldiers.

Besides monitoring compliance with the cease-fire agreement, UNPROFOR continued to control the borders of the UNPA's in order to prevent weapons from being brought in. However, due to restrictions on movement and insufficient personnel, the force could not monitor all the roads which gave access to the UNPA's. Moreover, it was impossible to control helicopters and trains which started operating following the economic agreement. In early July 1994, an association of displaced persons of Croatia imposed a blockade on all the crossing-points into or within the UNPA's, and severely restricted UNPROFOR's ability to carry out its mandate. The blockade was lifted on 19 August.

In the second half of the year, the relative stability in the area was endangered by a number of events which were triggered by developments in neighboring areas of Bosnia-Herzegovina. BiH army advances in the Bihac area led to a sudden influx of approximately 30,000 refugees into Sector North in August 1994. Their

---

[48] Interviews with Mr. Timothy Clifton, ECMM, Zagreb, 25 April 1995 and with Major Jan Segers, UNMO's, Zagreb, 26 April 1995.

[49] Interview with Major Jan Segers, UNMO's, Zagreb, 26 April 1995.

[50] *Ibid.*

presence created both security concerns and an unprecedented challenge to UNPROFOR and humanitarian organizations.[51] Furthermore, despite strong warnings by UNPROFOR, the Krajina Serb forces repeatedly intervened in the fighting by launching attacks from Ubdina airport into the Bihac area. An air raid on 18 November 1994 against the 5th Corps headquarters inside the Safe Area employed napalm and cluster bombs.[52] Following subsequent NATO air actions aimed at disabling the airfield on 21 November 1994, and the Dvor radar site on 23 November 1994, tension in all UNPA's increased dramatically, especially in Sectors North and South. From that month on, the involvement of Croatian Serb and Bosnian Serb forces in the Bihac area and the Croatian military activities in the Livno area near UNPA Sector South created new instabilities and challenges to the cease-fire agreement.

Mandate Enlargement, Resolution 959

Air attacks launched from Krajina territory into the Bihac Safe Area prompted the decision by the Security Council (Resolution 958 of 19 November 1994) to extend to the Republic of Croatia the authorization contained in Resolution 836 concerning the use of air power in and around the Safe Areas. On the same day, the Security Council also adopted Resolution 959, demanding that all parties put an end to "all hostile actions in and around the safe areas".[53] The obligation to abide by the rules established for the protection of the Safe Areas was thus extended to the Bosnian Muslims.

On 21 November 1994, Ubdina airfield was subject to an air strike conducted by NATO in accordance with Resolution 958. Thirty-nine aircraft attacked the tarmac, runway and surface-to-air missile sites and put them temporarily out of operation without destroying any of the aircraft on the ground.[54] Another NATO air strike against Bosnian Serb surface-to-air missile sites revealed that the Bosnian Serbs possessed sophisticated fire control and constituted a real threat to the alliance forces.

---

[51] Most of these refugees returned to Velika Kladusa in late December, according to UN Document S/1995/38 of 14 January 1995, p. 6.

[52] UN Document S/1994/1389 of 1 December 1994, p. 4.

[53] Resolution 959 of 19 November 1995, in United Nations, *The United Nations and the Situation in the Former Yugoslavia*, 23 January 1995, p. 181.

[54] Gustenau, "Die Neuordnung des Südslawischen Raumes", No 1, 1995, p. 66 mentions that, at the time, these forces consisted of 20 Galeb, Jastreb, MiG21 and Orao planes, as well as 10 helicopters.

Despite NATO intervention, Krajina Serb forces apparently continued their military engagements while Bosnian Serb forces showed no sign of relenting in their advance towards the Safe Area of Bihac and the town itself.

The Economic Agreement

The implementation of the cease-fire agreement had raised expectations that the parties would enter into comprehensive discussions on issues of mutual economic benefit, followed by talks on a final political settlement, under the auspices of the ICFY. Unfortunately, scheduled economic negotiations were repeatedly made impossible by provocative public statements, unrealistic preconditions for talks, and disagreements over modalities for the negotiations. Nevertheless, UNPROFOR continued to pursue local economic initiatives, particularly in and around the zone of separation.

On 27 October 1994, after an interruption of seven months, official talks between representatives of Croatia and the Serb Republic of Krajina resumed. These talks took place in the "mini-contact group" consisting of representatives from the UN, the European Union, the Russian Federation, and the United States. The negotiation package may have foreseen the return of Sectors East and West to Croatia and the constitution of a largely autonomous Serb region in Sectors North and South. Autonomy would extend to cultural, economic and communications matters, including the right to fly local flags and to possess local currency and citizenship. The president of the Krajina would automatically be the vice-prime minister of Croatia.[55] However, these negotiations did not lead to any concrete results due to strong opposition from the Krajina leaders, and when the Krajina army participated on the Bosnian Serb side in the Bihac area in mid-November, the negotiation climate further deteriorated.

Progress was, however, achieved in the economic field. The October talks led to a draft agreement on water, electricity, railways, the oil pipeline, and the Zagreb-Belgrade highway. This economic agreement was finalized and signed by representatives of the Croatian government and the Serb local authorities on 2

---

[55] Gustenau, "Die Neuordnung des Südslawischen Raumes", No 1, 1995, p. 61 ff., gives more details about these negotiations between the Krajina and Croat authorities on the future of the Serb Republic of Krajina. The issues negotiated corresponded to the main propositions formulated in the Z-4 plan in January 1995. An interview in Zagreb with Arne Nyberg, ECMM, on 25 April 1995, confirmed that the Z-4 plan was ready as early as October, but was not presented at that time since it might have hindered the successful implementation of the economic agreement.

December 1994. It also contained some disarmament aspects -- according to the concept of disarmament used in this study -- namely the de-mining required to open the water supply systems and the oil pipeline and to restore the electricity transmission lines. A joint commission, composed of two co-chairmen appointed by the Steering Committee of the ICFY, one representative appointed by each of the parties, and one representative of UNPROFOR, was responsible for implementing the economic agreement.

On 21 December 1994, the Zagreb-Belgrade highway was opened in Sectors West and East. UNCIVPOL established a Highway Command of 150 monitors to patrol the highway, together with monitors of the ECMM in areas under Croatian control. UNPROFOR military personnel provided security along the highway through Sector West, and UNPROFOR engineers made minor repairs to ensure safe conditions. Even though it was initially open only during daylight hours, the highway was used by hundreds of vehicles daily. After 6 January 1995, the highway was open on a 24-hour basis with traffic averaging 2,000 vehicles per day, and by 11 January, over 35,000 vehicles had used the highway.[56] By April, because it could be used by the populations from both sides and because it was protected by the UN, the highway had become a place for the local population to meet family members and friends from across the confrontation line.

The opening of the highway created a stimulus for the implementation of other aspects of the economic agreement. On 17 January 1995, work started on the repair and return to the Croatian Serbs of the generator poles of the Obrovac hydroelectric station which had been under the control of the Croatian authorities for four years. The Adriatic oil pipeline which passes through Sector North reopened on 26 January 1995, creating the possibility of significant revenue for Croatia from the shipment of oil to Central European customers. Finally, on 27 January 1995, the Economic Joint Commission held its first meeting in Knin.

Conclusions

During Phase III, the focus of UNPROFOR's activities in Croatia switched from an internal monitoring role in the UNPA's to an interpositional role. Separation and withdrawal zones were created along the whole confrontation line, and these zones became the only demilitarized and disarmed areas in Croatia. UNPROFOR also continued to prevent weapons from being introduced into the

---

[56] UN Document S/1995/38 of 14 January 1995.

UNPA's. However, restrictions imposed on the forces were severe, both in terms of available resources and in terms of cooperation from the parties. Resources were further stressed as UNPROFOR took over duties emanating from the economic agreement.

In implementing its new tasks, UNPROFOR encountered several obstacles. The most formidable were the increased restrictions on freedom of movement imposed by both sides together with a significant decrease in their willingness to cooperate. The number of violations of the cease-fire agreement increased, and in a number of cases disturbingly involved heavy weapons used by the Serbs. There was also a major increase in the number of UNPROFOR vehicles hijacked at gunpoint. All these factors severely hampered UNPROFOR's ability to carry out its mandate. The trend was clearly towards re-arming and not disarmament.

Events during this phase clearly showed that mutual interest by the parties and UNPROFOR's implementation capacity were important to the successful conduct of disarmament operations. Disarmament along the confrontation line served both sides for a while and did not considerably affect their strategic positions. However, beyond the zone of separation, the trend was towards re-arming and UNPROFOR's credibility was at its lowest. Despite these serious challenges to the cease-fire agreement, the Secretary-General concluded in his 14 January 1995 report that the agreements had generally been observed and had created a climate conducive to negotiations and to progress towards economic confidence-building measures.[57]

Towards the end of Phase III, UNPROFOR's primary tasks had developed beyond the maintenance of the cease-fire agreement to encompass the implementation of the economic agreement and the facilitation of cooperative dialogue between the parties. This three-step approach -- cessation of hostilities, economic normalization and political negotiations -- had been successfully pursued during this phase.

This climate was suddenly jeopardized when the Croatian Government decided, on 12 January 1995, not to agree to a continuation of UNPROFOR's mandate beyond March 1995. As UNPROFOR's review date drew nearer, the more the parties revealed the presence of heavy weapons. A UN representative pointed out, in April 1995, that "there are more arms and weapons in this theater than ever".[58]

---

[57] *Ibid.*

[58] Confidential interview, UNPROFOR, Zagreb, April 1995. The sources for the inflow of weapons into the area were Bosnia-Herzegovina, the Serb Republic of Yugoslavia, and Croatia.

Following President Tudjman's 12 January announcement, the "Zagreb-4" ambassadors -- comprising the US and Russian ambassadors to Croatia and Ambassadors Ahrens and Eide from the ICFY, presented a "Draft agreement on the Krajina, Slavonia, Southern Baranja and Western Sirmium" (the Z-4 plan) on 30 January 1995. This plan was not accepted by any party. But at the time research on this case study was concluded in June 1995, it was possible that this plan might constitute the basis for negotiations in view of a political settlement of the Krajina question.

Chapter 3
Disarmament Operations in Bosnia-Herzegovina

3.1. Introduction

While ethnic conflict began in Croatia after its independence became imminent, large-scale violence in Bosnia-Herzegovina erupted after its independence was recognized. In Bosnia-Herzegovina, no single ethnic group formed a majority. Out of a total population of 4.4 million in 1991, 31 percent were Serbs, 17 percent Croats, and 8 percent other minorities, including "Yugoslavs".[1] Most Serbs lived in rural areas, and approximately 60 percent of the land in Bosnia-Herzegovina belonged to them. The geographical distribution of the different ethnic groups in a number of dispersed, isolated enclaves further complicated the ethnic configuration of the country.

As in the Croatian conflict, the EC was initially the main force behind international peace efforts in Bosnia-Herzegovina. In Lisbon, at the end of February 1992 three Bosnian leaders representing their respective groups endorsed a proposal that Bosnia-Herzegovina become a confederation of three ethnic regions. The regionalization of the Republic into different "cantons" would guarantee the sovereignty of the three constituent peoples. The Bosnian Muslims thus renounced the unitary state, and the Bosnian Serbs consented to remain in the Republic. For the Bosnian Croats, who initially favored a partition of Bosnia-Herzegovina, independence from Belgrade was seen as a first step toward closer ties with Zagreb. Unfortunately, the Lisbon compromise was too vague, giving way to divergent interpretations and to continuing disputes among the parties.

Trouble began when the EC announced that Bosnia-Herzegovina would be granted recognition as an independent state once having held a popular referendum on the issue. The referendum process revealed the incompatibility of the positions adopted by the three constituent nationalities. The Muslim majority wanted an independent, sovereign state with strong central government, an objective which could only be achieved at the cost of increased conflict with the Bosnian Serbs and

---

[1] See James B. Steinberg, "International Involvement in the Yugoslavia Conflict", in *Enforcing Restraint -Collective Intervention in Internal Conflicts*, New York: Council on Foreign Relations Press, 1993, pp. 27-75.

the JNA. The Bosnian Serbs and especially the Bosnian Croats wanted the country to be partitioned, and their areas integrated with the Federal Republic of Yugoslavia (Serbia-Montenegro) and Croatia respectively. On the referendum question proper, as to whether to create an independent state of Bosnia-Herzegovina or to remain in what was left of former Yugoslavia, the division was different. Neither the Muslims nor the Croats in Bosnia-Herzegovina wanted to remain in an even more Serb-dominated rump-Yugoslavia. The Bosnian Serbs, on their hand, had no desire to become a "minority" in a new state, and they began to consolidate control over their territories and to proclaim "autonomous provinces". Although all three parties maintained the fiction of a three-way coalition cabinet, the government had already broken up long before the referendum. The referendum, held on 29 February and 1 March 1992, was boycotted by the Bosnian Serbs. Of all the votes cast, more than 99.4 percent, representing 62.7 percent of the total electorate, approved the creation of a sovereign Bosnia-Herzegovina, a confederation of sovereign and constitutive Croatian, Muslim and Serbian peoples.[2]

The EC then immediately announced that Bosnia-Herzegovina would be granted recognition as an independent state. Alja Izetbegovich declared the independence of the Republic of Bosnia-Herzegovina on 2 March 1992. The risk of war was imminent. Sarajevo was paralysed, and the first casualties were soon reported. Renewed negotiations under the presidency of the EC led to an agreement between the parties which would serve as a basis for further talks on the organization of Bosnia-Herzegovina into three constituent units, based on ethnic, economic and geographical criteria. These units would have equal rights and equal ability to issue laws. However, the question of the distribution of power between the Republic and the new units was not resolved. The debate was over the federation model, preferred by the Bosnian Muslims and Bosnian Croats, and the confederation model, advocated by the Bosnian Serbs.

On 7 April 1992, despite repeated warnings about the serious consequences such an action would entail, the EC countries and United States recognized the independence of Bosnia-Herzegovina, in the hopes that this would help to stabilize the political situation. At the same time, the Security Council called on the parties to cooperate with the European Community peace efforts;[3] however, these efforts heightened, rather than prevented, large-scale conflict in Bosnia-Herzegovina.

---

[2] Gustenau, "Die Neuordnung des Südslawischen Raumes", No 3, 1992, p. 232.
[3] Security Council Resolution 749 of 7 April 1992.

It is important to stress that UNPROFOR's mission in Bosnia-Herzegovina differed from other peace operations; it was never intended to be a "classical" peacekeeping operation in which the UN would deploy forces to separate the two sides and then try to forge a peaceful settlement of the dispute. On the contrary, the primary mission in Bosnia-Herzegovina was to use UN forces to provide protection for internationally-sponsored humanitarian assistance activities aimed at supplying and protecting the local inhabitants while an active military conflict raged among the parties. It was not until the Washington agreements of 1 March 1994, that UNPROFOR assumed an interpositional role between the Bosnian Muslims and Bosnian Croats, creating a zone of separation which was to be demilitarized and free of weapons.

From the perspective of UN peace operations, the conflict in Bosnia-Herzegovina unfolded in three phases. In each phase, the UN-led operations expanded and diversified. During the first phase, from April 1992 to June 1993, UNPROFOR had an exclusively humanitarian mandate. Activities concerning the monitoring of weapons or use of weapons, like those undertaken to open the Sarajevo airport, were aimed at assisting the distribution of humanitarian aid. Towards the end of this phase, UNPROFOR received a number of additional tasks, whose objectives deviated from the original humanitarian mandate. Following the crisis in Srebrenica, the second phase from June 1993 to February 1994 saw the enlargement of UNPROFOR's mandate to protect the Safe Areas and to conduct weapons withdrawal and control functions based on local cease-fire agreements reached for some of these Safe Areas. These additions were leading towards peace enforcement, but the limits of these peace enforcement operations were revealed by the Sarajevo crisis in February 1994. This crisis led to increased commitments by the United States and the Russian Federation to the international peace negotiations. Finally, the third phase, from February 1994 to January 1995, added to UNPROFOR's previous tasks the monitoring of the cease-fire agreements and an interpositional role along former confrontation lines. This was done in accordance with the Washington agreements signed between the Bosnian Croats and Bosnian Muslims. At the end of this phase, an important break-through was achieved with the signing of a brief cease-fire agreement between the Federation and the Bosnian Serbs.

3.2. Phase I: Disarmament and Weapons Control Measures as Facilitators of Humanitarian Aid Deliveries -- The Sarajevo Airport Agreement

The period between April 1992 and June 1993 was characterized by conflict escalation following the recognition of Bosnia-Herzegovina and the negotiations aiming at the "cantonalization" of the country. It was also marked by the collapse of existing political structures, and the strong resolution of the Bosnian Serbs to create the independent Republic of Srpska. At the same time, western Herzegovina, populated mainly by Croats, established closer links with Croatia; it was ruled by the laws of Croatia, and it used the Croatian Dinar as its official currency.

During this period, Bosnian Serb offensives concentrated on three main areas. A fierce struggle for the control of territory broke out between Serbs and Croats in the region of Posavina and at Bosanski Brod in the north of Bosnia-Herzegovina. Closely linked to the conflict taking place in Croatia, this "Operation Most" aimed at creating a land-bridge between the FRY (Serbia-Montenegro) and the Krajinas. In the east and south, urban centers with large Muslim populations were stormed by Bosnian Serbs, with support from the JNA. Bijeljina was the first to fall, followed by Zvornik and Bratunac. Srebrenica and Visegrad were encircled and regularly exposed to shelling. The aim of the war in this region was territorial acquisition. The last of the three areas of conflict was Sarajevo. Here a struggle took place primarily between the rural and the urban populations. Undertaken mainly for strategic reasons, this war combined Serb irregulars culled from the surrounding peasantry with JNA forces and heavy artillery to defeat the urban dwellers of Sarajevo. At the time, about 90,000 Serbs lived in Sarajevo, and they faced the devastation of their city side by side with their Muslim, Croat, Jewish and Yugoslav neighbors.[4] As the war continued, Sarajevo became a city divided between Serb-controlled and Muslim-controlled parts.

By July, the Bosnian Serbs had gained most of eastern Bosnia, the northern Posavina corridor (Brcko corridor), eastern Herzegovina and the Bosnian Krajina. Non-Serbs who had not fled during the fighting were now forced out in great numbers. By the end of December 1992, the war in Bosnia-Herzegovina had created a flow of approximately 2.7 million refugees and displaced people.

---

[4] Glenny, *The Fall of Yugoslavia*, 1992, p. 164.

At this stage, the UN's roles were primarily to provide humanitarian relief, to control and operate Sarajevo airport, to support and protect the land convoys, and to monitor the no-fly zone from the ground after it was established by the Security Council. Although the conflict continued, from this time on the front lines between the Bosnian Serbs and the Bosnian Muslim/Bosnian Croat forces remained fairly stable.

International Response to the Conflict

As the situation in Bosnia-Herzegovina continued to deteriorate, the international community adopted a multidimensional, multi-institutional strategy to address the conflict.[5] This strategy included: (a) economic sanctions to end the Federal Republic of Yugoslavia's support of the conflict; (b) humanitarian relief operations undertaken by the UN; and, (c) international negotiations for a political settlement of the conflict.

Economic Sanctions

The Bosnian Serb offensives in Bosnia-Herzegovina led to a change in international public opinion. On 11 May 1992, the EC foreign ministers took joint measures against the FRY. They clearly held it responsible for the deterioration of the situation in Bosnia-Herzegovina and threatened it with reinforced sanctions. On 12 May 1992, a declaration of the CSCE stated that "the pattern of clear, gross and uncorrected violations of CSCE commitments by the authorities in Belgrade and by the Yugoslav People's Army [was] now unmistakably established and that they [bore] the prime responsibility for the escalation of bloodshed and destruction in Bosnia-Herzegovina".[6] "They [CSCE] strongly condemn[ed] the shelling of Sarajevo and other cities by the JNA".[7] The CSCE member states also decided that action on matters relating to the crisis would be taken without the consent of the delegation of Yugoslavia.

On 15 May 1992, the Security Council adopted Resolution 752 calling for an end to interference in Bosnia by both the FRY and Croatia, to the involuntary expulsion of individuals, to any attempts to change the ethnic composition of the

---

[5] For a discussion about the international responses to the conflict in Bosnia-Herzegovina, see Steinberg, "International Involvement in the Yugoslavia Conflict", 1993, pp. 42 ff.

[6] Quoted in *Review of International Affairs*, No 1014, 1 March 1993, pp. 20 ff.

[7] *Ibid.*

population, and for non-interference with humanitarian relief.[8] On the grounds that the JNA had failed to withdraw from Bosnia-Herzegovina as requested by Resolution 752, the Security Council imposed, on 30 May 1992, comprehensive economic sanctions against the FRY (Serbia and Montenegro) based on Chapter VII.[9] These included an embargo on commercial exchanges, the closing down of civilian air traffic, the freezing of Yugoslav assets abroad, the suspension of scientific and technical cooperation and cultural exchanges as well as the interdiction of Yugoslav participation at international sporting competitions. The measures imposed by this resolution did not apply to humanitarian aid deliveries.

Some days after the mandatory sanctions had been adopted, the Secretary-General reported that the units of the former JNA which stayed in Bosnia-Herzegovina operated in fact independently from Belgrade, but that Croatia, on the other hand, had regular units operating in Bosnia-Herzegovina.[10] This statement questioned the appropriateness of the measures taken against the FRY in Resolution 757.

Humanitarian Intervention

The delivery of humanitarian aid was UNPROFOR's main mission in Bosnia-Herzegovina. On 8 June 1992,[11] the Security Council agreed to extend UNPROFOR's mandate to include the securing of Sarajevo airport, and later, authorized all measures necessary to facilitate the delivery of humanitarian aid.[12] However, since the military enforcement capacity originally intended was never provided for in the force, UNPROFOR had to rely on its ability to achieve the consent of all sides in order to fulfill its humanitarian mandate. The strong mandate founded on Chapter VII of the UN Charter was not consistent with the lack of resources given to UNPROFOR, which was asked to operate in an environment marked by hostilities both between the three warring parties and towards the UN itself.

Attempts to stabilize the situation in Bosnia-Herzegovina by locating UNPROFOR's main headquarters in Sarajevo, with Banja Luka as the main

---

[8] This resolution was based on the Secretary-General's report, UN Document S/23900 of 12 May 1992.

[9] Security Council Resolution 757 of 30 May 1992.

[10] Gustenau, "Die Neuordnung des Südslawischen Raumes", No 4, 1992, p. 320.

[11] Security Council Resolution 758 of 8 June 1992.

[12] Security Council Resolution 770 of 13 August 1992.

logistic base, blatantly failed and only complicated UNPROFOR's mission in Croatia. As war spread in Bosnia-Herzegovina, the UN was left with two choices: to expand UNPROFOR's area of operation and mandate, which at the time only covered Croatia, or to withdraw and await a cease-fire. After a visit to Bosnia-Herzegovina in early May, Undersecretary-General for Peacekeeping, Marrack Goulding, concluded that it was not feasible to undertake peacekeeping activities in Bosnia-Herzegovina beyond what had already been achieved.[13] UNPROFOR headquarters were successively moved from the beleaguered town of Sarajevo to Belgrade and then to Zagreb, indicating the unwillingness of the international community to become involved in the war.

In light of the conflict escalation, the ECMM called back all its observers, and the International Committee of the Red Cross (ICRC) ceased its activities in Bosnia-Herzegovina. The Secretary-General decided to accelerate the deployment of military observers from the UNPA's to Bosnia-Herzegovina by sending 40 military observers to the Mostar Region on 30 April 1992. On 14 May, when risks to their lives reached an unacceptable level, the observers were withdrawn, together with about two-thirds of UNPROFOR Sarajevo headquarters personnel. Some 120 military and civilian peacekeepers were left behind without any clearly defined mandate. By June 1992, they represented the only international presence attempting to mediate a cease-fire and to facilitate the delivery of humanitarian aid in Sarajevo.

Disarmament and Weapons Control Measures of the
Sarajevo Airport Agreement

As the devastation of Sarajevo continued and the conditions in the beleaguered town became unbearable, local negotiations allowed, at least, for humanitarian supplies to reach the civilian population in the city. These negotiations gained new momentum following a mortar attack on the Sarajevo market on 28 May 1992 which prompted wide media coverage and international outrage. It also changed the foreign policy positions of a number of countries. News of the attack provoked the departure of a Muslim delegation to the Lisbon peace negotiations and also marked the beginning of a series of Security Council

---

[13] David Rieff, "The Illusions of Peacekeeping", World Policy Journal, Vol. XI, No 3, Fall 1994, pp. 1-18.

resolutions imposing strict sanctions against the FRY[14] and leading to the deployment of UNPROFOR in Bosnia-Herzegovina. Furthermore, this incident led to the acceptance, in principle, of a military intervention should the sanctions not be effective, with NATO as the military instrument at the disposal of the UN. Although initially attributed to the Bosnian Serbs, neither UNPROFOR nor the Security Council wanted to formally and publicly establish the real identity of the perpetrators of the Sarajevo market attack.[15]

At the local level, under the leadership of UNPROFOR,[16] intensive discussions were engaged with the Presidency of Bosnia-Herzegovina, the leaders of the Croatian Democratic Party, and Bosnian Serb leaders Radovan Karadjic and General Ratko Mladic. These negotiations were aimed at stopping the fighting around Sarajevo airport and reopening it for humanitarian purposes under the exclusive authority of the United Nations. They were undertaken in the framework of the Security Council's request to "use the Secretary-General's good offices to achieve the objective of creating the Sarajevo security zone",[17] rather than being the outcome of a clearly defined policy as a resulting from the Blue Helmets' sense of their mission and their ability to find *ad hoc* solutions on the ground.[18] The negotiations led to the 5 June Sarajevo Airport Agreement[19] which ruled that:

a)   all anti-aircraft weapon systems would be withdrawn from any position from which they could engage the airport and its air approaches and would be placed under UNPROFOR supervision;

---

[14] Starting with Security Council Resolution 757 of 30 May 1992 imposing comprehensive sanctions on the FRY, including severing trade links, freezing government assets abroad, an oil embargo, a sporting and cultural ban, and cutting air links.

[15] The commander of the UN observers, General Lewis MacKenzie, attributes the responsibility for the "bread queue" massacre on 27 May 1992 to the Bosnian Muslims, who were trying to attract the attention of western public opinion. The confidential UN report was revealed by the *Independent* some months after the attack. See also Patrice Piquart, "Ex-Yougoslavie: vérités et mensonges au-dessus d'un champ de mines, *L'événement du Jeudi*, 4-10 March 1993, pp. 115-125; Vernet, Daniel and Jean-Marc Gonin, *Le rêve sacrifié*, 1994, p. 107; and Christitch, Kosta, *Le Point*, 26 February 1994.

[16] Mr. Cedric Thornberry, Director of Civil Affairs, and Col. John Wilson, Chief Military Observer at UNPROFOR headquarters in Sarajevo.

[17] Security Council Resolution 757 of 30 May 1992.

[18] See also Age Eknes, *Blue Helmets in a Blown Mission? - UNPROFOR in former Yugoslavia*, Research Report No 174, Norwegian Institute of International Affairs, p. 24.

[19] Contained in UN Document S/24075 of 6 June 1992.

b) all artillery, mortar, missile systems and tanks within the range of the airport would be concentrated in areas agreed by UNPROFOR and would be subject to UNPROFOR observation at the firing line; and,

c) security corridors between the airport and the city would be established and would function under the control of UNPROFOR to ensure the safe movement of humanitarian aid and related personnel.

In order to monitor the Sarajevo Airport Agreement, the Secretary-General asked, in his report to the Security Council of 6 June 1992, for the deployment of a UN contingent of 1,000 men.[20] On 8 June 1992, the Security Council decided to enlarge the mandate and strength of UNPROFOR accordingly.[21] It authorized the deployment of 60 military observers and related personnel and equipment to Sarajevo to supervise the withdrawal of anti-aircraft weapons and the concentration of heavy weapons at agreed-upon locations in the city. The deployment of additional units would be decided after "all conditions necessary for [UNPROFOR] to carry out the mandate approved by the Security Council, including an effective and durable cease-fire, [had] been fulfilled".[22] However, the cease-fire continued to be violated, and the heads of the European Community decided, on 27 June 1992 in Lisbon, to threaten military intervention if the hostilities continued to block the supply of the civilian population.

Following intensive work by UNPROFOR to establish modalities of implementation for the 5 June agreement, the Secretary-General reported that Bosnian Serb forces were withdrawing from the Sarajevo airport and that both sides -- Bosnian Serb and Bosnian Muslim forces -- had begun to concentrate their heavy weapons in locations to be supervised by UNPROFOR. On 29 June, the Security Council adopted Resolution 761 authorizing the immediate deployment of additional elements of UNPROFOR to take full operational control of the airport and to secure the delivery of humanitarian aid, thereby further formalizing UNPROFOR's role in Bosnia-Herzegovina.

The first group of 30 UNPROFOR personnel was deployed to the airport on 28 June 1992. French troops began to arrive on 1 July 1992 and a Canadian battalion arrived from UNPA West the following day. By 3 July 1992, all available UNMO's and troops, totalling roughly 1,100 people, were deployed at the airport and at other locations in Sarajevo.

---

[20] *Ibid.*

[21] Security Council Resolution 758 of 8 June 1992.

[22] *Ibid.*

On 29 June 1992, the first flight carrying humanitarian aid opened the airport, initiating a large-scale airlift operation. However, regarding the cease-fire and the establishment of secure corridors, the implementation of the agreement seemed less satisfactory. On 10 July 1992, the Secretary-General reported that a cease-fire in and around Sarajevo had not been fully established at any time since the UN flag was raised on 29 June.[23] Nor had the concentration of weapons under UNPROFOR observation been completed. Yet, these had been the measures to be implemented prior to the opening of the airport.

Although Sector Sarajevo was strengthened, first temporarily with a Canadian battalion and later by three smaller battalions from Egypt, France and the Ukraine, this did not represent a credible military force that could challenge the Serb forces in the surrounding hills.

Political Negotiations

In Bosnia-Herzegovina, as in Croatia, the international community initially adopted the "division of labor" approach. This method gave the UN responsibility for negotiating and monitoring cease-fires, while the EC was to lead the effort to find a political solution to the crisis. Unfortunately, this arrangement proved difficult to implement, and the EC and the UN decided to merge their efforts to find a political solution to the conflict. The London conference at the end of August followed by the Vance-Owen plan presented on 27 October 1992 constituted the first joint initiatives.

Disarmament Components of the London Agreement

In an effort to find a political solution to the crisis in Bosnia-Herzegovina, the EC, under Lord Carrington, brokered a cease-fire agreement signed in London on 17 July 1992 by the representatives of the three parties: Bosnian Serb leader Radovan Karadjic, Bosnian Croat leader Mate Boban, and the Bosnian Muslim Foreign Minister Haris Silajdzje. This agreement contained provisions concerning the control and monitoring of weapons. It ruled that parties would declare and put under international control all of their heavy weapons (fighter planes, artillery, mortars, rocket launchers, etc.). It also asked the Security Council to create, as

---

[23] UN Document S/24263 of 10 July 1992.

soon as possible, the conditions necessary for the implementation of this agreement.[24]

This provoked an immediate outcry from Secretary-General Boutros Boutros-Ghali, who criticized the EC for committing the UN without prior consultation. Furthermore, the Secretary-General considered that conditions did not yet exist for the UN to supervise the heavy weapons in Bosnia-Herzegovina, as envisaged in the London Agreement, mainly because of lack of cooperation from the belligerent parties.[25] This view was shared by the Security Council.[26] Following this dispute, the EC and the UN decided to merge their efforts and involve the UN directly in peace negotiations, beginning with a joint conference in London on 26-28 August 1992.

Weapons Control and Disarmament Measures of the London Conference

The London Conference on 26-28 August 1992 had as its main objective the coordination of the humanitarian and peace efforts of the different organizations and states involved in the conflict. It was designed to put pressure on the parties in Bosnia-Herzegovina to arrive at a political settlement of the crisis.[27] It outlined the terms for a political solution and approved a statement of principles as the basis for a negotiated settlement of the problems of former Yugoslavia. The parties also agreed to set up the open-ended International Conference on the Former Yugoslavia, with a permanent steering committee co-chaired by Cyrus Vance (on behalf of the UN) and Lord Owen, a former British foreign secretary who took over from Lord Carrington (on behalf of the EC).

While negotiations were to aim at achieving a political settlement, it was recognized that they also urgently needed to cover "the grouping of heavy weaponry under international control" and "the demilitarization of major towns and the monitoring of them by international observers". Furthermore, it was stated that an international peacekeeping force under UN auspices might be created by

---

[24] Gustenau, "Die Neuordnung des Südslawischen Raumes", No 5, 1992, p. 415.

[25] See UN Document S/24333 of 21 July 1992.

[26] See Statement of the President of the Security Council of 24 July 1992, in *The United Nations and the Situation in the Former Yugoslavia*, pp. 93-94.

[27] Gustenau, "Die Neuordnung des Südslawischen Raumes", No 5, 1992, p. 490.

the UN Security Council to maintain the cease-fire, control military movements and undertake other confidence-building measures.[28]

On the occasion of the London Conference, the representatives of the Bosnian Serbs indicated their agreement to: inform the UN within 96 hours of the positions of all heavy weapons to be grouped around the four towns of Sarajevo, Bihac, Gorazde and Jajce; to complete this grouping; and to put the storage sites under supervision of the UN within seven days.[29] However, this agreement was not respected, and one of the first tasks of the ICFY negotiators was to ask the Bosnian Serbs to put heavy weapons (artillery over 100 mm calibre, 82 mm mortars, tanks and rocket launchers) deployed around the four towns under UN control by 12 September 1992. This request was only partially honored.

Implementation of UNPROFOR's Mandate

The initial mandate, contained in Resolution 743, made provision for UNMO's to patrol certain limited areas in Bosnia-Herzegovina following the demilitarization of the UNPA's. This demilitarization did not occur, and until June 1992, this was the only mandate in Bosnia-Herzegovina.

Following the Sarajevo Airport Agreement, Security Council Resolution 758 of 8 June 1992 demanded all parties -- and this subsequently became UNPROFOR's mandate --"*to create the necessary conditions for unimpeded delivery of humanitarian supplies to Sarajevo and other locations in Bosnia-Herzegovina, including the establishment of a security zone encompassing Sarajevo and its airport*".[30]

During the summer of 1992, public pressure to take a more active approach to humanitarian relief increased, spurred on by horrifying revelations of human rights abuses and by reports on the war's devastating effects on the civilian population. Also, following attacks against convoy escorts and the shooting down of an Italian transport aircraft, pressure to reinforce the security and protection of UNPROFOR personnel increased, leading the Security Council to adopt measures to this end.

On 13 August 1992, after considerable debate, the Security Council adopted Resolution 770 which "called upon all states to take nationally or through regional agencies or arrangements all measures necessary to facilitate in coordination with

---

[28] London Conference, 27 August 1992, Statement on Bosnia.

[29] *Ibid.*

[30] Details about this agreement have been set out in earlier sections.

the United Nations" the delivery of humanitarian aid to Sarajevo and wherever needed in other parts of Bosnia-Herzegovina.[31] Based on Chapter VII of the UN Charter, this resolution provided a powerful base for the deployment of an international military presence in Bosnia-Herzegovina. Indeed, it had initially been planned as a humanitarian enforcement operation. However, the European countries that subsequently took responsibility for the operational planning also became the major troop contributors. They changed the concept of the operation, turning it into an intervention that followed standard peacekeeping procedures. Several factors contributed to the rejection of a large-scale military intervention as an option, namely the humanitarian consequences of such an action, the reluctance of UN troop contributors to send their forces on an enforcement mission, and the lack of clear objectives for such an intervention.

After a period of uncertainty over how to implement the provisions in Resolution 770, it was ultimately agreed that a new UN force, UNPROFOR II, would be deployed. Accordingly, the Secretary-General submitted, on 10 September 1992, a further report to the Security Council recommending the expansion of UNPROFOR's mandate and strength.[32] On 14 September 1992, it was decided that the operation should be formally integrated into the existing peacekeeping force as an expansion of UNPROFOR, and that its mandate would include the following tasks:[33]

a)   to provide support to the efforts of the United Nations High Commissioner for Refugees (UNHCR) to deliver humanitarian relief throughout Bosnia-Herzegovina, particularly through the provision of convoy protection when requested;

b)   to provide protection for other humanitarian agencies with the approval of the UNHCR;

c)   to protect United Nations facilities, including UNHCR storage centers, if so requested; and,

d)   to provide protection for convoys of released detainees when requested by the (ICRC) and with the concurrence of the Force Commander that the request was practicable.

---

[31]   Security Council Resolution 770 of 13 August 1992.
[32]   UN Document S/24540 of 10 September 1992.
[33]   Security Council Resolution 776 of 14 September 1992.

These duties proved to be the main tasks of UNPROFOR's Bosnia-Herzegovina Command, in terms of time and resources expended, during this first phase.

The organizational structure of the new Bosnia-Herzegovina UNPROFOR Command was rather unusual. It was composed of units from EC and NATO countries exclusively, which had responsibility for the military planning of the operation and for the financing of the nearly 8,000 man force.[34] Lt. General Satish Nambiar continued as the UN commander in former Yugoslavia; however, as commander for the Bosnia-Herzegovina operation, French Major General Philippe Morillon was nominated.

The Bosnia-Herzegovina Command consisted of Sector Sarajevo, which continued to perform the tasks arising from the 5 June 1992 Airport Agreement, and four new zones. In each zone, an infantry battalion group, possessing a high degree of self-sufficiency, was responsible for providing troops to protect UNHCR-organized convoys within that zone. The Command also included additional logistics and other support elements, some 80 UNMO's and 80 civilian staff members. UNPROFOR troops followed normal peacekeeping ROE, which authorized them to use force in self-defense only.

The financial arrangements for this mission constituted an innovation in UN peacekeeping operations. In fact, the additional contingents were financed and supported entirely by their national governments. This arrangement gave rise to some trouble, especially in regard to command and control issues.[35]

Nevertheless, as the war raged on with unrestrained ferocity, the new command was not able to implement much of its mandate nor to reach the objectives staked out in Resolutions 770 and 771. Furthermore, deployment of UNPROFOR's Bosnia-Herzegovina Command, which according to the initial planning comprised all of Bosnia-Herzegovina, could not be realized in areas under Serb control. According to UN analysts, only about one-quarter of the needed humanitarian supplies were reaching the target population, a situation which was to deteriorate further still as winter 1992/1993 approached. UNPROFOR's strict peacekeeping mandate, its limited military capacity, and the lack of cooperation between the belligerent parties severely limited the effective protection that UNPROFOR could provide to the humanitarian agencies. Also,

---

[34] This led some analysts to consider UNPROFOR Bosnia-Herzegovina Command as a *de facto* NATO operation. See Eknes, *Blue Helmets in a Blown Mission? - UNPROFOR in former Yugoslavia*, Research Report No 174.

[35] See UN Document S/24848 of 24 November 1992.

UNPROFOR's military resources were not in proportion with the successive tasks that the mission was given.

Evolution of UNPROFOR's Mandate:
Enforcement and Protection of the Safe Areas

The Security Council was clearly unwilling to act militarily in a comprehensive manner; however, member states found themselves compelled to react by public pressure on the Bosnia-Herzegovina issue. A number of resolutions intended to create an image of action were thus passed without being matched by an adequate strengthening of UNPROFOR's military presence. All this led to additional tasks for UNPROFOR. The ban on military flights in the airspace above Bosnia-Herzegovina, adopted by Resolution 781 of 9 October 1992, asked UNPROFOR to place observers at airfields in former Yugoslavia and to monitor air traffic to and from Bosnia-Herzegovina. The establishment of UN border control mechanisms, adopted by Resolution 787 of 16 November 1992, asked for the deployment of observers on the borders of Bosnia-Herzegovina, but this resolution was never implemented.[36] In addition, the establishment of the Safe Areas further overstretched UNPROFOR's resources and diverted even more staff attention and personnel on the ground away from what had been the mission's primary objective, namely to secure the delivery of humanitarian assistance throughout Bosnia-Herzegovina.[37]

No-fly Zone

On 13 March 1993, bombs were dropped on two villages east of Srebrenica by airplanes that UN observers could not identify, but which departed in the

---

[36] In a report to the Security Council of 21 December 1992, UN Document S/25000, the Secretary-General indicated that it would be necessary to give UNPROFOR a mandate which would include the right not only to search but also to turn back or confiscate military personnel, weapons, or sanctioned goods. He pointed out that a symbolic presence at selected crossing points would only undermine the already strained credibility of UNPROFOR, and proposed, therefore, an enlargement of UNPROFOR by some 10,000 additional troops. The Security Council later decided to send UN observers along the border (Resolution 838 of 10 June 1993). However, the Secretariat was not able to find countries willing to provide the 500 observers needed, and neither did the FRY want the observers deployed.

[37] Resolutions adopted in this respect were: 819 of 16 April 1993, 824 of 6 May 1993, and 836 of 4 June 1993.

direction of the FRY. Since the beginning of the monitoring of the "no-fly zone" in October 1992 and up to March 1993, the UN had reported some 540 violations.[38] This was the first time, however, that aircraft had been used in combat activity. On 17 March 1993, the Security Council demanded that the Bosnian Serbs explain immediately the violations and particularly the aerial bombardment of the two villages. The Security Council also requested the Secretary-General to ensure that an investigation be made into the reported possible use of the FRY's territory to launch air strikes against Bosnia-Herzegovina.

On 31 March, the Security Council adopted Resolution 816 which extended the ban on military flights to cover flights by all fixed-wing and rotary-wind aircraft in the airspace over Bosnia-Herzegovina.[39] It allowed NATO aircraft to shoot down planes violating the no-fly zone imposed on Bosnian airspace in October 1992 and became operational on 12 April 1993, when NATO fighters from France, the Netherlands and the United States began enforcement. It did not apply to flights authorized by UNPROFOR.

Safe Areas

On 16 April 1993, the Security Council, acting under Chapter VII of the Charter, adopted Resolution 819, demanding that all parties treat Srebrenica and its surroundings as a "safe area" free from any armed attack or any other hostile act. It demanded the immediate withdrawal of Bosnian Serb paramilitary units from areas surrounding Srebrenica and the cessation or armed attacks against that town. UNPROFOR was requested to be let into the town to arrange for the safe transfer of the ill and wounded and to assist in the delivery of humanitarian supplies.

This resolution did not formally imply an enlargement of UNPROFOR's mandate; it simply asked the warring parties to refrain from attacking the Safe Area. Subsequent enlargements and reinforcement of the troops came about in the next phase of UNPROFOR's activities in Bosnia-Herzegovina, with Resolutions 824, 836 and 844. In reality, however, UNPROFOR was already performing cease-fire monitoring and implementing disarmament provisions, as is shown in a separate section of this study.

---

[38] UN Document S/1994/300 of 16 March 1994.
[39] The early ban declared by Security Council Resolution 781 of 9 October 1992 concerned only military flights.

Disarmament and Demilitarization Measures
of the Vance-Owen Peace Plan

In the absence of a multinational military option to end the conflict in Bosnia-Herzegovina, international negotiations continued to pursue a political settlement of the conflict under the auspices of the EC, the UN and the ICFY. On 28 October 1992, the co-chairmen of the ICFY, Vance and Owen, presented a draft constitution for Bosnia-Herzegovina, representing a compromise between the divergent positions. It proposed seven to 10 largely autonomous provinces in charge of education, police, health, and law enforcement, and a central government responsible for defense, foreign policy, and trade. Although it was immediately refused by the Bosnian Serb and Bosnian Croat sides, this proposal served as a starting point for further negotiations.

In a new effort to reach a political settlement of the crisis, Lord Owen and Cyrus Vance presented on 2 January 1993, a new proposal for Bosnia-Herzegovina, including:

- the reorganization of Bosnia-Herzegovina into 10 provinces shown on a detailed map which was provided;
- the establishment of five major corridors between the provinces that would allow the safe passage of humanitarian aid and civilians;
- constitutional principles for the republic with a large measure of autonomy for the provinces within a decentralized state; and,
- cease-fire and demilitarization arrangements.

This was the first peace plan which implicitly put ethnic labels on the different provinces to be created in Bosnia-Herzegovina; it marked the beginning of what came to be known as the "map game".

The disarmament and demilitarization measures, contained in the "Agreement for Peace in Bosnia and Herzegovina" of the Vance-Owen plan, included the following elements:

1. The unconditional cessation of hostilities throughout Bosnia-Herzegovina and the separation of forces. The concrete steps envisaged in the process included an absolute cease-fire, the temporary freezing of the military situation, no forward deployments or offensive action, no movement of additional forces, the withdrawal of heavy weapons (direct and indirect fire), physical separation of forces in contact, and security and monitoring of the

demilitarized zone.[40]

The control measures included:

- the declaration of forces in being, including the location of minefields,
- the monitoring of front lines,
- the declaration of heavy weapons (12.7 mm calibre and above) in separation areas,
- the establishment of agreed lines on which forces might be located, and
- the staged withdrawal of forces culminating in their relocation to designated provinces.

2.   The opening of routes, to guarantee and ensure safe passage for the movement of civilians, commercial goods and humanitarian aid. On these "blue routes", inspected by UNPROFOR, "war-related material, weapons or ammunition [were] forbidden. If found, the items [would] be confiscated and subsequently destroyed under control of the UNPROFOR and the parties".[41]

3.   The demilitarization of Sarajevo, which "[was] based on one requirement: an effective cessation of hostilities".[42] The agreement implied that, first of all, the military situation should be frozen with no offensive action or forward redeployments allowed and that all heavy weapons be withdrawn from positions from which they could engage.[43] Furthermore, no movement or resupply of ammunition, explosives or incendiary devices was allowed.

4.   The monitoring of borders by UNPROFOR and ECMM in order to prevent interference from outside the Republic of Bosnia-Herzegovina, namely the transfer of irregular forces, weapons and ammunition.

The Vance-Owen Peace Plan was received favorably by the Bosnian Croat side only. The Bosnian Serbs accepted the plan as a basis for further negotiations but insisted on more favorable territorial arrangements, as the plan had allocated to them only 50 percent of the Bosnia-Herzegovina territory instead of the 70

---

[40] See UN Document S/25479 of 26 March 1993, p. 35.

[41] *Ibid.*, p.33.

[42] *Ibid.*, p. 38.

[43] According to the proposed agreement, all heavy weapons were to be withdrawn to designated locations from the following: Mojmilo, Dobrinja, Lukavica, Gornji, Kotorac, Vojkovici, Hrasnica, Sokolovici, Butmir, Ilidza, Otes, Stup and Nedarici.

percent they held at that time. The Bosnian Serbs also insisted on a constitutional framework allowing for more autonomy, and ultimately independence, for the provinces. For the Bosnian Muslims, it was exactly the decentralized organization proposed by the Vance-Owen plan which constituted the major point of discord. They also objected to some of the border delimitations. Despite intense international pressure upon the parties, changes in the wording[44] of the peace plan, and progress on certain issues,[45] negotiations collapsed at the end of January 1993. This period was also marked by new distrust and fears triggered by adverse developments in Croatia.

Although several other proposals were subsequently presented, namely a six-point program proposed by the United States and a peace proposal from the Russian Federation, the Vance-Owen plan remained the basis for negotiations on a political settlement of the conflict. On 1 and 2 May 1993, a summit conference in Athens assembled all the main political leaders in the conflict. Radovan Karadjic, the leader of the Bosnian Serbs, signed the Vance-Owen Peace Plan under strong pressure.[46] However, on 15 and 16 May 1993, in a referendum, the Bosnian Serbs rejected the Vance-Owen plan with a 96 percent majority and voted in favor of the independence of the Serbian Republic.

In order to implement the Vance-Owen plan, and particularly its manpower-intensive disarmament elements, some 50,000-60,000 peacekeepers were thought to be needed. The UN force would, upon request from the Bosnian Muslim side, include some 20,000 US troops and Europe would deploy the same number. As the US became increasingly reluctant to send ground troops into the Bosnian quagmire, support for the peace plan lagged. It is argued that, had the leading powers been more committed to the Vance-Owen plan, the Bosnian Serbs could have been persuaded to accept it.

The Vance-Owen plan was finally abandoned on 22 May 1993, when the United States, Russia, France, the United Kingdom and Spain established a "joint action plan" in Washington. This plan rejected military involvement and foresaw the creation of six security zones (Bihac, Gorazde, Sarajevo, Srebrenica, Tuzla and

---

[44] Namely the change of "the most important ethnic groups" in paragraph 1 and 4 of the original version, into "the three constituent peoples" in paragraph 1 of the version of 26 March 1993. See UN Document S/25479 of 26 March 1993, p. 8.
[45] The Bosnian Serb assembly in Pale had finally accepted the outlines of the plan on 19-20 January 1993.
[46] Western European Union, *The Yugoslav conflict - Chronology of events from 30 May 1991-8th November 1993*, ref. A/WEU/DEF(93)14.

Zepa) designed to protect the Muslim civilian population. According to General Cot, the creation of these safe havens was the only way for the international community to escape dishonor.[47]

The Vance-Owen plan was the last plan that would have kept Bosnia-Herzegovina together as a country in any true sense. The government, although decentralized, would have had coherence and authority. If the plan had been implemented, it would have been very expensive, but in the words of Lord Owen, "had it been fully backed by the United States we would have had peace in the early summer of 1993, and we would have now been reversing ethnic cleansing, and we would no longer be facing some of the present tragedies".[48]

Main Interests of the Parties

With 80 percent of the territory controlled by Bosnian Serbs and Bosnian Croats, the political and military situation of the Bosnian Muslims at the outset of the conflict was precarious. Their only assets were the international community's insistence on maintaining Bosnia-Herzegovina as a state within its borders, and possibly, an alliance with the Bosnian Croats. This coalition was essential in allowing the government to speak for well over half of the country's population. By January 1993, after the Bosnian Croats had accepted the Vance-Owen plan, the government "was still the recognized government for Bosnia-Herzegovina in name, but with the Croats laying claims to a self-governing Croat Herzeg-Bosna and the Serbs controlling 70 percent of the country, the authority of the government was exercised over less than 20 percent of the country".[49] During this first phase, however, President Izetbegovic had to abandon his initial objective of an unitary state, and to accept, first, a decentralized organization of the Republic, and later, a division according to ethnic criteria. The Bosnian Muslims were disappointed with the weak enforcement capacity of the UN peacekeeping forces deployed in Bosnia-Herzegovina. As the war went on, the Bosnian Presidency turned to providing incentives for the international community to transform UNPROFOR's mandate from humanitarian to enforcement purposes.[50]

---

[47] Interview with Lieutenant General Jean Cot.
[48] Speech by Lord Owen to the Foreign Press Association, 27 March 1995.
[49] *Ibid.*
[50] See Eknes, *Blue Helmets in a Blown Mission? - UNPROFOR in former Yugoslavia*, Research Report No 174, p.28.

Although the Bosnian Croats and Bosnian Muslims pursued divergent political objectives, the achievement of their aims often depended on some form of cooperation between them. However, interests clashed particularly in central Bosnia, where the Bosnian Croat forces (Hrvatsko Vijece Odbrane -- HVO), with the assistance of the Croatian Army (Hrvatska Vojska -- HV), attempted to gain control over areas which had been assigned to the Bosnian Croat side in the Vance-Owen plan. Ambiguity characterized not only the Bosnian Croats' relationship with the two other parties of the conflict but also the means chosen to achieve their objectives. Their approach included thus both negotiation and cooperation with the government but also military force.

The goal of the Bosnian Serbs was to achieve the right for all Serbs to live together in one state, a goal corresponding to the desire of the Bosnian Croats to join Croatia. Having achieved their military objectives by mid-1992, the Bosnian Serbs concentrated on consolidating their territorial gains and finding recognition for their state. The means chosen to secure these objectives were primarily military in nature.

In a situation where the parties' aims could only be reached by military means, disarmament operations like those foreseen in the Vance-Owen plan were not realistic. In fact, the only disarmament operation conducted by UNPROFOR took place after the Bosnian Serb siege led to the fall of Srebrenica and an agreement was signed to save the civilian population in the city.

Conclusions

UNPROFOR's main task during this first phase -- to assist in and to protect the delivery of humanitarian aid -- remained formally unchanged. However, UNPROFOR saw itself committing an increasing part of its resources to other tasks. It was in this context that the most important disarmament operation conducted by UNPROFOR during this phase took place in Srebrenica. This operation was not carried out in the framework of UNPROFOR's mandate. It was based on a local cease-fire agreement between the belligerent parties which included some disarmament elements. In this case, it was the spirit, not the letter, of the mandate that was decisive.

The original mandates, both for Sector Sarajevo and for the increased presence, were purely humanitarian. However, as the Security Council became more politically involved, it grew difficult to keep the peacekeepers outside the politics of the war. UNPROFOR was used as a source of information for the mediators and regional organizations and as an instrument to help implement political agreements. This resulted in the parties becoming steadily more hostile to the peacekeepers, and the original mission became impossible to accomplish fully.

It is argued that both overlapping interests between the warring parties and a credibility in the implementation of a mandate are essential for the success of a peacekeeping operation. In this connection, the on-going conflict severely hampered UNPROFOR's ability to provide assistance to the civilian population. Between April and June 1992, UNPROFOR's presence in Bosnia-Herzegovina was radically decreased because of escalating conflict. After the Sarajevo Airport agreement, lack of cooperation from the parties and insufficient implementation capabilities resulted in only one-quarter of the supplies reaching the targeted population. Despite these failures, or perhaps because of them, the UN Security Council felt pressure to act and continued to pass resolutions which further depleted UNPROFOR's resources. The monitoring of the no-fly zone and the establishment of the Safe Areas stretched the peacekeepers' limits and detracted them from their original humanitarian mission. The border control resolution was never even implemented by the UN.

At another level, the heavy weapons agreement reached at the London Conference in August 1992 was only partially honored, and the Vance-Owen plan proposed in October 1992, which constituted the basis for on-going negotiations, had to be abandoned in May 1993. In both cases, the international political will to implement the agreement was too weak; pressure on the parties to accept the arrangements decreased, and the momentum to find an agreement that met all parties' interests waned. In the case of Srebrenica, the decision taken by the Security Council even blocked a disarmament operation to be undertaken by UNPROFOR based on a locally-negotiated agreement.

At the end of this phase, UNPROFOR's peace operation in Bosnia-Herzegovina was characterized by the opening of a new front between the Bosnian Muslims and Bosnian Croats, by the escalation of conflicts around a number of Muslim enclaves, and by the strengthening of the concept of the Safe Areas. The parties were intent upon using military means and no mutually acceptable solution could be found. Disarmament was not realistic.

3.3. Phase II: Protection of Safe Areas and the Disarmament Components of UN-Brokered Agreements

The second phase of the conflict unfolded between June 1993 and February 1994. During this period, battles between the Bosnian Croats and the Bosnian Muslims took on the proportions of a full-fledged war in the central and southern parts of the country. The Bosnian Serbs, meanwhile, maintained their sieges around the enclaves, but otherwise consolidated their positions in more a or less defensive posture. Despite the desperate circumstances, however, the Bosnian government was able to strengthen its political and military situation.

During this period, the UN operation stepped up its humanitarian efforts to service about 2.7 million people. It was also assigned the task of Safe Area protection under a mandate established in Security Council Resolutions 824 and 836. To this end, UNPROFOR augmented its presence within the six designated Safe Areas -- Sarajevo, Srebrenica, Zepa, Gorazde, Tuzla, and Bihac -- and worked out procedures with NATO for the use of air power in support of ground operations. With a stronger commitment from the international community and especially the US, implementation of the mandate began developing in the direction of peace enforcement. This evolution culminated in the NATO decision to launch air strikes to enforce a weapons exclusion zone in Sarajevo in February 1994.

Position of the Parties

By June 1993, the Bosnian Croats had reached their main political-strategic objectives and found themselves increasingly siding with the Bosnian Serbs against the Muslims. The conflict escalation between Bosnian Croat and Bosnian Muslim forces, particularly in central Bosnia-Herzegovina, was accompanied by the pattern of atrocities and killing which so tragically characterizes civil wars.[51]

A Muslim offensive against Bosnian Croat villages in June led to a breakdown in the negotiations between these two former allies and a leaning of the Bosnian Croats towards the Bosnian Serbs. A new military offensive launched by Bosnian Croat forces in the areas of Mostar, Jablanica and Dreznica forced the

---

[51] For more details, see Statement by the President of the Security Council of 21 April 1993, *The United Nations and the Situation in the Former Yugoslavia*, p. 129.

UNPROFOR battalion in the area to redeploy under fire.[52] The Bosnian Croat forces refused access to the area (in particular to the city of Mostar) to military observers. The fighting intermittently blocked the main supply routes for humanitarian assistance into northern Bosnia, and further restricted the freedom of movement of UNPROFOR and UNHCR in the area. In relation to these developments, UNPROFOR and UNHCR initiated a humanitarian "Operation Lifeline" to keep the main routes open to help ensure the survival of up to 2.7 million people in Bosnia-Herzegovina during the winter.

Fighting in the second part of 1993 was centered in those areas where no agreement could be reached at the Geneva conference. It was dominated by Bosnian Muslim clashes with Bosnian Croats in Central Bosnia and the Neretva valley, the most violent being in the Mostar area. Bosnian Croat forces shelled the eastern, Muslim part of Mostar and blocked humanitarian aid deliveries to the encircled town. However, the structure of alliances remained extremely complex. Different alliances were forged from one conflict arena to the other, depending on the balance of forces and local command conditions.

Disarmament Components of the Invincible Package (Owen-Stoltenberg Plan)

Although the Vance-Owen plan had been abandoned in practice at the end of May 1993, it was never formally withdrawn and no other peace plan took its place on the negotiation table. By the summer of 1993, however, it had become clear that it was unrealistic to negotiate further on the Vance-Owen plan. Since the international community was unwilling to intervene militarily in the conflict in Bosnia-Herzegovina, the search for a peaceful settlement was becoming all the more urgent in order to prevent the conflict from spreading to other areas.

At a new round of negotiations starting in Geneva on 27 July 1993, Lord David Owen (EC) and Thorwald Stoltenberg (UN) proposed the creation of a "Union of Republics of Bosnia-Herzegovina", where the three constituent republics would be placed under the authority of a joint government with limited powers. The concept of a confederation for Bosnia-Herzegovina, first proposed in March 1992, was thus revived.

---

[52] See Statement by the President of the Security Council of 10 May 1993, *The United Nations and the Situation in the Former Yugoslavia*, p. 132.

While the Bosnian Serb and Bosnian Croat agreement to the proposed constitution on 30 July 1993 was expected, the Bosnian Muslim consent came as a surprise, since it meant that they had abandoned their hope for a unitary state. Further negotiations concentrated on the territorial division of the "Union", as well as the status of the Muslim enclaves of Gorazde, Srebrenica and Zepa.

On 20 August 1993, the two mediators arranged for negotiations between representatives from the three Bosnian parties, from Croatia and from the FRY on board of the HMS Invincible. They submitted a plan for the partition of Bosnia-Herzegovina into three Republics: 52 percent of the territory was allocated to the Bosnia Serbs, 31 percent to the Bosnian Muslims and 17 percent to the Croats.[53] A special status was proposed for Sarajevo and Mostar, which were to be administered under UN and EC mandate for two years. At the end of September 1993, the "Invincible Package" came to include the following provisions with regard to the disarming of warring parties. As a first step, it ordered the cessation of all hostilities and the demilitarization in all three republics within seven days of the signature. As a second step, within eight to 29 days after the signature, the parties were to start removing heavy weapons (larger than 12.7 mm) from the front lines. This process was to be finished within 60 days. Implementation of the Invincible Package was to be the responsibility of NATO and require a total of 50,000 troops. Half of the troops would be provided by the United States; France and Great Britain were to contribute 8,000 each.[54]

This plan was recommended by President Izetbegovic, who recognized that Bosnia-Herzegovina could not be kept together with force, but it was rejected by the Bosnian Muslim Parliament on 29 September 1993. A new approach for negotiations was adopted, focusing on humanitarian objectives and interim agreements, with the sole objective of alleviating the plight of the civilian population. In this context, the warring parties signed, on 18 and 29 November 1993 in Geneva, joint declarations on the delivery of humanitarian assistance, stating that UNHCR convoys would not be blocked or hindered. While it perhaps constituted a step in the direction of renewed negotiations, this declaration did not change the situation on the ground since local commanders did not feel obliged to respect the agreement. Only half of the humanitarian deliveries reached their destinations, and elements of all three sides deliberately fired upon relief convoys and UN personnel.

---

[53] Gustenau, "Die Neuordnung des Südslawischen Raumes", No 6, 1993, p. 551. The WEU chronology has slightly different figures: 30% for Muslims and 18% for Croats and 52% for Serbs.
[54] Gustenau, "Die Neuordnung des Südslawischen Raumes", No 1, 1994, p. 61.

Evolution of the Military Situation

Fighting had continued throughout the peace negotiation process and was generally centered in those areas where no agreement could be reached at the Geneva conference, as in central Bosnia and the Neretva valley. Following the break-down of the international peace negotiations, the warring parties revoked all former agreements, and the military and humanitarian situation in Bosnia-Herzegovina worsened. The situation became even more complex as command and loyalty structures split within each group. The authority of the state did not reach much beyond the Sarajevo area in practice, and the local Muslim political and military leaders acted to a great extent in an autonomous manner.[55] This resulted not only from a division of Muslim territories by the war, but also from the tarnished relationship between the government, who accepted the Stoltenberg-Owen plan, and the Bosnian Muslim parliament, who refused it.

The secession of the Bihac region in Northwestern Bosnia-Herzegovina further aggravated the split in the Bosnian Muslim political leadership. This region, containing 90 percent Muslim population, had been practically isolated from other Muslim regions for 17 months and depended for its survival on cooperation with the neighboring Serb Republic of Krajina and the FRY. Its Muslim leader, Fikret Abdic, had as his principal objective the physical survival of the Muslim population. The means to attain this was by maintaining cooperative relationships with the other ethnic groups. In October 1993 the Bihac area was declared "autonomous" from Sarajevo, and a new Muslim-Muslim front opened in November 1993.

Hostilities throughout the second part of the year were marked by Muslim-Croat confrontations, especially in the Neretva valley and in central Bosnia. The Bosnian Muslim forces realized significant territorial gains. Their success was attributed to several factors, especially the reorganization of their forces, loopholes in the weapons embargo, the creation of domestic production facilities, and the redeployment of forces from the Sarajevo area to central Bosnia. It was, to a great extent, also due to the weaknesses of the HVO forces in Central Bosnia.

On 3 August 1993, the four Bosnian Croat members of the Bosnia-Herzegovina presidency resigned, formalizing the end of the Muslim-Croat coalition, and on 28 August 1993, the Bosnian Croats proclaimed the creation of

---

[55] *Ibid.*, p. 64.

the Croat Republic of Herzeg-Bosna.[56] Fighting between Bosnian Croats and Muslims resulted in the displacement of almost half of the 900,000 Bosnian Croat population and the blockade, by Bosnian Croats, of humanitarian transport destined for the Muslim population.[57]

As the HVO experienced heavy losses, the Croat government was increasingly forced to send units from the Croatian Army into Bosnia-Herzegovina, and thus ran the risk of being labelled an aggressor and subject to sanctions by the international community as the FRY had been. On 1 February 1994, the Secretary-General reported that the Croatian Army had been directly supporting the HVO with manpower, equipment and weapons for some time.[58] The number of Croatian soldiers as well as cross-border movement of military equipment had apparently increased following successful offensives of Bosnian Government forces against the HVO. Despite the Security Council's demand for non-interference in Bosnia-Herzegovina,[59] some 5,000 Croatian Army troops were still believed to remain in that country.

The Sarajevo Market Incident

Meanwhile, fighting in and around Sarajevo continued unabated. A mortar attack on 5 February 1994 killed at least 68 civilians and wounded 142 others.[60] This incident, which came about shortly after all the three parties had agreed to a separate peace accord for Sarajevo in advance of an overall settlement, received immediate and extensive worldwide coverage from the media and considerably altered the political field on which the Bosnian conflict was being played. Most importantly, it triggered direct NATO, US and Russian involvement in the conflict. Furthermore, it led to a development in the concept of "safe areas" and an increase in UNPROFOR's strength. In this context, UNPROFOR was mandated to implement one of the most important disarmament operations conducted in Bosnia-Herzegovina (discussed in a separate chapter of this study).

---

[56] Which took over from the "Croatian Community of Herzeg-Bosna" proclaimed on 3 July 1992.

[57] Gustenau, "Die Neuordnung des Südslawischen Raumes", No 6, 1993, p. 553.

[58] See UN Document S/1994/109 of 3 February 1994.

[59] Presidential Statement of 3 February 1994, *The United Nations and the Situation in the Former Yugoslavia*, p. 154.

[60] The responsibility for this massacre was never officially established. See: David Binder, "Anatomy of a Massacre" *Foreign Policy*, Number 97, Winter 1994-1995, p. 77.

In a later stage, this new situation led to an American-negotiated coalition of Bosnian Muslim and Bosnian Croat forces, to NATO air strikes, and to a new international peace initiative by the five-member Contact Group headed by the United States. It marked the beginning of a new phase in UNPROFOR's mission in Bosnia-Herzegovina.

Safe Areas Mandate Enlargement: Monitoring the Withdrawal of Weapons

The Safe Areas concept was introduced by Resolution 819 of 16 April 1993, adopted at the peak of the Srebrenica crisis. It outlined the notion of Safe Areas, but did not formally entail an enlargement of UNPROFOR's mandate. The resolution simply asked the warring parties to refrain from attacking the Safe Area. It also asked the Secretary-General to increase UNPROFOR's presence in Srebrenica, but with the sole objective of monitoring the humanitarian situation in the Safe Area. On 6 May 1993, Resolution 824 extended this concept to include, in addition to Srebrenica, the towns of Sarajevo, Tuzla, Zepa, Gorazde, and Bihac. Under this resolution, UNPROFOR military observers were mandated: (a) to monitor the withdrawal of all Bosnian Serb military or paramilitary units from the towns to a distance at which they would cease to constitute a menace; and, (b) to monitor the humanitarian situation in the Safe Area.

Subsequent enlargements in the mandate proper came about in Phase II of UNPROFOR's activities in Bosnia-Herzegovina, with Resolutions 836 and 844. On 4 June 1993, Resolution 836 authorized the deployment of additional troops to protect the populations of the six Bosnian Muslim enclaves under siege by Serbian forces. In addition to assisting in the delivery of humanitarian relief to the population,[61] Resolution 836 extended UNPROFOR's mandate in the Safe Areas, in order to enable it: (a) to deter attacks against the Safe Areas; (b) to monitor the cease-fire in the Safe Areas; (c) to promote the withdrawal of military or paramilitary units other than those of the Bosnian Government from the Safe Areas; (d) to occupy key points on the ground; and, (e) to participate in the delivery of humanitarian relief to the population in the Safe Areas.

UNPROFOR was expressly authorized to take the necessary measures, including the use of force, in reply to bombardments of the Safe Areas by any of the parties or to armed incursion into them or in the event of any deliberate

---

[61] As provided for by Security Council Resolution 776 of 14 September 1992.

obstruction in or around those areas to the freedom of movement of UNPROFOR or of protected humanitarian convoys. Resolution 844 of 18 June 1993 further reinforced UNPROFOR's strength by 7,600 troops and authorized the use of air power, in and around the declared Safe Areas in Bosnia-Herzegovina, to support the force.

Problems associated with the realization of the Safe Areas proved to be numerous; in many instances, they were similar to problems encountered with UNPROFOR's initial deployment in the UNPA's. Although not as far-reaching as was intended in the Vance-Owen plan, the Safe Area Resolution 836 was still an ambitious initiative. The Force commander assessed that 34,000 additional troops with much more heavy equipment than traditionally associated with UN peacekeeping was needed in order to military ensure full respect for the Safe Areas.[62] However, member nations demonstrated limited willingness to stand by the resolution they adopted, and the Secretariat had to design a new "best case scenario". The Secretary-General therefore also presented a "light option" to implement Resolution 836, envisaging a minimal reinforcement of around 7,500 troops. This option would not completely guarantee the defense of the Safe Areas but would rely on the threat of air action as a deterrent. This option represented an initial approach with limited objectives. It assumed the consent and cooperation of the parties, provided a basic level of deterrence, and did not increase the levels of protection provided to UNHCR convoys. However, even this option proved to be too ambitious as weeks and months went by without much progress in its implementation. Not before spring 1994 were the 7,600 troops authorized on 13 June 1993 made available for the protection of the Safe Areas.

As summer 1993 went by, much of the heavy fighting shifted from the Bosnian Serb-Muslim front to the Bosnian Croat-Muslim front, and the Muslim pockets surrounded by Serb forces became less of a priority. By September 1993, the primary focus was the situation in the city of Mostar, a city not covered by the Safe Areas concept.

The first test of the Safe Areas came with the crisis in Sarajevo, as described in more detail in Chapter VI of this paper. The relentless bombardment of Sarajevo by Bosnian Serb forces had resulted in a large number of civilian casualties, disrupted essential services, and aggravated the severe humanitarian situation. UNPROFOR was unable to deter attacks on Sarajevo, and therefore started procedures for the Secretary-General to require the use of air power, which

---

[62] UN Document S/25939 of 14 June 1993.

was not uncontroversial. Specifically, there was deep skepticism about the viability, efficiency and the impact that the use of air power might have on UNPROFOR's humanitarian tasks. Discussions at the international level led to the North Atlantic Council decision of 9 February 1994 which called for the creation of a heavy weapons exclusion zone in Sarajevo and threatened air attacks in order to enforce implementation of this zone. Parallel to these efforts, local negotiations on the status and the demilitarization of Sarajevo resulted -- only hours prior to the announcement of the North Atlantic Council decision -- in an agreement between the parties to stop fighting and to withdraw heavy weapons or to put them under UN control. Compliance with this local agreement and with the North Atlantic Council decision was effective, and the Security Council decided not to carry out the air attacks.

As will be discussed in Chapter VI of this paper, overlapping interests of the parties was an important factor for the success in implementing the heavy weapons exclusion zone in Sarajevo. But equally important was the determination of the international community to enforce the reached agreement.

This operation was effective in that it stopped the shelling of Sarajevo. There was much optimism that the Sarajevo model could be successfully applied to a number of other enclaves. The withdrawal of the heavy weapons from Sarajevo did not necessarily mean, however, the end of the Bosnian Serb siege of the town. The use of air strikes and the conceptual and practical problems associated with such a military intervention continued to be a widely debated topic. This option marked the beginning of a new phase in UNPROFOR's activities in Bosnia-Herzegovina. It was to be tested again shortly after Sarajevo, this time relating to the Safe Area of Gorazde which will be discussed in section 3.4.

Border Control

Another component of the UN mandate relating to the management of arms during phase II concerned border control. A resolution asking for the deployment of observers along the borders of Bosnia-Herzegovina had been passed on 16 November 1992.[63] On 21 December 1992, the Secretary-General reported back to the Security Council that this would require some 10,000 additional troops.[64] No more action was taken on this matter until June 1993, when the Security

---

[63] Security Council Resolution 787 of 16 November 1992.
[64] UN Document S/25000 of 21 December 1992.

Council again called for deployment of UN observers along the border.[65] In his report of 1 July 1993, the Secretary-General presented two options for the deployment of international observers on the borders of Bosnia-Herzegovina and their respective requirements in terms of human and other resources.

Concerning the "strong" option, the Secretary-General considered it to be unrealistic to establish full control over the borders of Bosnia-Herzegovina as worldwide resources for additional peacekeeping troops were becoming increasingly stretched. Full border control implied the capability for UNPROFOR to deny passage and would thus supersede the national authorities in respect to certain border-control functions.

The second option concerned border monitoring. Observers would only observe and report on Bosnia-Herzegovina's borders, and would not be in a position to check the nature of goods coming into and out of the Republic. Even this more limited option would require substantial additional resources, and the Secretariat was not able to find countries willing to provide the 500 observers needed. Since member states would not provide the personnel resources and the material necessary for this task, there was no implementation of UNPROFOR's mandate on border monitoring during the period covered by this study.[66]

Conclusions

During the second phase of UNPROFOR's activities in Bosnia-Herzegovina, with war continuing and all parties relying on military means to obtain their principal objectives, UNPROFOR faced extremely difficult conditions under which to fulfill its mission. As fighting between the Bosnian Muslim and Bosnian Croats intensified and gradually spread northwards in central Bosnia-Herzegovina, the already very limited number of UN soldiers originally sent to protect the Safe Areas from Bosnian Serb attacks found themselves primarily engaged in reducing civilian suffering caused by fighting between the former allies in Central Bosnia. In the end, it became impossible to distinguish between the original mandate to assist in the delivery of humanitarian aid and the Safe Area operation. The mission also found itself exposed to a financial crisis, reflecting on the UN member countries' unwillingness to really become engaged in the conflict.[67]

---

[65] Security Council Resolution 838 of 10 June 1993.

[66] See also UN Document S/1994/300 of 16 March 1994.

[67] In mid-June 1993, the outstanding contributions to UN peacekeeping accounts amounted to $1,260 million in mid-June 1993, and unpaid assessments to $2,236.

In the second phase, UNPROFOR continued to face problems in securing the two major factors necessary for a successful peace operation: an agreement by the parties and credibility of mandate implementation. The Invincible Package, proposed in July 1993 and accepted by all sides in September 1993, was finally blocked because the Bosnian Assembly rejected the map of the plan. In the absence of an overall peace agreement, the parties agreed in November 1993 not to block the delivery of humanitarian aid. However, local leaders did not feel compelled to respect this accord, and it could not be fully implemented. Only about one-half of the humanitarian aid reached its target. In this phase, one major disarmament effort was successful, namely the protection of the Sarajevo Safe Area in February 1994. Success came because an agreement had been reached in the parties' interest, and because the UN, together with NATO, could back up enforcement with a credible threat.

In February 1994, an important change of position took place in the US which led to greater engagement in the Bosnia-Herzegovina conflict. This can be viewed as a result of the failure of the European-UN negotiation efforts, the new role of the Russian Federation in the conflict, and pressure from domestic public opinion following the events in Sarajevo. All these factors led to a new dynamic in international peace efforts, and a radical change in UNPROFOR's mandate during the third phase of this conflict.

3.4. Phase III: Controlling Heavy Weapons in the Safe Areas and the Disarmament and Demilitarization of Zones Adjacent to the Confrontation Lines

Introduction

Phase three of the conflict played out between February 1994 and January 1995. The fighting in the Safe Areas, initially in Sarajevo and subsequently in Gorazde, stopped as a result of UN-brokered arrangements accepted by the parties. These agreements, adapted to the specific situation in each Safe Area, included local cease fires, the interpositioning of UNPROFOR troops in certain areas, heavy weapons controls, anti-sniping restrictions, and greater freedom of movement for civilians in Sarajevo. In Sarajevo and Gorazde, these regulations were accompanied by the explicit threat of NATO air strikes. In other Safe Areas this threat was based on earlier Security Council resolutions.

In the wake of the UN-brokered cease-fire agreement of 23 February 1994 and the US-brokered Federation agreement signed in Washington on 1 March 1994, hostilities between Bosnian Croats and Bosnian Muslims stopped. The Bosnian Muslims slowly began to turn the tide of the war. As they were gaining strength in their strategic alliance situation and in their increasing military capacities, they were unwilling to accept a cessation of hostilities agreement proposed to them in June 1994, much to the dismay of the Bosnian Serbs. Such an agreement for a comprehensive cease-fire was reached on 23 December 1994, followed by a cessation of hostilities agreement for the duration of four months on 31 December 1994. The last months of 1994 were characterized by the Bosnian Muslims' advance in the Bihac pocket, and the Serb counter-action against Bihac.

Notwithstanding their advances in western Bosnia, the Bosnian Serbs continued to be politically isolated. Furthermore, they had to cover a long front line, and were vulnerable in certain areas. Trends started to go against them, and time was no longer on their side. Meanwhile, the Bosnian Muslims continued to gain strength militarily. As for the Croats, their interests could be best served by a quick end to the war in which neither side had serious loses. They wanted to preserve a breathing space amidst the larger Serbian and Muslim communities of Bosnia and to prevent any further encroachments of radical Islamic tendencies. The Federation agreement was the means to these ends.

During this third phase, the UN became not only a provider of aid and a protector of Safe Areas, but in more traditional terms, a peacekeeper and a peace-builder, both between the parties of the Federation, and also between the Federation and the Bosnian Serbs. To a lesser degree, UNPROFOR also carried out the heavy weapons control function in the exclusion zones, anti-sniping enforcement, and a number of other tasks in high-risk areas.

The Federation Agreement

In February 1994, following the failure of the European negotiation efforts and the increasing role of the Russian Federation in the conflict in former Yugoslavia, an important change of position in relation to the conflict took place in the United States. However, the US firmly excluded a military option to enforce a peace arrangement and vehemently rejected an intervention by ground forces to end the war. Efforts focused on the negotiation process.

US negotiation efforts led to a peace accord between the military representatives of the Bosnian Muslim Government and the Bosnian Croats, represented by Rasim Delic and Ante Roso respectively. It was signed on 23

February 1994 at a meeting hosted by UNPROFOR in Zagreb, Croatia. The two parties agreed to the immediate and total cessation of hostilities from 25 February 1994, a fixing of lines of contact and positions as of the time of the cease-fire, and the positioning of UNPROFOR forces at key points. The agreement further asked that all heavy weapons of 12.7 mm and more be put under UNPROFOR control or withdrawn to a minimum distance from the line of confrontation of 10 kilometers for mortars and 29 kilometers for artillery by 7 March 1994.[68]

Parallel to the efforts to end hostilities in Bosnia-Herzegovina, the US-led negotiations took place between representatives from Croatia and Bosnia-Herzegovina. These led to the signature of the Washington agreements on 1 March 1994, namely the "Framework Agreement establishing a Federation in the Areas of the Republic of Bosnia-Herzegovina with a Majority Bosniac and Croat Population", and the Outline of a Preliminary Agreement for a Confederation between the Republic of Croatia and the Federation.[69] These agreements constituted the basis for further negotiations in view of creating a federation of Muslims and Croats in Bosnia-Herzegovina, combined with a confederation arrangement between Croatia and Bosnia-Herzegovina. On 18 March 1994, the Federation Agreement was signed by the representatives of the Bosnian Muslim government and Bosnian Croats, Haris Silajdzic and Kresimir Zubak, while Presidents Tudjman and Izetbegovic initialled the Confederation Agreement. The Federation's constitution was subsequently ratified by the parliaments of the Bosnian Croats and the Bosnian Muslims.

The Federation agreement included the establishment of a unified military command and the development of comprehensive transitional arrangements. During the transitional period the existing command structures were to remain in place, and the following disarmament measures were to be undertaken: (a) immediate disengagement of the forces of both sides, with the aim of withdrawing to a safe distance to be specified in the military agreement; and, (b) withdrawal of all foreign armed forces from the territory of the Federation, except those present by the agreement of the Republic of Bosnia-Herzegovina or the authorization of the UN Security Council.

UNPROFOR had played an important role -- one which received little media attention and acknowledgement[70] -- in the implementation of all the military

---

[68] UN Document S/1994/216 of 25 February 1994.
[69] UN Document S/1994/255 of 4 March 1994.
[70] Interview with Sergio Vieira de Mello, Director of Policy Planning and Operations, UNHCR, Geneva, 13 June 1995.

aspects of the Federation agreement, bringing a large degree of stability and peace to central Bosnia and western Herzegovina. It monitored the cease-fire of February 1994 and the buffer zone between the parties, oversaw the separation of forces, and controlled heavy weapons through the establishment of weapons collections points and active sites.

Under the chairmanship of UNPROFOR, the Joint Policy Committee meetings first laid the groundwork for the mapping of the confrontation lines, the withdrawal of direct fire weapons to two kilometers from respective front lines, and the creation of a buffer zone. It also established observation posts to observe the buffer zone. Furthermore, it set up control posts on specified routes at the median point within the buffer zone in order to allow full freedom of movement for women and for men aged 16 or younger and 60 or older.[71]

The buffer zones became effective on 13 April 1994; the troops were withdrawn from them, and the only military personnel remaining in the buffer zone were so called "insurance platoons", armed with rifles, pistols and signal flares. These insurance platoons -- sometimes called observation posts -- were reduced by half in June 1994. An agreement to replace them with unarmed minefield parties along the confrontation line, with the task to ensure that civilians did not stray into minefields, was reached in October 1994.[72]

The notion of exclusion zones for different types of weapons led to the establishment of weapons collection points and active sites under UNPROFOR control. These were limited to a maximum of 12 for each party. An active site was a UN-controlled location inside the defined exclusion zone, within which could be deployed weapons or weapons systems of greater calibre than 12.7 mm for self defense purposes, including active defense, against a third party. These sites could be moved to a new location for tactical reasons provided that UNPROFOR or UNMO accompanied the guns to the new location. The sites and collection points were to be dismantled by mutual agreement between the BiH and the HVO after the separation of forces was completed. The concept of active sites was not unproblematic. Indeed, while it constituted a means for successfully disarming two parties, it had the potential to lead, at the same time, to a concentration of arms in a situation where the two confronted a third party.

Agreements to remove weapons from these sites and collection points were reached in some locations. However, these agreements were still placed on hold in

---

[71] According to UNPF, Compendium of Reference Documents, Index 1, October 1994.
[72] *Ibid.*

early October 1994, awaiting progress to be achieved elsewhere in the sector.[73] The requirement to proceed simultaneously -- as was the case for the UNPA's in Croatia -- brought down the evolution of the disarmament process to the speed of the slowest regions.

UNPROFOR was also instrumental in achieving a breakthrough in an agreement on freedom of movement in the Mostar area which was implemented on 23 May 1994. It played a vital role in monitoring the demilitarization of that city, a precondition for the establishment of European Union (EU -- formerly European Community) administration there on 23 July 1994. UNPROFOR also achieved demilitarization of Stari Vitez, starting with the establishment of a neutral area comprised of a municipal building (the garages), followed by the demilitarization of Stari Vitez and its surrounding area (the "civilianized area").[74] Demining operations were conducted in all the above-mentioned disarmament processes.

However, problems persisted in relations between the two communities, particularly with respect to freedom of movement within the territory of the Federation. Peace was fragile, and tensions in central and southern Bosnia-Herzegovina, which had witnessed some of the most intense fighting in the conflict, continued to require the vigilant efforts of the international community.

The Federation agreement for Bosnia-Herzegovina put the Bosnian Serbs in a difficult position. On the one hand, it presented a unique boost for their claim to an independent state or a confederation with the FRY. On the other hand, Serbian participation in the Federation could prevent it from being used as a Muslim-Croat alliance against the Bosnian Serbs. For the latter reason, Radovan Karadjic accepted the Bosnian Muslim-Croat Federation on 18 March 1994, and recommended it to the Bosnian Serb Parliament. On 24 March 1994, however, this assembly clearly rejected the possibility of entering a federation with the Bosnian Muslims and Bosnian Croats. This rejection was a reflection of a serious internal conflict between Radovan Karadjic, who was willing to compromise, and the more intransigent army commander, General Ratko Mladic.

---

[73] *Ibid.*

[74] UNPF, Compendium of Reference Documents, Index 2, October 1994.

Disarmament Operations in Gorazde

The question of air strikes came up again in April 1994 with reference to Gorazde after a period of intense pressures on UNPROFOR from the US and other countries.[75] An unusually high level of fighting had erupted in Gorazde, Zepa and Srebrenica at the end of March 1994. By 10 April 1994, the shelling of Gorazde by the Bosnian Serb Army had intensified to such a level that UNPROFOR initiated procedures to launch air strikes. At around 7:00 p.m., two American aircraft dropped three Mark 85 bombs on Bosnian Serb military targets, causing limited damage.[76] The following day, in view of the continuing Bosnian Serb shelling of Gorazde, UNPROFOR again requested close air support from NATO to protect UN personnel. Two NATO F/A-18A Hornets destroyed a Bosnian Serb tank that had been firing directly into the town and neutralized other military targets.

Despite intensive high-level diplomatic talks and the threat of air strikes, fighting continued. UN personnel, including military observers, faced confinement to accommodations or restrictions on their movements throughout Bosnia. Attempts were made to retrieve weapons from a collection site in Sarajevo. On 15 April 1994, a French NATO fighter, hit by ground fire over Bosnia, landed safely on an aircraft carrier in the Adriatic. The following day, a British Sea Harrier was shot down near Gorazde while undertaking reconnaissance for possible close air support.

This incident showed the difficulties of using high-precision weapons in this theater, this time not because of weather or terrain conditions, but for financial reasons. A senior British military officer summarized the problem of the efficiency of the surface-to-air missile attack on the Royal Navy Sea Harrier with the following words: "A £25 million plane was hit by an £8,000 missile while trying to target an old tank worth nothing".[77] On 18 April, heavy shelling of Gorazde resumed and UN personnel were evacuated. Five UNMOs and four UNHCR, two ICRC and two *Médecins Sans Frontières* personnel remained in the town.[78] Tension also increased in other areas of Bosnia-Herzegovina. In Sarajevo, Bosnian

---

[75] Bo Pellnäs, *Utan slut? - Kriget pa Balkan - bilder fran ett Fnuppdrag, Stockholm:* Albert Bonniers Förlag, 1995, p. 215.

[76] Gustenau, "Die Neuordnung des Südslawischen Raumes", No 4, 1994, p. 391. See also *UNPROFOR News*, May 1994, p. 3.

[77] See article by Michael Evans, *The Times*, 26 May 1995.

[78] *UNPROFOR News*, May 1994, p. 4.

Serb troops forcibly retrieved heavy weapons from two storage sites in Sarajevo on 19 April 1993; except for one tank, all weapons were returned later in the day.[79]

In view of the continuing crisis in Gorazde, NATO representatives in Brussels issued a decision asking the Bosnian Serb to cease attacks immediately, to pull back their units three kilometers from the center of the city by 12:01 a.m. GMT on 24 April 1994, and to give UN forces, humanitarian relief convoys and medical assistance teams free access to Gorazde. Non-compliance would lead to air strikes against Bosnian Serb heavy weapons and other military targets within a 20-kilometer radius of the center of Gorazde. That decision also called upon the government of Bosnia-Herzegovina not to undertake offensive military action from within that Safe Area.

In another decision, NATO also agreed to establish a "military exclusion zone" of 20 kilometers around Gorazde, which called for all heavy weapons, including tanks, artillery pieces, mortars, multiple rocket launchers, missiles and anti-aircraft weapons to be withdrawn by 12:01 a.m. GMT on 27 April 1994. In the event of non-compliance, Bosnian Serb heavy weapons and other military assets, as well as their direct and essential military support facilities, would be subject to NATO air strikes.

At the same time, in Belgrade, Yasushi Akashi and General de Lapresle had obtained a six-point agreement with the Bosnian Serb leadership which was included in the North Atlantic Council decision. The text of the Belgrade agreement was by and large identical to the provisions of the NATO decision.[80] Advance elements of an UNPROFOR convoy of some personnel, containing UNMOs, Civilian Police, soldiers, Civil Affairs and medical personnel, entered Gorazde soon after midnight on 23 April. On 27 April, at the expiration of the deadline for withdrawal of Serb heavy weapons from around Gorazde, Yasushi Akashi stated that it would not be necessary to request NATO to use air power. In a statement, the Secretary-General said that the international community had gone to the brink of war to attain peace on Bosnia-Herzegovina.[81] Despite a number of violations of the cease-fire by both parties during the first days following the NATO decision, the cease-fire was generally respected. The arrival in Gorazde, on the night of 23-24 April, of the first UNPROFOR convoy, largely contributed to this stabilization.

---

[79] *Ibid.*, p. 15.
[80] Interview with Mr. Sergio Vieira de Mello.
[81] UNPROFOR News, May 1994, p.15.

The withdrawal of Bosnian Serb forces from the three-kilometer zone was complicated by the need to separate the two opposing forces and by delays in the arrival of the required UNPROFOR forces. The right bank of the Drina river posed a particular problem, and no agreement could be reached between the parties on demilitarizing the three-kilometer zone. By 26 April 1994, however, substantial compliance had also occurred with respect to the required withdrawal of heavy weapons. Of the 32 sites visited by UNPROFOR in the 20-kilometer zone, all had been cleared of heavy weapons, apart from three weapons that were found to be immobilized. In subsequent patrols after the expiration of the deadline, three Bosnian Serb tanks and two anti-aircraft guns were found and escorted out of the zone. Investigation patrols continued to monitor the weapons exclusion zone.

In accordance with Resolution 913 and at UNPROFOR's request, the local commander of the Bosnian Muslim army submitted information on two heavy weapons in his possession. UNPROFOR patrols later found four additional undeclared heavy weapons (one anti-aircraft and three anti-tank weapons), and efforts continued to have the Bosnian Muslim heavy weapons placed under UNPROFOR control.[82]

It could not be established with certainty if the Bosnian Serb operation against Gorazde had been planned in advance or if it was a reaction to offensive actions by the Bosnian government's troops in the area.[83] The fact remains, however, that it resulted in large territorial gains by the Bosnian Serbs, the crushing of the BiH units and the encirclement of the overpopulated enclave of Gorazde, which became entirely dependent on UN assistance and Bosnian Serb goodwill. The deployment of UNPROFOR also ensured that Bosnian governmental units could not go back to their former positions. By end of April 1994, after the Gorazde incident, troops of all the warring parties began concentrating in the Brcko region.

Limitations to the Safe Areas Concept

Gorazde was a turning point in the UN's peacekeeping operation in the former Yugoslavia in the sense that it provoked questions about the concept of "safe areas". Gorazde -- more than Sarajevo, Srebrenica, Zepa, Tuzla or Bihac -- brought to light the contradictions and weaknesses in the "safe area" concept. Besides the fact that UNPROFOR did not have sufficient means to ensure the

---

[82] UN Document S/1994/600 of 19 May 1994, p. 4.
[83] Gustenau, "Die Neuordnung des Südslawischen Raumes", No 4, 1994.

safety of Gorazde, it was necessary to have the agreement of the parties concerning the implementation and the exact boundaries of the area to be protected. Most importantly, the Safe Area should have been safe in a reciprocal manner. That is, it should neither have been the object of attacks nor have served as a base from which attacks could be launched.[84] This problem was subsequently addressed by the Secretary-General, who however, up to the end of the period covered by this study, received no guidance from the Security Council. The Secretary-General was aware of the constraints on UNPROFOR regarding the performance of its responsibilities in the Safe Areas.[85] Furthermore, the exclusion zones around Sarajevo and Gorazde, although successful in protecting the civilian population from heavy weapons fire, were expensive and difficult to enforce. They could not be maintained indefinitely in the absence of a comprehensive cessation of hostilities or, at least, the demilitarization of those areas, which UNPROFOR continued to pursue for Sarajevo. Implementation of the disarmament components of the mandate were further complicated by the fact that UNPROFOR personnel, who were widely dispersed at weapons collection points, were vulnerable to any determined effort to remove weapons or take hostages. Also, it was possible for any side to hide weapons.

Another limitation inherent to the supervision and enforcement of weapons exclusion zones was that it placed additional constraints on UNPROFOR as an impartial force. It was not in the interest of the United Nations for its peacekeeping force to become a party to the conflict to which it was originally deployed to bring to an end.

Some argue that the Gorazde operation was not intended to protect UN personnel in Gorazde, but rather to demonstrate strength *vis-a-vis* the Bosnian Serbs, according to a doctrine of "deterrence" introduced by Generals Cot and Briquemont.[86] This is the way the Bosnian Serbs interpreted it. The lessons learned from Gorazde, however, were not about deterrence. Rather, they strengthened the Bosnian Serb belief that NATO air strikes could not constitute a real threat to them. For the Bosnian Muslims, who were trying to involve the international community -- especially NATO -- in the conflict against the Serbs, the operation led to the bitter realization that NATO would not be ready to enter

---

[84] UNPROFOR Head of Civil Affairs, Sergio Vieira de Mello, in an interview with *UNPROFOR News*, May 1994, p. 7.

[85] UN Document S/1994/1067 of 17 September 1994.

[86] Pellnäs, *Utan slut? - Kriget pa Balkan - bilder fran ett FN-uppdrag*, 1995, pp. 214 and 215.

into war on their side. Furthermore, UNPROFOR had played its last negotiating chip.[87] UNPROFOR also ran the risk of entering into war on the side of one of the parties to the conflict. It would have thus lost its main advantage in its efforts to achieve a peaceful resolution of the conflict: its impartiality.

The events in Gorazde led to the adoption of Resolution 914 of 27 April 1994 authorizing the increase of UNPROFOR's force by 10,000 troops. This was an indication that troop-contributing countries were no longer pressing for the withdrawal of UN troops from Bosnia-Herzegovina. Another consequence of the events in Gorazde was the increased engagement, which was now formalized, of the US and of the Russian Federation in the peace negotiations. In London, the UN, the US, the Russian Federation, Great Britain and France created, on 26 April 1994, a "Contact Group" to renew the peace process for Bosnia-Herzegovina.

The Contact Group Peace Plan

On 13 May 1994, the Contact Group presented a peace plan proposing a four-month cease-fire during which peace negotiations would take place. The cease-fire entailed a disengagement of troops along the existing confrontation lines combined with UNPROFOR's interposition. This plan was initially rejected by the Bosnian Serbs and the Bosnian Muslims. The Bosnian Serbs particularly criticized the partition of their territory (49 percent of the total territory of Bosnia-Herzegovina) into three separate, isolated areas.

At the beginning of June 1994, as peace negotiations were stagnating, the representatives of the Federation and the Bosnian Serb authorities initiated talks for another cease-fire agreement. Interests diverged between the parties concerning the duration of this agreement. On the one hand, the representatives of the Federation aimed at a short-term cessation of hostilities in order to prevent Bosnian Serb territorial gains from being consolidated. On the other hand, the Bosnian Serbs demanded a cease-fire lasting one year. On 8 June 1994, an initial agreement to end hostilities for one month was reached which allowed for continuing negotiations on a longer lasting cease-fire.

On 6 July 1994, the Contact Group presented a revised version of their plan to the conflicting parties. It contained the same percentage clause (51 to 49), but proposed a five kilometer-wide corridor in northern Bosnia, while the enclaves of Gorazde, Srebrenica and Zepa in eastern Bosnia (which would remain within the

---

[87] *Ibid.*, p. 216.

Federation) would be connected by corridors with Sarajevo. This plan was unique in that the parties could either accept or reject, but not negotiate it. Non-acceptance of the plan within two weeks was to entail massive sanctions.

The Bosnian Croats and Bosnian Muslims accepted the Contact Group plan; however, the Bosnian Serbs refused it despite intense pressure from the representatives of the Contact Group, the Russian Federation, and the president of the FRY. The Bosnian Serb Parliament, while remaining opposed to the peace plan, followed the recommendation of Radovan Karadjic and decided to organize a referendum on this issue on 27 and 28 August 1995. In practice, this was equivalent to a rejection of the plan. The Security Council answered by adopting Resolution 942 of 23 September 1994, calling for states to desist from any political talks with the leadership of the Bosnian Serb party and imposing strict economic sanctions. The international community was forced to recognize, however, that no pressure could quickly change of the position of the Bosnian Serbs and that the Russian Federation and the FRY were the only players capable of exercising any influence on them.

Interests of the Parties

While the Bosnian Serbs continued to demand the unification of all Serbs in one state, the Contact Group peace plan revealed clear differences between Belgrade and Pale. The Bosnian Serb leader Radovan Karadjic refused even very loose constitutional ties between the Serb Republic and the Bosnian Federation and insisted on the international recognition of his state. The FRY and its President Milosevic increasingly turned away from the demands of the Bosnian Serbs because of isolation and pressure from the Russian Federation. Support of the Bosnian Serbs had become an economic burden to the FRY. Furthermore, in the absence of a peace plan, the risk of renewed escalation of the conflict in Bosnia-Herzegovina between the Bosnian Serbs and the Bosnian Federation seemed imminent. The Yugoslav Army did not wish to find itself under pressure to become directly involved in the conflict. Conflict escalation was thus adverse to the interests of the FRY, and Milosevic welcomed the Contact Group plan on 6 July 1994. After the Bosnian Serb refusal of the plan, Belgrade broke its relations with and closed its borders to the Serb Republic. This split in the Serbian camp opposed nationalistic tendencies against the now more moderate line of President Milosevic, adding a new dimension to the conflict in former Yugoslavia.

The Contact group plan was clearly welcomed by the Croatian representatives and by the Croatian president of the Bosnian Federation, Kresimir Zubak, since the realization of the plan would allow 90 percent of the Croat population in Bosnia-Herzegovina to live within the borders of the Federation. The Bosnian Muslim position, however, was more ambiguous. With the pressure from the international community, a refusal of the plan was hardly possible, and if the fighting continued, it seemed unlikely that the Federation's army would be able to recover territory lost to the Bosnian Serbs. However, the Bosnian Muslims clearly approved of the international community's interest in maintaining the status of Bosnia-Herzegovina as a subject of international law within the internationally recognized borders. After acceptance by the Bosnian Croat and Bosnian Muslim parliaments, the parliament of the Federation of Bosnia-Herzegovina agreed to the Contact Group plan on 18 July 1994.

Military Developments

Two events marked the general military situation in Bosnia-Herzegovina at the beginning of this third phase. On the one hand, the cease-fire agreement and demilitarization of Sarajevo freed Bosnian Serb and Bosnian Muslim troops and material to be deployed to other fronts in North and Central Bosnia. On the other hand, the cease-fire agreements reached between the Bosnian Muslims and Bosnian Croats on 23 February 1994 in Zagreb led to an end of hostilities between these two parties. Heavy weapons were withdrawn or put under UNPROFOR control in the agreed-upon areas along the former confrontation lines, with the exception of twelve "active areas", where fighting was expected to resume with the Bosnian Serbs. UNPROFOR started also to take control of certain key positions along the 300 kilometer-long line of confrontation.

It became obvious during the summer of 1994 that, since their political-strategic objectives could not be achieved through negotiations, the Bosnian Army and political leadership would increasingly resort to military solutions. The Commander of the BiH, Rasim Delic, publicly announced on 27 June 1994 that the liberation war had begun and that the Bosnian army was strong enough to push back the Serbs.[88] Hostilities were concentrated in areas where fundamental disagreements between the parties had existed in relation to the Contact group plan, namely the Muslim enclaves in eastern Bosnia-Herzegovina, the Ozren mountains, Doboj and Sarajevo regions.

---

[88] See Gustenau, "Die Neuordnung des Südslawischen Raumes", p. 511.

In June 1994, the Bosnian Muslim military leadership tried, once more, to take control over the territories in the Bihac area controlled by Fikret Abdic. The Muslim units advanced some 13 kilometers towards Abdic's headquarters in Velika Kladusa, creating a flow of around 30,000 refugees into UNPA Sector North.[89] The Abdic forces started their counter-offensive at the beginning of July, with the support of Serbian artillery, both from Bosnia-Herzegovina and the Krajinas.

The months of October and November 1994, in anticipation of the approaching winter and because of the changing strategic situation, were characterized by a further conflict escalation. The success of the military operations undertaken by the BiH seemed to indicate that the conflict was reaching a strategic turning point. After having been disengaged on the fronts with the Bosnian Croats, the Bosnian army, better armed, organized, commanded, and motivated, was able to oppose the Bosnian Serb forces with increasingly strong troop concentrations. This improvement in military operational capacities and equipment was possible despite the arms embargo due to the cooperation of Croatia and the HVO, and also as a result of an increased domestic production of heavy weapons and munitions. Against the background of these military successes by Bosnian governmental troops, a solution to the conflict did not seem to lie in a negotiated settlement.

During most of this period, the Bosnian Serbs were severely constrained by a lack of fuel, spare parts and mobility. Besides trying to hold or recover territories, its only options for action were the shelling of the populations in the enclaves and Sarajevo and the provocation or hindrance of UNPROFOR. Only during the counterattack in the Bihac area (discussed below) were they able to retake initiative.

Lifting the Arms Embargo

The idea of lifting the arms embargo against Bosnia-Herzegovina had repeatedly been a subject of debate. It came up in the Security Council, in a revised version, and was used by the US to pressure the Bosnian Serbs into accepting the Contact group plan. This initiative was mainly based on the right to individual and collective self-defense. It had support from the General Assembly of the UN,[90] the

---

[89] UN Document S/1994/1389 of 1 December 1994, p. 3.

[90] See Resolution of the General Assembly of 3 November 1994 recommending the Security Council to lift the arms embargo against Bosnia-Herzegovina.

Congress of the United States, and the American people, but it went against the policies of the European NATO partners, especially those contributing ground troops to UNPROFOR. In their view, lifting the arms embargo would lead to an escalation of the conflict, jeopardize UNPROFOR's impartiality, and make it impossible for UNPROFOR to pursue its humanitarian mission in Bosnia-Herzegovina. The main troop contributing countries, including the Russian Federation, affirmed their intention to withdraw their contingents, should arms be allowed to flow into the conflict area.

Following the Security Council's refusal to adopt the proposition to lift the arms embargo on 9 November 1994, the US Administration announced that it would withdraw its cooperation from the monitoring of the embargo by 15 November 1994.[91] By the end of November 1994, the US Secretary of Defense William Perry revealed a shift in the American position when, contrary to the opinion prevailing in Congress, he declared himself opposed to the lifting the embargo, and proposed that the Bosnian Serbs join a "federation" with the Federal Republic of Yugoslavia.[92] This move was based on the view that an escalation of the conflict in Bosnia-Herzegovina might allow the conflict to spread to other parts of the area. By the end of November 1994, the international community again focused its efforts on a political solution in the context of negotiations in the Contact Group.

The Bihac Counter-Offensive

In August 1994, the self-declared Bihac "Autonomous Province of Western Bosnia", led by Fikret Abdic, was defeated by government forces. Victory over the Abdic forces allowed the Bosnian Muslim forces to concentrate their efforts on the remaining confrontation line with the Bosnian Serbs. On 26 October 1994, they penetrated the Serb lines on the Grabez plateau and achieved their largest territorial gain of the war. This offensive triggered a major counter-offensive by the Bosnian Serb forces, starting on 6 November 1994, which recovered the lost territories and advanced beyond the original confrontation lines to close in on the town of Bihac. This Bosnian Serb advance from the south and the east of the Bihac enclave was supported by shelling and air action from the Krajina Serb forces which advanced from the north and the west towards Velika Kladusa.

---

[91] Gustenau, "Die Neuordnung des Südslawischen Raumes", No 1, 1995, p. 60.
[92] *Ibid.*, p. 66.

Despite strong warnings by UNPROFOR, the Krajina Serb forces repeatedly intervened in the fighting by launching air attacks. An air raid on 18 November 1994 against the 5th Corps headquarters inside the Safe Area employed napalm and cluster bombs.[93] In an attempted attack the following day an aircraft crashed into a factory at Cazin, which resulted in a crash into an apartment block, causing civilian casualties.

These attacks on the Bihac Safe Area prompted the decision by the Security Council to extend to the Republic of Croatia the authorization contained in Resolution 836 concerning the use of air power in and around the Safe Areas.[94] In a parallel move, the Security Council also adopted on the same day Resolution 959, demanding that all parties put an end to "all hostile actions in and around the safe areas". The obligation to abide by the rules established for the protection of the Safe Areas was thus extended to the Bosnian Muslims. In spite of repeated efforts by UNPROFOR to obtain a cease-fire, the Bosnian Serb forces continued to advance towards the town. The 5th Corps of the Government Army, in its turn, launched mortar fire from within the Bihac Safe Area where its headquarters were located. These events highlight the problems of protecting the civilian population in the Safe Areas.

Already in his report to the Security Council on 9 May 1994, the Secretary-General concluded that "UNPROFOR found itself in a situation where many Safe Areas were not safe, where their existence appeared to thwart only one army in the conflict, thus jeopardizing UNPROFOR's impartiality, and where UNPROFOR's role needed to be adequately defined in a manner that would be compatible with the rest of the its mandate".[95] After Gorazde, the experience at Bihac demonstrated again, and even more strikingly, the inherent shortcomings of the Safe Areas concept. UNPROFOR's relationship with the Bosnian Serbs was at its worst, its forces were exposed to such a degree of intimidation and harassment that they could no longer fulfil their primary task of delivering humanitarian aid to the civilian population.

Winter Truce

By December 1994, the international community found itself confronted with a seemingly unsolvable dilemma. On the one hand, it was clear that it was

---

[93] UN Document S/1994/1389 of 1 December 1994, p. 4.
[94] Security Council Resolution 958 of 19 November 1994.
[95] UN Document S/1994/555 of 9 May 1994.

impossible to impose a peace arrangement on the Bosnian Serbs without their consent, and that UNPROFOR, subject to unacceptable risks and constant humiliation, was increasingly unable to fulfill its mandate. On the other hand, a withdrawal of the UN forces from Bosnia-Herzegovina would have painfully revealed the international community's incapacity to deal with blatant violations of international order. Moreover, the option of a pull-out was made unacceptable by the view that UNPROFOR's withdrawal would lead to an escalation of the war and a spill-over to other countries in the region.

The Contact Group peace plan remained the basis for negotiations, but some adjustments were made to account for new Bosnian Serb positions. On 2 December 1994, the Contact Group agreed that special relations could exist between the Bosnian Serbs and the FRY. On the territorial distribution, however, positions remained unchanged.[96] The Contact Group also insisted on the formal continuation of the Republic of Bosnia-Herzegovina, and showed, in this respect, consistency in its position. Unfortunately, this position had long ceased to reflect political realities.

During the last days of 1994, two major agreements were made between the warring parties: the Comprehensive Cease-fire Agreement and the Agreement on Complete Cessation of Hostilities. The Comprehensive Cease-fire Agreement was signed by representatives of the Bosnian Serbs and the Bosnian Muslims on 23 December 1994 after secret negotiations in Pale mediated by former US President Jimmy Carter.[97] The negotiation plan, originally presented by Radovan Karadjic, consisted of five elements: cease-fire, disengagement of troops under UNPROFOR control, peace negotiations on the basis of the Contact Group plan, freedom of movement for UNPROFOR and UN convoys, and an exchange of prisoners. Because it stated that the Contact Group plan would only serve as a basis for discussions, this proposed agreement was received with some skepticism by the UN and EU negotiators, by the Bosnian Government and also by President Milosevic.[98]

The agreement of 23 December 1994 contained the following provisions concerning the use of weapons and the disengagement of forces: (a) a general cease-fire along all lines of confrontation, expiring on 30 April 1995 and subject to renewal by the parties; and, (b) monitoring of the cease-fire by UNPROFOR. UNPROFOR was to "assess allegations of breaches, attempt to resolve them

---

[96] 51% for the Croat-Muslim Federation, 49% for the Bosnian Serbs.

[97] Attached to UN Document S/1995/8 of 6 January 1995.

[98] Gustenau, "Die Neuordnung des Südslawischen Raumes", No 2, 1995, p. 183.

where possible, and make public the results of its assessment, as appropriate".[99] Except in the area of Bihac, the cease-fire agreement was generally respected.

The accord also foresaw negotiations on the Agreement on Complete Cessation of Hostilities which was signed on 31 December 1994 and was to cover a period of four months.[100] The cessation of hostilities included the following measures: (a) the separation of forces in conflict to mutually agreed-upon positions and the positioning of UNPROFOR forces for observation and monitoring, to include interpositioning; and, (b) the prohibition of the use of all explosive munitions, and the use of weapons used to fire explosive munitions. In addition, talks were to begin immediately on the modalities for the withdrawal and monitoring by UNPROFOR of heavy weapons of 12.7 calibre and above. Furthermore, the agreement foresaw the restoration of utilities and the establishment of joint economic activities aimed at the normalization of life in all territories, *on a reciprocal basis.*

Unfortunately, a number of the provisions of the Cessation of Hostilities Agreement, aimed at consolidating the cease-fire and the situation on the ground, were not implemented. The lack of progress on fundamental political questions created a situation in which UNPROFOR could do little but delay a renewed outbreak of hostilities. In view of the general trend toward increased preparations for war by all parties, and in the absence of progress on political negotiations, this winter truce could not mean much more than a break before renewed escalation of the fighting as soon as the snow melted away.

Conclusions

After the Sarajevo market massacre of 5 February 1994, UNPROFOR played a stabilizing role and contributed to normalizing the situation in Bosnia-Herzegovina, particularly in and around Sarajevo. It also helped stabilize the entire confrontation line between the Bosnian Croat and Bosnian government forces following the 23 February cease-fire agreement. It played an important role in political negotiation efforts as well, and it helped to develop a solution to the Gorazde crisis and to prevent escalation in Brcko and the Posavina corridor by deploying military observers. Its mandate was enlarged and shifted from a humanitarian orientation to a more traditional peacekeeping force with cease-fire

---

[99] UN Document S/1995/8 of 6 January 1995.
[100] *Ibid.*

monitoring and interposition functions. The limits of enforcement of the mandate were illustrated in the Gorazde crisis, and a solution to the conflict in Bosnia-Herzegovina was again sought in negotiation efforts at the local and international levels. An important break-through came at the end of 1994, with the Comprehensive Cease-Fire Agreement and the Agreement on Complete Cessation of Hostilities.

Events during this third phase again reflect the importance of mutual agreements between the parties and credible mandate implementation in order to carry out successfully disarmament operations in a conflict situation. Successful operations were carried out in the context of the Federation and cease-fire agreements between Bosnian Muslims and Bosnian Croats, and also in Gorazde after the international community had gone to the brink of war. In both instances, the two pre-conditions were met.

Failures during the third phase occurred with the initial attempts to carry out disarmament in Gorazde, at a time when both agreement and enforcement capacity were missing. These two ingredients were also lacking in the response to the Bihac counter-offensive in August 1994, and in the attempts to find acceptance for the Contact Group plan. The analysis of this chapter reinforces the main assumptions of this study, namely that successful disarmament operations in conflict situations require a mutually acceptable agreement that meets the parties' interests and a credible implementation strategy which might include enforcement.

Chapter 4
Disarmament Operations in UN Sector West

4.1. Background

Of the four UN sectors which were created in Croatia under the Vance Plan, Sector West has probably been the least noticed. Sector East was created after the harrowing combats between Serbs and Croats for the city of Vukovar; Sector North was the closest to the Croatian capital Zagreb (only approx. 30 km away); and Sector South was built around the Krajina Serb capital of Knin. Comparatively, Sector West seemed somewhat featureless. This was, however, a mistaken view. Sector West had its own important features: its terrain and location.

Sector West is composed of three different zones which cut horizontally across the sector. The first zone lies north of the city of Pakrac and is a mix of flat terrain and hills. The second zone is formed of the elevations between the cities of Pakrac and Okucani; this zone only has a few roads in its terrain of hills and forests. The third, southernmost zone of Sector West lies between Okucani and the Sava river (which also comprises the border between Croatia and Bosnia). It is this third zone which constituted the key to the rest of the Sector. Indeed, the strategically important Zagreb-Belgrade highway runs through this part of the Sector. An East-West railway also crosses this zone.

The fighting between Serbs and Croats living in western Slavonia began rather early in the conflict, in the first week of March 1991. Sporadic clashes took place between the two communities, and a struggle erupted over the control of the local police forces. In July 1991, the Federal Army (then still called the JNA) intervened to separate the parties, but soon it became clear that the army was protecting the Serb population and supporting its secession from Zagreb. In September 1991, Serb forces launched an attack northwards across the Papuk Mountain range which failed to achieve its objectives due to strong Croat resistance and the difficult terrain. In December 1991, a Croat attack recaptured the Papuk Mountains and areas south of them. After this attack the confrontation lines froze, the conflict came to a relative standstill, and the world's attention shifted to the very violent combats around the city of Vukovar in eastern Slavonia.

105

The disarmament operation in Sector West received comparatively little media attention because the sector was identified as an easier, calmer sector. In fact, this sector was in some ways more difficult than the others. For example, this was the only sector in which both Croats and Serbs were living (other sectors were on Serb-held territory); the sector was isolated from the other sectors and the Bosnian Serbs had a strong influence over it; and a large part of the sector west was located on rather flat terrain which facilitated offensive military operations. In other words, Sector West was not necessarily an "easier" sector: it was made such by the efforts of UNPROFOR.

4.2. Voluntary Disarmament

The disarmament of Sector West began during the first days of June 1992 and was considered completed on 7 July 1992. It is interesting to note that while the Vance Plan called for the sectors to be demilitarized, most people in the sector were unaware of such provisions, and often, of the plan itself. Before the disarmament of the sector was initiated, the UN civil affairs representatives had to spend many hours on the road travelling back and forth across the sector to explain what the aim of UNPROFOR in the area would be. Initially, the reaction of both Croat and Serb combatants was one of disbelief; nevertheless, the information was disseminated and whatever action taken by UNPROFOR, it was to be completely unexpected.

For that purpose, a series of meetings had been organized under the auspices of the Sector Commander and the Civil Affairs coordinator with representatives of both armies and of the TDF's. During these meetings, UNPROFOR attempted to convince all parties of two things: (a) that they would not be given the opportunity to ignore the demilitarization of the sector; and (b) that UNPROFOR was indeed willing to use force to achieve its objective. These meetings also led to a local agreement on the modalities of implementation of the Vance Plan.

At this stage of the operation, intelligence proved crucial. It was important for UNPROFOR to gather information on: the type, number and location of weapons in the sector; the type of forces (regular, TDF, or para-military) present in the sector, and; which combatants originally were locals from the sector and which had been brought in from outside. This information was needed to achieve the following aims of the Vance-Owen plan: the withdrawal of all external forces, the demobilization of local forces, and the supervised storage or withdrawal of all weapons in the sector. UNPROFOR also pledged to take on the role as sole force responsible for the security of the entire sector.

The actual withdrawal of weapons from the sector began on 20 June 1992 (D-day) and was executed according to the local agreement signed between the parties which outlined the following phases:

Step 1 (D to D+4): Withdrawal of artillery, mortars, rocket launchers and tanks to 30 km from the UNPA limits.

Step 2 (D+5 to D+7): Disarmament and demobilization of the Territorial Defense Forces and other non-police forces.

Step 3 (D+8 to D+9): Withdrawal of armored personnel carriers, anti-aircraft systems, heavy machine guns and short-range anti-tank weapons to 10 km from the UNPA limits.

Step 4 (D+10 to D+14): All remaining troops withdrawn to at least 5 km from the UNPA limits.

Step 5 (after D+15): Minefield lifting by unarmed parties from the Yugoslav Army and the HV under UNPROFOR supervision and security.

By 7 July 1992, the disarmament of the sector was considered completed. All weapons and forces had been withdrawn to their assigned limits, weapons within the sector had been put under exclusive UNPROFOR control (i.e., *not* under a so-called "dual-key" arrangement), and all forces within the sector had been demobilized. In fact, even a ban on wearing any uniform was enforced by UNPROFOR. The weapons, however, remained the property of the parties who retained the right to carry out maintenance work on them.

Although the disarmament of the sector itself had been successful, many problems and difficulties still arose. Joint searching operations had to be organized with the UN Civilian Police, the local police forces and the UNPROFOR forces. Such searches were organized with the aim of confiscating any illegal weapons still located within the sector, including hunting rifles and handguns (although special hunting permits were issued by UNPROFOR). The only weapons authorized by UNPROFOR were side arms for the local police. It can be noted here that, as a rule, confiscated weapons were not returned to their owners. Furthermore, matters were complicated by the strong suspicion on the part of both Croats and Serbs that UNPROFOR was not impartial. Indeed, both parties were extremely well-informed about any developments taking place in the other half of the sector and viewed them with great suspicion. Impartiality was, therefore, crucial to the acceptance by all parties of the UNPROFOR operations.

The key to the successful demilitarization of Sector West was the decision to fully involve the local authorities on both sides in the disarmament operations. It was made clear to them that with their assistance and full cooperation, UNPROFOR would provide a number of services to their respective zones of control such as: the so-called "peace building activities" which included meetings on demarcation lines, the "village visitation programme" which provided displaced persons with the opportunity to visit their villages in the opposite sector, and the distribution of humanitarian aid and the repair of destroyed civilian infrastructures (the "rehabilitation cum reconstruction programme").

As often happens in conflict areas, the Croat and Serb military authorities within Sector West had a more important role than their civilian counterparts. Far from being disturbed by this, UNPROFOR skillfully exploited the situation. By requesting frequent meetings with local civil authorities, by insisting on their presence during all meetings and negotiations, and by providing them with goods and services which they were then asked to deliver to the local population, UNPROFOR re-established the civil authorities as a relevant social and political component of Sector West. This, in turn, secured at least a minimum degree of cooperation from the civil authorities.

4.3. First Challenge to the Disarmament of Sector West

The efforts put into building a relationship of trust with the local authorities proved invaluable during the Croatian attack of 22 January 1993 against Krajina Serb villages in Sector South and in the adjacent "pink zone". Although this attack occurred relatively far from Sector West, tensions in the sector escalated as soon as news of the action spread. On 27 January Croat forces took control of the Peruca Dam thereby triggering an angry Serb reaction; VSK soldiers penetrated UNPROFOR-controlled depots and seized the weapons. The Serbs were infuriated by the inability of UNPROFOR to protect them against Croatian attacks, and they blamed their casualties on the fact that their heavy weapons had been put into UNPROFOR collection sites. Serb TDF commanders in Sector West, also fearing a surprise HV attack, mobilized their forces and moved them to combat positions;

furthermore, TDF commanders were considering taking control of the weapons placed under UNPROFOR supervision.

Faced with such a crisis, the Sector Commander, General Zabala, and Civil Affairs representative, Mr Gerald Fisher, immediately tried to convince the Serbs that UNPROFOR would protect them and that they should not seize their weapons and move to the confrontation lines. After a tense and difficult night, the Serbs finally agreed to give up any radical action. This was not, however, enough to ease tensions; the Croats had been informed of the Serb movements, had moved their forces to the confrontation lines, and were preparing for a Serbian attack. Once again, Civil Affairs representatives and UNPROFOR officers had to engage in lengthy negotiations to convince the Croats to return to their assigned areas. Finally, both sides returned to their agreed positions after reaching an agreement for demilitarization and the crisis subsided. The agreement in Sector West had proven strong enough for the time being, but 18 months later, the stability of Sector West was to be tested again.

4.4. Second Challenge to the Disarmament of Sector West

While Sector West had indeed been demilitarized, this demilitarization had been harder to achieve in the southern (Serb-controlled) part of the sector. There were a number of reasons for this, including the proximity of the border between Sector West and the Serb-controlled area of Bosnia and the relative proximity of Banja-Luka. This made it very difficult to monitor VRS movements across the border. Furthermore, because the Serbs often restricted the movements of UNPROFOR personnel, they did not have good intelligence about VSK, or particularly VRS, operations. As a result, Serb forces regularly continued to move across the southern part of Sector West. While this was not too problematic in the parts of the sector under the control of the Nepalese and Jordanian battalions, it was far more dangerous in the area controlled by the Argentinean battalions as this area was adjacent to the confrontation line.

To all parties involved, it was increasingly obvious that the situation was worsening. Fire was being exchanged across the line of confrontation between the Croats and the Serbs. These exchanges were threatening an important road on the Croat-held side, the Dragovic road, which was the only direct road across the sector under Croat control. Furthermore, a number of incursions by Serb commandos had taken place, and the city of Pakrac came regularly under Serb fire. For their part, the Croats had deployed "special" police forces (in reality paramilitaries) along the line of confrontation and shot regularly at the Serbs. While the Sector Commander had allowed the Croats to maintain a number of police observation posts with 6 assault rifles each, the Croats regularly pressed for more observation posts. To make matters worse, during the last days of July 1993, UNPROFOR began to suspect that an entire VRS brigade (about 1,500 men) had crossed the border between Croatia and Bosnia and had deployed in the sector. Finally, the bulk of the Canadian battalion had to be redeployed to another sector, and the Argentinean battalion was to take the responsibility for both sides of the line of confrontation (the two other battalions of the sector, the Jordanian and the Nepalese battalions, were deployed in the area under Serb control). Under these circumstances, the Argentineans decided that they had no choice but to take action.

4.5. Limited Coercive Disarmament

The UNPROFOR operation initiated on 4 September 1993, was preceded by a meeting between UNPROFOR representatives, the Croat chief of police, and a Croat special representative of the Ministry of Internal Affairs. The Croats were told that all unauthorized police posts were to be dismantled within 72 hours, and that if this was not done, UNPROFOR would act unilaterally. The Croats complied reluctantly and the goal was met only after a full week. The Argentine battalion made daily controls on all Croat posts and registered all the serial numbers of the Croat weapons; all unauthorized weapons were seized.

All this action took place under the careful scrutiny of the Serb observation posts on the other side of the line of confrontation. Not only were the Serbs capable of observing all the activities of UNPROFOR directly from their observation posts, but they seemed to have very good and timely intelligence on events in the Croat-controlled part of the sector. This actually had a positive impact on the subsequent actions of UNPROFOR: having seen what was happening on the Croat side, the Serbs were not truly surprised when they were told by UNPROFOR that the area under their control also had to comply with the UNPROFOR mandate, including disarmament and demobilization. Specifically, the Serbs were repeatedly told that, if they would not disarm and demobilize voluntarily, UNPROFOR would compel them to do so by force. They were also given a week to retreat from the line of confrontation.

The Argentines waited for 48 hours, but nothing happened: obviously, the Serbs had not taken UNPROFOR seriously. The Argentine battalion began its operation by seizing weapons from all armed individuals in the streets. The disarmed individuals were given receipts for their weapons which they could show to their superiors. Finally, on 4 September the Argentine battalion acted directly against the Serb observation posts along the line of confrontation.

The total force used by the battalion commander was comprised of three infantry companies, plus two Canadian APC companies in reserve for a total force of 47 APC's. Four days before the action, the battalion commander had visited every single Serb post, and every officer involved new exactly what was expected of him. Furthermore, the Serbs had been told at every single encounter "pushka no, pushka no, kucha, kucha" (or "gun no, gun no, home, home" in pidgin Serbocroatian). Besides, there was little the Serb soldiers could do: their telephone lines had been cut during the night (these posts did not have radios); they were vastly outnumbered (2-5 Serbs per position against 18 UNPROFOR men supported by APC's); and the Argentineans had dispatched 10 men and 1 APC along each road leading from the Serb barracks to the observation posts. This was done in order to block the Serb soldiers coming to replace the night shift, therefore, no reinforcements showed up. All weapons were seized, and the soldiers were sent away with receipts for all their seized guns. By 8:00 a.m. The action was finished.

While the operation was a success, UNPROFOR was still concerned about the reaction of the Serb commanders. How would they respond when informed of the UNPROFOR action? In fact, the Serbs strongly protested; they also made threats to the effect that they would retake their weapons by force. Such actions, however, never materialized. After a period of tension, calm returned to the sector; the disarmament operation was a success.

Successful as it was, this action still fell short of truly enforcing the mandate to the letter-- far from it. The main achievement of UNPROFOR's action was that Croats and Serbs no longer shot at each other across the line of confrontation. This was, in fact, to the benefit of both sides because of the exchange of goods between the two communities across the line of confrontation (i.e., the black market). But the Serb-controlled part of the sector was far from demilitarized: no action had been taken against the Serb forces in the areas under the control of the Nepalese and Jordanian battalions, and no action whatsoever was taken against the VRS brigade in the sector. It was only in the relatively narrow stretch between the limit of the area of responsibility of the Argentine battalion and the two other battalions and the line of confrontation that action had been taken. The heaviest weapon seized was a 50 mm gun. The Serb-controlled section of Sector West, about one-third of the sector, or 600 square kilometers, lay north of the Sava river and the Bosnian Prosara mountains. The river is the natural border between Croatia and Bosnia-Herzegovina. On the southern side of the Sava river, on the Bosnian side,

UNPROFOR believed that powerful VRS brigades were deployed. These brigades, contrary to the low-readiness Serb TDF forces in the Sector West, were very well-trained, armed, and commanded, and they were formed entirely of combat-ready and well-disciplined men. In other words, it was likely that, from a Serbian perspective, the TDF forces in the sector were primarily tasked with occupying the ground and "showing the flag". Considering their low level of readiness -- they were, after all, mainly composed of locally drafted men -- and their lack of equipment (as evidenced by the few 50 mm guns and lack of radio communications in their observation posts), it is unlikely that these TDF forces were ever intended to be tasked with the defense of the sector.

Thus, it is likely that even though the Serbs were angered by the UNPROFOR action, they did not see it as compromising their security in an unacceptable way. After all, what were the exact risks for the Serbs in accepting the UNPROFOR insistence on removing their observation posts from the line of confrontation and on seizing weapons (mostly Kalashnikov assault rifles) from individual men in the streets? In other words, the sector probably did not have the means to defend itself militarily, and UNPROFOR was accepted simply because it represented the best chance to defend the sector from a Croat takeover by political means.

From the Croatian prospective, matters were even simpler: the UNPROFOR action freed the important Dragovic road from the threat of Serbian attack, reduced the number of incursions of Serbian commandos in the Croat-controlled area, and removed the constant fire attacks against the city of Pakrac. Similarly, the Croats did not really have to fear a Serbian attack northwards simply because the Serbs did not have the means to conduct such a large-scale offensive operation, hence the lack of true resistance on the Croat side.

It is likely that Croats and Serbs accepted the UNPROFOR action simply because it was advantageous to both sides, or at least, not worth opposing by force. Clearly, disarmed individuals on both sides protested, sometimes vehemently, against the operation. But it remains likely that, for all the posturing and protest, both Serbs and Croats accepted the "tough" stance of UNPROFOR because it suited them. Under other conditions, it is likely that the reaction of the warring parties would have been different.

4.6. The Collapse of Sector West

The situation, however, had changed during the course of 1994-1995 due mainly to the fact that the military balance seemed to be shifting away from the

Serb forces. The US-backed Muslim-Croat coalition put an end to the infighting between Muslims and Croats and resulted in a united opposition facing the Serbs. Furthermore, due to a massive violation of the arms embargo, the Muslim-Croat coalition managed to re-arm itself with weapons ranging from small arms to MiG-21 aircraft, tanks and even long-range multiple-rocket launchers.[1] Most of the heavier systems, however, went to the Croats (the Muslims received primarily infantry weapons). The resulting picture of the political and military equations was changed fundamentally in a number of ways:

1. The nature of the conflict changed from a multi-party civil war to a two-party conflict with the Bosnian Serbs and the Krajina Serbs on one side and the Muslims, the Bosnian Croats and the Croats on the other side. In terms of manpower, this meant that roughly 60,000 Serbs were then facing a coalition of about 220,000 well-equipped soldiers. By 1994 the Serb's lack of manpower became acute.

2. Three factors had made things even more difficult for the Serbs: the embargo on all supplies imposed by Yugoslav President Milosevic which denied the Serbs badly needed supplies, fuel in particular; the very long front lines which favored tactical breakthroughs; and the international willingness to enforce the existence of six UN Safe Areas, three of which were situated in key strategic locations (Tuzla, Bihac and Sarajevo) and which contained the headquarters of four Muslim Army Corps (the 2nd in Tuzla, the 5th in Bihac, and 1st and 6th in Sarajevo). These corps totaled approximately 49 brigades and 75,000 soldiers.[2] This was most important for the military balance because these Safe Areas negated the only military advantage held by the Serb forces: their superiority in artillery. Indeed, under these circumstances, about one half of the Muslim forces were protected from anything larger than sporadic artillery attacks.

3. Finally, according to well-informed sources, President Milosevic had indicated to President Tudjman as early as 1993 that "the issue of the Serb Krajina was a Croatian matter", thereby implying that Yugoslavia would not intervene in support of the Krajina Serbs if a violent conflict erupted in

---

[1] "Orkan Appears in a BiH Service", *Jane's Intelligence Review Pointer*, April 1995, p. 1.

[2] "The Army of Bosnia-Herzegovina", *Jane's Intelligence Review Pointer*, March 1994, p. 3.

Croatia. President Tudjman, furthermore, was under strong pressure from a large segment of the Croatian population to do something about the Krajina problems.

In light of these developments Sector West acquired new importance. It was the only sector that held a number of lucrative targets (the E70 Zagreb-Belgrade highway, oil resources and few population centers), was politically safe to strike (both the international community and Belgrade having signalled that it was a "Croatian matter") and was militarily easy to conquer.

Indeed, while the Serb TDF forces were relatively well-equipped with artillery, APC's and tanks, all these were stored under UNPROFOR supervision. In case of a surprise attack by the HV, the Serbs would not have had time to seize the weapons and deploy them in useful combat positions. Secondly, while any HV movement of troops would have been impossible to conceal from the Serb intelligence, it could have been concealed in a number of other events (sometimes referred to as "noise"). As early as February 1993, a restricted ECMM document warned that, due to the high level of military activity in the area around Sector West, it would be very difficult to identify a military buildup in advance of an operation. Even if such a buildup had been detected, it would have been only one among many others which had not resulted in an attack; therefore, it would have been costly for the Serbs (both politically and in terms of resources) to react with a mobilization to every detected buildup. Possible reinforcements from Bosnian Serb forces south of the Sava river would have been unlikely due to the overstretched deployment of the VRS forces and their acute shortage of resources.

The Croatian attack of May 1995 was not really a surprise for those aware of this situation. Indeed, a number of other restricted ECMM documents from January and February 1993 very accurately predicted the HV attack plan. According to the ECMM monitors, the Croats would attack from both sides of the UNPA along the E70 highway, cut the UNPA in half, take positions along the Sava river and then turn north and fight any TDF forces which had not surrendered immediately after being surrounded. This is exactly what happened.

Interestingly, the operation did not reflect highly on the level of military proficiency of the HV; the key bridges in Jasenovac and Bosanska Gradiska were not destroyed by the Croatian Air Force (one plane was reportedly shot down and most bombs fell about 2 km away from their targets), the Sava river banks were only secured on the fourth day of the operation, and the Serb forces were not disarmed rapidly. Clearly, the Bosnian Serb forces could have launched an attack across the Sava and along the two 10 km-long asphalt main roads which lead to the E70 highway. At a minimum, the VRS could have opened artillery fire anywhere along the 25 km highway stretch running across the UNPA. The Serb reaction was, however, different.

While Radovan Karadjic announced on CNN that he would give assistance to the Krajina Serbs and while Knin announced that no negotiations with Zagreb would take place, the military reaction of the Serb coalition was limited; Krajina Serbs launched only two attacks with their multiple rocket launchers against Zagreb and shelled a number of other Croatian cities. This clearly was a retaliatory attack designed to punish and frighten the Croats for their attack on UNPA West, but it had no military purpose. Both the Krajina Serbs and the Bosnian Serbs vigorously denounced the Croatian assault against a UN Protected Area in which they had surrendered their heavy weapons only after receiving explicit and repeated security guarantees by UNPROFOR. They accepted, however, the military inevitability of the loss of a sector impossible to defend against a decisive Croatian attack.

4.7. Mandate Implementation:
UNPROFOR Responsible for the Security of Sector West

There is a direct link between the issue of UNPROFOR's mandate and the circumstances under which the HV attack took place. Indeed, the E70 highway had been at the center of numerous negotiations between Zagreb and the Krajina. Finally, these negotiations had resulted in an agreement to open this highway to traffic. The Croats had then warned the Serbs that, if they attempted to re-close the highway, force would be used.

The incident used by Zagreb as a reason for attacking UNPA West began when a Croat slashed the throat of a Serb at a fuel station on the E70 highway. The Serb's brother used a Kalashnikov assault rifle to shoot at Croatian cars thus killing several people. In response to these events, the Serbs closed the highway and the Croats launched their offensive.[3] As indicated above, UNPA West presented an ideal target for a Croatian attack, and the events on the highway were used only as pretexts. This being said, a number of comments can be made about UNPROFOR's performance in the months preceding the attack.

---

[3] The Croats used 7,200 troops in the attack against Sector West. "A Good Season for War", *Time Magazine*, 15 May 1995, p. 28.

First, prior to these events, weapons and armed soldiers had returned to the sector. Furthermore, the Sector Commander -- having taken responsibility for the security of the sector -- should have been held at least partially responsible, if not for the first stabbing incident, then certainly for the attack on Croatian vehicles on the highway. Of course, it might be argued that UNPROFOR simply did not have the means to secure the safety of the highway. In that case, it remains unclear as to what exactly UNPROFOR was referring when the Sector Commander said that he was "personally responsible" for the entire sector, and not only the highway. This issue of personal responsibility can also be raised regarding the Croatian offensive itself. According to the Croat government, the attack on UNPA West resulted in 400 deaths. It was also reported by the Swiss TV channel DRS that over 100 artillery shells had been fired at the town of Okucani during the attack. Under these conditions it remains a matter of speculation as to what UNPROFOR meant by "taking responsibility for the security of the sector".

More generally, a question can be raised regarding the difference between a "UN Protected Area" (as defined in Croatia) and a "UN Safe Area" (as defined in Bosnia). Specifically, why should a counterattack against the 5th Muslim Corps in Bihac trigger a NATO airstrike and a Croatian attack on Okucani not do so? After all, the Croatian attack on UNPA West triggered a flow of thousands of refugees from western Slavonia which greatly contributed to the ethnic cleansing of the sector.[4]

One could, of course, argue that the difference lies in the fact that the attack against UNPA West was executed by the internationally recognized government of Croatia within the internationally recognized borders of Croatia; conversely, the Bosnian Serb counterattack against the Muslim 5th Corps, and even more so the Krajina Serb Air Force bombing raid against Bihac, were executed by internationally non-recognized insurgents against the forces of an internationally recognized government and the 5th Corps was deployed within the internationally recognized borders of Bosnia-Herzegovina. But, in fact, such a position raises many more questions. Indeed, if internationally recognized forces can use force against non-recognized insurgents, what was the purpose behind the creation of the UNPA? Who was being protected against whom? Should it be understood that UN safe zones and UNPA's are meant only to protect governmental forces and their supporting ethnic/cultural groups? Or were they designed to protect all those

---

[4] 13,200 Serbs fled Western Slavonia after the Croat attack, according to UN relief workers. See "'Explosive Mood in Croatia Worries UN", *Financial Times*, 10 May 1995.

in these areas but only against an attack across an international border? In reference to UNPA's, the Vance Plan says:

> The role of the United Nations troops would be to ensure that the areas remained demilitarized, and that all persons residing in them were protected from fear of armed attack.[5]

The UN Security Council Resolution 824 of 6 May 1993, which extended the concept of the "UN Safe Area" from Srebrenica to other cities in Bosnia-Herzegovina declared that:

> The capital of the city of the Republic of Bosnia-Herzegovina, Sarajevo, and other such threatened areas, in particular the towns of Tuzla, Zepa, Gorazde, Bihac, as well as Srebrenica, and their surroundings should be treated as safe areas by all parties concerned and should be free from armed attack and from any other hostile act.[6]

If one looks at these two statements, further questions come to mind. One could, for example, ask why Mostar was not considered as an "other such threatened area" when it was torn apart by heavy fighting between Bosnian Muslim and Bosnian Croat HVO forces until February 1994. Or why in June of 1994, when the Muslim 5th corps attacked Bihac killing many people and creating a flow of refugees of approximately 25,000 people,[7] was this not considered as an "armed attack" or "hostile act" against a UN Safe Area?

Clearly, there is a link between the Croat attack on Sector West, the inability of UNPROFOR to either prevent or react to this attack, and the nature of the mandate as well as the way the mandate was executed in the sector.

---

[5] Vance Plan, Annex III, "Concept for a United Nations Peace-Keeping Operation in Yugoslavia, as Discussed with Yugoslav Leaders by the Honourable Cyrus R. Vance, Personal Envoy of the Secretary-General and Marrack Goulding, Under-Secretary-General for Special Political Affairs", November/December 1991.

[6] Security Council Resolution 824 (1993), 6 May 1993, in United Nations, *The United Nations and the Situation in the Former Yugoslavia*, p. 131.

[7] Report of the Secretary-General Pursuant to the Security Council Resolution 959, UN Document S/1994/1389.

4.8. Did UNPROFOR and the Serbs Sacrifice UNPA West to Political Considerations?

One last issue needs to be raised about the events in Sector West: the issue of military means. Indeed, it is often said that UNPROFOR did not have the means to truly protect the sector. But is this really so?

The attack proceeded (predictably) along the E70 highway axis coming from both east and west. The Croats used over 7,000 troops in this operation. These were supported by APC's, tanks and a few helicopters. The operation began at 5:30 a.m. on 1 May 1995 with a preparatory artillery barrage of 65 artillery pieces and 20 tanks followed by an attack of two HV special purpose brigades, the 101st and 103rd. According to *Jane's Intelligence Review Pointer*, the main reason for the Croatian success was the reconnaissance information provided by the US CIA's Gnat 750 remote-piloted vehicles which helped the Croats identify weak points in the Serb defenses.[8] By 10:45 a.m. Jasenovac had fallen; and by 1:30 p.m. the next day the city of Okucani fell to the HV assault.

UNPROFOR forces did nothing to oppose the attack, and according to certain reports, actually complied with a Croatian order to immediately withdraw from the confrontation line. Colonel Alexander Oliinik, quoted in the Russian Armed Forces newspaper *Krasnaia Zvezda*, claims that the order to evacuate the observation posts, the checkpoints and the E70 highway was given to the Sector Command at 2:30 a.m. by the Croatian operational command, and that at 4:30 a.m. the UNPROFOR headquarters (HQ) in Zagreb ordered UNPROFOR forces in the sector to abandon their positions along the E70 Zagreb-Belgrade highway.[9] This information was corroborated by other independent sources in the area.

Was such a withdrawal the only option left, particularly in military terms? The UN forces in the sector were composed of three battalions totalling over 2,000 men. These forces were equipped with APC's, mortars and light infantry weapons. The most powerful UN force ever deployed in this sector, the Canadian battalion with 60 APC equipped with TOW anti-tank guided missiles, had been redeployed to another sector and had never been replaced. As a result, it is clear that the UNPROFOR forces left in the sector could not have stopped the HV attack with their limited forces.

---

[8] Tim Ripley, "Croat Surgical Strike Successful", *Jane's Intelligence Review Pointer*, June 1995, p. 2.

[9] "Khorvatskii 'blitzkrieg' i nasha politika na Balkanakh", *Krasnaia Zvezda*, 18 May 1995, p. 3.

But this does not mean that UNPROFOR had no better options and that the sector was bound to be retaken by the HV. Keeping in mind that ECMM monitors had described the scenario for a HV attack very accurately as early as January 1993,[10] the following steps could have been taken during the 28 months prior to the HV attack. Basically, the only lucrative target for a HV attack was the Zagreb-Belgrade highway. Hence, rather than attempting to deny the entire sector to a Croatian attack, another approach could have been to deny the HV rapid control of the highway. Considering the terrain and the forces involved, it would have been possible with limited resources to hold the highway long enough to significantly raise the military and political costs of such an attack for Zagreb: two battalions, particularly if well chosen, could have held this road long enough (ideally, a Canadian and a Russian battalion). A third, assumably less capable, battalion could have been given the responsibility of the northern part of the sector. Finally, the HV superiority in armor could have been countered by a suitable but simple preparation of the terrain.[11] Had such tactics been used, the Serb forces would have been given enough time to defend themselves and the risks for the HV would have been significantly increased.

Clearly, such a posture would have entailed its own risks. An attack on Pakrac could not have been meaningfully opposed by UNPROFOR (but neither was there any opposition during the actual attack) and there would have been the risk of taking casualties. However, it is also difficult to understand how any force could protect any sector if it was not willing to take military action, and any military action implies the possibility of taking casualties.

In the opinion of a former UNPROFOR battalion commander in UNPA West, even the UN forces then present in the UNPA during the Croatian attack could have opposed the HV assault (albeit at greater risk): with 2,000 UN soldiers mainly concentrated on the defense of one stretch of highway and the potential of Serb reinforcements, it is dubious whether the Croats would have felt confident about the success of their plans. Hence, the decision to take no action cannot be explained solely by military arguments: it was a political decision.

Again, the issue of the mandate formulation and interpretation is at the center of the problem: if the Sector Commander had "promised to provide security to the

---

[10] ECMM Information Briefing, "Croatian Armed Forces Capabilities and Intentions", 21 January 1993; and ECMM Information Briefing, "Potential for Croatian Attack in UNPA West", 22 February 1993.

[11] See, for example, "Wo selbst der Panzer steckenbliebt: Bauen und Uberwinden von Barrikaden", *Wehrausbildung*, No 5, 1994, pp. 266-269.

Serbian population in case of a Croatian attack",[12] if the nature of the Croat attack was known for over two years to the UNPROFOR HQ in Zagreb, and if the military capabilities to deter such an attack were at least partially available to the Sector Commander, then why was there no action taken whatsoever? Why was the Sector Commander authorized to commit UNPROFOR to the defense of the sector's population? What exactly did the Security Council have in mind when it created the UN Protection Area? How was this protection extended to the local population?

The same questions have been asked about the protection of the Safe Areas in Bosnia, with the major difference being that in Bosnia NATO airpower capabilities were made available to the UN and that at least on a number of occasions (Sarajevo, Gorazde, Bihac, and Sarajevo again) some, although limited, action was taken. Nevertheless, UNPROFOR's performance in its protective role left all parties in the conflict embittered towards the UN.

Another troubling set of questions can be raised concerning the Serbian reaction to the Croat attack. Indeed, it is difficult to understand precisely why the Serb response was so limited. Resistance inside the sector was short and limited in magnitude. As it was widely reported in the press, Krajina Serb forces in Sectors North and South responded to the attack by shelling the cities of Sisak, Karlovac, Dubrovnik and Zagreb as well as the Pleso airport. However, these attacks were very limited in scope. A far more effective response could have been to attack and cut off either the E70 highway from Sector North or from Bosnia, or to do the same with the highway running from Zagreb and Karlovac southward along the Dalmatian Cost. Such action never occurred.

The Serb forces in the sector might have been taken by surprise and might have lacked the weapons to oppose the Croatian attack. As for the Bosnian Serb lack of reaction, it can in part be explained either by the fact that most of their forces were busy fighting in the Bihac, Kurpres-Knin and Brcko areas, or by a political decision to abandon a sector difficult to defend. What remains unclear is the reason why the Krajina Serb forces in Sector North did nothing against the HV forces attacking UNPA West. Had these forces used their artillery on HV forces attacking from the West, it would have made the operation far more difficult for the Croat forces, particularly if these strikes had been supported by artillery strikes from the Bosnian Serb forces south of the Sava river. Again, political considerations seemed to have prevailed.

---

[12] ECMM Information Briefing, "Croatian Armed Forces Capabilities and Intentions", 21 January 1993.

Chapter 5
Demilitarization and Disarmament Operations in Srebrenica

5.1. Background

Srebrenica is the largest Muslim enclave in the eastern part of Bosnia-Herzegovina. It is surrounded by areas with Bosnian Serb majority populations, lies some 20 kilometers from the border to the FRY, and constitutes an important communications link between the Bosnian Serb areas and the FRY. The town of Srebrenica had a peacetime population of just under 10,000[1] which, according to the 1991 census, was 70 per cent Muslim and 25 per cent Serb. The enclave was allocated to the Bosnian Muslims by the Vance-Owen Peace Plan for Bosnia-Herzegovina. By April 1993, because of an influx of displaced persons from surrounding villages destroyed by the Bosnian Serbs, the enclave held some 70,000 people, and the town itself some 20,000 to 28,000 people.[2]

At the outset of the war in Bosnia-Herzegovina in April and May 1992, Serb paramilitaries, backed by the JNA, stormed into eastern Bosnia and overwhelmed a number of predominantly Muslim towns such as Zvornik, Visegrad and Foca. A great number of refugees flooded into remote Muslim enclaves, the largest of which was the Srebrenica municipality. Attempts by Bosnian Serb forces to capture this enclave were repeatedly foiled. From hilltop defensive positions, Srebrenica's Muslim fighters, although vastly outgunned, kept the Serbs at bay and often inflicted heavy losses on their enemy. During this period, they only had three armed squads of 40 or 50 men each, fighting with little coordination

Towards the end of summer 1992, Srebrenica's military commanders received reinforcements of special forces units from Sarajevo. At this point, they changed their tactics and mounted a series of lightning counter-offensives. They drove the Serbs back as far as the Drina river, which forms the border between the FRY and Bosnia-Herzegovina. Dozens of Serb villages were burned to the ground and many

---

[1] *The Guardian*, 17 April 1993.
[2] UN Document S/25700 of 30 April 1993.

of their inhabitants killed by the Bosnian Muslims.[3] This offensive caused panic among local Serbian army leaders, who called in reinforcements from Serb-held regions in northern Bosnia. These extra troops enabled the Serbs to halt the Muslim advance. During the autumn and winter of 1992, a ferocious guerrilla war raged with neither side gaining or losing much ground. Living conditions in Srebrenica steadily worsened. The municipality was practically surrounded, and Serb artillery and fortified positions were strong.

The UNHCR was first alerted to the deteriorating conditions in Srebrenica in November 1992. Initial relief efforts failed when Bosnian Serb women and children barred aid trucks from crossing the Drina, although they eventually relented. Only days after the first food consignments arrived in Srebrenica, however, the enclave's forces launched another devastating offensive in which Bosnian Serb villages were again a target.

The Bosnian Muslim offensive suddenly stopped at the end of January 1993. By the end of February, the Bosnian Serbs began gaining the upper hand again, and the Muslim forces were slowly driven back to the hills and scarps surrounding the enclave as the Bosnian Serbs tightened their grip on the region. As Bosnian Serb forces drew closer, thousands of uprooted civilians fled to the relative safety of the last Muslim outpost in the region, and living conditions in Srebrenica became intolerable. By April 1993, some 28,000 people had sought refuge in the already hard-pressed town.

On 26 March 1993, after a meeting with UNPROFOR commanders, General Radko Mladic, commander of the Bosnian Serb forces, suggested at a press conference in Belgrade the surrender of the Muslim forces in Srebrenica and asked the combatants to hand their arms over to UNPROFOR. His proposition was repeated two weeks later, but the commander of the Bosnian Muslim forces, Sefer Halilovic, refused to negotiate until 16 April 1993, when the Bosnian Serb forces announced the imminent fall of Srebrenica. The Bosnian Serb forces were only one kilometer from the center of the town.

5.2. The Local Agreement

By 17 April 1993, Srebrenica was under intense shelling; it was surrounded and totally isolated. The situation forced the Bosnian Muslim commander to agree

---

[3] *The Guardian*, 17 April 1993.

to a settlement in which only the Muslim side was to disarm under the supervision of UNPROFOR. This agreement, reached in Sarajevo, is reproduced in the Annex of this volume.

Negotiations regarding this settlement had been initiated at least one month before the Security Council was informed that the fall of the city was imminent and that a cease-fire agreement was being discussed in Sarajevo. The negotiations involved UNPROFOR's Force Commander, and UNPROFOR participated actively in the drafting of and in convincing the Bosnian Commander to sign the agreement. The Bosnian Muslims were reminded that no outside support would be forthcoming and that they were entirely defenseless. UNPROFOR acted in an emergency situation. Had this agreement not been reached, a massacre would most probably have taken place; this justifies the Force Commander's actions which went beyond the mandate proper that he had been given.

The Srebrenica deal was signed early on 18 April 1993 by General Ratko Mladic, the Bosnian Serb commander; General Sefer Halilovic, the Bosnian army chief; and General Lars-Eric Wahlgren, the Swedish UN commander for former Yugoslavia. It was reportedly reached after 14 hours of hard bargaining.[4] It included the following disarmament provisions:

- the demilitarization of Srebrenica would be completed within 72 hours of the arrival of the UNPROFOR company on 18 April 1993;
- all weapons, ammunition, mines, explosives and combat supplies (except medicines) inside Srebrenica would be handed over to UNPROFOR under the supervision of three officers from each side with control carried out by UNPROFOR; and
- no armed persons or units except UNPROFOR would remain within the city once the demilitarization process was completed. Responsibility for the demilitarization process was to remain with UNPROFOR.

These disarmament provisions contradicted Resolution 819 and subsequent Safe Areas resolutions, as explained in the next section. It is not clear, therefore, if the Security Council was informed about the details of these negotiations or not. The report of the investigation team seems to suggest that the Security Council did not know about the negotiations leading to the conclusion of the Srebrenica

---

[4] *The Guardian*, 19 April 1993.

agreement.[5] On the other hand, a UN representative interviewed in Geneva, who was present when the agreement was concluded in Sarajevo, maintains that UNPROFOR reported the progress made at the local negotiation table. However, the Security Council acted independently of what was happening on the ground, and the adoption of Resolution 819 came as a surprise to UNPROFOR.[6]

5.3. The Security Council Resolutions on Safe Areas

On 16 April 1993, the Security Council, acting under Chapter VII of the Charter, adopted Resolution 819, in which it demanded that all parties treat Srebrenica and its surroundings as a "safe area" which should be free from any armed attack or any other hostile act. It demanded the immediate withdrawal of Bosnian Serb paramilitary units from areas surrounding Srebrenica and the cessation of armed attacks against the town. The Council requested the Secretary-General to take steps to increase the presence of UNPROFOR in Srebrenica in order to arrange for the safe transfer of the ill and wounded from Srebrenica and its surrounding areas and to assure the unimpeded delivery of humanitarian assistance. This was done in the context of the original, humanitarian mandate.

The concept of Safe Areas was elaborated in Resolution 824 of 6 May 1993. The Security Council declared that in these Safe Areas, the following should be observed:

a)   the immediate cessation of armed attacks or any hostile act against these Safe Areas, and the withdrawal of all Bosnian Serb military or paramilitary units from these towns to a distance wherefrom they ceased to constitute a menace to their security and that of their inhabitants, to be monitored by UNMO's; and

b)   full respect by all parties of the rights of UNPROFOR and the international humanitarian agencies to free and unimpeded access to all safe-areas in the Republic of Bosnia-Herzegovina, and full respect for the safety of the personnel engaged in these operations.

---

[5] The report of the investigation mission is contained in UN Document S/25700 of 30 April 1993.

[6] Interview with Victor Andrew.

Resolution 824 also declared that, in addition to Srebrenica, Sarajevo and other such threatened areas, in particular the towns of Tuzla, Zepa, Gorazde, Bihac and their surroundings, should be treated as Safe Areas by all the parties concerned. It authorized the strengthening of UNPROFOR's mandate by an additional 50 military observers to monitor the humanitarian situation in those areas. Subsequently, Resolution 836 of 4 June 1993 further elaborated on the Safe Areas concept and enabled UNPROFOR to deter attacks against these areas.

5.4. Mandate Interpretation

Although founded on Chapter VII of the UN Charter -- as had also been the case for UNPROFOR's humanitarian mandate in Bosnia-Herzegovina -- Resolution 819 did not, in reality, allow the use of force if the Bosnian Serb forces decided not to comply. Furthermore, the introduction of the Safe Areas concept did not imply any enlargement of UNPROFOR's mandate. As a matter of fact, the Resolution simply asked the parties to show restraint; it did not provide any details about UNPROFOR's role in protecting these areas.[7] Resolutions 824 and 836 made the rules clearer in some instances. In others cases, such as with Resolution 836 and Srebrenica, the Security Council contradicted the agreement reached between the parties on the demilitarization of the area by expressly allowing Bosnian Muslim military or paramilitary units to stay in the Safe Areas.

In order to put pressure on the Bosnian Serbs and to assure compliance with Resolution 819 as well as with earlier resolutions, the Security Council tightened the sanctions against Belgrade. By voting Resolution 820, the Security Council thus played its last non-military card from the range of measures it could take to put pressure on Belgrade. The non-aligned countries would, as a next step, press for the lifting of the arms embargo against the Bosnian Muslims.

Divergent views have been expressed concerning the relationship between Resolution 819 and the local agreement. Lieutenant General Wahlgren and General Morillon have stated that, without such Security Council action, the agreement for the demilitarization of Srebrenica would not have been reached.[8] UN

---

[7]   Interview with John Almstrom, Senior Political Advisor, Office of the Special Representative of the Secretary-General, UNPROFOR Headquarters, Zagreb, 24 April 1995 and interview with Victor Andreew. The mandate was, however, enlarged subsequently, with the adoption of Resolutions 824 and 836.

[8]   UN Document S/25700 of 30 April 1993.

representatives interviewed in Zagreb in April 1995 indicated, by contrast, that the Security Council resolution did not affect the local agreement, namely because of the shortcomings of the Safe Areas concept. It certainly had a negative impact, however, on the implementation of the Safe Areas over the years in that it did not require the demilitarization of the Safe Areas, while it expressly demanded the withdrawal of Bosnian Serb paramilitary units from them. Resolution 819 gave little incentive to the Bosnian Muslim party to demilitarize Srebrenica in accordance with the local agreement. In this respect, the Security Council resolution did not facilitate the negotiations; rather, it was counterproductive and eliminated UNPROFOR's chances to find a durable settlement in Srebrenica.[9]

5.5. Implementation of the Disarmament Elements of the Srebrenica Agreement

The implementation of the disarmament elements was complicated by the confusion over the applicability of the Safe Area Resolution 819. It was further hampered by the relatively long time frame of 72 hours during which the demilitarization and withdrawal of Bosnian Serb units and the deployment of UNPROFOR troops were expected to proceed simultaneously and in a reciprocal manner.

On 21 April 1993, UNPROFOR's Force Commander reported that 170 UNPROFOR troops, civilian police and military observers had been deployed in Srebrenica to collect weapons, ammunition, mines, explosives and combat supplies. By noon on 21 April 1993 they had successfully demilitarized the town. Although General Mladic would have preferred for the arms collected by UNPROFOR in Srebrenica to be destroyed on the spot,[10] the collection and storage of weapons was done following the same techniques used in the UNPA's in Croatia. Weapons were stored in an intact state and remained the property of the party handing them in. The actual operation was limited to three weeks in time. Since April 1993, as of this writing, there has not been any disarmament in Srebrenica. In the view of an UNPROFOR representative, however, it would be possible to go back to the agreement if this question arose again.[11]

---

[9] Interview with Victor Andreew.
[10] *Le Monde*, 20 April 1993.
[11] Interview with John Almstrom.

Unfortunately, the disarmament of Srebrenica was not fully accomplished at the outset.[12] Less than half of the weapons in the area were handed in. Armed parties began entering the area, weapons began flowing in, and a formal, organized military structure was established in the pocket. Neither did the Serbs withdraw all of their heavy weapons either. Srebrenica remained within the reach of Bosnian Serb weapons, and subject to Serb control of the access routes.

A Security Council fact-finding mission visited the region from 22 to 27 April 1993. It described Srebrenica as the "equivalent of an open jail in which its people [could] wander around but [were] controlled and terrorized by the increasing presence of Serb tanks and other heavy weapons in it's [sic] immediate surroundings".[13] On its visit to UNPROFOR observations posts in the mountains surrounding the city, the mission found that new trenches had been dug during the previous weeks, and that tanks and heavy weapons could be seen at a distance of 900 meters from one observation post. The mission stated that, evidently, the Serb paramilitary forces were not ready to withdraw. On the contrary, they were larger than they were when Resolution 819 was adopted and were increasing their pressure on the town.[14]

Evidently, the Bosnian Serbs did not feel bound by the decision taken in the Security Council, and expected demilitarization to proceed according to the agreement that they had reached with the Bosnian Muslim side. They held the view that the Safe Areas were contrary to international law, especially to the 1949 Geneva Conventions requiring such areas to be demilitarized in order to receive protection.[15] Accordingly, it was reported by the Commander of the Canadian Battalion that the Bosnian Serbs had "their own interpretation of the demilitarization agreement".[16] UNPROFOR's Chief of Staff at Kiseljak was more explicit when recognizing that "even though the Security Council [was] obviously an important organ of the United Nations it [was] of no importance to the Serbs in the area".[17] Another difficulty with re-establishing an acceptable security situation in Srebrenica was the small territory given to the Safe Area. It covered merely 4.5 by 0.5 kilometers. For the area to be considered "safe", it needed to be

---

[12] Interview with John Almstrom; interview with Victor Andreew; and UNIDIR, *Practitioners' Questionnaire,* No. Y-097.

[13] UN Document S/25700 of 30 April 1993.

[14] *Ibid.*

[15] Interview with John Almstrom. See also reference to the Geneva conventions in UN Document S/1995/444 of 30 May 1995.

[16] UN Document S/25700 of 30 April 1993.

[17] *Ibid.*

greatly expanded, and Bosnian Serb forces needed to withdraw to points from which they could not attack, harass or terrorize the town.

Despite these shortcomings, it must be stressed that, even though Srebrenica was not a successful disarmament operation as such, it successfully brought about military stability. Fighting ceased -- or rather shifted to the Muslim-Croat confrontation line -- and the living conditions of the civilian population improved considerably.

5.6. The Parties and Their Motivations

It is suggested in this study that overlapping interests are important for the success of a multinational force's disarmament operation. An attempt will therefore be made to briefly analyze the parties' interest in the Srebrenica disarmament operation.

The Bosnian Muslims

In April 1993, Srebrenica was about to fall into the hands of the Bosnian Serbs and the Bosnian Muslims forces were facing a certain defeat. The situation for the civilians was dramatic and the casualties were numerous. In view of the imminent fall of Srebrenica, an arrangement with the other party was in the interest of the Bosnian Muslims, and the price to be paid was demilitarization. But the Bosnian Muslims were not left empty-handed since the adoption of Resolution 819 redressed the situation in their favor, and in any case, the implementation of the demilitarization component of the Srebrenica agreement was never completed.

The Bosnian Serbs

The Srebrenica agreement was also in the Bosnian Serbs' interest. From a military point of view, they could have fought their way through the town. However, to penetrate into Srebrenica could hardly have served the military objective of the Bosnian Serbs. Their intention was to reduce the town's defenses in order to be able to communicate freely with the FRY. Furthermore, since UNPROFOR was to guarantee the implementation of the Srebrenica agreement and its demilitarization component, the Bosnian Serbs had no reason to oppose UNPROFOR's mission. In the Srebrenica agreement, they had reached their aims, namely a smaller pocket, the demilitarization of the town, and an end to the bad image that the siege of Srebrenica was giving to the Bosnian Serbs. An escalation of the crisis would have advanced the Security Council decision to tighten sanctions against the Bosnian Serbs and the FRY. This move would have embarrassed the government of the Russian Federation, strengthened Boris Yeltsin's nationalistic-minded adversaries, and jeopardized the development of democracy in the Russian Federation.[18]

Srebrenica was interpreted as a Bosnian Serb victory. On 18 April 1993, buoyed by the Muslim "surrender", the Bosnian Serb leader, Radovan Karadjic, stated that "The Muslims had to accept peace and help to hand over their weapons to the UN".[19] The Serbs seemed to have reached all their objectives after almost a year of besieging Srebrenica.

5.7. Consequence of the Crisis: Mandate Enlargement

Acting under Chapter VII of the UN Charter, on 4 June 1993 the Security Council further expanded UNPROFOR's mandate to enable it to protect the Safe Areas with Resolution 836. UNPROFOR was then able to deter attacks against itself, to monitor the cease-fire, to promote the withdrawal of military or paramilitary units other than those of the Bosnian Government, and to occupy some key points on the ground. The Security Council authorized UNPROFOR to take necessary measures, including the use of force, in response to bombings of the Safe Areas, to armed incursion into them or to any deliberate obstruction to the freedom of movement of UNPROFOR or of protected humanitarian convoys. The Security Council also decided that member states, acting under its authority nationally or through regional arrangements, might take all necessary measures to support UNPROFOR through the use of air power in and around the Safe Areas.

In his report dated 14 June 1993, the Secretary-General indicated that it would be necessary to deploy additional troops on the ground and to provide air support.[20] The UNPROFOR Force Commander had estimated an additional requirement of approximately 34,000 troops to obtain deterrence through strength. The Secretary-General stated, however, that it was possible to start implementing the resolution under a "light option", with a minimal troop reinforcement of around 7,600. This option represented an initial approach and had limited objectives. It

---

[18] According to the *Le Monde* issue of 19 April 1993, quoting Vitali Churkin.

[19] Ian Traynor, "Serb Forces Rejoice in Conquest", *The Guardian*, 19 April 1993.

[20] UN Document S/25939 of 14 June 1993.

assumed the consent and cooperation of the parties and provided a basic level of deterrence. The Secretary-General also reported that he had initiated contacts with member states and had invited NATO to coordinate with him the use of air power in support of UNPROFOR. He pointed out that the first decision to initiate the use of air resources in this context would be taken by him in consultation with the members of the Security Council. Subsequently, Resolution 844 of 18 June 1993 authorized an additional reinforcement of UNPROFOR by 7,600 troops and reaffirmed the use of air power to support the force in and around the declared Safe Areas in Bosnia-Herzegovina.

5.8. Options of Intervention and Their Implications

Events in Srebrenica fueled the widespread frustration felt by UN troops and humanitarian organizations involved in relief efforts. They showed the international community's failure to address the main cause of the civilian population's suffering, the war, while trying to alleviate this suffering by providing humanitarian aid. They also revealed the deep gaps between the numerous and forceful Security Council resolutions, and the scarce means that the international community was actually ready to put at UNPROFOR's disposal. But the important question remains: would a more forceful military engagement under UNPROFOR's authority have led to an early end to the bloodshed in Bosnia-Herzegovina? In this connection, it is worth studying the different military options discussed during the Srebrenica events and their implications for the mandate. These options were:[21] to maintain the safe zones; to arm the Bosnian Muslims; to perform air strikes on supply lines; to perform air strikes on artillery positions; to perform air strikes inside the Federal Republic of Yugoslavia; or, to deploy a full-scale peacekeeping force.

Maintaining safe zones

UNPROFOR's authorization to defend itself and aid deliveries could be interpreted as justifying the use of force in order to set up and to protect effectively the safe havens. However, a number of countries argued that such enforcement

---

[21] Based on a number of articles published in the daily press, but particularly in *The Guardian* of 17 April 1993 and *Financial Times* of 16 April 1993.

would need a new resolution and a redefinition of the UN military role. The advantage of creating safe havens was that they would be able to ensure the lives of the civilian population, mainly Muslims. At the same time, however, securing Muslim enclaves could be interpreted as UN acceptance of Bosnian Serb war gains. Such action, furthermore, undermined the Vance-Owen map which sought to avoid dividing Bosnia along purely ethnic lines. In order to enforce effectively the safe zones concept, UNPROFOR would have had to expand considerably, and probably also include US ground forces. Deploying these new troops would have taken weeks, during which time existing UNPROFOR forces would have been in danger, and the supply of humanitarian aid heavily disturbed. Finally, in the words of the UN Secretary-General, the "safe areas must be safe for everyone", and that they must therefore be demilitarized.

Arming the Bosnian Muslims

Security Council Resolution 713 of 25 September 1991 imposed an arms embargo on all republics of the former Yugoslavia. Arming the Bosnian Muslims would have called for a new resolution. Supporters of this alternative maintained that allowing the Bosnian Muslims to acquire weaponry and to defend themselves would avoid a Western military intervention and would appease Islamic countries. Critics, on the other hand, feared an increase in the other warring parties' arms holdings and a polarization between the permanent members of the Security Council. Such an action would have set off a new Balkan arms race, bringing even more bloodshed, and thwarting the UN's humanitarian mission.

Performing air strikes

(i) strikes on supply lines

The UN's basic mandate in Bosnia was to deliver food and medicine and to employ "all necessary means" to do so. To the extent that Bosnian Serb actions blocking humanitarian aid convoys depended on spare parts, ammunition and oil from the FRY, it could be argued that a decision to bomb the Bosnian Serb supply routes would have been covered by the existing mandate. This is, however, a doubtful interpretation of the mandate. While this option would have eventually reduce military viability, it would not have had any serious short-term effect on the Bosnian Serb military resources. This was probably the least effective air strike option for loosening the Bosnian Serb grip.

(ii) strikes on artillery positions

Strikes on artillery positions could be covered by the "all possible means" authorization. Such operations would destroy some weapons and forced the Serbs to move others, and they might have weakened Bosnian Serb sieges of a number of Muslim enclaves. However, wooded mountain terrain made identifying a great number of dispersed and mobile targets extremely difficult. This action could have also triggered Bosnian Serb action against UNPROFOR troops. While the Bosnian Muslims might have been willing to incur casualties in order to destroy some of the Serb heavy artillery, the mandates of UNPROFOR and the humanitarian aid agencies would have been undermined.

(iii) strikes on the Federal Republic of Yugoslavia

Such a punitive action would have required a new Security Council mandate for UNPROFOR. It could have shocked President Milosevic into forcing Bosnian Serb leaders to sign the Vance-Owen plan. However, this option could also have broadened the conflict to Kosovo and Macedonia, and it is far from certain that the Bosnian Serbs would have submitted to pressure from Belgrade. Most Western governments had deep reservations concerning such air strikes, and the Russian Federation would probably have vetoed a Security Council authorization.

Deploying a full-scale peacekeeping force

A full-scale peacekeeping operation, such as presented in NATO's provisional plans, would imply putting together a force of perhaps 65,000-75,000 troops with air support, which could be sent into Bosnia-Herzegovina once a genuine cease-fire was established. It could not have been established in the framework of the existing mandate. This operation would be prepared to tackle flare-ups, but not to manage a breakdown in the local cease-fire. Tasks would include ensuring the withdrawal, demilitarization and disarmament of warring militias and the establishment of an effective police. But the record of UN forces conducting such tasks in Serb-controlled parts of Croatia does not augur well. Its success would depend to a great extent on US and Russian Federation participation, and a considerable increase in resources put at the disposal of the peacekeeping force by the contributing states.

5.9. Conclusions

In a general mood of relief and optimism, the solution of the Srebrenica crisis was seen as a victory for the United Nations. On 18 April 1993, General Philippe Morillon, the commander of the UN troops in Bosnia, insisted that the deal he helped broker was a triumph for the UN. "We have achieved exactly all our objectives from the beginning of this crisis", the French officer stated, "Yesterday we saved the city. We have saved thousands of lives there. I hope the despair and the panic is now over".[22] It was hoped that the creation of Safe Areas would alleviate the suffering of the civilian population in other enclaves.

Srebrenica was the first test of the Safe Areas concept, which, in the view of the Secretary-General, was applied with a greater degree of effectiveness there than in the other areas.[23] The two warring parties had agreed upon a cease-fire on the confrontation line, deployment of UNPROFOR troops, medical evacuation, ad hoc demilitarization, freedom of movement and other related measures. Although the implementation of these agreements was far from complete and faced many problems, UNPROFOR was able to deploy troops on the ground. Its presence had an important preventive role; as one UN representative expressed, "if you have international eyeballs on the scene, some things will not happen".[24] He added that the media also had a preventive role.

The warring parties' failure to comply fully with the Srebrenica agreement has been described in previous sections. There were also disappointments on the part of the international community. They represented the missed occasions in the Srebrenica disarmament operation. By not meeting even the minimum troop reinforcement requirements proposed by the Secretary-General and approved by the Security Council, the troop-contributing countries severely limited UNPROFOR's presence in the Safe Areas, including Srebrenica. UN forces had to use peacekeeping techniques that relied on the consensus of the parties and they were thus unable to handle any crisis emerging between the parties. A lack of resources also critically affected UNPROFOR's ability to carry out disarmament operations while ensuring the security of the parties. In the view of a UN representative in Zagreb, this was an impossible situation. "Unless we are prepared to defend those enclaves militarily it is difficult to ask them to give up their weapons. We could only act as intermediaries and carry out mutually agreed

---

[22] *The Guardian*, 19 April 1993.
[23] UN Document S/1994/555 of 9 May 1994.
[24] Interview with John Almstrom.

stabilization measures".[25] This disarmament operation clearly showed the importance of obtaining a local agreement that meets the parties' interests. However, the lack of support from the international community for implementing this agreement did not allow for disarmament to be carried out other than in a symbolic manner.

The Srebrenica crisis resulted in a number of Security Council resolutions which elaborated on the Safe Areas concept and tightened sanctions. Also, a debate ensued on the use of force. Lord Owen, for a long time opposed to any western military intervention other than for humanitarian purposes, envisaged for the first time the use of force against the Bosnian Serb militia to end the siege of Srebrenica. US President Clinton, confronted with the news of the attack on Srebrenica, declared that he did not exclude any option, except the deployment of troops on the ground.[26] However, for it to be successful, any of the military options mentioned above would need a clear long-term objective.

---

[25] *Ibid.*
[26] *Le Monde*, 18-19 April 1993.

Chapter 6
Creating the Heavy Weapons Exclusion Zone of Sarajevo

6.1. Background

Sarajevo is one of the oldest cities in Europe and one with a truly ecumenical vocation. As the capital of Bosnia-Herzegovina, situated in the Miljacka plain, it bears the characteristics of the urban architecture of three successive periods which marked its history: the Ottoman, the Austro-Hungarian and the post-World War period. During the latter, the population passed from 99,000 (1948) to 526,000 (1991), and a number of neighboring small villages along the principal communications roads became industrial suburbs, like Hadzici, Blazuj, Hrasnica, Vogosca and Ilidza. This industrialization during the Tito era was motivated by the political will to promote the development of the area and also by strategic reasons. In fact, Sarajevo, located in mountainous terrain in the center of former Yugoslavia, was considered to be very difficult for any foreign aggressor to conquer.

Situated between 530 and 750 meters above sea level, Sarajevo is surrounded by a number of mountains of more than 1500 meters: in the north the Ozren, in the south-east Trebevic, and in the south-west Igman and Bjelasnica. Despite these mountain barriers, Sarajevo is by no means isolated. It is situated at the intersection of roads leading from the Adriatic to the plain of the Sava river via Mostar, and from the Sandjak and Federal Republic of Yugoslavia to western Bosnia via Travnik.

At the beginning of the war in Bosnia-Herzegovina, Sarajevo had, like the rest of the country, a very mixed population.[1] None of its ethnic groups constituted an absolute majority: 49 percent of the population was Muslim, 30 percent Serb, seven percent Croat. An unusually high proportion of citizens, namely 11 percent, declared themselves "Yugoslavs" and did not associate themselves with a

---

[1] Unlike the other republics and their capitals.

particular ethnic group.[2] Sarajevo was a model of ethnic and religious tolerance, yet it was still unable to avoid the escalation of war following the international recognition of Bosnia-Herzegovina.

The Bosnian Serbs, opposed to the independence of Bosnia-Herzegovina, proclaimed the Republic of Srpska and claimed Sarajevo as their capital. From the heights of the surrounding mountains, they could shell the city and cut it off from all outside communication. The Serbs also controlled a number of neighborhoods in Sarajevo itself. At the beginning of the war the Bosnian Serbs had a triple objective: to create a homogeneous Serb population in the areas under their control, to dominate the communication lines between the north-east and the south-east of Bosnia-Herzegovina, and to cut the territorial links between the Muslim populated areas in Bosnia-Herzegovina and the Sandjak Muslims in the FRY.[3] The partition of Sarajevo along the Miljacka river was one of the objectives leading to the creation of a Greater Serbia and part of the deal between Bosnian Serbs and Bosnian Croats concerning the partition of Bosnia-Herzegovina.[4] Only in negotiations during August 1993 did the Bosnian Serbs renounce their goal of partitioning Sarajevo when they accepted UN administration of the city combined with its demilitarization.[5]

On 5 February 1994, a 120-mm mortar round fired at the Markadale marketplace killed at least 68 civilians and wounded about 200 others in the worst single incident of the 22-month war. Although the Bosnian Serbs were initially accused of perpetrating this act, it has proven impossible, up to this date, to identify the culprit. The Sarajevo marketplace shelling received immediate and extensive coverage from the media worldwide and was strongly condemned by the international community. It altered the political field on which the Bosnian conflict was being played. It tested the limits of the "safe areas" concept, provoked the first NATO engagement in Europe since its foundation, incited the first involvement of US forces in combat in Europe since the end of World War II, and it drew Russia into the hapless circle of Balkan problem-solvers. It also led to an American-negotiated coalition of Bosnian Muslims and Bosnian Croats, to

---

[2] Michel Foucher, (ed.), *Fragments d'Europe - Atlas de l'Europe médiane et orientale*, Paris: Fayard, 1993, p. 211. Foucher does not indicate the nationality/ethnic origin of the remaining 3%.

[3] *Ibid.*, p. 208.

[4] Foucher, *Fragments d'Europe - Atlas de l'Europe médiane et orientale*, 1993, p. 208, and Daniel Vernet and Jean-Marc Gonin, *Le rêve sacrifié*, Paris: Odile Jacob, 1994, p. 99 ff.

[5] International Conference on Former Yugoslavia (ICFY), "Background to the 'Sarajevo First' Initiative", Geneva, 10 February 1994.

American air strikes on Bosnian Serb targets, and to a new international peace initiative, the Contact Group peace plan.

6.2. Evolution of the Safe Areas Concept

The situation in Sarajevo in February 1994 has to be seen against the background of the Safe Areas decisions. In Resolution 836 of 4 June 1993, the Security Council extended UNPROFOR's mandate in the Safe Areas and enabled it to deter attacks. UNPROFOR was expressly authorized to take the necessary measures, including the use of force, in response to bombing of the Safe Areas by any of the parties, to armed incursion into their territory, or to any deliberate obstruction of the freedom of movement of UNPROFOR or of protected humanitarian convoys in or around these areas. In this context, the Secretary-General could request the use of air power.

At a meeting in Brussels on 10 and 11 January 1994, NATO members reaffirmed their readiness, under the authority of the Security Council, "to carry out air strikes in order to prevent the strangulation of Sarajevo, the Safe Areas and other threatened areas in Bosnia-Herzegovina".[6] However, countries contributing forces on the ground were opposed to this enforcement option.[7] Furthermore, the lack of appropriate military assets available to UNPROFOR in Bosnia-Herzegovina put in doubt the viability of this option. Even if such action would have been feasible from a military point of view, there was deep skepticism about the efficiency of air strikes against Bosnian Serb positions. These positions could only partly be neutralized, and Bosnian Serb retaliation could completely halt the delivery of humanitarian aid, UNPROFOR's main mission. At the end of January 1994, even UN Secretary-General Boutros-Ghali vehemently opposed any form of military intervention, as this would, in his view, escalate the conflict to an all-encompassing Balkan conflict.

At the same time as the UN headquarters in New York seemed to rule out all forms of enforcement actions, the new UNPROFOR commander in Bosnia-Herzegovina, General Rose, requested the right for his soldiers to get immediate air support should their security be in danger.[8] Deep divergences seemed to persist

---

[6] United Nations, *The United Nations and the Situation in the Former Yugoslavia*, p. 21.

[7] Canada was particularly concerned about the security of its UNPROFOR contingent in Srebrenica.

[8] Austrian Press Agency 408, 24 January 1994.

between the Secretary-General and the commanders on the ground on a number of essential questions.

With respect to the question of whether air strikes would require a new resolution by the Security Council,[9] the Secretary-General noted that UNPROFOR's mandate concerning the Safe Areas in Bosnia-Herzegovina had been adopted under Chapter VII of the UN Charter, and that UNPROFOR did not have to seek the consent of the parties for operations falling within its mandate. Furthermore, the Secretary-General distinguished between close air support involving the use of air power for self-defense, which had already been authorized by NATO, and air strikes for pre-emptive or punitive purposes. NATO forces were not authorized to launch the latter type of air strikes without a decision of the North Atlantic Council.

6.3. The NATO Decision

Following the Sarajevo marketplace explosion, on 6 February 1994 the Secretary-General requested that NATO obtain "a decision by the North Atlantic Council to authorize the Commander-in-Chief of NATO's Southern Command to launch air strikes, at the request of the United Nations, against artillery or mortar positions in and around Sarajevo which are determined by UNPROFOR to be responsible for attacks against civilian targets in that city".[10] Late at night on 9 February, in a move intended to put an end to the strangulation of Sarajevo, the North Atlantic Council issued a statement calling "for the withdrawal, or regrouping and placing under UNPROFOR control, within ten days, of heavy weapons (including tanks, artillery pieces, mortars, multiple rocket launchers, missiles and anti-aircraft weapons) of the Bosnian Serb forces located in the area within 20 kilometers (about 12.4 miles) of the center of Sarajevo, and excluding the area within two kilometers (about 1.2 miles) of the center of Pale". It also called upon the Muslim-led Government of Bosnia-Herzegovina "to place the heavy weapons in its possession within the Sarajevo exclusion zone described

---

[9] In two declarations of 14 and 15 January 1994, the Russian Federation confirmed its position that every form of use of force in Bosnia-Herzegovina should be preceded by consultations of the Secretary-General with the Security Council. At the time, a consensus in the Security Council regarding air strikes was obviously not forthcoming.

[10] United Nations, *The United Nations and the Situation in the Former Yugoslavia*, p. 23.

above under UNPROFOR control, and to refrain from attacks launched from within the current confrontation lines in the city" within the same period.

The North Atlantic Council decided that, from midnight on 20 February 1994, heavy weapons of any of the parties found within the Sarajevo exclusion zone, unless controlled by UNPROFOR, would, along with their direct and essential military support facilities, be subject to NATO air strikes. These strikes would be conducted in close coordination with the Secretary-General. This decision was based on Resolution 836 which gave UNPROFOR the right to use force, including air support, if either the Safe Areas or the liberty of movement of UNPROFOR or humanitarian convoys were violated. However, this resolution did not clarify the responsibility for the intervention.

For the Russian Federation, who would only accept a NATO intervention in case of imminent threat to the UN forces, the North Atlantic Council decision constituted a transgression of the UN mandate. NATO's call for the parties both the Serbs and the Muslims to place the heavy weapons deployed in the Sarajevo area under UN control or to withdraw them from the area was close to the Russian Federation's position. It could not agree, however, with the interpretation of a number of NATO members who saw this decision as "a one-sided ultimatum to the Bosnian Serbs, who [were] being threatened by air strikes".[11]

This issue was discussed in the Security Council on 14-15 February 1994. Although most of the Member states widely supported the North Atlantic Council decision, several either opposed it or expressed concern that, as a result of air strikes, UNPROFOR might become a target for retaliatory measures. No Security Council resolution or statement was issued in this regard.

6.4. The Local Cease-Fire Agreement

NATO headquarters in Brussels was not the only decision-making and negotiating forum for the creation of the Sarajevo heavy weapons exclusion zone. In fact, the NATO ultimatum was preceded by a local agreement secured under UN leadership. In order to better understand these local negotiations, it is necessary to recall the context in which they took place. This context shows that, at the time, substantial progress in negotiations on UN administration and

---

[11] *Ibid.*, p. 24.

demilitarization of Sarajevo had just been made, and the market incident created a new momentum.

The demilitarization of Sarajevo, and of the Safe Areas in general, had been on the agenda since the establishment of the concept of Safe Areas. It was in this context that the "Sarajevo First" initiative was taken by the co-chairmen of the ICFY. The proposal to put Sarajevo under UN administration for a period of two years was made on the basis that, during this period, solutions not apparent during war time could emerge to provide a long term resolution of the issue.[12]

Meeting in Geneva on 19 January 1994, the three parties agreed to UN administration of Sarajevo. However, there was no agreement on an overall settlement at that time. The Bosnian Serbs finally agreed to negotiate the immediate implementation of the UN administration of Sarajevo, including demilitarization and lifting the siege of the city. The parties agreed to meet again on 10 February 1994 to discuss confidence-building measures.

On 5 February 1994, in preparatory consultations for a confidence-building measures meeting later that day at Sarajevo Airport, UN negotiators received assurance from the Bosnian Serbs that they were ready to agree to the UN administration and demilitarization of the Sarajevo District in advance of a final settlement in Bosnia-Herzegovina. The Bosnian Serbs had given up their demand that the city be divided into a Muslim and a Serb part, and the mediators hoped to reach a final agreement on the status of Sarajevo within days, possibly within the same week.[13] This important development was about to be discussed in the confidence-building meeting at Sarajevo Airport when a shell landed in the marketplace of Sarajevo and the meeting had to be suspended.[14] In view of this new political situation, the ICFY negotiators took action to follow up the implementation of a separate political and military peace agreement involving the Sarajevo district as the first step to an overall peace settlement for Bosnia-Herzegovina.[15]

The Sarajevo market incident created a new momentum for these negotiations. A few hours prior to the announcement of the North Atlantic Council decision of

---

[12] ICFY, "Background to the 'Sarajevo First' Initiative", 10 February 1994.

[13] See *The International Herald Tribune*, 11 February 1994.

[14] ICFY, Press Statement Issued on Saturday, 5 February 1994, 19:00 hours, concerning "A Separate Peace for Sarajevo". According to the ICFY, the Bosnian Serb agreement to negotiate for UN administration and the demilitarization of Sarajevo prior to a final settlement for Bosnia-Herzegovina was again confirmed on 6 February 1994.

[15] UN Document S/1994/173 of 14 February 1994.

9 February 1994, Lieutenant General Rose, Yasushi Akashi and UNPROFOR's Sector Commander for Sarajevo had brokered an oral agreement between the Bosnian Serb army and Bosnian Muslim army representatives. The agreement contained 4 points:

(i) the completion of a cease-fire as of 12:00 p.m. on 10 February 1994;
(ii) the withdrawal of all weapons and artillery which should be put under UNPROFOR control;
(iii) the positioning of UNPROFOR troops on sensitive and key positions; and,
(iv) the establishment of a joint commission under UNPROFOR's Commander for the Sarajevo district, Lt. General Soubieru.

The first meeting of the Joint Commission on the following day was to put this oral agreement in writing. At that time, already on 9 February, even *before* the North Atlantic Council decision, there was a willingness on the side of the Bosnian Serbs to remove heavy artillery from the Sarajevo area.[16] There was no fundamental difference in the contents of this local agreement compared with the NATO ultimatum. The wording of the peace accord in Sarajevo and the wording of the North Atlantic Council decision were the same except that the latter indicated the distance of 20 kilometers beyond which the heavy weapons were to be withdrawn. The new UN commander for Bosnia, Lieutenant General Sir Michael Rose, had communicated to Yasushi Akashi the full extent of what was agreed locally. This information was then fed back to the Council in Brussels and the same wording taken up in the statement.[17]

Interviews conducted with UN officials in Zagreb, as well as briefings with UNPROFOR commanders in Geneva, stressed the importance of the local agreement -- which was consensual -- relative to the NATO decision, which was associated with enforcement. It was also significant that NATO had been informed about progress on the local agreement and that it did not act before the agreement was obtained. In the opinion of a UN official in Zagreb, it would not have been possible for the Bosnian Serbs to agree to withdraw their heavy weapons if NATO

---

[16] It is important to note that the local agreement preceded the NATO decision, a fact which was confirmed by a number of primary sources, briefings in Geneva and interviews in Zagreb. Press coverage often placed the local agreement after the NATO decision, and completely ignored the existence of this agreement as the deadline for calling on air strikes was approaching.

[17] Interview with Lieutenant General Sir Michael Rose, "Sarajevo: A Model for Peace", in *UNPROFOR News*, March 1994.

had produced an ultimatum first. As things were, the Bosnian Serbs had agreed to the substance of the North Atlantic Council decision before the decision was taken.[18]

6.5. Interests of the Parties

In the following sections, the interests of the parties with respect to the Sarajevo agreement in general, and its disarmament components in particular, will be identified, and other key actors will be noted.

The Bosnian Muslims

For the Bosnian Muslims, it was important to stop the shelling of the capital. Media coverage of the marketplace incident and the North Atlantic Council decision were favorable to their cause and prompted a greater interest from, and involvement of, the international community in the conflict. For the Bosnian Muslims, the active intervention of the United States on their side in the Geneva peace negotiations was "a dream come true, something they have been working hard to achieve since the start of these negotiations".[19]

The implementation of the disarmament elements of the North Atlantic Council decision led to a withdrawal of Bosnian Serb heavy weapons from the weapons exclusion zone and to the placing under UN control of the 286 heavy weapons remaining in the zone. From the Bosnian Muslim side, about 80 heavy weapons were handed in.[20] The disarmament element of this arrangement, including the monitoring necessary to ensure that it was respected, resulted in an increased commitment on UNPROFOR's behalf to assure the security of Sarajevo.

The terms of the North Atlantic Council decision were clearly more favorable to the Bosnian government's cause than those of a complete demilitarization of Sarajevo agreed on at an earlier stage in the context of the ICFY negotiations. Under the heavy weapons exclusion zone regime, the Bosnian Muslims were able to maintain military forces in the Sarajevo area which was the headquarters of the 1st and 6th Muslim Army Corps.[21]

---

[18] Interview with John Almstrom.

[19] David B. Ottawa, *The International Herald Tribune*, 12-13 February 1994.

[20] *The Geneva Post* and *Die Welt* of 23 May 1995.

[21] Warren Zimmermann, "The Army of Bosnia-Herzegovina", *Janes Intelligence Review Pointer*, March 1994, p. 3.

The Bosnian Serbs

The Bosnian Serbs, having recognized that they could not take Sarajevo by force,[22] agreed to withdraw their weapons and to have UNPROFOR freeze the situation in Sarajevo. They were not indifferent to the fate of the important Serb population in Sarajevo who suffered from shelling, snipers, and food and medicine shortages. There was no purpose of gaining control of a town consisting of ruins and ashes. No one wanted a new Vukovar. Furthermore, according to interviews conducted with UN officials, the Bosnian Serbs were tired of the bad image that the endless and, from a military point of view, frustrating shelling of Sarajevo was giving them. They therefore welcomed the opportunity to deploy their forces and equipment to other conflict areas.

In this context it is important to stress that the Bosnian Serbs were acting according to the agreement reached between them and the Bosnian Muslims, and not in response to the NATO decision when they withdrew their heavy weapons. Undoubtedly, however, the threat of airstrikes helped to ensure the parties' compliance to the creation of the weapons exclusion zone. Lieutenant General Rose said this truce was different because the Serbs were under greater international pressure and had agreed to pull back their weapons.[23] However, the dimension given to the NATO ultimatum might have complicated the implementation of the local agreement.

The intervention of Vitali Churkin, the Russian special envoy to the former Yugoslavia, unblocked discussions concerning the implementation of the agreement, namely the exact meaning of "UN control" of the weapons. This clarification provided the Bosnian Serbs with much-desired security guarantees in the form of 800 Russian soldiers perceived to be an allied force. Of equal importance was the fact that the agreement allowed disarmament to become an honorable action and not a sign of weakness or defeat.

NATO

The political decision to issue the ultimatum was made by the 16 regular NATO ambassadors in Brussels after consultation with their capitals. In effect, however, it was the clear determination of President Bill Clinton to put the United

---

[22] Interviews in Zagreb indicate that this would have been possible from the military point of view, but that such an action would have had disastrous political consequences.

[23] *The International Herald Tribune*, 11 February 1994.

States behind this threat, along with strong French support, that motivated the British, the Canadians, and the Greeks -- the countries with the biggest reservations towards NATO intervention -- not to block it. Although NATO demonstrated unity, the political implications of the threat of air strikes remained vague. Air strikes would not put an end to the war in Bosnia-Herzegovina. Rather, they would carry the risk for the NATO countries to be dragged in as a party to the conflict. Furthermore, the execution of air attacks could result in one of the parties leaving the negotiating table in Geneva, thus putting UNPROFOR's humanitarian mission in Bosnia-Herzegovina -- the mandate proper for the UN intervention -- into jeopardy.

The failure of the Bosnian Serbs to comply with the ultimatum would have put NATO in a very delicate situation. It might have lost credibility if it did not enforce its decision. On the other hand, if the war dragged on or was escalated, this would have split the allies, damaged the UN system and undermined NATO. But the North Atlantic Council decision also had advantages according to UN representatives interviewed in Zagreb and Geneva, namely the credible enforcement of the local agreement reached between the Bosnian Serbs and Bosnian Muslims. It was helpful, but it was a dangerous game.

The United States

As the United States committed itself for the first time to enter peace negotiations among Bosnia's warring factions, its only objective was "to reduce the carnage caused by the shelling or the potential to shell Sarajevo".[24] The US had consistently backed the territorial integrity of Bosnia, but was unwilling to use force to maintain it. Seeing no military solution, the United States began to embrace partition, and to concentrate all its efforts on achieving a political settlement.

On 11 February 1994 peace talks in Geneva took a new turn with the start of active US participation in the search for a settlement to the 22-month-old conflict in Bosnia-Herzegovina. One administration official described this shift in attitude as designed "to get the Bosnian Muslims to understand that we are not going to help them win this war, and that within pretty small margins they are not going to end up with much more, and that the international community is seriously losing

---

[24] *The International Herald Tribune*, 11 February 1994.

patience".[25] The NATO ultimatum also allowed the Clinton Administration to portray the initiative as proof of American foreign policy leadership. The Administration could also down-play the diplomatic defeat caused by the Europeans' rejection in May 1993 of the President's proposal to arm the Bosnian Muslims. But in reality, the threat of NATO air strikes in Bosnia was "neither a carrot nor a stick but an aspirin".[26]

The Russian Federation

The Russian Federation, a consistent opponent of any use of force in the Bosnian conflict, had been left out of the debate concerning the use of air strikes. This debate took place not within the UN Security Council, as the Russian Federation would have wished, but between the Secretary-General and NATO in the context of previous UN resolutions.

On 17 February 1994, Vitaly Churkin obtained a pledge from the Bosnian Serbs to fulfill the terms of the North Atlantic Council decision. He surprised UN officials in Bosnia with the announcement that the Russian Federation, a traditional ally of the Serbs, would send 800 troops to bolster the UN peacekeeping operation there. While excluded from the process leading to the NATO decision, the Russian Federation obtained a decisive *droit de regard* on the actual implementation of the decision. It did so by getting directly involved in local negotiations concerning the modalities of the withdrawal of Bosnian Serb weapons from the weapons exclusion zone and by weighing compliance with the Sarajevo agreement against deployment of Russian troops in Bosnian Serb controlled areas. Moscow's clever intervention, considered to be "Russia's greatest diplomatic coup in 10 years" made air strikes unnecessary.[27] It strengthened the position of the Russian Federation in Balkan politics and reaffirmed Moscow's status as a world power.

6.6. Implementation of the Agreement

On 11 February 1993, the Bosnian Serbs reluctantly started to withdraw heavy weapons from the areas surrounding Sarajevo, and UNPROFOR was

---

[25] Ibid.
[26] R.W. Jr. Apple, *The International Herald Tribune*, 11 February 1994.
[27] J.F.O. McAllister, *Time*, 7 March 1994.

deployed along the confrontation line. Following the intervention of Vitali Churkin, the Bosnian Serbs agreed on 17 February 1994 to withdraw all their heavy weapons within two days to the distance set by NATO.

The Bosnian Serbs agreed to extensive and unhindered UNPROFOR patrolling within the weapons exclusion zone covering the 20-kilometer radius from the center of Sarajevo. Heavy weapons not withdrawn from the exclusion zone were grouped and placed in eight separate collection points under the control of armed UNPROFOR elements.[28] Although the Bosnian Serbs had already removed most of their weapons from the exclusion zone, on 21 February 1993 UNPROFOR reported that they had handed over a total of 260 weapons to the UN forces. The great majority of the heavy weapons from the Bosnian Muslim units in the exclusion zone were also put under UNPROFOR's control.[29] Implementation of the ultimatum was rendered difficult because of the lack of insufficient UNPROFOR troops to manage the large amount of weapons put under their control during the two days preceding the deadline. Furthermore heavy snowfall hindered movements of troops and weapons. Compliance with the ultimatum was effective, however, and the Security Council decided, on 20 February 1994, not to recommend that air strikes be carried out at that time.

However, the withdrawal of heavy weapons from Sarajevo did not mean the end of the Bosnian Serb blockade of the town.[30] This question, as well as the demilitarization of the town, needed to be addressed in a subsequent political settlement concerning the status of Sarajevo. The isolated nature of the Safe Areas meant that a land blockade would have decisive impact even after the removal of the heavy weapons. No such settlement was achieved, but a series of economic agreements, reconstruction programs and confidence-building measures allowed the population in Sarajevo to go back to a relatively normal life.

The implementation of the disarmament mandate corresponded to the parties' interests. It brought security to the population in Sarajevo and allowed the Bosnian Serbs to redeploy some of their troops and weapons. It was successful in that there was little shelling in Sarajevo after this agreement. But there were problems associated with the establishment of weapons collection points: they were related to limitations on UNPROFOR's power and practical application problems. As a matter of fact, the weapons collection points were stabilizing and destabilizing at the same time. In Sarajevo, there were eight separate collection points.

---

[28] United Nations, *The United Nations and the Situation in the Former Yugoslavia*, p. 25.
[29] Gustenau, "Die Neuordnung des Südslawischen Raumes", No 3, 1994, p. 275.
[30] UNIDIR, *Practitioners' Questionnaire*, No. Y-013.

UNPROFOR would have preferred fewer, but at the initial stage, because of time and personnel restraints, this was the only way to consolidate the weapons. The distance between the collection points made it easier for the Bosnian Serbs to accept UN control. This was their stabilizing effect. On the other hand, the weapons collection points had a destabilizing effect. Because of their dispersion and UNPROFOR's limitations, the Bosnian Serbs were able to re-take their weapons at any time.

Could the disarmament operation have been carried out more efficiently? Discussions in Geneva in April 1994 with UNPROFOR's Force Commander, General Jean Cot, indicate that the weapons exclusion zone around Sarajevo could have been established more efficiently if he had immediately obtained an additional 2,000 to 3,000 troops to better control the regrouping.[31] UNPROFOR would also have needed additional means, such as helicopters, radars of trajectography, a better use of communications, and specialized units intelligence. Intelligence was specifically seen as an indispensable means for carrying out UNPROFOR's mandate because "a neutral UN on a war theater is not a blind and deaf UN".[32] Some of this equipment was introduced after Sarajevo, and it greatly increased troop efficiency.

It should also be mentioned that not all weapons could be regrouped at the sites designated by the UN. In some instances, as on the Tilava Hill, the mission of the UN forces was to survey the weapons and prevent any use of them. These weapons were under visual control only.[33] The task could also have been improved if exceptions to the heavy weapons exclusion zone had been dealt with. For example, the Bosnian Muslim's refusal to permit verification on Mt Igman or Bosnian Serb refusal to permit access to the Hadzici workshop or Jahorina area should have been avoided. But at the time, stopping the shelling of Sarajevo and re-installing the humanitarian lifeline presented a greater urgency than negotiating these issues.[34]

The implementation of the heavy weapons exclusion zone also presented a number of practical problems. The need to disperse the troops charged with controlling the regroupment of arms was a major handicap for the eventual use of air strikes. As a consequence, force protection measures rendered the

---

[31] Interview with Lieutenant General Jean Cot.

[32] UNIDIR, *Practitioners' Questionnaire*, No. Y-002.

[33] See Roger Cohen, "In the Sarajevo Hills, Flexibility Toward the Serbs", *International Herald Tribune*, 23 February 1994.

[34] UNIDIR, *Practitioners' Questionnaire*, No. Y-013.

implementation of the disarmament operations in Sarajevo more difficult. Other practical problems centered on the presence and the use of heavy weapons in the vicinity of hospitals and apartment buildings and the impossibility of neutralizing them without causing civilians to pay an unacceptably high toll.[35]

6.7. Conclusions

The Sarajevo February 1994 disarmament operation faced many particular problems. Unlike the situation in Srebrenica, the military situation in Sarajevo was at a stalemate: neither of the parties was able to defeat the other. An arrangement based on overlapping interests, reciprocity and consensus was therefore essential. Either party could interpret the outcome as a victory for its own cause. Nevertheless, the disarmament operation largely benefitted from the dynamics in the negotiation process created after the market shelling.

Before turning to the question of whether the Sarajevo model could be applicable to other disarmament and peace operations, it is necessary to define the model. For some it is the identification of overlapping interests among the warring parties combined with a firm engagement to monitor the local agreement. For others, it is a "show force and strike" model. In the first model, UNPROFOR is a mediator, and diplomatic skills are essential. In the second model, UNPROFOR plays the role of a military force.

For Lieutenant General Rose, the Sarajevo model was focused on achieving an agreement to develop a peace plan. The first step was a cease-fire, and the second was the positioning of UN troops. The third step was the withdrawal of both sides' troops, and the fourth, finally, was the establishment of a joint commission to analyze the remaining problems.[36] If this approach was successful in bringing peace to Sarajevo, it could be applied in other areas before an overall settlement of conflict is reached.

For others, the Sarajevo model consisted in "waving the big stick and making it clear it [would] be used".[37] However, the use of air strikes was a delicate undertaking. It would have jeopardized UNPROFOR's impartiality in the conflict which was crucial for attaining its main objective of delivering humanitarian aid

---

[35] Interview with John Almstrom; interview with Sergio Vieira de Mello.

[36] "Sarajevo: A Model for Peace", *UNPROFOR News*, March 1994, pp. 1, 3-4.

[37] William E. Schmidt, *The International Herald Tribune*, 21 February 1994.

to some 2.7 million people. Prudence was considered crucial due to past experience with warring parties in Bosnia restricting convoys and the risk of UN personnel being used as a human shield.

In actuality, however, the Sarajevo model relied on a combination of these two factors: an agreement that met the parties' interest, together with credible implementation. The Sarajevo disarmament operation in February 1994 was, for the most part, successful. Taking advantage of the special momentum created after the market place shelling was essential: the tide of public opinion was clearly against the war, and decision-making and implementation were done quickly and decisively. But most importantly, the disarmament operation was based upon an agreement which met the parties' mutual interests and was backed by the credible use of force.

Could the Sarajevo model be applied elsewhere? In an interview, Lieutenant General Rose stated, "The logic is if it works in Sarajevo then there is no reason why it shouldn't work elsewhere", while specifying Mostar, Maglay and the Lasva Valley.[38] However, the situation there and in the Safe Areas was different, both with respect to the interests and strengths of the parties, as well as to the negotiation dynamics. It must also be recognized that there is no way to maintain an island of peace in a sea of war. Since Sarajevo, a number of specific, local agreements have been reached. They could have accelerated the process of achieving a peaceful political settlement, but they could never replace it.

February 1994 was a turning point in the evolution of the conflict in Bosnia-Herzegovina insofar as the US and the Russian Federation took a more active role in ending hostilities. The Owen-Stoltenberg plan was abandoned as a basis for negotiations and realities on the ground seemed to indicate that the partition of Bosnia-Herzegovina into a Muslim-Croat part and a Serb part could not be avoided. These parts would be under the influence of the Western countries and the Russian Federation, respectively.

In the view of Russian, American and European diplomats, the withdrawal of heavy weapons from Sarajevo after a NATO bombing ultimatum and Russian intervention had created the best chance in two years to achieve a negotiated end to the war in Bosnia-Herzegovina. Were there missed occasions? In the view of General Cot, the psychological shock induced by the massacre in the old market could have been better exploited, at the political level, to extend the disarmament

---

[38] *UNPROFOR News*, March 1994.

measures. Particularly, he considered the failure to obtain the demilitarization of Sarajevo as a missed opportunity.[39]

What are the lessons to be learned? Several elements enabled the establishment of the Sarajevo weapons exclusion zone and allowed the population to return to a relatively normal life for a little more than one year. These elements included: reciprocity and common interests between the parties; a face-saving option for all parties during negotiations; the flexibility of the parties to adjust to new circumstances; the ability of UNPROFOR to deploy and act quickly in order to fully take advantage of the element of surprise; and the determination on all sides to implement reached agreements. However, local disarmament operations and peace operations have a limited lifetime and cannot replace an overall political settlement. In April 1995, one UN official interviewed in Zagreb said:

> "It is difficult to establish peace in one particular area when there is war going on somewhere else. I am amazed with our not having more trouble in Sarajevo because the war goes on in the rest of the country." [40]

In the absence of an overall political settlement, troubles could erupt at any moment, and they did.

---

[39] Interview with Lieutenant General Jean Cot.
[40] Interview with John Almstrom.

Chapter 7
Conclusions

The chronological section of this study outlines the variety of efforts undertaken by peacekeepers in the former Yugoslavia. In terms of disarmament operations specifically, the three examples explored in Chapters IV, V and VI differ widely from one another. The operations in Sector West, Srebrenica, and Sarajevo each involve a particular approach in terms of international decisions and local agreements. At first sight, the three cases present few common characteristics which could be used to build a model for future peacekeeping missions.

In the case of the disarmament operation in Sector West, action was taken based on a 18 month-old peace plan and the original mandate for UNPROFOR in Croatia. It was a limited enforcement action with no media attention and no interference or pressure from the international community. Neither did it have a major impact on the parties' strategic position, nor did it influence their fundamental interests. In Srebrenica, the seemingly imminent victory of one of the warring parties gave rise to a local disarmament and demilitarization agreement. The Srebrenica operation was based on this agreement, but ironically, it was severely hampered by the actions of the Security Council. Resolution 819 declared Srebrenica a Safe Area but did not recognize the necessity of disarming the units present in the town. In Sarajevo, finally, the disarmament agreement was negotiated following a stalemate at the front. It had gained momentum when strong international pressure was brought upon the parties. In this situation, the North Atlantic Council's threat of airstrikes played a decisive role by forcing the parties to respect their local agreement.

Despite these differences, some commonalities can be identified. In all three cases, the timeliness of the operation was decisive in implementing the disarmament arrangements. In Sector West, the surprise element and the Serb force's lack of communications with its headquarters were essential for the success of the operation. It was important that disarmament by UN forces be conducted before the parties organized, before they came to know the details of the multinational forces' rules of engagement,[1] and before they could test the limits of international resolve. Later, disarmament would have been impossible. Only a new crisis and a new agreement could have brought about another chance to conduct disarmament. In Srebrenica, confusion related to the defeat of the Muslim forces would have made effective disarmament possible. In Sarajevo the parties' determination to respect the accord on the withdrawal of heavy weapons was secured only a few days before the expiry of the North Atlantic Council decision. This put an enormous strain on the UN forces tasked to take control of these weapons. Had UNPROFOR been given more personnel, resources and equipment, the heavy weapons surrounding Sarajevo could have been managed more effectively.

In all of these cases, disarmament was achieved during the presence of a real or perceived superior UNPROFOR strength, and with a credible threat of forceful implementation. Equally important, however, it came about the result of the interest and determination of the parties. None of the disarmament operations conducted by UNPROFOR significantly changed the strategic situation of the warring parties, and even at the tactical level, the real impact on the balance of the forces' power was limited. In war, no side would agree to give up its most important means of defense; therefore, a full-scale enforced disarmament operation is only feasible as long as the security concerns of the parties are met. Hence it is important to identify and take advantage of mutual interests in order to create a relatively secure environment in which both parties can feel that progress is being made toward achieving their goals.

Disarmament is closely linked to the notion of security, and this relationship is at the heart of the main conclusion to be drawn from the Croatia and Bosnia-Herzegovina case studies. For disarmament to be possible in the context of a multinational conflict resolution effort, it is necessary that the security needs of the party to be disarmed must be fully and credibly assumed by the multinational force. The failure to do so led the Krajina Serbs, for example, to re-arm after the Croat incursion in January 1993 and explains why the Safe Areas could never be demilitarized and disarmed. The failure to meet security demands was also the main reason for the abandoning of the Vance-Owen plan.

Some critics maintain that the recipe for a successful disarmament operation lies in finding negotiated agreements and overlapping interests between the parties.

---

[1] Interview with Brigadier-General P. Peeters, Chief Military Negotiations and Assessment Team, UNPROFOR, Zagreb, 26 April 1995. See also UNIDIR, *Practitioners' Questionnaire*, Nos. Y-094, Y-030 and Y-060.

Others say that the determining factor is the credible threat or use of force. This research shows that, in the cases where disarmament operations were carried out effectively, a combination of both factors was vital for the mission's success. In all of the examined cases where disarmament failed, one or both of these critical factors were missing. In all of the successes, by contrast, both of the two crucial ingredients were present: (1) a mutually acceptable agreement which met the parties' interest; and, (2) the credible threat, or use, of force to compel the implementation of the agreement.

Biographical Notes

Managing Arms in Peace Processes: Croatia and Bosnia-Herzegovina

Thakur and Carlyle A. Thayer). He is a Swiss citizen and lives in Geneva, Switzerland.

Barbara Ekwall-Uebelhart is currently working as a consultant in international affairs and human rights at the Lutheran World Federation in Geneva. Prior to her research at UNIDIR's DCR Project, she studied at the University of Geneva where she obtained a post-graduate "diplôme d'études supérieures en études européennes" at the Faculty for Economic and Social Sciences (1992-1994), specializing in European security studies. Her diploma thesis, a pluri-disciplinary analysis of the European antitrust policy, "La mise en oeuvre de la politique communautaire de contrôle des concentrations", has been published in the European studies series at the University of Geneva. She holds a Bachelor of Arts degree from the University of Stockholm, Sweden, and certificates in international relations, development studies and economics from the University of Uppsala, Sweden. Because of the experience acquired while living in a number of countries and working with the Swiss Foreign Ministry, the CSCE Conference in Stockholm, the OECD in Paris, and the UNDP in Hanoi, Mrs. Ekwall Uebelhart is particularly interested in international relations and peace and development research. Following up on her work carried out at the DCR Project, she is currently focusing on peacekeeping, the security of civilian populations in multilateral peacekeeping operations and conflict resolution in the former Yugoslavia.

Andrei Raevsky received his B.A. in International Relations from the School for International Service of the American University, Washington DC, with specializations in International Relations and Russia/USSR Area Studies. He received his M.A. in International Relations from the Paul Nitze School of Advanced International Relations of John Hopkins University, Washington DC, with specializations in Strategic Studies and International Economics. He was a Research Associate with the United Nations Institute for Disarmament Research (UNIDIR) and the Primary Project Researcher for the UNIDIR Project on Disarmament and Conflict Resolution. He has published two research papers at UNIDIR entitled *Development of Russian National Security Policies: Military Reform* and *Russian Approaches to Peacekeeping Operations* (with Major General N.I. Vorob'ev); articles in different journals including the *Journal of Slavic Military Studies* and *Le Trimestre du Monde;* and a chapter on the problems of command and control during peacekeeping operations in *UN Peacekeeping in the 1990s,* published by Westview Press (edited by Ramesh

Thakur and Carlyle A. Thayer). He is a Swiss citizen and lives in Geneva, Switzerland.

Part II:

Bibliography

GENERAL UN PEACEKEEPING

Blechman, Barry M. and Pamela L. Reed, "The Lessons of Cambodia and Somalia", *The World and I*, June 1994, pp. 32-37.

Clemons, Elgin, "No Peace to Keep: Six and Three-Quarters Peacekeepers", *New York University Journal of International Law and Politics*, Vol. 26, No 1, pp. 107-141.

Dobbie, Charles, "A Concept for Post-Cold War Peacekeeping", *Survival*, Vol. 36, No 3, Autumn 1994, pp. 121-48.

Dorn, A. Walter, "Keeping Watch for Peace: Fact-Finding by the UN Secretary-General", in *Verification in the 1990s*, J. Alman, *et al.* (eds), Amsterdam: VU Press, 1992, p. 308-317.

Durch, William, (ed.), *The Evolution of UN Peacekeeping*, New York: St. Martin's Press, 1993.

Goulding, Marrack, "The Evolving Role of the United Nations in International Peace and Security", *Irish Studies in International Affairs*, Vol. 3, No 4, 1992, pp. 1-8.

_____, "The Evolution of United Nations Peacekeeping", *International Affairs*, Vol. 3, No 69, 1993, pp. 451-464.

Guillot, Philippe, "The United Nations and Internal Conflict Resolution: Promoting Western Standards of Democracy Through Multidimensional Peace Suport Operations", *The Elsa Law Review*, No 2, 1994, pp. 93-107.

Henn, Francis, "UN Peacekeeping: The Mirror Should be Polished", *Contemporary Review*, Vol. 264, No 1541, June 1994, pp. 281-287.

Lyons, Gene M., "A New Collective Security: The United Nations and International Peace", *The Washington Quarterly*, Spring 1994, pp. 173-197.

Mackinlay, John, "Improving Multifunctional Forces", *Survival*, Vol. 36, No 3, Autumn 1994, pp. 149-173.

Mackinlay, John and Jarat Chopra, "Second Generation Multinational Operations", *The Washington Quarterly*, Vol. 15, No 3, Summer 1992, pp. 113-131.

Naarden, Gregory L., "UN Intervention After the Cold War: Political Will and the United States", *Texas International Law Journal*, Vol. 29:231, Spring 1994, pp. 231-256.

Roberts, Adam, "Humanitarian War: Military Intervention and Human Rights", *International Affairs*, Vol. 3, No 69, 1993, pp. 429-449.

_____, The Crisis in UN Peacekeeping, *Survival*, Vol. 36, No 3, Autumn 1994, pp. 93-120.

Ruggie, John G, "Wandering in the Void. Charting the UN's New Strategic Role", *Foreign Affairs*, Vol. 72/5, November/December 1993, pp. 26-31.

Smith, Hugh, "Intelligence and UN Peacekeeping", *Survival*, Vol. 36, No 3, Autumn 1994, pp. 174-192.

Sorel, Jean-Marc, "L'ONU et le règlement des crises", *Problèmes politiques et sociaux*, No 725, 8 avril 1994, 61 p.

Sutterlin, James S., *Military Force in the Service of Peace*, Aurora Papers No 18, Ontario: Canadian Centre for Global Security, 1993.

_____, *The United Nations and The Maintenance of International Security: A Challenge to be Met*, Westport and London: Praeger, 1995.

Törnudd, Klaus, "Integrating Disarmament and Arms Regulation with UN Peace Activities", *Disarmament*, Vol. XVII, No 2, 1994, New York, pp. 49-57.

Weiss, Thomas G., "Intervention: Whither the United Nations?", *The Washington Quarterly*, Vol. 17.1, Winter 1994, pp. 109-127.

FORMER YUGOSLAVIA

Agrell, Wilhelm, *Fran början för sent - Väst och de jugoslaviska nationalitetskrigen*, Stockholm: Natur och kultur, 1994.

Allied Forces Southern Europe, "Operation Deny Flight", *Fact Sheet*, 13 January 1995.

"The Army of Bosnia and Herzegovina", *Jane's Intelligence Review*, March 1994, p. 3.

"Audiatur et altera pars or Real Causes of the Crisis in Former Yugoslavia", *Review of International Affairs*, Vol. XLIV, 1 March 1993, pp. 1-28.

Barkey, Brett D., "Bosnia: A Question of Intervention", *Strategic Review*, No 4/93, Fall 1993, pp. 48-59.

Baskin, Mark, "Building Peace with Patience", *UNPA's Monitor*, No 1, 9 September 1994.

Bebler, Anton, "Der Krieg in Jugoslawien 1991-1992", *Oesterreichische Militärische Zeitschrift*, No 5/1992, pp. 397-410.

Berdal, Mats R., *Wither UN Peacekeeping?*, Adelphi Paper, No 281, 1993.

_____, *Peacekeeping in Europe*, Adelphi Paper, No 284, Papers from the 35th Annual Conference of the IISS from 9-13 September 1993, London: IISS/Brassey's.

Berkowitz, Bruce D., "Rules of Engagement for UN Peacekeeping Forces in Bosnia", *Orbis*, Fall 1994, pp. 635-646

Binder, David, "Anatomy of a Massacre", *Foreign Policy*, No 97, Winter 94-95, pp. 70-78.

Brown, Michael, "Yugoslavia's Armed Forces - Order of Battle", *Jane's Intelligence Review*, August 1991, pp. 366-373.

Carter, Hodding, "Punishing Serbia", *Foreign Policy*, No 96, Fall 1994, pp. 49-56.

Charlier, Thierry, "Les Moudjahidins américains en Bosnie", *Defense 2001*, No 2, January 1995, pp. 8-10.

_____, "Coulisses de la Bosnie", *Defense 2001*, No 1, December 1994, pp. 17-23.

Cohen, Lenard J., "The Disintegration of Yugoslavia", *Current History*, November 1992, pp. 369-375.

Collins, John M., "Balkan Battlegrounds: US Military Alternatives", *CRS Report for Congress*, 2 September 1992.

Collinson, Christopher, "Bosnia this Winter - A Military Analysis", *Jane's Intelligence Review*, December 1993, pp. 547-546.

_____, "Bosnian Army Tactics", *Jane's Intelligence Review*, January 1994, pp. 11-13.

Cornu, Yves, "La fausse défaite serbe", *Le Point*, No 1119, 26 February 1994, pp. 36-39.

"The Croatian Forces in Bosnia and Herzegovina", *Jane's Intelligence Review*, March 1993, p. 103.

Curtis, Glenn E. (ed.), *Yugoslavia: A Country Study*, Area Handbook Series, Federal Research Division, Library of Congress, 1992.

Debay, Yves, "Printemps de guerre en Bosnie", *RAIDS*, No 107, April 1995, Paris: Histoire & Collections, 1995, pp. 30-35.

_____, "Bosnie: an III pour les casques bleus", *RAIDS*, No 107, April 1995, Paris: Histoire & Collections, 1995, pp. 36-41.

Dempsey, Judy, "Le conflit serbo-croate et la Bosnie-Herzégovine", *Politique étrangère*, 1992, pp. 269-280.

Dick, C.J., "Serbian Responses to Western Intervention in Bosnia-Herzegovina", *SSRC Occasional Brief*, No 14, 24 August 1992, Soviet Studies Research Centre.

_____, "Prospects for Conflict Termination in Former Yugoslavia", *SSRC Occasional Brief*, No 20, 7 May 1993.

Dizdarevic, Zlatko, "Playing Host to some Dubious Guests", *Time*, 7 March 1994, pp. 42-43.

Dizdarevic, Zlatko, and Gigi Riva, *J'accuse l'ONU*, Paris: Calman-Lévy, 1995.

Duder, Dusco, "Yugoslavia: New War, Old Hatreds", *Foreign Policy*, Summer 1993.

Duic, Mario, "Jugoslawien: Entwicklung und Zerfall - Zweiter Weltkrieg, Bürgerkrieg - Volksrepublik", *Oesterreichische Militärische Zeitschrift*, No 4, 1993, pp. 322-331.

Dunn, J.F., "Ukrainian Attitudes to the Crisis in former Yugoslavia", *CSRC Occasional Brief*, No 21, June 1993.

Durieux, J., "Leçons de la crise Yougoslave", *La Revue Politique*, No 5, September-October 1994, pp. 17-44.

Eknes, Age, *Blue Helmets in a Blown Mission? - UNPROFOR in former Yugoslavia*, Research Report No 174, Norwegian Institute of International Affairs, December 1993.

Fischer, Gerard, *Experience from Implementing the Mandate Given to the United Nations Protection Force (UNPROFOR) in United Nations Protected Area (UNPA) Sector West*, unpublished paper, Geneva, March 1993.

Foucher, Michel (ed.), *Fragments d'Europe - Atlas de l'Europe médiane et orientale*, Paris: Fayard, 1993.

Galtung, Johan, "Yugoslavia: The End of the Nightmare in Sight?", *Review of International Affairs*, Vol. 44, No 1023, 1 January 1994, p. 4.

Garde, Paul, *Vie et mort de la Yougoslavie*, Paris: Fayard, 1992.

Ghebali, Victor-Yves, "L'ONU et les organisations européennes face au conflit Yougoslave", *International Geneva Yearbook*, Vol. 8, 1994, pp. 22-43.

Glenny, Misha, *The Fall of Yugoslavia*, London: Penguin, 1992.

——————, "Heading off War in the Southern Balkans", *Foreign Affairs*, May/June 1995, Vol. 74, No 3, pp. 98-108.

Goodby, James E., "Peacekeeping in the New Europe", *The Washington Quarterly*, Vol. 15, No 2, Spring 1992, pp. 153-171.

Gow, James, "Deconstructing Yugoslavia", *Survival*, Vol. 33, No 4, July-August 1991, pp. 305-306.

——————, "Military-Political Affiliations in the Yugoslav Conflict", *RFE/RL Research Report*, Vol. 1, No 20, 15 May 1992, pp. 16-25.

——————, "The Remains of the Yugoslav People's Army", *Jane's Intelligence Review*, August 1992, pp. 359-362.

——————, "The Future of Peacekeeping in the Yugoslav Region", *Brassey's Defence Yearbook 1993*, pp. 179-198.

_____, "Belgrade and Bosnia - An Assessment of the Yugoslav Military", *Jane's Intelligence Review*, June 1993, pp. 243-253.

_____, "Towards a Settlement in Bosnia: The Military Dimension", *The World Today*, Vol. 50, No 5, May 1994, p. 96-99.

_____, "To Win on Points - Stalemate in Bosnia", in *The World in Conflict 1994/1995*, Jane's Intelligence Review Yearbook, Coulsdon, Surrey, 1995, pp. 54-57.

Gow, James and Lawrence Freedman, "Intervention in a Tragmenting State: The Case of Yugoslavia" in Nigel Rodley (ed.), *To Loose the Bands of Wickedness: International Intervention in Defence of Human Rights*, Brassey's, 1992.

Gow, James and Hans-Christian HAGMAN, "What future for UNPROFOR?", *Jane's Intelligence Review*, Vol. 7, No 4, pp. 166-169.

Gustenau, Gustav E., "Die Neurodnung des Südslawischen Raumes", *Oesterreichische Militärische Zeitung*, February 1991 to February 1995.

Higgins, Rosalyn, "The New United Nations and Former Yugoslavia", *International Affairs*, Vol. 3, No 69, pp. 465-483.

Isby, David C., "Yugoslavia 1991 - Armed Forces in Conflict", *Jane's Intelligence Review*, September 1991, pp. 394-403.

James, Alan, "The UN in Croatia: An Exercise in Futility?", *The World Today*, May 1993, pp. 93-96.

Kearns, Ian, "Croatia: The Politics Behind the War", *The World Today*, London: Royal Institute of International Affairs, April 1993, pp. 62-64.

Kim, Julie, "Bosnia-Hercegovina Federation: One Year of Muslim-Croat Cooperation", *CRS Report for Congress*, Congressional Research Service, The Library of Congress, 18 April 1995.

Klein, Edith S., "Obstacles to Conflict Resolution in the Territories of the Former Yugoslavia", *Peacekeeping and the Challenge of Civil Conflict Resolution*, Proceedings of the Sixth Annual Conflict Studies Conference, David A. Charters (ed.), University of Brunswick, 1994, pp. 149-167.

Lewis, Flora, "Reassembling Yugoslavia", *Foreign Policy*, No 98, March 1995, pp. 132-144.

Lough, J.B.K., "Constraints on Russian Responses to the Yugoslav Crisis", *CSRC Occasional Brief*, No 22, 15 June 1993.

Macinnis, John A., "The Rules of Engagement for UN Peacekeeping Forces in Former Yugoslavia: A Response", *Orbis*, Winter 1995, pp. 97-100.

Malcolm, Noel, *Bosnia, a Short History*, London: Macmillan, 1994.

Mc Allister, J.F.O., "Next, Friendly Persuasion", *Time*, 7 March 1994, pp. 41-42.

Markotich, Stan, "Croatia: Stalemate over Krajina", *RFE/RL Research Report*, Vol. 3, No 26, July 1994.

Merlino, Jacques, *Les vérités yougoslaves ne sont pas toutes bonnes à dire*, Paris: Albin Michel, 1993.

Milivojevic, Marko, "Croatia's Intelligence Services", *Jane's Intelligence Review*, September 1994, pp. 404-409.

—————, "Slovenia - An Arms Bazaar", *Jane's Intelligence Review*, November 1994, pp. 496-497.

Nambiar, Satish, "United Nations Operations in Former Yugoslavia: Some Reflections", *UNIDIR Newsletter*, No 24, December 1993, pp. 18-22.

Patrick, Charles R., "Tactics of the Serb and Bosnian-Serb Armies and Territorial Militia", *Conflict Studies Research Centre*, A96, March 1994.

Pellnäs, Bo, *Utan slut? - Kriget pa Balkan - bilder fran ett FN-uppdrag*, Stockholm: Albert Bonniers Förlag, 1995.

Piquard, Patrice, "Ex-Yougoslavie: vérités et mensonges au-dessus d'un champ de mines", *L'événement du jeudi*, 4-10 mars 1993, pp. 115-125.

Ripley, Tim, "Croatia's Strategic Situation", *Jane's Intelligence Review*, Vol. 7, No 1, pp. 29-31.

Ronen, Dov, *The Origins of Ethnic Conflict: Lessons from Yugoslavia*, Working Paper No 155, Canberra: Australian National University Research School of Pacific Studies, 1994.

Rostow, Eugene V., "Is UN Peacekeeping a Growth Industry?", *Joint Forces Quarterly*, 4/94, pp. 100-105.

Schear, James A., "International Intervention into Civil Conflict: The Case of Bosnia and Herzegovina", presentation given at a conference on *Managing Chaos: Coping with International Conflict into the 21st Century*, at the United States Institute of Peace, 1 December 1994.

Schultz, Kerstin, *Build Peace from the Ground up - About People and the UN in a War Zone in Croatia*, Lund: The Transnational Foundation for Peace and Future Research, 1994.

"The Serbian Army in Bosnia and Herzegovina", *Jane's Intelligence Review*, May 1994, p. 3.

Smith, Mark, "Attacks on Gorazde: Russian Perceptions and their Implications", *CSRC Occasional Brief*, No 30, May 1994.

Stark, Hans, *Les Balkans - Le retour de la guerre en Europe*, Collection RAMSES, Paris: IFRI, 1993.

Stedman, Stephen John, "Alchemy for a New World Order", *Foreign Affairs*, May/June 1995, Vol. 74, No 3, pp. 14-18.

Steinberg, James B., "International Involvement in the Yugoslavia Conflict", in *Enforcing Restraint - Collective Intervention in International Conflicts*, New York: Council on Foreign Relations Press, 1993, pp. 27-75, pp. 368-387.

Tiihonen, Ilkka, *What Hapened in Yugoslavia? Lessons for Future Peace-Keepers*, manuscript prepared for National Defense University, 1993.

United States General Accounting Office, *Humanitarian Intervention - Effectiveness of UN Operations in Bosnia*, Briefing Report to the Honorable Robert S. Dole, US Senate, April 1994.

Van Heuven, Marten, "Rehabilitating Serbia", *Foreign Policy*, No 96, Fall 1994, pp. 38-48.

Vego, Milan, "The Army of Serbian Krajina", *Jane's Intelligence Review*, October 1993, pp. 438-445.

_____, "The Muslim Defence Industry in Bosnia and Herzegovina", *Jane's Intelligence Review*, May 1994, pp. 213-214.

_____, "The New Yugoslav Air and Air Defence Forces", *Jane's Intelligence Review*, July 1994, pp. 297-303.

Vernet, Daniel and Jean-Marc Gonin, *Le rêve sacrifié*, Paris: Odile Jacob, 1994.

Warnes, Kevin, *Developing more Effective Regional Peacemaking Structures: Western European Intercession in the Yugoslav Conflict (1990-1993)*, Working Paper No 153, Canberra: Australian National University Research School of Pacific Studies, August 1994.

Woehrel, Steven, "Bosnia-Herzegovina: Summary of the Debate On a Unilateral Lifting of the Arms Embargo", *CRS Report for Congress*, Congressional Research Service, The Library of Congress, 11 April 1995.

Zamenica, John, *The Yugoslav Conflict*, Adelphi Paper, No 270, 1992.

Zimmermann, Warren, "Origins of a Catastrophe. Memoirs of the Last American Ambassador to Yugoslavia", *Foreign Affairs*, Vol. 74, No 2, March/April 1995, pp. 2-20.

INTERVIEWS

John Almstrom, Senior Political Advisor, Office of the Special Representative of the Secretary-General, UNPROFOR Headquarters, Zagreb, 24 April 1995.

Victor Andreew, Senior Advisor, UNHCR, Geneva, 9 June 1995.

Captain Giles Casalta, French Army, Geneva, 12 April 1995.

Timothy Clifton, ECMM, Zagreb, 25 April 1995.

Lieutenant General Jean Cot, former UNPROFOR Force Commander, Geneva, 12 April 1995.

H.E. Sune Danielsson, Ambassador of Sweden, Zagreb, 15 April 1995.

Elmar Dinter, International Conference on the Former Yugoslavia, Geneva, May-June 1995.

Gerard Fischer, Senior Economist, UNCTAD, former Chief of Civilian Affairs in Sector West, Geneva, March-June 1995.

Captain Steve Guiney, Deputy Chief OPS OFFR, UNMO's, Zagreb, 26 April 1995.

Bent Jensen, European Community Monitoring Mission, Zagreb, 24 and 25 April 1995.

Svetlana Jovic, expert, Geneva, 14 March 1995.

Lieutenant Colonel Ewen Loudon, Chief of Operations Officer, UNMO's, Zagreb, 26 April 1995.

General Carlos Roberto Matalon, Sector Commander, Sector West, Daruvar, 21 April 1995.

Lieutenant General Satish Nambiar, former UNPROFOR Force Commander, Geneva, 8 March 1995.

Elisabeth Nauclér, Civil Affairs Representative, Croatia Command, UNPROFOR, Zagreb and Geneva, April-May 1995.

Major Michael Nixon, UNPROFOR, Croatia Command, Zagreb, 24 April 1995.

Roderick de Normann, ECMM, Zagreb, 24 April 1995.

Arne Nyberg, ECMM, Zagreb, 25 April 1995.

Brigadier-General P. Peeters, Chief Military Negotiations and Assessment Team, UNPROFOR, Zagreb, 26 April 1995.

Colonel Ivan Peric, Stara Gradiska, 22 April 1995.

Colonel Norris Pettis, Croatia Command, UNPROFOR, Zagreb, 24 April 1995.

Major Jan Segers, UNMO's, Zagreb, 26 April 1995.

Sergio Vieira de Mello, Director of Policy Planning and Operations, UNHCR, Geneva, 13 June 1995.

General Carlos Zabala, Military Attaché, former Commander of Sector West, Geneva, March-April 1995.

UNITED NATIONS RESOURCES

UN Documents

United Nations, *Charter of the United Nations*, New York: United Nations, 1993.
United Nations, *The United Nations and the Situation in the Former Yugoslavia*,
    Reference Paper, 23 January 1995.
United Nations Protection Force, *UNPROFOR News*, United Nations Press and
    Information Office, September 1993-June 1994.
VANCE PLAN, Annex III *"Concept for a United Nations peace-keeping
    operation in Yugoslavia, as discussed with Yugoslav leaders by the
    Honourable Cyrus R. Vance, Personal Envoy of the Secretary-General and
    Marrack Goulding, Under-Secretary-General for Special Political Affairs*,
    November/December 1991.

Reports of the Secretary-General:

From 1992: S/23280; S/23592; S/23777; S/23836; S/23844; S/23900;
S/24075; S/24188; S/24263, Add.; S/24305; S/24307; S/24333; S/24353,
Add.; S/24600; S/24795; S/24848; S/25000.

From 1993: S/25221; S/25248; S/25264, Corr. 1; S/25318; S/25403;
S/25479; S/25519, Ann; S/25646; S/25700; S/25709; S/25777, Corr;
S/25993; S/26470, Add. 1; S/26828; S/26922.

From 1994: S/1994/109; S/1994/154; S/1994/173; S/1994/216;
S/1994/255; S/1994/291; S/1994/300; S/1994/333; S/1994/367;
S/1994/555; S/1994/600; S/1994/1067; S/1994/1074; S/1994/1124;
S/1994/1375; S/1994/1389.

From 1995: S/1995/6; S/1995/8; S/1995/38; S/1995/222; S/1995/320;
S/1995/444.

UNIDIR Primary Sources

United Nations Institute for Disarmament Research, *Analysis Report Of
Practitioners' Questionnaires On Weapons Control, Disarmament, and*

Demobilization During Peacekeeping Operations: Former Yugoslavia.
Geneva: UNIDIR, unpublished draft.

United Nations Institute for Disarmament Research, *Practitioners' Questionnaire On Weapons Control, Disarmament, and Demobilization During Peacekeeping Operations,* Nos. Y002, Y009, Y010, Y013-17, Y024-28, Y030, Y042-48, Y054, Y057, Y060, Y063, Y069, Y071, Y074, Y075, Y080, Y088, Y090, Y094, Y095, Y097, Y126, Y136, Y137-139, Y147, Y149, Y151, Y159, Y160, Y169, Y172, Y174. Geneva: UNIDIR, unpublished survey responses.

United Nations Institute for Disarmament Research, *Preliminary Analysis of Practitioners' Questionnaires on Weapons Control, Disarmament, and Demobilization During Peacekeeping Operations: Former Yugoslavia.* Geneva: UNIDIR, internal memo.

Briefings and Interviews with External Reviewers and Military Experts

UNIDIR DCR Project Military Expert Team: Col Roberto Bendini, Argentina; Lt Col Jakkie Potgieter, South Africa; Lt Col Ilkka Tiihonen, Finland.

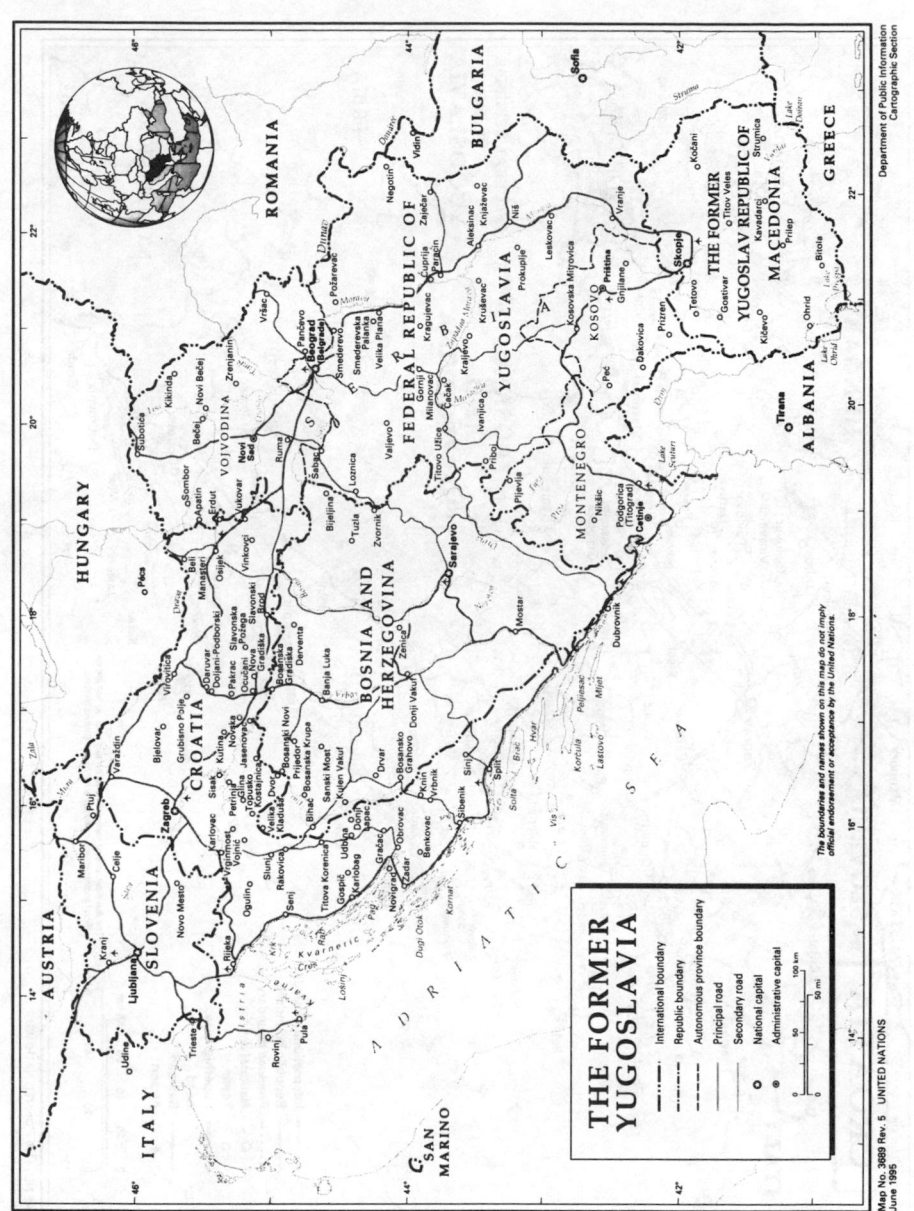

THE FORMER
YUGOSLAVIA

International boundary
Republic boundary
Autonomous province boundary
Principal road
Secondary road
National capital
Administrative capital

Department of Public Information
Cartographic Section

The boundaries and names shown on this map do not imply
official endorsement or acceptance by the United Nations.

Map No. 3689 Rev. 5   UNITED NATIONS
June 1995

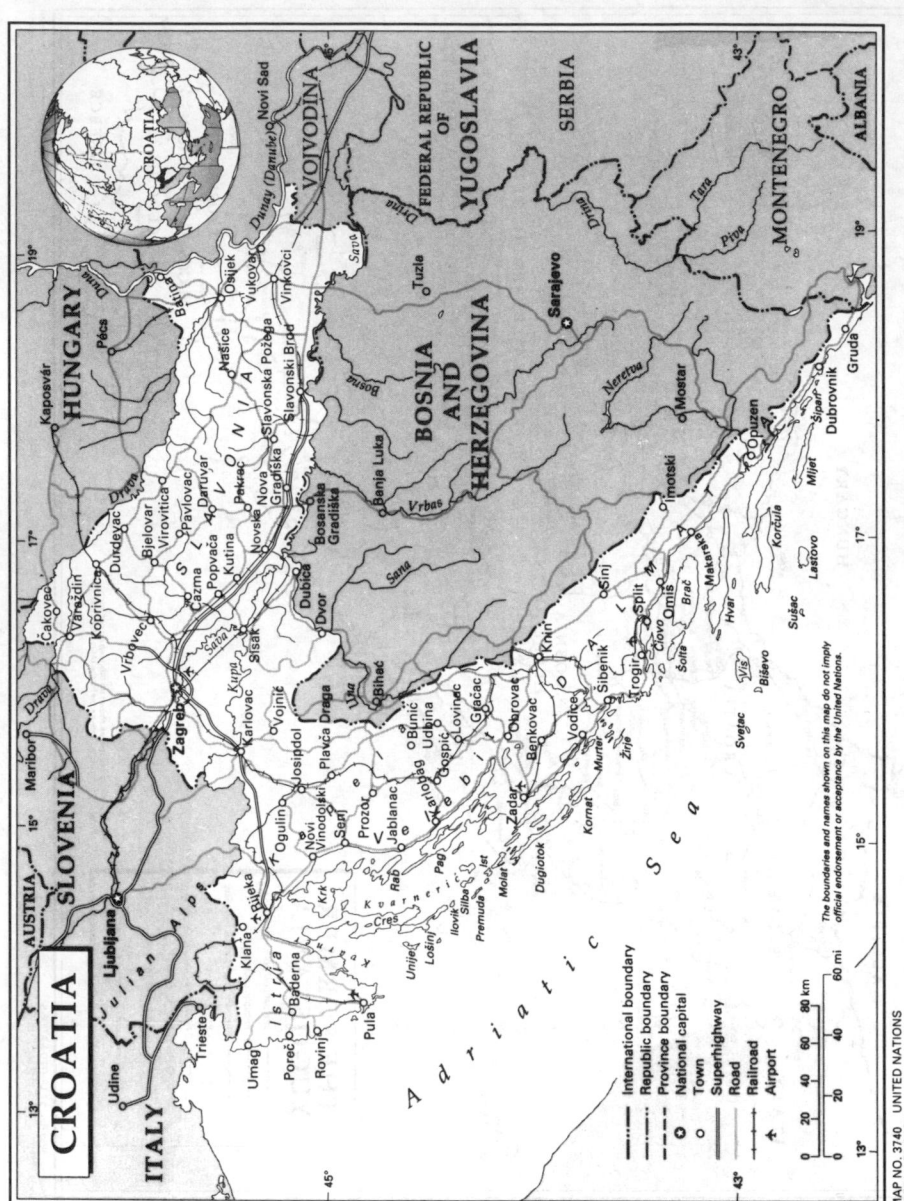

BOSNIA AND
HERZEGOVINA

- - - - - - International boundary
- · - · - Republic boundary
- - - - Province boundary
⊙ National capital
○ Town, village
✦ Major airport
Railroad
Main road
Secondary road

The boundaries and names shown on this map
do not imply official endorsement or acceptance
by the United Nations.

0 10 20 30 40 50 60 70 80 km
0   10   20   30   40   50 mi

MAP NO. 3729   UNITED NATIONS
DECEMBER 1993

UNPROFOR Area of Operations

HUNGARY

SLOVENIA
Zagreb

EAST

WEST

Osijek

CROATIA

Vukovar

NORTH

Bihac

Banjaluka

Brcko

BOSNIA AND
HERZEGOVINA

Tuzla

SOUTH

Srebrenica

Knin

Zepa

Sarajevo

Gorazde

Mostar

FEDERAL REPUBLIC
OF YUGOSLAVIA

LEGEND

International Border
Approximate Line of
Confrontation
UN Protected Area
Highway

0   40   80 km

ALBANIA

Note: approximate lines of confrontation as of early December 1994; for the sake of clarity
Bosnian Croat/Bosnian Muslim lines of confrontation are not shown.

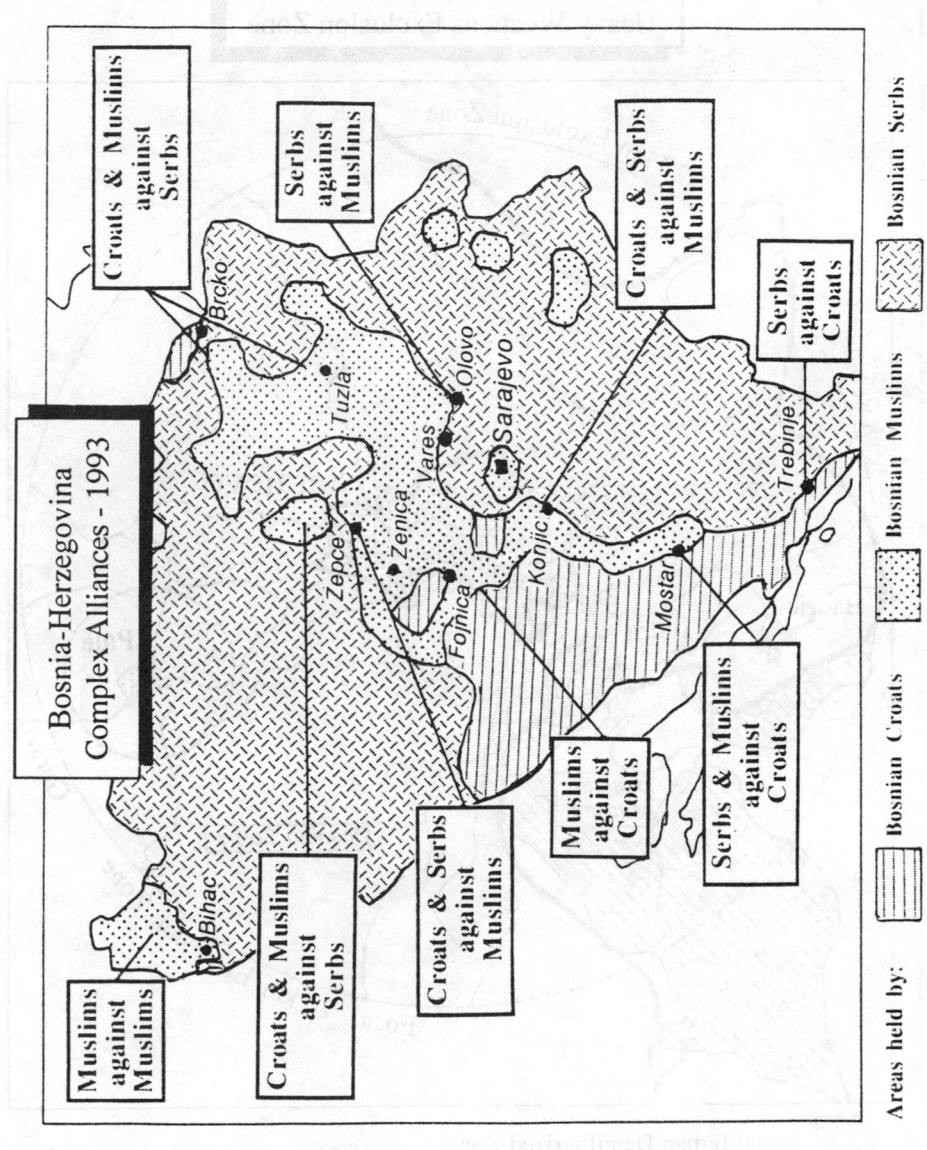

Bosnia-Herzegovina
Complex Alliances - 1993

Croats & Muslims against Serbs

Serbs against Muslims

Croats & Serbs against Muslims

Serbs against Croats

Muslims against Muslims

Croats & Muslims against Serbs

Croats & Serbs against Muslims

Muslims against Croats

Serbs & Muslims against Croats

Brcko

Tuzla

Olovo

Sarajevo

Vares

Zenica

Zepce

Fojnica

Konjic

Trebinje

Mostar

Bihac

Areas held by: Bosnian Croats   Bosnian Muslims   Bosnian Serbs

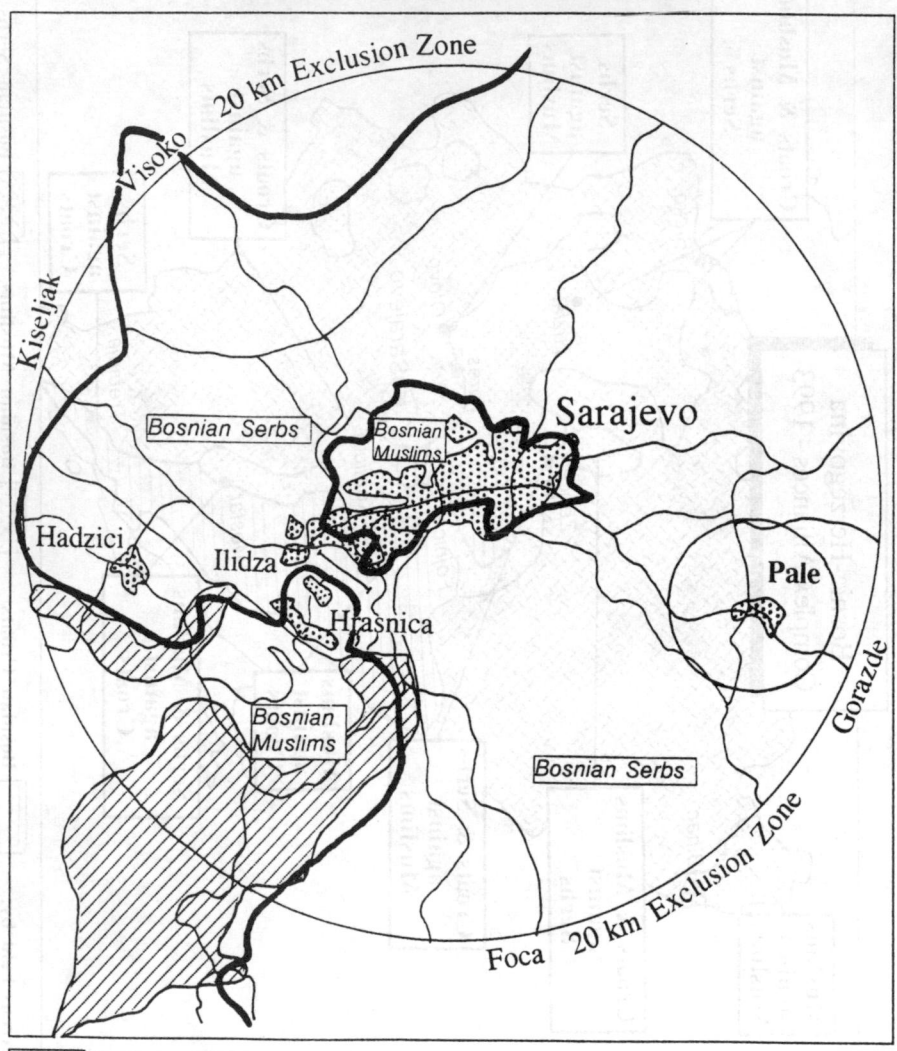

Sarajevo
Heavy Weapons Exclusion Zone

Mount Igman Demilitarized Zone

Urban areas

Front lines

ANNEX I

Important Security Council Resolutions for UNPROFOR's Disarmament Mandate in Croatia

Number	Date	Decision
713	25.09.1991	States that the conflict in Yugoslavia poses a threat to international security and imposes arms embargo
721	27.11.1991	Agrees, in principle, to send troops to former Yugoslavia
724	15.12.1991	Endorses the Vance Plan for Croatia
727	8.01.1992	Decides to send monitors to Yugoslavia
740	7.02.1992	Decides to send more monitors to Yugoslavia
743	21.02.1992	Establishes UNPROFOR
749	7.04.1992	Authorizes the deployment of troops
762	30.06.1992	Rules the deployment in the "pink zones"
769	7.08.1992	Asks UNPROFOR to perform immigration and customs functions at UNPA boundaries which are international borders
779	6.10.1992	Asks UNPROFOR to ensure demilitarization of the Prevlaka Peninsula
802	25.01.1993	Asks Croatian forces to withdraw behind the original cease-fire lines
820	17.04.1993	Strengthens the sanctions regime against the FRY and decides that trade with UNPA's be submitted to Croatian control
807	19.02.1993	Chapter VII; allows UNPROFOR to use force in self-defense
908	31.03.1994	Extension of close air support to Croatia; welcomes cease-fire agreement between Croatia and local Serb authorities in the UNPA's
847	30.06.1993	Chapter VII; allows UNPROFOR to use force to ensure its freedom of movement for all its missions in Croatia and in Bosnia-Herzegovina
958	19.11.1994	Extends use of air strikes in and around safe areas to Croatia
981	31.03.1995	Establishes new mandate for Croatia (UNCRO)

Important Security Council Resolutions for UNPROFOR's
Disarmament Mandate in Bosnia-Herzegovina

Number	Date	Decision
743	21.02.1992	Authorizes deployment of military observers in Bosnia-Herzegovina
749	7.04.1992	Asks parties in Bosnia-Herzegovina to cooperate with the EC peace efforts
752	15.05.1992	Asks for an end to outside interference in the Bosnian conflict
757	30.5.1992	Imposes mandatory, comprehensive economic sanctions on the FRY
758	8.06.1992	Enlarges UNPROFOR's mandate to include securing the Sarajevo airport
761	29.06.1992	Decides to send additional elements to take full operational control of Sarajevo airport and to secure humanitarian aid
770	13.08.1992	Authorizes all measures necessary to facilitate the delivery of humanitarian aid in all parts of Bosnia-Herzegovina
776	14.09.1992	Decides to enlarge UNPROFOR's mandate in Bosnia-Herzegovina to provide protection for UNHCR-organized humanitarian convoys, as well as for convoys of released detainees if requested by the ICRC
781	9.10.1992	Bans military flights in Bosnian airspace
787	16.11.1992	Considers that observers should be deployed on the borders of Bosnia-Herzegovina with the FRY
816	31.03.1993	Bans all fixed-wing and rotary-wing aircraft over Bosnia
819	16.04.1993	Declares Srebrenica a safe area
824	6.05.1993	Extends the concept of safe area to Sarajevo, Tuzla, Zepa, Gorazde and Bihac
836	4.06.1993	Acting under Chapter VII of the UN charter, enables UNPROFOR to deter attacks against the safe areas, to monitor cease-fires and to occupy key points on the ground

844	18.06.1993	Reinforces UNPROFOR's strength by 7600 troops to implement safe areas mandate, and authorizes air power to support these troops
847	30.06.1993	Applies Chapter VII of the UN charter to ensure the security of UNPROFOR and its freedom of movement for all its missions
900	4.03.1994	Asks for a plan of action for the normalization of life in Sarajevo, and requests a report on the feasibility and modalities for the application of the safe area concept to Maglaj, Mostar and Vitez
908	31.03.1994	Enlarges mandate to carry out tasks in relation to Muslim-Croat cease-fire agreement
942	23.09.1994	Condemns Bosnian-Serb refusal to accept peace plan and asks states to desist from any political talks with Pale
959	19.11.1994	Asks for an end to hostile actions in and around safe areas (concerns Bosnian-Muslim party too)
982	31.03.1995	Establishes new UN mandate for Bosnia-Herzegovina (UNPROFOR)

ANNEX II: THE VANCE PLAN[1]

Concept for a United Nations peacekeeping operation in Yugoslavia, as discussed with Yugoslav leaders by the Honorable Cyrus Vance, Personal Envoy of the Secretary-General and Marrak Goulding, Under-Secretary-General for Special Political Affairs

November/December 1991

General Principles

1. A United Nations peacekeeping operation in Yugoslavia would be an interim arrangement to create the conditions of peace and security required for the negotiation of an overall settlement of the Yugoslav crisis. It would not prejudge the outcome of such negotiations.

2. The operation would be established by the United Nations Security Council, acting on a recommendation, from the Secretary-General. Before making such a recommendation, the Secretary-General would need to be satisfied that all concerned in the conflict were, in a serious and sustained way, abiding by the arrangements, including an unconditional cease-fire, agreed at Geneva on 23 November 1991.He would also need to receive, through his Personal Envoy, categorical assurances that all the Yugoslav parties concerned in the conflict accepted the concept which he intended to recommend to the Security Council and that they would provide all necessary assistance and cooperation to enable the peacekeeping operation to carry out its functions.

3. The military and police personnel required for the operation would be contributed, on a voluntary basis in response to a request from the Secretary-General, by the Governments of Member States of the United Nations. The contributing States would be approved by the Security Council and what they would provide, on the recommendation of the Secretary-General after consultation with the Yugoslav parties.

---

[1] UN document S/23280

4. All members of the peacekeeping operation would be under the operational command of the Secretary-General and would not be permitted to receive operational orders from the national authorities. They would be required to be completely impartial between the various parties to the conflict. Those personnel who were armed would have standing instructions to use force to the minimum extent necessary and normally only in self-defense.

5. In accordance with its normal practice, the Security Council would probably establish the operation for an initial period of six months. Subject to the Council's agreement, the operation would remain in Yugoslavia until a negotiated settlement of the conflict was achieved. The Secretary-General would submit regular reports to the Security Council, normally every six months. These reports would contain his recommendations on extension of the operation's mandate.

6. The operation would be financed collectively by the Member States of the United Nations. But the various Yugoslav authorities would be expected to make available to the United Nations, free of charge, as much as possible of the accommodation and other facilities and supplies, such as food and fuel, that would required by the operation. They would also be asked to conclude with the United Nations agreements concerning the privileges, immunities and facilities which the operation and its members would need in order to carry out their functions, especially complete freedom of movement and communications.

Basic Concept

7. United Nations troops and police monitors would be deployed in certain areas in Croatia, designated as "United Nations Protected Areas". These areas would be demilitarized; all armed forces in them would be either withdrawn or disbanded. The role of the United Nations troops would be to ensure that the areas remained demilitarized and that all persons residing in them were protected from fear of armed attack. The role of the United Nations police monitors would be to ensure that the local police forces carried out their duties without discriminating against persons of any nationality or abusing anyone's human rights. As the United Nations Force assumed its responsibilities in the United Nations Protected Areas (UNPA's), all JNA forces deployed elsewhere in Croatia would be relocated outside that republic. The United Nations Force would also, as appropriate, assist the humanitarian agencies of the United Nations in the return of all displaced persons who so desired to their homes in the UNPA's.

The United Nations Protected Areas

8. The UNPA's would be areas in Croatia in which the Secretary-General judged that special arrangements were required during an interim period to ensure that a lasting cease-fire was maintained. They would be areas in which Serbs constituted the majority or a substantial minority of the populations and where inter-communal tensions have led to armed conflict in the recent past. As already stated, the special arrangements in these areas would be of an interim nature and would not prejudge the outcome of political negotiations for a comprehensive settlement of the Yugoslav crisis.

9. There would be three UNPA's: Eastern Slavonia, Western Slavonia and Krajina. They would comprise the following *opstine* or parts of *opstine*:

Eastern Slavonia:	Beli Manastir
	Those parts of Osijek which lie east of Osijek city
	Vukovar
	Certain villages in the extreme eastern part of Vinkovci
Western Slavonia:	Grubisno Polje
	Daruvar
	Pakrac
	The western parts of Nova Gradiska
	The eastern parts of Novska
Krajina:	Kostnjnica
	Petrinja
	Dvor
	Glina
	Vrgin Most
	Slunj
	Titova Korenica
	Donji Lapac
	Gracac
	Obrovac
	Benkovac
	Knin

Before the deployment of the Force began, the exact boundaries of the UNPA's would be decided by an advance party of the United Nations Force, after consulting local leaders.

The Deployment and Functions of the United Nations Force

10. The function of protecting the inhabitants of the UNPA's would be shared between the United Nations Force's infantry units and its civilian police monitors. The infantry would ensure that the UNPA's remained demilitarized. The police monitors would ensure that the local police carried out their duties without discrimination against any nationality and with full respect for the human rights of all residents of the UNPA's.

11. The infantry units would be deployed throughout the UNPA's. They would be lightly armed but would use armored personnel carriers and helicopters. They would control access to the UNPA's by establishing checkpoints on all roads and principal tracks leading into them and at important junctions inside them. At these checkpoints they would stop and, if necessary, search vehicles and individuals to ensure that no military formations or armed groups entered the UNPA's and that no weapons, ammunition, explosives or other military equipment were brought into them. They would patrol extensively inside the UNPA's on foot, and by vehicle and helicopter. They would also investigate any complaints made to them about violations of the demilitarized status of the UNPA's. Any confirmed violations would be taken up with the offending party and would, if necessary, be reported by the Secretary-General to the Security Council. If serious tensions were to develop between nationalities in a UNPA, the United Nations Force would interpose itself between the two sides in order to prevent hostilities.

12. The civilian police monitors would also be deployed throughout the UNPA's. They would be unarmed. They would have no executive responsibility for the maintenance of public order but they would closely monitor the work of the local police forces. To this end, they would be co-located with police headquarters in each region and *opstine* and would accompany the local police on their patrols and their performance of other duties. They would investigate any complaints of discrimination or other abuse of human rights and would report to the Chief of the United Nations Force any confirmed cases of discrimination or abuse. They would require free and immediate access to all premises and facilities of, or under the control of, the local police forces.

13. The United Nations Force would also include a group of military observers. They would be unarmed, in accordance with normal United Nations practice. They would initially be deployed in the UNPA's to verify the demilitarization of those areas. As soon as demilitarization had been effected, the military observers would be transferred to parts of Bosnia-Herzegovina adjacent to Croatia. Their functions there would be to patrol extensively, to liaise with the local authorities and to warn the Chief of the United Nations Force if inter-communal tension threatened to disturb the peace and tranquility established by the Force in the UNPA's. Their good offices would be available to help resolve local difficulties and to investigate allegations of inter-communal tension or aggression. The exact locations in which the military observers would operate would be decided by the advance party of the United Nations Force, after consulting local authorities. There would be a small detachment of military observers at Dubrovnik.

14. The military and police personnel of the United Nations Force would arrive in Yugoslavia as soon as possible after the Security Council decided to establish the Force. They would be deployed simultaneously in all three UNPA's. The Force's assumption of responsibility for the protection of these areas would be synchronized with the demilitarization process. To this end, close coordination would be required with the commanders of the forces currently deployed in each of the UNPA's and agreed timetables would be established in order to link deployment of the United Nations Force with the demilitarization of each area.

Demilitarization of the UNPA's

15. On the basis of the agreed timetables, demilitarization of the UNPA's would be implemented as rapidly as possible, in the following way:

(a) All units and personnel of the Yugoslav National Army (JNA) and the Croatian National Guard, as well as any Territorial Defense units or personnel not based in the UNPA's, would be withdrawn from them;

(b) All Territorial Defense units and personnel based in the UNPA's would be disbanded and demobilized. Disbandment would involve the temporary dissolution to the units command structures. Demobilization would mean that the personnel involved would cease to wear any uniform or carry any weapons, though they could continue to be paid by the local authorities;

(c) The weapons of the Territorial Defense units and personnel based in the UNPA's would be handed over to units of JNA or the Croatian National Guard, as the case might be, before those units withdrew form the UNPA's. Alternatively, they could be handed over to the United Nations Force for safe custody during the interim period, if that arrangement was preferred by the units concerned;

(d) All paramilitary, irregular or volunteer units or personnel would either be withdrawn form the UNPA's or, if resident in them, be disbanded and demobilized.

16. It would be the responsibility of each unit, before it withdrew or was disbanded, to remove any mines which it had laid while deployed in the UNPA's.

17. The implementation of the above arrangements for demilitarization of the UNPA's would be verified by the United Nations Force.

Relocation of the Yugoslav National Army

18. In parallel with the assumption by the United Nations Force of its protective functions in the UNPA's, any JNA units deployed elsewhere in Croatia would be relocated to places outside that republic. A timetable for this relocation would be agreed between the Chief of the United Nations Force and the Federal Secretary for National Defense of the Socialist Federal Republic of Yugoslavia. All Serbian territorial, paramilitary, irregular and volunteer units (other than those disbanded and demobilized in the UNPA's) would similarly withdraw from Croatia. These withdrawals would be verified by the military observers of the United Nations Force.

Local Police Forces

19. The maintenance of public order in the UNPA's would be the responsibility of local police forces who would carry only side-arms. Each of these forces would be formed from residents of the UNPA in question, in proportions reflecting the national composition of the population which lived in it before the recent hostilities. The local police forces would be responsible to the existing *opstine* councils in the UNPA's. Any existing regional police structures would remain in place, provided that they were consistent with the principle described above concerning the national composition of the local police forces.

Return of Displaced Persons to Their Homes

20. In accordance with established international principles, the United Nations policy is to facilitate the return to their homes of all persons displaced by the

recent hostilities who so desire. The lead in this matter is being taken by the humanitarian agencies of the United Nations. If a United Nations Force were established in Yugoslavia, it would provide all appropriate support to this effort in the UNPA's. The United Nations police monitors would have an especially important role in this regard.

Organization of a United Nations Force

21. If a peacekeeping operation were established to carry out the above-described functions, it would be commanded by a civilian Chief of Mission who would receive his instructions from, and report to, the Secretary-General of the United Nations. As already stated, the Secretary-General would himself report regularly to the Security Council, whose guidance he would seek if any difficulties arose in implementation of the Force's mandate. Under the authority of the Chief of Mission, there would be a Force Commander, with the rank of a Major General, who would command the military elements, and a Police Commissioner, who would command the civilian police monitors. The headquarters of the Force would be located at Banja Luka, with sub-offices at Belgrade and Zagreb.

22. To carry out the functions described above, the Force would require approximately 10 infantry battalions, 100 military observers and 500 police monitors, together with the necessary civilian and military support personnel. This would indicate a strength of somewhat over 10,000 persons.

ANNEX III: THE DARUVAR AGREEMENT

1. On February 18, 1993 in Daruvar, in the presence of the UNPROFOR members (signatures illegible),

    the meeting was attended by following persons:

    VELJKO DZAKULA   ZLATO KOS
    DUSAN ECMOVIC   ZDRAVKO SORICC
    MILAN VLAISAVLJEVIC   IVAN VOLF
    MLADEN KULIC   VLADIMIR DELAC
    DORDE LOVRC   ZELIMIR MALNAR
    MILAN RADAKOVIC

2. In the whole area covering the former municipalities of Daruvar, Grubisno Polje, Nova Gradiska, Novska and Pakrac, that are now under the protection of UNPROFOR, the following will be provided:

    a) complete reconstruction of electric power and water supply systems;

    b) passenger car traffic on all roads, including the Zagreb-Belgrade highway; further negotiations will also cover commercial traffic;

    c) repair of the Novska-Nova Gradiska railroad;

    d) repair of the telecommunication system (in accordance with the results of the preliminary assessment of the current state made in August 1992, in the presence of the representatives of both parties);

    e) founding of the joint committee for normalization of living conditions of populated UNPA areas, with particular emphasis on observation, followed by restitution of social activities, health, education and sports;

    f) undisturbed and regular meetings at checkpoints under the supervision of UNPROFOR;

    g) return of all displaced persons;

h) permission for the civilians with residences on both sides of the demarcation line to work on their estates (it is especially significant and important in this moment to guarantee the safety of the farmers during the future harvest period);

i) meetings of the representatives of local authorities, in order to discuss matters of future cooperation;

j) placing of containers according to the achieved agreement; and

k) a joint committee should be formed for the preparation of the implementation and observation of all items of the Agreement

3. The Agreement is signed by the representatives:

(signatures)

The representative of UNPROFOR:

(signatures)

ANNEX IV:
AGREEMENT FOR THE DEMILITARIZATION OF SREBRENICA[1]

At a meeting held at Sarajevo on 17 April 1993, Lt.-Gen. Mladic and Gen. Halilovic, in the presence of Lt.-Gen. Wahlgren, representing UNPROFOR, acting as a mediator, agreed on the following:

1. A total cease-fire in the Srebrenica area effective from 0159 on 18 April 1993. Freezing all combat actions on the achieved lines of confrontation including supporting artillery and rocket fire.

2. The deployment of a company group of UNPROFOR into Srebrenica by 1100 18 April 1993. This company group is guaranteed safe and unhindered passage from Tuzla to Srebrenica by both sides.

3. The opening of an air corridor or between Tuzla and Srebrenica via Zvornik for evacuation of the seriously wounded and seriously ill. The air corridor opens at 1200 18 April 1993 and continues on 19 April, weather permitting, for as long as it takes to evacuate all the existing seriously wounded and seriously ill. The helicopters will fly from Tuzla to Zvornik and land for an inspection at Zvornik which will not cause unnecessary delay to the evacuation. The seriously wounded and seriously ill will be evacuated after identification by UNPROFOR in the presence of two doctors from each side and ICRC. All categories of seriously wounded and seriously ill will be evacuated by air, unhindered by either side. The number of seriously wounded and seriously ill is believed to be approximately 500. This will be verified on 18 April 1993 by UNPROFOR, and the result notified to each side.

4. The demilitarization of Srebrenica will be complete within 72 hours of the arrival of the UNPROFOR company in Srebrenica (1100 hours 18 April 1993; if they arrive later this will be changed). All weapons, ammunition, mines, explosives and combat supplies (except medicines) inside Srebrenica will be submitted/handed over to UNPROFOR under the supervision of three officers form each side with control carried out by UNPROFOR. No armed persons or units except UNPROFOR will remain within the city once the demilitarization process is complete. Responsibility for the demilitarization process remains with UNPROFOR.

---

[1] UN Document S/25700

5. A working group will be established to decide the details of the demilitarization of Srebrenica. This group will study in particular: the action to be taken if the demilitarization is not complete within 72 hours; the correct treatment for any personnel who hand over/submit their weapons to UNPROFOR. The working group will report to Lt.-Gen Wahlgren, Lt.-Gen. Ratko Mladic and Gen. Sefer Halilovic. The first report will be made at a meeting to be held at Sarajevo airport on Monday, 19 April 1993, at 1200.

6. Both sides are to submit a report on the minefields and explosive obstacles in the Srebrenica area to UNPROFOR. Each side is to clear its minefields under the supervision of UNPROFOR.

7. Neither side is to hinder the freedom of movement. The UNHCR and ICRC are to investigate allegations of hindrance of movement in Srebrenica and Tuzla in particular.

8. Humanitarian aid will continue to be allowed into the city as planned.

9. The officers and the doctors supervising the demilitarization process are under the protection of UNPROFOR; their safety is to be guaranteed by both conflicting sides.

10. The working group is to make recommendations on carrying out an exchange of the prisoners, the killed and the wounded according to the principle "all for all" in the region of Srebrenica within 10 days. This is to be under the control of the ICRC.

11. All the disputed issues are to be resolved by a mixed military working group or at another meeting of the respective delegations of the conflicting sides under the mediation of Lt.-Gen. Wahlgren.

Signed:

Gen. Sefer HALILOVIC   Lt.-Gen. Ratko MLADIC

Witnessed by:

Lt.-Gen. Lars-Eric WAHLGREN

The 18th day of April 1993

ANNEX V: RESOLUTION 824 (1993)

Adopted by the Security Council at its
3208th meeting, on 6 May 1993

The Security Council,

Reaffirming all its earlier relevant resolutions,

Reaffirming also the sovereignty, territorial integrity and political independence of the Republic of Bosnia and Herzegovina,

Having considered the report of the Mission of the Security Council to the Republic of Bosnia and Herzegovina (S/25700) authorized by resolution 819 (1993), and in particular, its recommendations that the concept of safe areas be extended to other towns in need of safety,

Reaffirming again its condemnation of all violations of international humanitarian law, in particular, ethnic cleansing and all practices conducive thereto, as well as the denial or the obstruction of access of civilians to humanitarian aid and services such as medical assistance and basic utilities,

Taking into consideration the urgent security and humanitarian needs faced by several towns in the Republic of Bosnia and Herzegovina as exacerbated by the constant influx of large numbers of displaced persons including, in particular, the sick and wounded,

Deeply concerned at the continuing armed hostilities by Bosnian Serb paramilitary units against several towns in the Republic of Bosnia and Herzegovina and determined to ensure peace and stability throughout the country, most immediately in the towns of Sarajevo, Tuzla, Zepa, Gorazde, Bihac, as well as Srebrenica,

Convinced that the threatened towns and their surroundings should be treated as safe areas, free from armed attacks and from any other hostile acts which endanger the well-being and the safety of their inhabitants,

Aware in this context of the unique character of the city of Sarajevo, as a multicultural, multi-ethnic and pluri-religious centre which exemplifies the viability of coexistence and interrelations between all the communities of the

Republic of Bosnia and Herzegovina, and of the need to preserve it and avoid its further destruction,

Affirming that nothing in the present resolution should be construed as contradicting or in any way departing from the spirit or the letter of the peace plan for the Republic of Bosnia and Herzegovina,

Convinced that treating the towns referred to above as safe areas will contribute to the early implementation of the peace plan,

Convinced also that further steps must be taken as necessary to achieve the security of all such safe areas,

Recalling the provisions of resolution 815 (1993) on the mandate of UNPROFOR and in that context **acting** under Chapter VII of the Charter,

1. **Welcomes** the report of the Mission of the Security Council established pursuant to resolution 819 (1993), and in particular its recommendations concerning safe areas;

2. **Demands** that any taking of territory by force cease immediately;

3. **Declares** that the capital city of the Republic of Bosnia and Herzegovina, Sarajevo, and other such threatened areas, in particular the towns of Tuzla, Zepa, Gorazde, Bihac, as well as Srebrenica, and their surroundings should be treated as safe areas by all the parties concerned and should be free from armed attacks and from any other hostile act;

4. **Further declares** that in these safe areas the following should be observed:

(a) The immediate cessation of armed attacks or any hostile act against these safe areas, and the withdrawal of all Bosnian Serb military or paramilitary units from these towns to a distance wherefrom they cease to constitute a menace to their security and that of their inhabitants to be monitored by United Nations military observers;

(b) Full respect by all parties of the rights of the United Nations Protection Force (UNPROFOR) and the international humanitarian agencies to free and unimpeded access to all safe-areas in the Republic of Bosnia and Herzegovina and full respect for the safety of the personnel engaged in these operations;

5. **Demands** to that end that all parties and others concerned cooperate fully with UNPROFOR and take any necessary measures to respect these safe areas;

6. **Requests** the Secretary-General to take appropriate measures with a view to monitoring the humanitarian situation in the safe areas and to that end, authorizes the strengthening of UNPROFOR by an additional 50 United Nations military observers, together with related equipment and logistical support; and in this connection, also **demands** that all parties and all others concerned cooperate fully and promptly with UNPROFOR;

7. **Declares** its readiness, in the event of the failure by any party to comply with the present resolution, to consider immediately the adoption of any additional measures necessary with a view to its full implementation, including to ensure respect for the safety of United Nations personnel;

8. **Declares also** that arrangements pursuant to the present resolution shall remain in force up until the provisions for the cessation of hostilities, separation of forces and supervision of heavy weaponry as envisaged in the peace plan for the Republic of Bosnia and Herzegovina, are implemented;

9. **Decides** to remain seized of the matter.

Part III:

Questionnaire Analysis

DISARMAMENT AND CONFLICT RESOLUTION PROJECT
The Disarming of Warring Parties
as an Integral Part of Conflict Settlement

PRACTITIONERS' QUESTIONNAIRE ON:
WEAPONS CONTROL, DISARMAMENT, AND
DEMOBILIZATION DURING PEACEKEEPING OPERATIONS

ANALYSIS REPORT: FORMER YUGOSLAVIA
COMPILED BY: COL ROBERTO BENDINI
COMPLETED BY: LT COL JAKKIE POTGIETER
DATE: 25 AUGUST 1995

Note to Readers: The responses which appear in this analysis have been reproduced directly from the respondents' answers to the DCR *Practitioner's Questionnaire*. Changes, if any, have been made only to correct spelling, grammar, and sentence structure; all efforts have been made to maintain the integrity of the original responses. Illegible portions of the original written responses have been indicated with ellipses.

Reference Number:
UNIDIR/UNPROFOR/002

Analysis Report of Practitioners' Questionnaires

Number of questionnaires analyzed: 51

IDENTIFICATION INFORMATION

1. OPERATION

    a. **Name of operation:** UNPROFOR

    b. **Location of operation:** Former Yugoslavia

    c. **Time frame covered by questionnaires:**

        (Y002) 01/07/93-15/03/94
        (Y009) 00/08/92-00/02/93
        (Y010) 00/09/92-00/04/93
        (Y013) 16/10/93-14/07/94
        (Y014) 00/07/93-00/07/94
        (Y015) 00/03/94-00/11/94
        (Y016) 04/04/94-13/10/94
        (Y017) 23/03/93-21/09/93
        (Y024) 00/03/92-00/08/94
        (Y025) 00/09/92-00/06/93
        (Y026) 00/03/92-00/08/92
        (Y027) 00/04/93-30/06/94
        (Y028) 13/03/92-14/09/92
        (Y030) 01/02/92-07/03/93
        (Y042) 10/03/93-10/03/94
        (Y043) 26/11/92-26/11/93
        (Y044) 10/08/92-11/08/93
        (Y045) 13/08/93-13/08/94
        (Y046) 01/04/93-16/04/94
        (Y047) 17/07/93-17/07/94
        (Y048) 23/01/92-23/01/93
        (Y054) 00/03/92-00/03/93

(Y057) 00/03/92-00/04/93
(Y060) 03/03/92-02/03/93
(Y063) 00/07/92-00/07/94
(Y069) 22/03/92-12/04/93
(Y071) 26/03/92-23/09/92
(Y074) 00/03/93-00/09/93
(Y075) 00/03/92-00/11/92
(Y080) 00/10/93-00/10/94
(Y088) 21/01/93-21/07/93
(Y090) 13/12/93-13/06/94
(Y094) 00/02/95-25/04/95
(Y095) 00/10/94-00/04/95
(Y097) 12/07/93-24/01/94
(Y126) 00/08/93-00/08/94
(Y127) 22/07/92-22/06/93
(Y129) 00/04/93-00/11/93
(Y130) 00/03/94-00/09/94
(Y136) 00/06/93-00/12/94
(Y137) 00/10/93-00/04/94
(Y138) 14/03/93-04/05/94
(Y139) 01/10/93-02/11/94
(Y147) 01/07/93-30/04/94
(Y149) 22/09/93-13/04/94
(Y151) 22/07/94-21/07/95
(Y159) 20/03/94-20/03/95
(Y160) 00/03/93-00/03/94
(Y169) 00/04/92-00/12/93
(Y172) Dates not available.
(Y174) Dates not available.

2. **RESPONDENTS**

   a. **Primary Role:**

      UN Civilian: 04
            Chief   : 02
            Other   : 01
      (One respondent did not specify).

Military Officer: 45
        Commander   : 23
        Other   : 22

Humanitarian Relief Operator and/or NGO personnel: 00

National Official: 01

b. Primary Function/Mission:

Military: 46

HQ Staff	: 12	Military Observer	: 13
Infantry	: 11	Armour	: 02
Artillery	: 01	Engineer	: 05
Medical	: 02	Aviation	: 03
Transport	: 03	Logistics	: 05
Mil Police	: 02		

Civilian: 03

Civil Affairs	: 02	Staff HQ's	: 00
Representative	: 00	Relief Coordinator	: 00
Relief	: 00	Volunteer	: 00
Other	: 01		

Note: One respondent did not indicate his/her primary role and two did not indicate their primary mission on the questionnaire.

c. Regular Activities:

Convoy Operations	: 22	Convoy Security	: 20
Base Security	: 17	Patrolling	: 38
Search Operations	: 20	Check Point Operations	: 22
Cease Fire Monitor	: 40	Humanitarian Relief	: 29
Weapons Inspection	: 30	Weapons Inventories	: 23
Weapons Elimination	: 08	Cantonment Construction	: 12
Cantonment Security	: 11	Special Operations	: 07
Information Collection	: 37	Police Operations (Mil)	: 10
Disarmament Verification			: 22

Cease-fire Violations Investigation   : 36
Voluntary Weapons Collection   : 21
Involuntary Weapons Collection   : 15

Other:
Casualty evacuation, refugee and movement control, route maintenance and construction, military information officer, technical assistance, storage, counter blockade operations, helicopter inspections, exchange of POW's and bodies, demining, engineering tasks and construction, liaison with local authorities, criminal investigation, protection of refugees and minorities, mediation and negotiation with warring parties.

SECTION ONE

(Note to readers: Two caveats should be kept in mind when surveying the respondents' answers to the Practitioner's Questionnaire. First, in answering the questionnaire, respondents were instructed to answer only those questions which pertained to their specific mission and/or function; as a result, most respondents did not answer all of the "yes" or "no" questions. The number of responses for each question, therefore, will not always add up to the total number of respondents. Second, respondents often provided additional commentary for questions they should have skipped -- they may have answered a question with "no", for example, and then elaborated on their answer in the space provided for the "yes" respondents. For this reason, certain questions may contain more responses than the number expected.)

I.   IMPLEMENTATION OF THE PEACE AGREEMENT:

Q1.1   Was there a disarmament component in the original peace agreement and/or relevant UNSC Resolution? (If no, go to Section II.)

Yes: 43   No: 06

Q1.2   **If yes, was the disarmament component a central feature of the agreement?**

Yes: 35   No: 07

Q1.3   **Describe the desired outcome of the disarmament component vis-à-vis the peace agreement.**

(Y002) Plan Vance: départ de l'armée fédérale des zones contrôlées par les Serbes croates, [et] stockage des armes lourdes serbes.
[Vance Plan: departure of the JNA from zones controlled by the Serbs in Croatia and the storage of Serbian heavy weapons.]

(Y009) Disarmament was reached only in the Protected Areas, and it was only for the Armed Forces. A lot of weapons were hidden in houses by the civilian population.

(Y010) The four UNPA's were to be demilitarized. All heavy weapons were to be withdrawn outside the UNPA or put into UN-controlled storage. Except for police pistols no weapons were permitted to be held or used by either side.

(Y014) Serebrenica: BiH Army should be unarmed. UN forces should protect them.

(Y015) Disarm Croats/Muslims of heavy weapons as part of Washington Agreement (1994). Sarajevo exclusion zone - heavy weapons removal (Bosnian Serb Army).

(Y016) Separation of Croats and Serbs, creation of zone of separation under exclusive control of UNPROFOR, establishment of weapons exclusion zones, weapons storage, demining, return of populations. Phase Two was to be economic agreement. Phase Three was to be comprehensive political agreement.

(Y017) The complete demilitarization of the UNPA's as rapidly as possible.

(Y024) Only light arms were supposed to be used after the disarmament actions within the UN Protected Areas.

(Y026) Weapons to be withdrawn to UN controlled stores, weapons to be taken out of area, all personnel to be demobilized, civilian police to be supervised, [and] displaced persons to [be returned] to area.

(Y027) From March 1992 to January 1993 the disarmament worked reasonably well, less so [from] January 1993 to June 1993, [and] then not at all until April 1994 when weapons were put into storage sites.

(Y030) Disarming of warring parties in [the] UNPA was carried out in accordance with [the] Cyrus Vance Plan. There was a relapse after a few months with many ex-combatants having access to their weapons although weapons were not carried openly.

(Y042) Disarmament helped to achieve cease-fire and in general prevent the many violations [that] used to take place in the area and achieve a good psychological feeling among the warring parties.

(Y043) Collection of heavy weapons, [re-]construction of damaged buildings, construction of infrastructure, [and delivering] humanitarian aid to isolated places.

(Y044) Reach peace agreement [...] for the people to be safe, convoys for the humanitarian aids will be [protected] and help the people, exchange of prisoners, bodies, others.

(Y047) Separate the local police and [...] while they [were] inside [the] zone of separation if there was any violation of cease-fire agreement and report to HQ.

(Y048) Withdrawal of heavy weapons to 15-20 km from [the line of confrontation]. Opening new crossing point. Helped [the delivery] of humanitarian aids for civilian people.

(Y054) Withdrawal or disarmament of all armed forces. Collecting of weapons to be kept under UN custody. Local police to be armed only by short arms.

(Y057) It would allow for long-term issues to be settled while halting hostilities.

(Y060) Was partly achieved, until the setback as a result of the Croatian offensive on 22 January 1993.

(Y063) Disarmament to provide for establishing pre-war ethnically proportioned police forces and thereby make possible the return of displaced persons.

(Y069) The agreement of the Cyrus Vance Plan.

(Y071) The mandate was based on the Vance peace plan for Croatia: disarmament of the warring parties, local police only to stay in the UNPA's, return of the refugees (never carried out).

(Y074) Disarm all personnel in the UNPA's to create conditions for peace discussions.

(Y075) Total demilitarization of the Protected Area.

(Y080) Under Vance Plan - disarmament of occupied areas.

(Y094) It was successfully carried out because it was immediately done after the Cease-Fire Agreement.

(Y095) They were mentioned as a secondary role instead of a main role and perhaps the most important.

(Y126) The disarmament component was not very successful. This was due to the fact that the warring factions hindered the work of UN personnel. Also weapons collected by the UN were sometimes seized by the warring factions.

(Y127) It was not workable due to disagreement among the factions.

(Y130) In central Bosnia, the separation of forces and re-introduction of civil utilities, [and] in eastern Bosnia, the security of the Gorazde Safe Area.

(Y136) The disarmament was established, but later on broken due to attack from one of the warring parties.

(Y137) Necessary to avoid further harassment of UN troops and civilians.

(Y138) Involved parties should, as a part of the agreement, let the UN control all heavy weapons in the area.

(Y147) Phase 1: withdrawal of heavy weapons. Phase 2: demobilisation and disarmament of territorial defence forces and paramilitary groups. Phase 3: withdrawal of troops. Phase 4: demining.

(Y149) Create atmosphere of security and confidence in order to permit the return of refugees (final result) and to start peace talks.

(Y159) Monitor the [Cease-fire Agreement] throughout the implementation of a 2 km-wide zone of separation between the parties (fully demilitarized) and two zones at 10 and 20 km with military control.

(Y160) Disarmament component worked hardly and both sides were agreed, but since the beginning the peace agreements were violated.

(Y174) Disarmament of combatants to reduce conflict and facilitate eventual negotiations regarding territory.

Q1.4　　**Was there a timetable planned for implementation?**

Yes:　31　　　　No:　10

Q1.5　　**If so, did it go as planned?**

Yes:　09　　　　No:　23

Q1.6　　**If not, why? Give three reasons.**

(Y009) Ability of the negotiator to implement the mandate. The time frame of the party was slow.

(Y014) BiH army did not handover all arms. UNPROFOR had not forces enough to protect them. There were always incidents at the confrontation line.

(Y015) Unwillingness on part of [the Bosnian Serb Army], unwillingness on part of UN/NATO to enforce in areas that were in [the Total Exclusion Zone] but did not affect Sarajevo proper.

(Y016) Failure by Krajina Serbs to withdraw from all forward positions as agreed to in cease-fire agreement. Failure to place all heavy weapons in approved storage sites. Failure to cease military operations against each other.

(Y024) Continued hostilities, escalation of crisis [in] Bosnia-Herzegovina, lack of cooperation [between the] UN and conflicting parties.

(Y027) Warring factions attack [in] January 1993 (Croatian-instigated). Direction from Knin government to take out arms in January 1993. Deep distrust on all sides.

(Y030) Disarming was initially agreed upon and implemented by all warring parties. Reluctance by UNPROFOR to insist on disarming.

(Y042) There is no deadline or time limit to peace agreement.

(Y043) Because there was no cooperation of warring parties.

(Y044) There is no commitment from the parties.

(Y045) Not so often and according to the situation of the cease-fire agreement between the two parties and the time of implementing the cease-fire agreement.

(Y048) Both parties did not comply with [their] commitments.

(Y057) [Sector West] achieved its aim within the set time frame (same cannot be said of other sectors).

(Y060) Primarily because of the deep suspicions of the belligerents and the fact that the situation on the ground had changed considerably since the mandate was formulated.

(Y069) Suspicious fear between the two [parties]. The other sectors did not have success. Political influences.

(Y071) From April 4,1992 the priority became the evolution of the situation in Bosnia-Herzegovina. The force HQ was in Sarajevo with almost no communications. The action of high-ranking officials focused on Sarajevo (where there was at that time no mandate and no UN troops).

(Y075) Parties did not comply [with] the agreement. Distrust. Weapons hidden inside the area. Belligerent acts carried out by uncontrolled groups.

(Y080) Unwillingness of SRK, lack of will from UN, continuous threats/action by HV.

(Y095) Delays, no experience, [and no knowledge of] how to implement.

(Y126) Due to mistrust among the parties. The inability of the UN forces on the ground to effectively supervise the implementation. The urge among the parties for land and victory.

(Y127) The Serbs were not committed to the timetable, the Serbs mistrusted [the] UN who was to supervise the program, [and the] UN did not have [the] power to implement [the timetable].

(Y130) Non-compliance by warring factions, timetables too tight for negotiation, [and] insufficient troops to cover the task.

(Y136) The agreement about location was broken several times. Demining was stopped and the warring parties denied to go on.

(Y138) Lack of willingness (political) from the parties.

(Y147) Local authorities are not respecting the agreement. Lack of political will. Mandate is too restricted. Transformation of regular troops into "police forces".

(Y149) Reticence of one party, practical difficulties of the same party, [and] lack of internal chain of command.

(Y160) Serb population in Croatia. Serb population in Bosnia-Herzegovina. Croat population in Bosnia-Herzegovina.

(Y169) Problems with the parties involved. Problems with the arrival of the military contingents.

Q1.7 **If there were delays in the implementation, summarize their impact on the disarmament process.**

(Y009) It creates a lack of confidence in the other party.

(Y016) Resulted in non-implementation of demobilisation of military units in exclusion zones as originally planned. Continued distrust and non-compliance created mistrust of opponent's intentions.

(Y024) Total failure in three of the four sectors in Croatia 1992.

(Y030) Delays should be accepted, but lack of persistence by UNPROFOR [was] one of main reasons why disarming failed.

(Y042) Delays caused [the] opening [of] new check/control/observation points and made our mission more difficult.

(Y043) There were delays in disarmament process.

(Y044) Delays cease-fire. Delay for the humanitarian aid.

(Y045) Fighting each other (the two parties). For example, Croatian army and the Serbian army in Krajina.

(Y047) There was a delay between the local level and high level because of the delay of information reaching the high level. Both parties did not see the peace agreement.

(Y048) Delays to reach [a] cease-fire agreement.

(Y057) No delays.

(Y060) The security situation did not allow the return of displaced persons.

(Y069) Cease-fire violations between two [parties].

(Y071) The Sector Commander had to deal quite alone with the Vance plan. [He was] hampered by [the] incoming of the battalions [which] happened too late (certain contingents) [and by] UN logistics [which were] ineffective until August except for [the police].

(Y075) The main activities of the disarmament process were accomplished as planned, without delays.

(Y095) Danger [of starting] the war again. Intent to take the armaments out of the zone of UN for reinforcement.

(Y126) The delays caused frustrations among UN personnel and disrupted the disarmament process.

(Y127) There was no implementation, [...] the factions kept their weapons, and the plan collapsed, died a natural death.

(Y130) Occassional loss of UN credibility in the short term.

(Y138) It delayed the whole process.

(Y149) Delay of about one week.

(Y160) No answer because we [have] been serving in former Yugoslavia in the second part of [the] mandate.

(Y174) The disarmament process did not take place.

Q1.8   **Did the existing agreements hinder you at any time from conducting disarmament measures?**

Yes: 21   No: 14

Q1.9   **If so, mention some of the ways in which you felt hindered.**

(Y009) It had to be done step by step, implementing the same measures in each party.

(Y014) All over the mission they made a lot of rules that made trouble for us.

(Y016) Cease-fire agreement made no mention of armored personnel carriers, machine guns and various types of anti-tank weapons on new lines of separation. Agreement did not specify or empower UNPROFOR military units to disarm violators found in the zone. This was eventually changed. Clear confiscation policy should have been stated in the cease-fire agreement. Local joint commissions and higher level commissions should have included civil authority, police and military engineers from respective sides.

(Y017) Please [...] read 3.6.

(Y026) UN agreements and plans did not take account of local facts. UN plans and directives were too unprecise.

(Y027) Too much interference in local negotiation process. Distrust and cheating on all sides. Misunderstanding by senior UN officials of actual progress and problems, i.e., too many resolutions [and] not enough action.

(Y030) Developments in one UNPA may have affected implementation of disarming in other sectors. Political decision at highest level.

(Y042) Allowing the warring parties to carry weapons on the cease-fire line [...] led to [the] carrying [of] weapons in wider areas [and] limited us to disarming warring parties only [at] checkpoints.

(Y043) There was doubt with some parties about the mission.

(Y045) According to my knowledge there were many ways in which it was impossible to conduct disarming due to the enmity of the Serbian people and army [toward the] UN.

(Y060) The premise on which the agreements [were based] had changed; and in fact one of the parties did not have direct influence (or claimed not to have) over the authorities in the UNPA's, in view of the changed situation.

(Y069) The fact of being under the local law.

(Y074) We were not allowed to conduct cordon and search operations without specific justification.

(Y075) Limitations for weapons searching.

(Y080) Not included.

(Y095) Excessive official routine (bureaucracy).

(Y126) Restrictions on UN patrols. Roadblocks aimed at denying information to UN military observers. Arrest and threats against UN personnel by all the parties to the conflict.

(Y127) Our movement was restricted; therefore, [we] had problems [...] monitoring the exact arms caches.

(Y136) The agreements were okay but the warring parties did not follow the agreements.

(Y147) Restriction of freedom of movement. No border control - unlimited import of weapons.

(Y149) Insufficient mandate of UN forces. Insufficient procedures. Freedom of movement.

(Y159) While airfield monitoring (at Banja Luka), the location agreed with [the] UN to perform the duties had no direct view to the airfield. Monitoring directly from towers [would] be wiser. The Croatian side agreed for a daily plan for the patrols to be conducted in each area (the day before). Saying where [you are] going to patrol tomorrow seems not the best way to monitor any army.

(Y160) Because high percentage of Serb population in Croatian territory will not be pushed out from Croatia. Muslim population in [Bosnia-Herzegovina] attacked by Serbs.

(Y174) Agreement was not a problem but commitment to enforce it was.

Analyst's Comments:

   Many agreements and Security Council Resolutions marked the course of UNPROFOR's mission, but they were not always applied in an evenhanded manner. Localized agreements were reached in different parts of the former Yugoslavia, and some Security Council Resolutions were only applicable to particular, defined areas. The interpretation of the disarmament components of the different agreements was for this reason very complex. Practitioners completed the questionnaires without indicating their units or area of deployment. It is hence impossible to determine a framework of reference for any single questionnaire, and to be of any use, this analysis must therefore concentrate on general issues and commonalities only.
   Table 1 illustrates the balance of responses to the Yes/No questions in Section I. From this data, some basic conclusions can be drawn. First, the vast majority of the respondents admitted that the agreements or resolutions they were working with contained both an important disarmament component and a timetable for implementation. Second, the responses to questions 1.5 and 1.8

were not so positive. The majority of the respondents did not feel that the timetable was executed as planned (although this question was only answered by 63% of the total respondents), and most respondents conceded that existing agreements hindered their disarmament operations at one time or another.

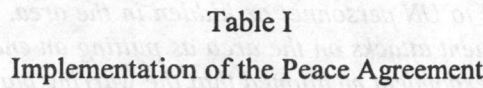

Table I

Implementation of the Peace Agreement

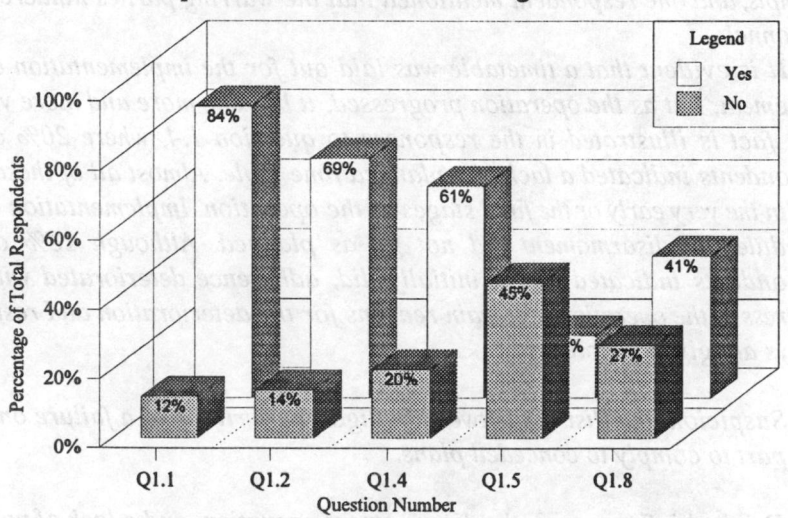

Each agreement or Security Council Resolution signalled a new stage in the evolution of the operation up to the end of 1994. Almost all of them included components for disarmament or demobilization. When asked to describe this component, 75% of the total respondents did so. Thirty-nine percent of these indicated that the disarmament of the warring parties in the UNPA's was the goal of the disarmament component of the peace agreement. Seventeen percent of those responding mentioned the separation of the parties as part of the desired outcome of their mission, and fourteen percent mentioned the storage of weapons under UN supervision. The return of displaced persons, the establishment of weapons exclusion zones, and the creation of conditions suitable for peace negotiations were each noted by 11% of those responding. Various respondents also indicated that the establishment and supervision of civilian police forces, the delivery of humanitarian aid, and the conducting of demining operations were desired outcomes of their disarmament missions.

A few respondents also added their opinions on the success or failure of this aspect of their mission. One respondent (Y094) noted that his mission was successful because it was carried out promptly after a cease-fire agreement. Six respondents offered explanations for the failure of their missions. Half of these pointed to the easy access that the warring parties had to weapons that they had either surrendered to UN personnel or hidden in the area. Two respondents pointed to subsequent attacks on the area as putting an end to disarmament attempts, and one respondent mentioned that the warring parties hindered UN personnel.

It is evident that a timetable was laid out for the implementation of the agreement, but as the operation progressed, it became more and more vague. This fact is illustrated in the responses to question 1.4, where 20% of the respondents indicated a lack of a planned time table. Almost all of these took part in the very early or the final stages of the operation. Implementation of the schedule for disarmament did not go as planned. Although 18% of the respondents indicated that it initially did, adherence deteriorated with the progress of the operation. The main reasons for the deterioration and resulting delays are given as follows:

- Suspicion and distrust between belligerent parties and a failure on their part to comply to conceded plans.

- Political influences on the disarmament operation, and a lack of political will to enforce the agreements with equal exacting measures on the belligerents. A lack of persistence by UNPROFOR during the early stages of the operation was also noted by one of the respondents (Y030, Q1.7).

- Mandates were not ratified in time to keep pace with the changing situation on the ground.

- Inexperience of UN officials and troops and the poor ability of negotiators on the ground.

- Lack of contributing countries to adhere to the timetable for deployment - causing shortages of personnel and gaps in the tasking tables.

- _The presence and action of thugs not necessarily belonging to any of the belligerents, pursuing their own interests and confusing the situation on the ground._

Resulting delays inadvertently had an impact on the outcome of the disarmament operations. One can easily reason that the effect is far reaching. A window of opportunity existed during which UNPROFOR could have had a major impact on the disarmament of the belligerent parties. This opportunity was missed. From the view point of the respondents, the impact of the delays was as follows:

- _The operation was intricate and it became difficult to carry out. This in turn led to frustration and friction between members of the different components of UNPROFOR._

- _Lack of confidence in UNPROFOR on the side of the belligerent parties resulted in non- compliance with the agreements._

- _Seizure of implementation of disarmament operations._

- _Adverse effects on the delivery of humanitarian aid._

- _Increasing violations of the cease-fire agreements leading to the start of the war again._

- _Total failure of UNPROFOR in three of the four sectors in Croatia._

Twenty-nine percent of all the respondents were not hindered by the agreements reached in carrying out their disarmament tasks. This, however, relates to what the tasks were. It was impossible to deduce from their responses what specific tasks they had to perform. Factors that did hinder some of the respondents can be summarized as follows:

- _UN agreements and plans that did not take local conditions into account. Directives were not precise. Important elements of disarmament arrangements were left out of directives._

- *Due to the constant changes in the situation, the policy applied was not homogeneous in all sectors or applicable to all belligerents. Political decisions on higher levels allowed for different sets of rules to be applied.*

- *Specific military operations, like cordon and search operations, were not permitted, even when requested.*

- *Parties were allowed to carry weapons in one area, and weapon free zones in other areas could not be implemented due to inexact arrangements and no commitment to enforce basic agreements.*

- *Excessive bureaucracy.*

II. MANDATE:

Q2.1   **At the start of your mission, were you informed of the part of the mandate regarding disarmament?**

Yes: 36   No: 12

Q2.2   **How was the disarmament component expressed in your mission mandate? (Summarize.)**

(Y002) Voir plus haut 1.3. [See above, Q1.3.]

(Y009) It was generally expressed.

(Y010) Tanks [and] artillery [were to be withdrawn to] 30 km outside UNPA or be stored under UN control. [Armored personnel carriers] 10 km outside UNPA or stored. Armed soldiers 1 km outside UNPA [and] all forces inside to be demobilized.

(Y014) Written agreement and rules.

(Y015) Monitor [the] Sarajevo [Total Exclusion Zone] [and] monitor [the] Washington Agreement which included control of weapon collection points.

(Y016) Withdrawal of all forces at least 1000 meters, withdrawal of artillery, tanks, mortars and air defense weapons to 10 and 20 km lines. Eventual withdrawal of all military within specified distance. No weapons or uniformed personnel within the zone of separation. Lifting of all mines by both parties.

(Y017) UNPROFOR is responsible [for] the demilitarization of the UNPA's, though the withdrawal and disarmament of all armed forces from all the UNPA's.

(Y024) Very clearly as a step towards the return of refugees to their origins.

(Y025) No idea.

(Y026) Yugoslav Army (JNA) to withdraw. Disarm and demobilize local militias. Police to carry side-arms only. (From memory - for details, see the Vance Plan).

(Y027) Vance Plan and subsequent amendments received in writing plus original [UN Security Council Resolution] and subsequent resolutions.

(Y028) As a general goal.

(Y030) See [the] Cyrus Vance plan. Warring parties should disarm and the carrying of long weapons in the UNPA's should not be allowed.

(Y042) The disarmament was [along] 3 cordon lines. [Within] the first line [at] 5 km, [no one was] to wear military clothes [or] long arms. [Only] short arms [were allowed] for the police. [Within the second] line [at]10 km, no mortars or [armored personnel carriers] or medium range [weapons were allowed]. [Within] the third line [at] 20 km, no tanks or artillery. Inside the UNPA no weapons [were allowed] at all.

(Y043) Withdrawal of heavy weapons for 30 km, withdrawal of medium weapons for 10 km, [and] withdrawal of light weapons for 5 km.

(Y044) Withdraw the weapons [specified] in the agreement [to the specified number of] kilometers [...].

(Y047) It was only helping the UN militarily.

(Y048) Withdrawal [of] heavy weapons 30 km from [the confrontation line].

(Y054) UNPROFOR is responsible for demilitarization through the withdrawal or disbandment of all armed forces into the UNPA's and must ensure the UNPA's remain demilitarized.

(Y060) That the JNA was to withdraw from the UNPA's, the Territorial Defense Force was to disband and heavy weaponry was to be placed under joint control of the UN and the local authorities; police were only to be equipped with "side arms".

(Y063) UNPROFOR would be deployed in Safe Areas, and these areas would be demilitarized. All armed forces would be either withdrawn or disbanded.

(Y069) By a document of the UN mandate [and] through a briefing [in] the UN HQ.

(Y071) The four sectors had to reach a local agreement on the practical modalities (including time schedule) with the warring parties. They had very little help from the force HQ until August 1992 (re-setting up in Zagreb).

(Y074) Not in [the] mandate, but in tasks. Error [...] was in the mandate. UNPROFOR is responsible for ensuring that the UNPA's are demilitarized through the withdrawal or disbandment of all armed forces in them.

(Y075) Units and weapons withdrawal (out of the area). Demobilization, disarmament, [and] weapon storage. Prevention of reintroducing weapons [with] checkpoints [and] vigilance.

(Y080) As in the Vance plan.

(Y094) Heavy weapons, artillery, armor and aircraft should be stored in magazines under UN control. No long arms should be used by police or military forces.

(Y095) The areas would be demilitarized. All armed forces in them would be either withdrawn or disbanded and all persons residing in them were protected from fear of armed attack.

(Y097) La composante désarmement concernait exclusivement la maitrise des armements et encore de facon limitée. Il s'agissait de l'opération DENY FLIGHT (interdiction de survol) et du stockage des armes légères dans deux zones de sécurité (SREBRENICA et ZEPA) pour lesquelles un accord avait été signé entre Bosniaques (Musulmans) et Serbes de Bosnie.
[The disarmament component dealt exclusively with the control of arms and only in a limited way. It was due to Operation DENY FLIGHT and the storage of light arms in the two security zones (Srebrenica and Zepa) that there was an agreement signed between the Bosnian Muslims and the Bosnian Serbs.]

(Y126) The collection and concentration of all heavy weapons under UN control in order to stop hostilities.

(Y127) Warring factions, especially the Serbs, [were] to put their weapons under UN control. They were to be centralized at points unders UN guards.

(Y130) In accordance with UN [Security Council Resolution] 913.

(Y136) Withdrawal of weapons and storing of these (for the Krajina Serbs, disarming); later, separation zones. Demining of area. Freedom for the UN troops to inspect/have control of the weapon [stores].

(Y138) As a part of the education (training) from my home country, this was fully informed.

(Y147) Very vague. Generalities which made different interpretations possible.

(Y149) Control of heavy weapons.

(Y160) Only inside UNPA's - United Nations Protection Areas.

(Y174) Disarmament was mentioned briefly in introductory briefing.

Q2.3   How did you interpret the mandate you received?

(Y002) A mon arrivée, le 1 juillet 1993, le plan Vance était encore en vigueur mais de façon formelle: à la suite de l'attaque croate du 23 janvier 1993 dans la Dalmatie du Sud, les Serbes avaient repris presque tout leur armement lourd dans les dépôts.
[When I arrived on July 1, 1993, the Vance Plan still existed but only formally: following the Croatian attack

on January 23, 1993 in Southern Dalmatia, the Serbs had taken almost all their stored heavy weapons.]

(Y009) It was summarized in an operational order from the Sector Commander.

(Y010) Exactly as given.

(Y015) To do so with [...] the willingness of belligerent parties.

(Y016) As stated in 2.2 above except to include withdrawal of all machine guns, [armored personnel carriers], [and] anti-tank wire guided weapons from lines of separation. Confiscation of all weapons, ammunition, and explosives found in zone of separation, use of force to remove offenders or negotiate removal in conjunction with local commanders.

(Y017) [It] was my responsibility [to] impede, in my [area of responsibility], the presence of troops belonging to the warring parties [and] even the movement through the UNPA of trucks or other kind of vehicles, small groups or single soldiers, militias or civilians carrying weapons. And if some of this [did] occur, I [was to] push these people outside the UNPA and capture their vehicles and weapons.

(Y025) Normal control mission. Our duty was to construct the containers for the UN.

(Y026) Establish a knowledge of [the] area, monitor the withdrawal of JNA, [and] monitoring in general.

(Y027) To supervise and insist on [the] disarming process.

(Y030) The mandate was not transformed into mission-wide and generally accepted implementation guidelines. Interpretation as regards implementation [was] left to

[the] Sector Commander and [the] Head [of] Civil Affairs.

(Y042)   Within the UNPA I should confiscate any long weapons and store them in a double-lock magazine. Outside the UNPA I should report any violations to the agreement.

(Y043)   By daily [patrols] and investigation.

(Y044)   Daily patrolling for checking the weapons in [...] storage.

(Y047)   I did what [...] was in the mandate.

(Y048)   By daily patrol and checking weapons storage areas.

(Y054)   After the withdrawal was completed, I assumed total responsibility over the UNPA including [its] security.

(Y057)   [The] mandate was general, [and this] gave [the] local UN commander a lot of leeway.

(Y060)   As above.

(Y063)   All weapons had to be moved out of the area or destroyed.

(Y069)   Like a problematic mission.

(Y071)   No interpretation of the initial mandate [for] Croatia (Vance Plan). But while focusing on Bosnia-Herzegovina [...] not enough attention was paid to the initial mandate [and there was] no mandate at all and no troops in Bosnia.

(Y074)   This action was already completed when I arrived. However, I know that all weapons were confiscated on site by UNPROFOR personnel.

(Y075) It was very clear. No interpretation needed.

(Y080) Did not - only monitoring capacity.

(Y088) To cooperate in humanitarian assistance and relief operations.

(Y094) It is important that the mandate should be enforced all the time in all its contents because when small violations are tolerated they tend to escalate and become intolerable.

(Y095) It said a lot of words but nothing clear and concrete about disarmament.

(Y097) DENY FLIGHT était une opération dangereuse dans le sens ou elle n'expliquait pas de risques particuliers mais pouvait avoir une influence directe sur les négociations si on la considérait exclusivement sous son aspect militaire.
[DENY FLIGHT was a dangerous operation in the sense that it did not entail particular risks but could have a direct influence on the negotiations if considered exclusively with respect to its military aspect.]

(Y127) To monitor the handing over [of weapons] and the centralization of the warring factions' arms.

(Y130) Whichever way was appropriate to execute my mission.

(Y136) The original mandate was not working when I arrived [in] the mission area. The later agreements were quite detailed and interpretation was not necessary.

(Y137) We were supposed to assist other units as necessary to keep the roads and airways open for UNHCR humanitarian aid. Force was to be used only for self-defense.

(Y147) Too restricted. Unrealistic with regard to the disarmament component.

(Y149) Store weapons in storage sites or return them at certain distance from separation line.

(Y159) To interpret it was easier [than] applying it on the ground [...].

(Y160) I was totally [in agreement] with the mandate.

(Y174) Confused due to lack of information.

Q2.4   **Did the way the disarmament component was expressed hinder or assist your disarming task?**

Hindered: 09   Assisted: 27

Q2.5   **If it was a hindrance, how would you have preferred your mandate to read?**

(Y016) Should have been worded much more clearly, so as to leave no "loopholes" for misinterpretation.

(Y027) Clearly state time lines and method of turn-in of weapons.

(Y030) Hindrance as there were no clear cut guidelines for implementation throughout all sectors.

(Y060) There were two significant parts. [First], in sectors other than Sector West, the Croatian forces were not required to disarm or move away from the confrontation line. This posed problems in that the Serbs would not give up their weapons unless the Croatians pulled back. Second, the very concept of "side arms" was open to interpretation.

(Y075) More freedom of action.

(Y097) DENY FLIGHT devait être sous contrôle des Commandants de la FORPRONU et non sous contrôle de l'OTAN. Le commandement ne se partage pas!
[DENY FLIGHT should have been under the control of the commanders of UNPROFOR and not under the control of NATO. The command cannot be divided!]

(Y127) It was hindered because the troops did not have enough protection to resist the warring factions taking back weapons that had already been centralized.

(Y137) Disarming would have to be described in detail, but lack of usable forces in Bosnia would be a major problem due to hostage-games from the warring factions.

(Y147) Enlarged mandate with regard to the use of force. Time frame for [...] disarmament.

(Y159) On the Croatian side, a way not only to protest any violation but an effective way to withdraw the weapons and avoid [their] return to the area.

(Y174) Mandate was not communicated properly to UN elements.

Q2.6   Were your actions/freedom of action during disarmament operations influenced by external factors other than the mandate?

Yes: 24   No: 13

Q2.7   If so, which ones?

(Y009) Each party was living a different situation, so we had to deal with it.

(Y010) Croatian attack into Sector South in January 1993 caused Serbs to rearm in the UNPA.

(Y014) The warring parties made their own rules [at the] local level.

(Y016) Application and interpretation of cease-fire agreement [...] was not well implemented by some units. Higher level joint commissions were unable to maintain initial momentum of cease-fire agreement. Situation in Bosnia influenced implementation and comprehensive peace plan solution. Lack of economic agreement progress.

(Y017) Subsidiary disarmament agreements. National policy "instructions".

(Y026) Lack of freedom of movement, lack of trust in [the] UN, [and] lack of knowledge among locals about [the] mandate.

(Y027) Higher HQ interference by civilian (HCA) and military components who had little understanding of local situations. The result was chaos.

(Y030) The unfolding situation in Bosnia. As a result, [there was] reluctance by all warring parties to adhere to timetable.

(Y042) Orders started flowing from [top to bottom] to make the procedures more flexible until it reached [confiscating] weapons only [at] your own checkpoints. You cannot really forbid any warring party or [...] stop them doing what they really want to [do].

(Y047) There were a lot of new resolutions influencing the mandate. All parties were not agreed to the peace agreement.

(Y048) Both parties did not cooperate most of the time. Sometimes depending on individual commanders.

(Y057) [...] the physical terrain (river Sava splitting Serb forces) [...] gave an advantage in disarming and having a direct control if the rules were broken (simplified task).

(Y060) Primarily the two aspects I have mentioned in 2.5 above.

(Y063) The parties resumed their war activities, and weapons had not been moved out or destroyed in the first disarmament operation.

(Y069) Political problems between both sides. Bad propaganda [against the] UN.

(Y071) Conflict in Bosnia-Herzegovina: freedom of action of force headquarters seriously hampered and even aggravated by the temporary relocation in Belgrade. Almost normal functioning of force headquarters in Zagreb at the end of the mandate.

(Y075) The respect for private property (where irregulars hid weapons).

(Y097) Négociations à Genève, évolution de facto du mandat au gré des résolutions du Conseil de sécurité mais sous approbation d'un nouveau mandat ou d'une adoption de celui-ci.
[Negotiations in Geneva, *de facto* evolution of the mandate according to the resolutions of the Security Council but under a new mandate or the adoption of one.]

(Y130) The media.

(Y137) Threatening letters from the warring factions claiming their rights to area control.

(Y149) Restriction of freedom of movement by both parties.

(Y159) There are too many factors. Sometimes political and
military or even to test the UN reaction.

(Y160) Psycho-social environment of population. No respect [for
the] mandate in Croatia and [Bosnia-Herzegovina].

Analyst's Comments:

The main efforts of disarmament operations were concentrated in either Croatia or Bosnia-Herzegovina. Operations evolved differently in both regions and had different mandates. To clarify this, specifically for analysis of the disarmament components, the following framework applies:

- *In the case of Croatia three distinct phases of disarmament operations can be identified. In the first phase, spanning operations from January 1992 to January 1993, disarmament and demobilisation were based on the Vance Plan and enhanced by the UNPA's (United Nations Protection Areas). The second phase stretched from January 1993 to December 1993, during which time the disarmament and demobilisation achieved in the first phase were reversed. The third phase started with the Christmas Truce of December 1993 and stretched until January 1995. During this phase UNPROFOR positioned itself between the belligerent parties and conducted disarmament and demobilisation operations in the zone of separation.*

- *Operations in Bosnia-Herzegovina can likewise be divided into three phases. The first phase, from April 1992 to June 1993, was a time when UNPROFOR had an exclusively humanitarian mandate. Tasks concerning disarmament were limited to those assisting the delivery of humanitarian aid. The second phase, from June 1993 to February 1994, included the expansion of UNPROFOR's mandate to protect Safe Areas and control weapons based on local cease-fire agreements. During the third phase, from February 1994 to January 1995, further expansion of the mandate included the monitoring of the cease-fire agreement. UNPROFOR also positioned itself between belligerent parties on the confrontation line in this theatre of operations.[1]*

The responses reflect most of the elements of the different mandates. Clear reference is made by some of the respondents to specific mandates and plans which in general correlate with the original mandates. The evolution of the operation and the subsequent changes to the mandates are also evident in the responses. The following, however, need to be mentioned:

- *Twenty-four percent of the respondents to Question 2.1 indicated that they were not informed about the disarmament components of their specific mandates. No relationship was found between the different respondents except for the fact that they were all military personnel. They were almost all deployed in the operation at different times (although overlapping), and judging from their responses, they represented more than four nationalities. This in reality means that the information and orders they received about their different tasks were not very thorough. Considered from a military point of view, this is unacceptable.*

- *Many of the answers given do not correspond to distances, time periods, etc. (Y048, Y044, Y043, Y042). The answers also do not correspond to the actual figures given in the mandates. This must be attributed to either bad memory or to inadequate information as discussed above.*

- *Some responses, no matter from what theater of operations/time frame, are disturbing:*

   (Y014) The warring parties made their own rules [at the] local level.
   (Y015) To do so with [...] the willingness of belligerent parties.
   (Y095) It said a lot of words but nothing clear and concrete about disarmament.
   (Y174) Confused due to lack of information.

---

[1] This framework is laid out in Barbara Ekwall-Uebelhart and Andrei Raevsky, *Managing Arms in Peace Processes: Former Yugoslavia*, Geneva: UNIDIR, 1995, unpublished draft.

One cannot but wonder what the effectiveness of disarmament and demobilization operations were, when the officers that were supposed to execute the mission responded in this way. The fact to be noted is that the operations to disarm and demobilize the different belligerent parties started on shaky legs. This may be one of the main reasons why it was never completely achieved.

Peacekeeping operations, more often than not, take place in political, military and cultural environments which are, by nature, highly fluid and dynamic. A lack of clarity may result, caused by factors such as unresolved political issues, an unclear understanding or description of the end result for an operation, or difficulty in gaining international consensus. The least civilian heads of missions and military commanders can do to keep this issue from affecting the objective of the operation is to strive to gain as much clarity as possible when formulating mandates and mission statements for operations. In response to Question 2.4, only 9 respondents indicated that they were hindered in their tasks by the way in which the mandate was expressed. In contrast, fifteen indicate some form of vagueness, confusion or complexity in executing the mandate in the preceding questions. Apparently these respondents were not hindered by the fact that they did not understand their tasks on disarmament or were unable to execute the mandate.

Respondents felt that their mandates could have been improved or clarified by the following:

- *The wording of the mandates must be clear and without room for "loop holes". This may not necessarily mean that it must be prescribing or restricting to the agency responsible for execution. What it does mean is that the rules of the game must be clear to all the players on the field. The mandate must not allow for change or interpretation to benefit the interpreter: it must set the guidelines clearly and without room for question.*

- *The mandate must be communicated properly. Once the mandate is set, and the rules have been agreed upon, it must be communicated to both the force responsible and the belligerent parties.*

- *The rules, once agreed upon, must be valid for every party to the agreement. Slackening of the rules on one front may create anxiety on another and result in non-compliance by some or all of the belligerent parties.*

- *Some form of retribution must be built into the mandate. Belligerent parties must know what is expected of them, and what will happen if they do not comply with the agreements.*

External factors often influence the execution of a mandate. The commanders on the different levels usually appreciate the situation and all given factors in order to plan the execution of their mandate or mission. No matter how thorough the planning process, there are always unforeseen influences that can drastically influence the desired result. Some of the major influences on a mission are those external factors that you are unable to forecast or plan for. Although not all responses to Question 2.7 relate to this category, we can summarize them as follows:

- Lack of trust between all parties concerned; no respect for the force or its mandate by belligerent parties; and lack of cooperation from the different parties. *Although the different belligerent parties may have at one point in the operation agreed to the same set of rules, there is no guarantee that they will honor their agreement. The situation on the ground can change with such rapidity that they can pull out of the agreement at any time. Although the military commander must anticipate this and have a contingency plan ready to minimize the effect, the responsibility to get the parties back on track is a political one. The political officers must keep their ears on the ground and step in once they detect a deviation from the agreement. Only their vigilance and capability to negotiate with the party concerned can stem the influence on the rest of the operation.*

- Political objectives. *Although the influence of political objectives is mentioned time and again by respondents as negative, it is important not to lose perspective on the issue. Political objectives drive the decisions to engage in peacekeeping operations in the first place. Secondly, political objectives drive military decisions at every level. Commanders should adopt plans and courses of action that support these objectives. The UN approach is to apply effective policies and strategies which combine the instruments of power (political, economic, informational and military). The careful application and coordination of these instruments determines the success or failure of any peacekeeping mission. The nature of each situation, coupled with the desired end result, guides the head of the mission in selection and balance of the instruments at his disposal. The resulting policy is then implemented through the different activities (political, military, economic and informational) to advance the objectives of the UN for the mission. It is therefore possible that the practitioners on one level of activity will not comprehend the effect of a given situation on the full scope of the operation, and that they will feel hindered by decisions and actions on the highest level. Two important factors about political primacy stand out. First, military personnel at all levels should understand the operation's political objectives. Second, commanders should remain aware of changes in the political objectives which demand an adjustment of military operations. Sometimes these changes may be subtle, yet failure to recognize them and adjust may lead to operations that do not support the attainment of political objectives.*

- Diplomatic activities. *The military component of any peacekeeping operation supports political objectives and their implementing diplomatic activities. Military support improves the chances of success in the peace process by lending credibility to these activities and demonstrating resolve to achieve viable political settlements. Diplomatic activities, however, must be coordinated and directed by the set political objectives of the mission. It is somehow disturbing to notice that several respondents mention the interference of national diplomatic activities with operations under UN command. These "side line" activities can seriously affect the accomplishment of international political objectives and should be avoided.*

- Terrain. *Terrain is often mentioned as a hindering factor. It is, however, one of the given factors that the military commander must deal with in his operational appreciation. The aim of this appreciation is to determine what the terrain allows the commander to do, and what restrictions it places on the execution of his mission. It also allows him to anticipate how the belligerent parties will use terrain to further their aims or what restrictions are placed on their activities. Rather than allowing terrain to hinder the execution of operations, the utilization of the terrain and the circumvention of restrictions should be reflected in the operational plan.*

Lessons learned at the this stage are fairly obvious:

- *Disarmament and demobilization can only take place with the full consent of belligerent parties. If this is unobtainable, coercive measures are the only other viable option. The forces that are designated to execute the operation must have the fire power, resources and political backing to enforce the agreement on the party(ies) not complying with the intentions thereof.*

- *Where disarmament operations are in effect, weapons, equipment and personnel must be kept at different locations. These locations must be properly secured to prevent any faction from re-arming itself. The Serbs succeeded in January 1993 in removing their compounded weapons from UNPROFOR storage sites and in re-arming themselves. Had these weapons been immobilized, or the essential parts needed for firing stored at different locations, the Serbs would have been unable to re-arm themselves.*

- *Where predetermined disarmament objectives are vital to the successful outcome of a whole mission, they must not be abandoned in preference of time or political favor.*

- *The events that took place in the former Yugoslavia during January 1993 are testimony to the ability of conflict to re-ignite without strong and sustained disarmament efforts.*

III. SUBSIDIARY DISARMAMENT AGREEMENTS:

Q3.1   Did the warring factions enter into a separate disarmament agreement?

Yes: 20   No: 26
(If no, go to question 4.)

Q3.2   If so, describe the agreement.

(Y013) In the case of Sarajevo under threat of NATO airstrikes on 11 February 1994 the warring parties agreed to [a]

Total Exclusion Zone in which heavy weapons were collected under UN control in weapon collection points [on] or, before 21 February 1994, withdrawn. In the case of Gorazde a military exclusion zone was established and heavy weapons were to be withdrawn by Bosnian Serbs outside of [the] zone. In [the] case of Zepa, [the] area was to be demilitarized by [the] June 1993 agreement.

(Y016) See comments at 2.2.

(Y017) Serbians were allowed to maintain their TDF troops deployed inside the UNPA. They were able to wear uniforms and to carry their light weapons openly. Also Serbians operated [their] own checkpoints.

(Y024) Each of the sectors negotiated their local agreements with varying results according to the umbrella plan (Vance Owen Plan). Creation of the buffer zones later on was initialized by local active Sector Commanders.

(Y027) Gentlemen's agreements [of] November 1993-March 1994 which resulted in a cease-fire agreement.

(Y030) Agreement to disarm was agreed by warring parties in the sector. Then direct negotiations under UNPROFOR's umbrella.

(Y043) There was local agreement between local commanders.

(Y044) Agreement between [the] two commanders from the two parties.

(Y047) There was a separation zone between the two parties but neither of the parties followed the peace agreement.

(Y054) Withdrawal of artillery, mortars, rocket launchers and tanks. [Then] disarmament and demobilization of Territorial Defense Forces and other non-police forces.

Withdrawal of [armored personnel carriers], anti-aircraft systems, heavy machine guns and short range anti-tank weapons. Withdrawal of all remaining troops. Completion of minefield lifting by both sides under UNPROFOR supervision and security.

(Y063) They agreed on weapons collection and demobilization. Only armed police forces were approved in the areas of concern. Croatia proper was included, partially, in this agreement.

(Y088) To concentrate all weapons bigger than 12.70 mm in established depots under UN control.

(Y095) Rules of disengagement which said [that] the parties shall provide UNPROFOR with lists stating unit by unit the number of tanks, [anti-aircraft] guns, artillery pieces and other indirect weapons which are to be deployed outside the 10 and 20 km lines. These list should also state the exact locations with grid references to which the weapons will be redeployed.

(Y097) Un accord prévoyait le retrait des armes lourdes (Serbes) hors d'une zone d'exclusion autour de ZEPA et GORAZDE allant de pair avec un rassemblement des armes légères (Musulmans) sous contrôle FORPRONU dans les zones de ZEPA et GORAZDE.

[An agreement scheduled the withdrawal of heavy arms (Serbian) in an exclusion zone around Zepa and Gorazde coupled with a collection of light arms (Muslim) under the control of UNPROFOR in the Zepa and Gorazde zones.]

(Y129) A number of cease-fire agreements were agreed and broken during the period. As a result, weapons were never moved back from the front lines.

(Y130) Local agreements negotiated to take account of local issues. For example, the establishment of [an] active site for the collection of Croat and Muslim heavy weapons for defensive operations against the Serbs.

(Y136) Agreements about zone of separation. Control and inspection of weapon stores.

(Y137) No heavy weapons within 20 km of Sarajevo.

(Y147) Creation of a separation zone [through the] withdrawal and storage of heavy weapons. Control of storage sites.

(Y149) Forbidden zones/weapon system: 1 km zone - small weapons, 10 km - heavy weapons, 20 km zone - [...] storage sites for artillery tanks.

Q3.3   **Was the agreement formulated with the mandate in mind or independent of the mandate?**

Mandate-oriented: 15   Independent of mandate: 05

Q3.4   **Were there any contradictions between the mandate and the agreement?**

Yes: 08   No: 11

Q3.5   **If so, which ones?**

(Y013) Mandate essentially dealt with delivery of humanitarian assistance while [the Demilitarized Zone, the Total Exclusion Zone, and the Military Exclusion Zone] were zones affecting [the] holding of weapons.

(Y016) Original Vance Owen Plan was superseded by subsequent events in Bosnia Croat offensive launched in January 1993. Agreement did not permit UNPROFOR military units to monitor or implement cease-fire agreement behind Croat front lines. Only UN Military Observers were permitted behind Croat lines even though Croat lines were inside of UNPA boundaries.

(Y017) The mandate established that all troops must be withdrawn from the UNPA's, and UN forces must perform the disarmament of all individuals that remain inside the UNPA's. That agreement was against the spirit of the mandate, because [it] allowed the military deployment of one warring faction inside the UNPA.

(Y027) Local issues by the military to at least have a local cease-fire put into effect. Political concerns could be tackled later.

(Y047) There was entry to the zone [of] separation from both sides carrying weapons [...], [a] violation of the cease-fire agreement.

(Y057) On [the] Serb side (beyond Sava river) it was a different country (Bosnia-Herzegovina). The exclusion zone could not be implemented. The war in Bosnia-Herzegovina complicated matters.

(Y063) The police forces were extended to paramilitary units, so the intended reduction in forces was not achieved.

(Y136) The mandate described disarming of all Serbian troops in the Krajina area, but the Krajina Serbs opened all weapon stores on January 1993 (due to Croatian Attack) and took out all weapons and established military units.

Q3.6   What was the impact of the agreement on the mandate?

(Y013) Delivery of humanitarian assistance should have been made easier in that shelling stopped in Sarajevo and Gorazde. However the isolated nature of Sarajevo, Zepa and Gorazde in fact meant that a long blockage had the decisive impact even when heavy weapons were removed.

(Y017) The impact was that we only could apply the whole mandate in one part of our operation, and if I wanted to apply the mandate to the Serbs I had to ask for permission to do it. That situation hindered the fulfillment of our mission. The Croats claimed against the agreement and accused us of partiality and permanently asked for permission to deploy troops inside the UNPA (like Serbs) for security reasons, and they threatened us proclaiming if UNPROFOR did not push out the Serbians, they will perform some kind of military operation to clean the area.

(Y016) Mandate changed from implementation of Vance Owen plan to implementation of cease-fire agreement. In most areas of Croatia, main tenets of Vance Owen plan including cease-fire were never realized.

(Y027) Initially reasonably well, however, mistrust by all sides caused problems. There were some decisions taken that affected the success.

(Y030) As described above, [the] agreement's implementation was naturally influenced by other political events in the region.

(Y047) 90% of our time was to help the military and monitor the zone of separation so that enabled us to do [what] the mandate was found for.

(Y054) The withdrawal and disarmament of both sides was the key [to] the success in the implementation of the mandate.

(Y057) Total control was achieved by UN in [Sector West].

(Y063) The mandate's intention to [translate] a military reality into a civil reality was delayed and finally reversed by the Croatian attack on Maslenica [on] 22 January 1993 and the subsequent mobilization. [On the] 29 March 1994, the withdrawal of heavy weapons and demilitarization was revitalized by a new agreement which was implemented.

(Y088) Because the agreement was not respected there was no impact on the mandate.

(Y095) The same as mentioned in part I.1.7.

(Y130) It supported the mandate.

(Y137) It made UNHCR-traffic easier for a while.

(Y147) Small step forward in the implementation.

Analyst's Comments:

Since it was not the chief role-player, there was very little that the UN could have done to slow down the process in order to enforce compliance with the agreements reached. The lesson to be learned from this experience is that once an agreement is reached on disarmament and the role it plays in the whole process, the process becomes subject to the successful execution of disarmament. In the case of the former Yugoslavia, successful settlement of the disputes is not possible without containing the military force of the warring parties. Disarmament and demobilization are therefore cornerstones of the building of peace. UNPROFOR made the decision to build the building without securing the foundation and paid the price.

IV. TOP-DOWN CHANGES: CONSISTENCY OF THE MANDATE AND ITS IMPACT ON THE DISARMAMENT COMPONENT:

Q4.1 **Did the mandate change while you were engaged in the UN/national operation?**

Yes: 19   No: 31
(If not, go to question 5.)

(Y010) There was no formal change, however, Croatian attack did, in effect, change the mandate.

(Y095) No. Until now. It will change in July 1995.

Q4.2 **If so, what was(were) the change(s)? (Describe the most important aspects.)**

(Y002) Pour la Bosnie-Herzégovine, les résolutions 826, 836, etc. ont ajouté le concept de zone de sécurité au mandat initialement humanitaire (accompagnement de l'aide humanitaire).
[For Bosnia-Herzegovina, Resolutions 826, 836, etc., added the concept of security zones to a mandate which was initially humanitarian (accompanying humanitarian aid).]

(Y010) Serbs mobilized and went back into uniform [and] prepared defenses.

(Y013) Mandate changed in that UNPROFOR in case of Sarajevo, Gorazde and Zepa became responsible for monitoring [the Total Exclusion Zone, the Military Exclusion Zone, and the Demilitarized Zone] respectively.

(Y024) Increased demands to control the area which was expanding day by day.

(Y026) Hard to define now as there was a "mission creep" from the beginning.

(Y027) Too many resolutions to list, however, UN recognition of Croatia caused Serbs' distrust of the UN.

(Y028) The area of operations.

(Y030) No changes but amendments in the form of [a General Assembly] resolution.

(Y045) The political and the security situations.

(Y046) Changing from police work to [a] 90% humanitarian aid mission.

(Y057) It was modified to include [Bosnia-Herzegovina]. This happened after we had achieved [the] disarmament [of] troops only.

(Y060) The situation that emerged in Bosnia-Herzegovina affected everything that was being done in Croatia.

(Y063) The new mandate emphasized Croatian sovereignty, pointing out Croatian sovereignty to be re-established in [the] pink zones within [the] mandate period.

(Y080) [The Vance Plan was] ignored; then [we] moved on to [the cease-fire agreement] on 29 March 94.

(Y097) Mandat humanitaire: protection des zones de sécurité, protection armée des convois, utilisation possible de l'appui aérien rapproché, mission d'interposition sur le Mont Igmann.
[Humanitarian mandate: protection of the security zones, armed protection of the convoys, possible utilization of close air support, mission of interposition on Mount Igmann.]

(Y129) UN Resolutions on Bosnia came out at regular intervals from April to November 1993.

(Y138) New Security Council resolutions changed part of the mandate.

(Y172) Instigation of demilitarized zones/safe areas/weapons collection.

(Y174) Expanded to include Bosnia and humanitarian roles.

Q4.3   Did this (these) change(s) affect your disarmament operations?

Yes: 09   No: 09

Q4.4   If so, how? (Name the three most important effects.)

(Y002) L'affaire de Srebrenica, en avril 1993 (juste avant mon arrivée) s'est traduite par le désarmement des Bosniaques à l'intérieur de la poche. Disarmement incomplet qu'il serait intéressant d'étudier auprès des acteurs directs (ICFY doit pouvoir donner des éléments).
[The affair of Srebrenica in April 1993 (just before my arrival) was translated by the disarmament of Bosnians in the interior of the zone. Incomplete disarmament which would be interesting to study through the primary actors (ICFY must be able to provide some elements).]

(Y010) Attempted on several occasions to remove weapons from storage sites. Intense pressure to allow soldiers to rearm.

(Y013) Resources dedicated to monitoring heavy weapon exclusion zones were previously resources dedicated to observing impact of shelling.

(Y024)   The whole operation (including the disarmament) [was] always late. When the mandate was changed it very seldom was followed by increasing the resources in time.

(Y027)   Serbs refused to cooperate with further disarmament.

(Y060)   As in 4.2.; because the Krajina Serb life line was through Bosnia-Herzegovina.

(Y138)   Made the implementation more difficult.

(Y174)   Resources were stretched, situation became confused, [and] less commitment to disarmament due to changes in priorities.

Q4.5   **If disarmament was affected, was it still possible for you to implement disarmament measures as first envisaged?**

Yes: 09   No: 04

Q4.6   **In the context of 4.5, did you have to change or abandon procedures?**

Change: 07   Abandon: 03

Q4.7   **If you changed procedures, what were the changes? (Mention the three most important ones.)**

(Y010)   Permitted officers, as well as police, to carry side arms. Number of search operations curtailed.

(Y013)   Put in place procedures regarding [the Total Exclusion Zone] or MBZ monitoring, visiting uncollected heavy weapons, and monitoring accepted abnormalities such as Hadzici Armored Rebuilding Facility.

(Y015)   Focus went from disarmament to control and accountability of heavy weapons.

(Y016) Establishment and implementation of confiscation policy. Establishment and implementation of destruction of weapons, arms, explosives. Destruction of mines [...] when found [...] to impede UN forces' freedom of movement.

(Y026) Apply more flexibility.

(Y027) Political situation (Croat attack) meant [that there was] no support to continue the process. Dual key system changed.

(Y030) It is difficult to answer the type of change. More likely that stalemate occurred, and that after negotiations, disarming continued.

(Y047) The local police should fill in an application form to enter zone of separation [...] 48 hours [in advance]. This was changed to 24 hours or less than that.

(Y060) Abandonment was forced upon UNPROFOR by the Croatian offensive of 22 January 1995.

(Y080) Movement of WSS. Movement/imposition of LOW's.

(Y136) The disarmament according to the mandate was, in my time in the mission area, more or less a farce. If everything was quiet, you could inspect the weapons; if not quiet, you [were] not allowed to inspect the weapons.

Q4.8   Were you adequately informed of changes when and as they occurred?

Yes: 11   No: 03

Q4.9 Were you able to implement alternative measures immediately?

Yes: 06   No: 08

Q4.10 If not, why? (Give the three most salient points.)

(Y016) Changes required changes to UNPROFOR's rules of engagement. Changes took time to implement. Some national contingents were not willing or equipped to make/implement changes. Mine lifting, cordon and search operations, lack of [armored personnel carriers] and firepower [and] training.

(Y027) Time, mistrust, [and] inadequate direction from HQ (and sometimes directions were in conflict).

(Y030) Because no instructions were issued. All implementation issues were left to sector command.

(Y047) It was out of my hands.

(Y063) Not necessary as operational aims were not changed although [the] mandate changed. In general, mandates were primarily seen as a political surrogate for the satisfaction of Croatian politicians, while the situation on the ground set [...] the agenda.

(Y080) Monitoring only.

(Y172) Lack of resolve at [the] political level (UN). Lack of interest by warring factions at [the] local level.

(Y174) Resources inadequate. Confused directions/instructions.

V. BOTTOM-UP CHANGES: DISPUTES AMONG THE WARRING PARTIES ARISING DURING THE MISSION:

Q5.1   Was there a mechanism or a provision for the settlement of disputes if and when these emerged?

Yes: 35   No: 05

Q5.2   If so, what type of mechanism/provision did you have (i.e., mission, special agreement, the UN process, special commission, etc.)?

(Y009) Special agreement.

(Y010) Unilateral meeting with both sides chaired by the Sector Commander and Chief Civil Affairs Officer.

(Y013) UN had to act as bridge for disputes as [the] Bosnian Government refused to meet with Bosnian Serbs on a joint commission to discuss heavy weapons collection or withdrawal issues.

(Y015) Mission [and] joint committee process.

(Y016) Cease-fire agreement, local joint commission, sector joint commission, HQ UNPROFOR joint commission, special representative to [the] Secretary-General.

(Y017) UN process [and] special agreement.

(Y026) We had to build up a system, starting with meetings with both sides separately, using the "good office" system [and] meetings with local authorities.

(Y027) UN process.

(Y030) Direct negotiations between parties. Negotiations with parties on separate occasions (shuttle negotiations to reach agreements).

(Y042) Mission.

(Y044) UN special agreement.

(Y048) UN process [of] reaching an agreement [...] with both parties and forming sub-commissions from warring parties and UNPROFOR.

(Y054) The Sector Commander and the Chief of Civil Affairs were the authorities to settle any dispute.

(Y060) Negotiations with the parties and in specific cases, by appointment of special commissions.

(Y063) Joint commissions on various levels.

(Y069) Mission.

(Y074) Negotiations between the two sides on an informal basis.

(Y080) [...], tripartite meetings (ECMM), [and] [...] meetings (UN).

(Y088) Joint commissions, liaison officers, [and] military observers.

(Y090) Special commision to make arrangements and select the collection points.

(Y094) Special commissions [were] divided in three levels according to their participants: lower level (Battalion Commander), sector level (Sector Commander), central level (Force Commander).

(Y097) Réunions nombreuses entre commandants en chefs, entre "Civil affairs" et "ministres" des différents partis, nombreuses réunions à l'échelon local (UNMO'S etc.). [Numerous meetings between chief commanders, civil affairs officers and ministers of the different parties, numerous meetings at the local level (UNMO's, etc.).]

(Y126) UN process.

(Y127) Observer mediation and negotiations.

(Y129) [A] joint commission between [the] warring parties [was] chaired by UN officers [with the] UNHCR and ECMM in attendance.

(Y130) Local commissions were established containing UN and warring faction representatives.

(Y136) Meetings with the warring parties on all levels.

(Y137) Commanders from the warring factions would sometimes meet for discussions/negotiations arranged by the UN Force Commander. UN helicopters were often used to bring the parties together on short notice.

(Y138) Special agreement and special commission.

(Y147) Joint commission on force, sector and battalion level.

(Y149) Mechanism: joint local and control commissions at all levels, with both parties. Persistency: UN authority.

(Y151) Local joint commission composed of local authorities and UNPROFOR officials.

(Y159) The joint commission meetings (local, sector, general).

(Y160) Special commission (civil affairs).

(Y172)   UN process.

(Y174)   Local liaison arrangements involving UN military observers [and] commanders.

Q5.3   **What kind of regulations were agreed between the parties and the peacekeepers for the collection of arms?**

(Y009)   Same steps had to be followed by both parties. Heavy weapons had to be deposited first and then small weapons. Weapons in custody had to be controlled by [peacekeepers] and parties.

(Y010)   All weapons seized by UN after agreed time were retained by UN. Local police were present at all search operations. Ammunition [and] mines seized by UN were destroyed for safety reasons.

(Y013)   In Sarajevo, the warring parties were told to collect heavy weapons in mutually agreed upon sites. These sites were subject of negotiation as [were] the definitions of what constituted "heavy", "central" and "20 km radius". [The] Gorazde Agreement allowed Bosnian Serb weapons to be withdrawn outside [the Military Exclusion Zone].

(Y015)   Weapon collection points for heavy weapons only. There was no disarmament of small arms.

(Y016)   Mortars, artillery, tanks and air defense artillery were to be stored in pre-approved storage sites and would be inspected on a regular basis to ensure compliance. No weapons or personnel were to be allowed in the zone of separation.

(Y017)   I did not accept the existence of weapons on both sides of my [area of responsibility]. When we found [a] weapon, we captured it. Both sides knew my rules.

(Y026) System of withdrawal of arms to fixed distances from confrontation line. Heavy [and] then light weapons to agreed stores.

(Y027) Vance Plan allowed for weapon collection sites under dual key and that Croats could not bring weapons (unless pistols) into Sector West. April 1994 cease-fire allowed for weapon collection sites - again under UN monitoring but no dual key.

(Y030) Collection of heavy and long weapons and storing in depots with double key.

(Y042) To collect weapons in double lock magazines and the UN forces will protect civilians against any aggression.

(Y044) Collect the weapons under UN controlling.

(Y045) It was understood that they can collect the arms according to the agreement between the local army and UN peacekeepers and military observers, but the local armies can get [them] back in case of invasion by the other side.

(Y047) The regulation was given to the UN [...].

(Y048) Withdrawal of heavy weapons to 15-30 km according to [the] Cyrus Vance Plan.

(Y054) The weapons had to be delivered to UNPROFOR on the storage sites.

(Y057) UN troops were responsible for weapon storage with key access controlled by [the] UN and [the] Serbs. In exchange for the weapons, [the] UN guaranteed [the] safety of [the] population.

(Y060) Joint control as specified in the Vance Plan.

(Y063) Weapons to be cancelled were defined by calliber, WCP by distance to frontline and a control system, and verification measures [were to be] agreed.

(Y069) Special routes and checkpoints to control.

(Y080) None.

(Y088) Peacekeepers were not allowed to collect weapons. The parties declared their inventories [in] the storage sites where peacekeepers conducted inspections on a daily basis.

(Y090) To choose demobilization area. To choose several routes to arrive at selected points. To choose collection points. To choose way for destruction. To [certify the entire] process.

(Y094) That the weapons would either be withdrawn out of the sector or be stored in magazines under UN control.

(Y095) There were no kind of regulations.

(Y097) Aucune; tout se faisait à l'initiative des "négociateurs" sur place.
[None; everthing was done on the initiative of the negotiators on the ground.]

(Y127) The agreement was with UN HQ and not the peacekeepers on the ground.

(Y129) None.

(Y130) There were many different agreements arising from negotiations over several months.

(Y136) Different lines, distance to the confrontation line, for different weapons.

(Y137) Only heavy weapons around Sarajevo where collected under UN control to my knowledge.

(Y138) All heavy weapons in specific areas under UN control.

(Y149) Demilitarization of different zones, identification of the storage sites, definition of the withdrawal routes for heavy weapons, count procedures, registration of heavy weapons.

(Y151) Weapons collection points established by [the] warring factions and monitored by [the] UN. No use of heavy weapons.

(Y159) Initially several weapons collections points were agreed.

(Y160) Inside UNPA's, each warring party had weapons magazines collected and guarded by the UN forces, in their own areas (one on Croat side and one on Serb side).

(Y172) Central collection points under UN security.

(Y174) Identification and concentration in local areas remained, however, under the control of parties.

Q5.4   **What kind of negotiations/regulations were agreed at the top and lower levels with respect to the storage of arms?**

(Y009) The above mentioned [Q5.3] were agreed at the top military level. I don't know what was agreed at the top (political) level.

(Y010) Two locks to each site - one controlled by [the] UN, one by [the] faction. Visits authorized in small groups with prior notice for cleaning/accounting. UN guards at all sites.

(Y013)   Negotiations established locations of sites for collection and assured [...] UN control but did not lay out [provisions for] long-term storage such as what could be done to preserve weapons ([...] barrels, etc.).

(Y015)   UN would control access.

(Y016)   Weapons moving within the exclusion zones had to be escorted by UNPROFOR for the purpose of maintenance and training. No large quantities of weapons were allowed to be withdrawn. No transit through exclusion zones of heavy weapons. Mines if lifted by respective party engineers could be retained. No weapons, [ammunition], or explosives could be stored within old positions in the zone of separation.

(Y017)   On the Serb side were depots for the storage of arms with "double-key" system, but all of them were outside of my [area of responsibility].

(Y026)   On top level, general directives. On lower level, detailed agreements.

(Y027)   See above.

(Y030)   The same as under 5.3.

(Y042)   The main principle that [the] UN store and keep the weapons [and at] the same time provide security and protection to the local population in the UNPA's.

(Y044)   Storage [of] weapons under [...] UN [supervision].

(Y045)   Storing the arms within stores close to [the] UN. Headquarters use the local army protection at hand.

(Y047)   It was to the UN military.

(Y048) The negotiations were on the level of [the] Sector [Commander] and Corps [Commanders] at the lower level up to Battalion [Commander] (UNPF) and Brigades Commander of warring parties.

(Y054) All arms were collected at different storage points and kept under the permanent supervision and protection of UNPROFOR personnel, and the parties had access to them once a week for maintenance purposes.

(Y057) All negotiations were under [the] direct control of [the] Sector Commander. UNPROFOR HQ was not involved.

(Y069) The storage of arms under UN control.

(Y074) Weapons depots were set up under joint UN/party control. If a situation occurred which threatened the safety of that party, the UN would release their weapons to them.

(Y080) All arms into storage and [...] checked by UN/ECMM.

(Y088) Weapons were stored in perfect condition with sentries from their parties, and military observers could only check and report on the number of weapons stored or missed on the sites on a daily basis.

(Y094) Regarding the maintenance of the stored weapons to be done on a regular basis or in special cases upon requirement of the parties.

(Y095) Only for the maintenance of them.

(Y097) Aucune; il n'y a eu en fait aucun stockage d'armes pendant ma période de commandement.
[None; in fact, there was no storage of arms during my period of command.]

(Y126) The negotiations had to do with the creation of weapon storage areas separately for Serbs and Bosnian government forces. These storage areas were UN-administered.

(Y127) Weapons to be under lock at central points which will be guarded by UN peacekeepers.

(Y129) None.

(Y130) I cannot describe all the various agreements that were made in only 4 lines and certainly out of [the] context of the situation we were in.

(Y137) See 5.3.

(Y138) To give in weapons at certain times in certain places.

(Y147) Dual key, inspection of storage sites, [and] patrolling in the withdrawal areas.

(Y149) Brigade levels, battalion level.

(Y151) As above.

(Y159) As some weapons should be stored out of 20 km and the area was not so wide, [a] special and particular agreement was reached.

(Y160) On some occasions the Serb forces burst into the above-mentioned magazines. Sector Commander sent complaint letter to Serb Sector Commander and informed [...] upper command.

(Y172) UN security, double locking, daily inspection.

(Y174) As above.

Q5.5   **Was there a conflict between these *new* agreements and the *original* agreement and/or mandate?**

Yes: 15   No: 20

(Y063)   Small arms were allowed [and] widespread.

(Y090)   [The Demilitarized Zone] (Zepa), [Total Exclusion Zone] (Sarajevo), [and] [Military Exclusion Zone] (Gorazde) were in addition to [the] original agreements.

VI. PROTECTION OF THE POPULATION DURING THE MISSION:

Q6.1.   **Did you consider the protection of the population when negotiating disarmament clauses with the warring parties?**

Yes: 31   No: 10

Q6.2.   **Was the protection of the population a part of your mission?**

Yes: 31   No: 14

Q6.3   **If so, did you have the means to do so?**

Yes: 18   No: 16

(Y097)   Non; je n'ai jamais reçu les renforts prévus dans les résolutions du Conseil de sécurité.
[No, I never received the reenforcements scheduled in the resolutions of the Security Council.]

Q6.4   **What were the three most important means at your disposal to achieve this objective?**

(Y010)   Large numbers of [armored personnel carriers] which permitted rapid deployment and protection for roadblocks, checkpoints and search operations. Excellent thermal and night vision devices. Large numbers of well-armed and trained soldiers.

(Y013) To protect civilians, military observers had the deterrent factor of being able to report what was happening. In some cases this observation alone was a deterrence. In other cases mere reporting was not enough to stop [the] slaughter of civilians.

(Y015) Military force, moral high ground, financial or material resources (fuel for roads, food, etc.).

(Y016) Active civic program to educate population on terms of cease-fire agreement. Escorting civilians and providing protection patrol in sensitive areas. Physical protection of mixed villages and regular patrols. Presence within area of operations to provide [the] greatest confidence possible, especially near confrontation lines.

(Y017) My own battalion.

(Y024) As a construction unit only by being present and showing the flag.

(Y026) A well-trained and disciplined unit. Proper armament, even if not armed heavily enough. Good surveillance equipment.

(Y027) One excellent battalion (fully equipped and trained) of the force deployed. Useful UNCIVPOL organization and process. Lengthy and involved negotiations at local levels. It worked well until higher HQ got involved.

(Y030) Information to population through [the] media. Discussing and explaining [the] process to local administrations.

(Y042) My own [armored personnel carriers]/company size. SAS/landrovers with machine guns and four information companies. The back up support from other UN units and NATO close air support.

(Y044) [Cease-fire]. Withdrawal [of] the weapons.

(Y045) Given the opportunity to observe our control [of] the arms. Being armed to defend yourself increased [the] danger.

(Y047) To protect the minority of people and to let them feel secure and safe.

(Y048) There were no actual means to achieve this except the word of honor of the warring parties and the availability of UN [peacekeeping forces] at locations.

(Y054) Four   infantry   battalions.   Military   police. UNPROFOR/[UNCIVPOL].

(Y057) Personal guarantee of Sector Commander for safety of all. One full mechanized battalion to enforce control. Military Sector Commander and Civil Affairs Coordinator planned everything together (first-rate relationship).

(Y060) Purely negotiation and good will, when it was available.

(Y069) The UN monitoring [of] local police. The agreement between UN and local authorities. The UN propaganda.

(Y074) Patrols, verification of access to the UNPA, UNCIVPOL monitors.

(Y075) The normal means of the infantry battalion. Cooperation with local and UN police.

(Y094) Troops (under direct command), Civil Affairs Coordinator, UNCIVPOL, UNHCR.

(Y095) Humanitarian relief, press and information.

(Y097) Des unités deployées dans les zones de sécurité et sur le terrain. L'appui aérien rapproché, mais pratiquement impossible à utiliser dû à la lenteur de réactions des Nations Unies, au manque de troupes sur le terrain. Les réunions avec les commandants en chef des trois parties en guerre.
[The units which were deployed in the security zones and on the ground. Close air support, but this was practically impossible to use because of the slow reactions of the UN and the lack of troops on the ground. Meetings between the chief commanders of the three warring parties.]

(Y126) By observing and reporting weapons violations in UNPA's for prompt action. By following up and monitoring the actions of forces passing through an area in order to report any violations. Meeting with heads of factions in order to relay grievances of locals to them and come to terms on how to avoid violations.

(Y130) The ability to interpose my forces, [the] establishment of observation posts/checkpoints, [and] a robust and professional approach.

(Y136) UNPROFOR did not achieve this objective because the [...] troops were not able to take [...] charge in the area. It was the warring parties who decided what the troops could do or not. The UN troops were not able/willing to put strength behind the words.

(Y137) The partly firm attitude of the BHC Force Commander forcing the warring factions to negotiate. NATO aircraft with air-to-ground capability. Armored firepower ([armored personnel carriers] and tanks).

(Y138) UN observers, UN forces and the world threat [of an] embargo.

(Y147) Military units: patrolling [and] interpositioning. Civilian police (UN): patrolling [and] investigation. Demining.

(Y149) UNPROFOR military troops, UNCIVPOL, UNMO's and civil affairs.

(Y151) Patrol of potential conflict areas/zones. Transfer of civilian population to safe areas. Air strikes in case of extreme provocation [or] danger.

(Y160) Cooperation of UNHCR, Red Cross, etc.

Analyst's Comments:

   Protective tasks include the safeguarding of individuals, communities and installations. Protective measures tend to use up manpower. A commander should therefore balance protective requirements against the need for more operational measures. Measures used for protection can be any one or combination of the following:

-   *precautionary measures such as basic security safeguards;*
-   *tactical measures such as escorts and pickets;*
-   *contingency measures including such things as evacuation plans, rapid deployment forces, etc.;*
-   *protected areas which aim to create the conditions under which communities can respect and observe the law without outside interference or attack; and*
-   *control measures such as prohibitions and restrictions (curfews, roadblocks, searches, patrols, etc.) with the aim to:*
    -   *deter violent or criminal activity,*
    -   *restrict the potential for riotous assemblies,*
    -   *limit the illegal traffic of war supplies or contraband,*

- *apprehend wanted persons, and*
- *detect patterns of activity and gain information.*

The application of accepted military doctrine for conventional operations, which was designed around the four Geneva Conventions of 1949 relating to the protection of victims of war, seems to be of little importance to belligerent parties in the former Yugoslavia. The value of human life and human rights seems to be over shadowed by the pursuits of the belligerent parties. Evidence has shown that some belligerent parties even use their own population as a shield against attacks from other forces or acts of retribution by UNPROFOR/NATO. When the belligerent parties do not even value the lives and rights of their own peoples, the Force Commander can employ whichever protection measures he chooses, but the population will still suffer casualties. (This is indeed the case in the former Yugoslavia.)

UNPROFOR was deployed in areas in Croatia designated as United Nations Protected Areas (UNPA's) in which the Security Council judged that special interim measures were required to ensure that a lasting cease-fire was maintained. The original UN plan was envisaged to protect the population and rested on two key elements, namely: the removal of the JNA from all of Croatia and the demobilization of the UNPA's. It also involved the restoration and continued functioning of the local authorities and police. The mandate called on UNPROFOR to ensure that the UNPA's were demilitarized, through the withdrawal or disbandment of all armed forces inside them, and that all persons inside them were protected from fear of armed attack. To achieve this UNPROFOR was authorized to control access to the UNPA's, to ensure that the UNPA's remain demilitarized and to monitor the functioning of the local police. Disarmament per se was not mentioned in the Security Council Resolution, but it was implied, and good ground was made in removing and compounding heavy weapons in the area. This unfortunately was undone in January 1993 when the Serbs broke into several storage areas and reclaimed their weapons.

As can be seen from the responses, the main measures of protection were indeed employed. But the declaration of the UN Protected Areas/UN Safe Areas, and the subsequent efforts to rid them of arms and heavy weapons, were not successful. The reason for this does not lie in the concept of Safe Areas, but in the lack of will to enforce them with all means at the disposal of the force. Humanitarian operations continued to be seriously obstructed. Access to the population in need was repeatedly denied or sabotaged for political or military purposes, especially by the Bosnian Serb and Bosnian Croat sides. Threats against the security of UNPROFOR and UNHCR personnel were frequent and strained the relief and protection issues even more.

One of the tasks of the military component was to protect what little infrastructure and fixed assets remained in the theater of operations and which were of importance to the UN mission and the region. Light and medium indirect fire weapons and missiles were constantly used by some of the belligerent parties to attack their opponents' infrastructure, population, and forces, sometimes with devastating effect. Yet in its effort to disarm the belligerent parties of these weapons, UNPROFOR remained reluctant to exercise its mandate to compound or destroy them.

SECTION TWO

VII. FORCE COMPOSITION AND FORCE STRUCTURE

Q7.1   Was the force composition for your mission area unilateral or multilateral?

Unilateral: 01   Multilateral: 48

Q7.2   Describe the three most important advantages in acting in the manner described in 7.1.

(Y002)   Réduire les risques d'accusation de non-neutralité par les parties en conflit.
[Diminish the risks of accusations of non-neutrality by the parties to the conflict.]

(Y009)   Credibility, impartiality, and the support of the international community.

(Y010)   Proved the UN is multinational organization with a single purpose.

(Y013) Symbol of international concern. Normal UNMO team had at least 2 or 3 nationalities so catered for several biases (Islamic, East European, NATO, Nordic, etc.) rather than strength (weapons) for security.

(Y014) Neutral, representatives from many countries, different views of problems.

(Y015) Impartiality, experience, perspective of sub-unit commanders.

(Y016) Unity of commitment by large number of countries to mission. Impartial appearance to belligerents. Ability to generate required number of troops for large missions.

(Y017) Allows the improvement of capabilities of each battalion, allows the exchange of information, [and] facilitates the knowledge of different procedures.

(Y024) Large support from the outside world. Different views [of] the crisis.

(Y025) The costs [were] divided up [between] many countries. Internationalism. Disperse knowledge.

(Y026) No single nation was dominating. Improved "independence" of the force. A physical show of world community.

(Y027) Procurement of sufficient troops. Showed a world-wide support for the UN [Security Council Resolution]. Spread the wealth of talent to be employed in the best place.

(Y028) Neutrality.

(Y030) Contributing countries have different strengths and weaknesses (impossible to answer).

(Y042) Make the force of many nations against one nation rather than one against one and to avoid hatred and revenge. Mutual military, plans, ideas, [and] experience [lead to] cooperation. Avoid religion problems with the warring parties.

(Y043) Its strength [was] the impartiality.

(Y044) UN units well-trained. Doing well on the ground. Good coordination.

(Y047) Taking action was taken from all multilaterally.

(Y048) Skill and knowledge, cooperation, [and good] training.

(Y054) Stronger moral support from the world community. Different experiences in peacekeeping. More possibilities of getting well-experienced people in UN missions.

(Y057) Avoids the pitfalls associated with one single force (its weakness).

(Y060) Greater involvement of the international community; more integration of personnel from various countries; the understanding of one another.

(Y063) International legitimacy.

(Y069) Professional knowledge. The UN guarantee. The UN support.

(Y074) Expertise from the different nations. Varying degrees of language skills in English. Credibility in the eyes of the two parties.

(Y080) Complete experience [...].

(Y088) Balance national interests. Avoid biases from specific countries. Spread responsibility [...] among people from different countries.

(Y090) Cooperation, possibility of covering more extension in areas, flexibility.

(Y094) The only advantage is to comply with UN integration of military forces.

(Y095) More and new experience (personnel and professional); more knowledge about equipment, vehicles, weapons, etc.; more impartiality and control between themselves.

(Y097) Reflet de la communauté internationale. Reflet des trois parties en guerre; par example à Sarajevo: Ukrainiens, Slaves, orthodoxes; Egyptiens, musulmans; France, chrétiens.
[Reflection of the international community [and] of the three warring parties. For example in Sarajevo: Ukrainian Orthodox Slavs; Egyptian Muslims; French Christians.]

(Y126) It had the support of the world body. Financially it was self-supporting. More experiences were employed in solving problems.

(Y127) Different views were expressed.

(Y129) UN seen as multinational, [and] therefore, representative. Eased [the] burden of [the] peacekeepers.

(Y136) Impartiality, neutrality, [and] the different training of officers.

(Y137) Several nations would react if serious harassment toward UN personnel took place.

(Y138) Broad political back-up from participating countries. Major peacekeeping experience present. Nations present with a higher level of sophisticated technical equipment and education for using it.

(Y147) Procedures improved by "watching" the other unit.

(Y149) Respect of neutrality.

(Y151) Effective command and control. No coordination problems. No cultural differences.

(Y159) It shows impartiality.

(Y160) Exchange of ideas among the components. Support each other all the time.

(Y169) Impartiality is granted.

(Y174) Broad base of national representation.

Q7.3 **Describe the three most important disadvantages in acting in the manner described in 7.1.**

(Y002) Composition des Etats Majors selon la règle de la proportionalité aux effectifs engagés. D'où beaucoup d'officiers incompétents et non motivés. Des bataillons très inégaux en équipement, entraînement, motivation etc...
[Composition of the major states according to the proportionality of the pledged forces. So many officers were incompetent and unmotivated. Some batallions were very unequal in equipment, training, motivation, etc.]

(Y009) Command and control issues, differences in training, differences in equipment.

(Y010) Major disparities in equipment and training. Serious language problems.

(Y013) Warring parties initially suspicious [of] certain nationalities. Communications between different nationalities in Force sometimes a problem. Cultural differences between different nationalities required tolerance.

(Y014) Different experience and training. Too many from the "third world". Everybody was not so active or interested.

(Y015) Incompetence of third world armies/contributing nations, equipment deficiencies, bias or partiality of other nations.

(Y016) Varying levels of experience among contributing nations. Compatibility of equipment and sufficient types of equipment. Language commonality.

(Y017) The most important were the different points of view [on] the fulfillment of the mandate. Level of risk that the different battalions were [exposed] to [...]. Procedures and language problems at low levels.

(Y024) Units without any kind of proper experience were deployed. [This was a] disaster in some areas. In some areas total lack of support/cooperation by the local population.

(Y025) Cooperation. Different cultures.

(Y026) Different _modus operandi_, too wide a cultural gap, [and] locals could play on [these] cultural differences.

(Y027) Standards of units vary greatly from excellent to poor. Wide variety of equipment. UN accepted forces made available simply for the number count, not for capability.

(Y028) Big differences in competence of troops, material and training level.

(Y042) The forces [do] not [have] the same capabilities and efficiency. Language difficulties. Different resources of spare parts and technical aid.

(Y043) Sometimes [there was a] lack of coordination.

(Y044) [...]. Different habits.

(Y047) There was no disadvantage.

(Y048) Language problems [and] time to adapt to the culture of others.

(Y054) Different qualities of personnel, even some low [quality] people. Different levels of professionalism, with some partly-trained and equipped soldiers. Difficulties with the chain of command because of national interferences.

(Y057) Some forces are excellent [and] others a joke. Language and procedures vary greatly. Some forces come unprepared and are totally dependent on the UN for everything.

(Y060) Language, procedures, [and] some distrust between former NATO/Warsaw Pact antagonists.

(Y063) [Heterogeneous] command structure. Situation perception and concept differences between contigents. Dynamic operations impossible.

(Y069) Language problems. Different customs. Different military education.

(Y074) Different methods of executing the tasks (inconsistent), poor equipment in some continents, varying staff experience in the HQ.

(Y075) Different procedures.

(Y080) Work ethic, idleness, national interests.

(Y088) Difficult coordination of field procedures. Communications problems. Different way of thinking could cause clashes among participating nations.

(Y090) Languages fluency, UN/DIS coordination.

(Y094) No uniform code of military justice to enforce discipline between different nationalities, language, different doctrine of employment.

(Y095) Difficulties in communication (language), lack of capacity and training in this type of mission for some countries, difficulties [working] in an organization which includes civilian members.

(Y097) Tour de Babel - très difficile à commander, aucune homogénéité des contingents, imixtion inacceptable des nations contributrices dans la conduite des opérations.
[Tower of Babel - very difficult to command, no homogeneity in the contingents, inacceptable interference by contributing nations in the conducting of operations.]

(Y126) Language was a problem as the locals had to deal with people speaking different languages. English was a problem [for] some military observers. There were traces of racism displayed by some UN personnel.

(Y127) Some participants had different agendas [than] what the UN wanted. Because of country alliances, problems were handled with an eye on relationships.

(Y129) Languages, communications, [and] doctrines all different.

(Y136) The lack of UN experience, the lack of military training, [and] the language problem.

(Y137) Several units where unfit for their task (ethnic or climatic factors), confusion due to language problems, [and] different equipment (non-NATO standard).

(Y138) Absence of unitary policy for commanding control. Lack of good administrative regulations. Vague organizational structure on the civilian component in the force HQ.

(Y139) Composed of soldiers not speaking English.

(Y147) Different concepts about the execution of the mission. Lack of confidence by one of the conflicting parties. Language problems.

(Y149) Language problems, no common procedures, different level of competencies [and] capacities.

(Y151) Less transparent and perceived suspicions continue about each other.

(Y159) Lack of common military training, real communication.

(Y160) Different ways of action for the same proposal. Different capabilities (no equals) among battalions.

(Y169) I don't see any.

(Y172) Lack of ability to communicate. Lack of willingness to coordinate and cooperate with each other. Lack of effective direction and command due to multi-lateral headquarters.

(Y174) Unprofessional, ill-disciplined and trained troops. Lack of standard operating procedures. Lack of communication.

Q7.4   **If you worked in a multilateral context: how important was consensus (with peacekeepers from other countries) for the achievement of disarmament and demobilization components during the operation?**

(Y009) It was very important.

(Y010) Consensus is important but the support and backing of the local sector HQ is critical.

(Y013) Consensus was required for military observer reporting.

(Y014) Very much.

(Y015) Not.

(Y016) Extremely important.

(Y017) It was the most important point.

(Y026) A military formation in the field does not need consensus as the commander has the right to command.

(Y027) Consensus was not a problem as we had the agreement in hand. Supplementing them was a different matter given the diversity of religion, race, training etc.

(Y030) Sector Commander would - give directives for implementing components. There was no problem as regards consensus.

(Y042) Very important because the warring parties will start comparing the procedures between this country and other ones and they take benefit from the differences.

(Y043) Very good cooperation.

(Y044) To reach agreement of [cease-fire violations] or peace agreement in the area.

(Y047) [It] was not important.

(Y048) The impartiality of UN forces assisted in this achievement.

(Y054) Not so important.

(Y057) Very little in some cases. Western army staffs took control because others (with rare exceptions) were incompetent.

(Y060) Not relevant as it was a UN force.

(Y063) Consensus was established through [the] mandate [...]. Disarmament, a dynamic UN operation, was only made possible by Canada's and France's commitment of troops.

(Y069) Was very important.

(Y074) Extremely important, even critical. If all continents do not apply the same determination to disarm the two sides, the UN [loses] credibility and some nations are accused of being over-zealous.

(Y075) The most important thing is the commander's ability, not consensus.

(Y080) Total.

(Y088) Not important.

(Y090) Total, because the mandate was very clear.

(Y094) At the beginning it was very important.

(Y095) Always the same, very low.

(Y097) Ce concensus est très important. En outre, l'impartiabilité est une donnée essentielle du comportement des Casques bleus dans une telle situation.
[This consensus is very important. Furthermore, impartiality is an essential characteristic of the behavior of the Blue Helmets in such a situation.]

(Y126) It was [easier] to achieve consensus because most peacekeepers did not have any [personal] interest in the situation.

(Y129) Vital.

(Y130) The military chain of command functions, hence consensus was not an issue.

(Y137) Very important, but hardly obtainable.

(Y138) Consensus was most important.

(Y139) Very important.

(Y147) Extremely important.

(Y149) Very important, while each party was hiding behind the most "easy" UN component.

(Y159) It was not so important. Applying to the [Cease-fire Agreement] was paramount.

(Y160) It was normal for these circumstances.

(Y169) Was very important but there was not disagreement at any time.

(Y172) Very important.

(Y174) No significant problem in consensus only in carrying operation out.

Q7.5.   Was adequate consideration given to the disarmament component as the mission evolved?

Adequate:　　　30　　　Inadequate:　　　17

(Y097) Adéquate pour autant que la maîtrise des armements a toujours été au centre des préoccupations.
[Adequate as long as the control of arms was always at the center of attention.]

Q7.6   If it was inadequate, explain how this affected your mission (mention the three most important issues).

(Y013) Procedures to deal with heavy weapons exclusion zones were developed at short notice under threat of NATO airstrikes. Long term strategy could have led to consistent policy; for example, [a] trade-off between UN troops needed to control weapons collection [...] and these troops becoming a shield of hostages against further airstrikes.

(Y017) Because I had two ways. First, act immediately against the violation, maybe against the wishes of Force Commander or Sector Commander. Second, wait for orders. That delays allows the violator to improve. Fourth position because the "status two situation" gave him a great benefit.

(Y025) The warring factions can use the weapons.

(Y043) There was [a] delay in processing the mission.

(Y057) Sector West succeeded despite [the] UN because it had excellent leaders. Two battalions out of four were adequately trained.

(Y063) As small arms were widespread [and] at the disposal of the population, protection of endangered ethnic minorities demanded [an] unproportionately large number of troops.

(Y071) Fighting between warring parties was [making it] very difficult to accomplish our tasks.

(Y074) Requirement for authority [to] conduct cordon and search [operations] without specific justification.

(Y088) Fighting between warring parties was continuously making [it] very difficult to accomplish our tasks.

(Y095) Less trust in our forces. More difficulties [in achieving] the objective.

(Y127) The UN did not consider the fact that the war was still going on and the disarmament could only materialize when there was a cease-fire. [...] saw it as a weakling in some of the policies of war.

(Y129) No guidelines other than a [...] of disarmament - heavy weapons first.

(Y136) Not possible to fulfill the mandate/agreements. Security threat against UN personnel. Restricted movements.

(Y137) Convoys were stopped by armed factions. Helicopters and [aircraft] at risk for being shot down by [anti-aircraft artillery] or missiles. The fighting and shelling of civilian targets kept on.

(Y151) Did not affect the mission as disarmament was not one of our objectives.

(Y169) The inadequate storage of the weapons allowed the parties to continue using them, [e.g.,] cases of Krajina and Sarajevo.

(Y172) We kept getting shot at. Local forces would not cooperate.

(Y174) Parties [were] not committed to pursuing disarmament and therefore [it was] not achieved. No means to force them to disarm.

Q7.7   Did the force composition identify a specific structure to support the disarmament component of the mandate?

Yes: 14   No: 32

Q7.8   If so, what was it?

(Y014) By rules.

(Y015) Not necessary, it was just one function of many and was never a high priority.

(Y016) UN military units [and] UN military observers.

(Y017) The battalions' structure.

(Y030) [With the] Sector Commander's guidance, the force [composed] a plan of action for [the] implementation of [the] disarmament component.

(Y042) A light/heavy infantry company within its sector forms a force to cordon the objective area and a part of the force to inspect the suspected area and a reserve force at every level ready to deal with any emergency case.

(Y047)   The UN forces.

(Y057)   Battalions to control.

(Y069)   The battalions' composition and the HQ structure.

(Y090)   [Storing] depots of armament till the moment of destruction.

(Y094)   The force has to be divided in different elements, i.e. control, security, administration, [and] liaison.

(Y138)   Head of civil affairs with civilian police under command and control.

(Y149)   Joint commissions at all levels.

(Y159)   The UN battalions in their [areas of responsibility].

Q7.9   **Did the force composition allow for verification and monitoring measures for the control of weapons and disarmament?**

Yes: 34   **No: 12**

(Y097)   Oui, AURAIT permis.
         [Yes, should permit.]

Q7.10   **If so, what were they?**

(Y009)   I was authorized by the mandate through the operational order of the [Force Commander].

(Y010)   Use of storage sites [and] patrols in the UNPA. Use of UNMO's/ECMM team outside the UNPA.

(Y013)   Once there was a need then forces were allocated to the task, such as radar units to monitor mortar usage.

(Y014) Regular inspections of weapon stores.

(Y015) Physical control, inspection, enforcement.

(Y016) See 7.8.

(Y017) The battalion structure itself.

(Y024) Military observers as an independent organization.

(Y030) The approximate number and location of weapons was assured by UNPROFOR intelligence officers. After weapons were withdrawn monitoring was carried out regularly.

(Y042) The [battalion] sector divided into companies' sector with a reserve at the [battalion] level and the sector level.

(Y054) Detailed orders were issued through the chain of command.

(Y057) The battalions did the controlling.

(Y063) Patrolling in exclusion zones and double lock systems on weapons collection sites.

(Y069) Checkpoints and patrolling.

(Y074) Inspections, patrols.

(Y075) Professional proficiency.

(Y080) Monitoring-checks, etc.

(Y090) [Store] and destroy.

(Y094) Inform the warring parties, control the execution of tasks, secure the areas, inventory and record the weapons which are stored [as well as] those withdrawn and those still on the field.

(Y126) Inspections were done on a daily basis by UN observers to look at weapon sites and areas.

(Y127) The observers were given additional tasks to monitor the disarmament.

(Y130) Patrols, observation posts and checkpoints.

(Y137) Helicopters could sometimes check front lines and areas supposed to be weapon-free zones.

(Y139) Patrolling [and] helicopter surveillance.

(Y149) Checkpoints, links of storage sites, [and] UN badges for local police.

(Y151) Observation, patrolling, inspection.

(Y159) UNMO's on the Croatian side and UN battalions's on Serb side.

(Y160) In some cases each battalion supported the other battalions to achieve the proposal.

(Y169) To check the storage areas and have our [...].

(Y174) UNMO's.

Q7.11   Was the chosen force structure appropriate for executing the mission?

Yes: 28   No: 16

(Y010) Varied widely depending upon the nation involved.

(Y097) Non, insuffisante
[No, insufficient.]

Q7.12 **Were the units efficient for the mission given?**

Yes: 28   No: 17

(Y010) Varied widely.

(Y026) Some units were indeed inefficient.

(Y097) Oui, la plupart.
[Yes, most were.]

Q7.13 **Were the units appropriate for conducting the disarmament operations?**

Yes: 23   No: 21

(Y010) Varied widely.

(Y026) Some units were indeed inefficient.

(Y097) Oui, la plupart.
[Yes, most were.]

Q7.14 **Were your units augmented with specific personnel and equipment for the disarmament mission?**

Yes: 08   No: 37

(Y026) There was no need for that, as a special organization was created for the task.

Q7.15 **If so, what additional capabilities did they provide? (List the five most important ones.)**

(Y013) Additional observers were deployed to monitor heavy weapon use. Eventually some observers were relieved by deployment of radars designed to locate mortars or artillery firing. The radar unit [was] located next to the observer HQ so observers could investigate findings of radar unit.

(Y016) Understanding and interpretation of agreement. Well-equipped, highly mechanized unit. Well-disciplined and well-led troops. Thorough understanding of low level conflict resolution. Aggressive proactive implementation of agreements.

(Y017) One mortar 120mm platoon.

(Y042) Engineer capabilities. Work as reserve (company size) at sector level. Help blocking the roads to push warring parties to leave a new checkpoint. Show of force to push warring parties [to] listen to our demands. Help humanitarian aid due to lack of [a] number of working members.

(Y057) One engineer regiment was brought in for demining.

(Y090) [One] more battalion.

(Y126) Weapon specialists. Ammunition technicians. Mine detection equipment.

(Y130) Command and control, knowledge of weapons systems, [and] communications.

Q7.16   If you were a commander, were you briefed by HQ's prior to your disarming mission and before your arrival in the area of operations?

Yes: 24   No: 07

Q7.17   Did the security situation in the mission area allow for weapons control an disarmament operations?

Yes: 25   No: 21

(Y097) Oui, partiallement.
[Yes, partially.]

Q7.18   If not, what steps were required in order to establish and maintain a secure environment?

(Y009) An important part of the force was carrying out security operations in order to maintain a secure environment.

(Y014) Cease-fire [and] mine clearing.

(Y024) To stop the continuing hostilities [and] fix [...] fire after which to start disarming. However, all efforts collapsed in Croatia [in] January 1993 when the Croatian army attacked [the] Majlenica-Zemunic area.

(Y026) Establishment and maintainence of cease-fire, mutual trust, [and] investigation of breaches of the cease-fire.

(Y045) To give the local authorities the trust in UN [peacekeeping] which was not effective.

(Y047) The step was to disarm weapons.

(Y048) By enforcing the agreement [with] extra UN forces and NATO.

(Y054) Negotiate an agreement. Obtain the withdrawal of the armies. Provide security to the whole UNPA. Convince both sides [of] your neutrality.

(Y060) The basis of the agreement needed broader acceptance and the force should have been better armed.

(Y088) General cease-fire agreement. Access for UN to fighting units up to battalion level. Access for UN to weapon inventories of the parties. Effective control of depots under UN control.

(Y097) La signature du "Military agreement", le 11 août 1993 aurait dû permettre de conduire des opérations de maîtrise des armements prévues dans l'Accord.
[The signing of the military agreement on 11 August 1993 should have permitted the beginning of the arms control operations scheduled in the accord.]

(Y126) Local factions could be informed so that they act more friendly to UN personnel. Local factions to be stopped from firing close to UN personnel.

(Y127) The war was still going on and these [...] could give out their weapons. This was no cease-fire.

(Y129) Cease-fire agreements, military (UN) patrols, [and] military (UN) convoy escorts.

(Y137) The roads would have to be UN controlled. Artillery units would have to be threatened by air-attacks in areas where they were capable of firing at cities or UN installations. Border control means.

(Y139) More troops and UN weapons.

(Y147) Cooperation of the local civilian and military authorities. Appropriate mandate: use of force. More troops.

(Y151) Greater willingness of warring factions through joint commission activity. Effective embargo on supply of military aid. More powers for effective retaliation in case of need.

(Y160) Checkpoints were established at all access points around the UNPA's.

(Y169) The situation in Yugoslavia was very confused in this aspect.

(Y172) Stop the fighting. Effective [rules of engagement] for UN units.

Q7.19 **Did these force protection measures affect the accomplishment of the disarmament operations positively or negatively?**

Positively: 17   Negatively: 10

Q7.20 **Elaborate on the impact mentioned in 7.19 above.**

(Y002) Je me réfère aux opérations de regroupement des armes lourdes égales ou supérieures au calibre 12 (exemple: l'obus de 5 février 1994 à Sarajevo). La grande dispersion des unités pour contrôler les regroupements d'armes a été un handicap majeur pour l'application éventuelle de frappes aériennes.

[I am refering to the operations for the collection of heavy weapons equal or greater than 12 caliber (e.g. the shelling of 5 February 1994 in Sarajevo). The widespread dispersion of the units for controlling the arms collection was a major disadvantage for the eventual application of airstrikes.]

(Y009) Negotiations between political leaders were essentia! to accomplish the mission.

(Y026) When there is no shooting from [the] opposite party, you might persuade people to hand in their weapons.

(Y030) Initially negatively. To remove weapons from the combatants is a sensitive issue and often makes the combatants and the force as a whole feel defenseless.

(Y042) The measures helped to see the area clean [and] without long arms.

(Y043) There was [a] threat to the lives of personnel of [the] UN [peacekeeping force].

(Y045) Distrust of the local army [toward the] UN.

(Y047) The peace agreement was not functioning.

(Y054) The disarmament process ran smoothly and without major problems.

(Y069) The measures were according [to] the agreement of the disarmament operations.

(Y074) Sound security measures give [a] positive impression to belligerents and therefore make the force more credible.

(Y080) We were not arrested/harassed.

(Y094) The disarmament operation is a demonstration of [...] UN authority and gives security.

(Y095) They were mentioned in VII. 7.3 and 7.6.

(Y126) The measures to a large extent were positive. In a lot of instances, however, the warring parties aimed direct and indirect weapons at UN troops.

(Y129) The measures allowed humanitarian aid to be delivered.

(Y147) To show the willingness and resolve of the force.

(Y149) In fact, no impact, no problems.

(Y151) Nowhere effective disarmament control could be exercised.

(Y159) The structure was adequate, but the parties did not help to perform the operations.

(Y160) In one way positively because UN forces had [...] proper control of locals, but sometimes [it] was negative because some people (no regular) took different ways [...].

Q7.21   Were command and control/operational procedures adequate for your task?

Yes: 28   No: 12

Q7.22   If not, mention three examples which demonstrate their inadequacy.

(Y009) Intelligence did not exist, [...] lack of an efficient logistical support, inadequate communications.

(Y024) Lack of proper force level communications during the first 6 months. HQ/ UNPROFOR was relocated several times, [and there was] no contact [with] the superiors for long time.

(Y026) Lack of clear tasks, lack of information, [and] lack of coordination.

(Y043) As a UNMO you [could not] defend yourself.

(Y063) The UNMO organization was not operationally integrated. The quality of force staff officers was too poor. Reporting from units [was] too slow: only UNMO's had adaquate and quick communications.

(Y071) "Cooperation" between military engineers, military logistics and the Administrative Office never worked properly, due to the system (separate chains of command) and not to the individuals (relationship has been quite good).

(Y097) Manque de structures du commandement. Ambiguïté concernant la subordination réelle des contingents.
[Lack of command structure. Ambiguity concerning the hierarchy of the contingents.]

(Y137) Air operations should be manned 24 hours. Sometimes missions could not be carried out due to lack of HQ coordination, lack of [navigational] aids to operate in bad weather. Bad intelligence information (too late and insufficient [...]).

(Y139) There is no centralized [command and control] of air assets in UNPROFOR.

(Y172) Inability of HQ to provide any backup force. Inability of HQ officers to communicate with each other on an effective level. Lack of command or direction from a high level.

(Y174) Lack of personnel resources, lack of equipment, lack of plans/policy/direction.

Q7.23 **Summarize your salient experiences with command and control/operational procedures while on this mission.**

(Y009) On the military side, chain of command was excellent except [for the] lack of intelligence; UN logistical support was very slow.

(Y014) There were some problems [regarding] how to use UNMO organizations contra UNPROFOR forces. Sometimes we did [...] the same things.

(Y017) First, the command and control system must allow the commander [...] complete control over all positions, patrols, [operations, and] CP. Deployed in the field (24 hours/day). He must receive reliable information in the same moment that [...] incidents occur. Second, the UN operational procedures are correct and are good guidelines to preform almost all the duties.

(Y025) Position of power must be clear. Good communications.

(Y026) Directly superior HQ was in total disarray. Lack of operational procedures. Lack of   common training and standards. Language problems.

(Y028) Usually these procedures worked in a normal military way. In the beginning of the operation some troops did not obey the orders given by HQ but made national decisions.

(Y030) A straightforward operation which by and large was completed as foreseen.

(Y042) Command and control [...] depended on written procedures supported by the higher commanders' guidance and oral orders; the help provided to the units to solve any problem with the warring parties at a higher level; and the field visits to the sectors to supervise the mission fulfilled.

(Y047) The decision was not taken by ourselves.

(Y054) Necessity of issuing clear and detailed orders. Effective liaison with all parties involved. Importance of unity of command. Reliable means of communication. Comprehensive and reliable military information.

(Y060) The dedication of various components of the force, the positive response of all components, [and] variation in procedures had obvious disadvantages.

(Y063) Lack of direction. Lack of ability to react [to] events or [to] forecast events. Pretension, vanity and military "Yes Sir" culture and lack of delegation generated operational stagnation.

(Y069) The communications procedures. The UN [standard operating procedure].

(Y071) It [...] proved to be impossible to [correctly supply] the force from the very beginning [...].

(Y074) [Standard operating procedures] must be published by HQ. All components of the force must know/use the same [standard operating procedures]. We must be perceived by the parties as being competent, professional, and in control.

(Y075) A well organized unit [UN battalion] does not have any problem with command and control in this kind of mission.

(Y080) First passage of information both ways. Cooperation with all sides [in the Serbian Republic of the Krajina].

(Y090) Normally without problems. From time to time, some UN/DIS coordination between civilian and military components.

(Y094) Dissemination of information to all those concerned. Provide all the necessary support to the warring parties so as to complete the disarmament. Clearly explain the benefit of such measures. Give open and visible security to all the operations. Guarantee return of weapons when the situation returns to normality.

(Y095) I have no experience with command and control to mention.

(Y097) Problèmes de "commandement" avec l'ONU, l'OTAN. Refus d'ordre par certains contingents.
[Command problems with the UN and NATO. Refusal of orders by certain contingents.]

(Y126) The inability of some military observers to speak English created problems. Some UN observers were civilians and this adversely affected the operation. Some UN personnel, particularly Russians and some Western Europeans, seemed interested in outcome of operations.

(Y127) [...]. There was a centralized command and the Sectors also had sectoral command with positions also having their commanders.

(Y129) Little direct command and control [and] many guidelines issued.

(Y130) The procedures were established on the ground by the Ground Force Commander. Communications were critical.

(Y137) Too slow processing [...] request of air support [...]. In general too weak [a] response towards harassment.

(Y139) Confusing.

(Y147) Direct and easy access/contact with force HQ. Uniform procedures.

(Y149) One UN component used NATO procedures. Another UN component did not.

(Y151) Air strike on Ubdina airfield in Sector South took [place] five days after initiation of request. By then the target was fully aware and strike went in without any effect.

(Y159) The UNMO organization was often mixed with the sector/UNPROFOR organization, so the chain of command was not as clear as it should have been.

(Y160) Knowing the situation in the mission area, I suggest to use the force to prevent casualties in proper forces (UN).

(Y169) Commanders, communications, and [standard operating procedures] were good.

(Y172) Continually sent into front line areas without suitable vehicles, enough troops, any back-up, [and] no contingency plans.

(Y174) [Command and control] inadequate or nonexistent.

Q7.24 **What additional support (special capabilities/force multipliers) did you receive which helped the disarmament mission? List the three most important ones.**

(Y002) Sarajevo, 5 février 1994. Regroupement d'armes lourdes: hélicoptères, radars de trajectographie, unités spécialisées dans le renseignement.
[Sarajevo, February 5, 1994. Collection of heavy weapons: helicopters, trajectographic radars, special intelligence units .]

(Y009) None.

(Y014) Manpower, vehicles, radios.

(Y017) One mortar 120mm platoon.

(Y026) No need as I brought the [necessities] from [my] home [country].

(Y030) None that I recall.

(Y042) Communications [network].

(Y057) One company of engineer regiment.

(Y060) None.

(Y063) NATO air surveillance.

(Y074) We required better lift/transport in one of the battalions. This would have been a multiplier.

(Y080) None.

(Y090) Logistic support (vehicles). Personnel support (surveillance).

(Y094) None.

(Y095) Anything.

(Y097) Aucun. [None.]

(Y126) Injection of more troops from Europe and Asia. More weapons and armored vehicles.

(Y127) The warring factions at their local levels cooperated any time observers insisted on the importance of disarmament.

(Y130) Improved communications.

(Y136) Nothing at all.

(Y147) None.

(Y149) None.

(Y151) Availability of NATO air power.

(Y172) None.

(Y174) None.

Q7.25   Were they adequate?

Yes: 09   No: 10

Q7.26   **If not, what other capabilities would you have needed to make your mission more effective? (List the most relevant.)**

(Y009) More personnel, more [armored personnel carriers], better communications equipment [and] intelligence capability.

(Y017) Anti-tank weapons.

(Y047) To secure ourselves first [and then] to secure the others.

(Y054) Military information system. Mobile means of communication.

(Y060) Positive political support would have been a great help - from members of the international community. An effective public information system.

(Y063) [Sarajevo] collection points were never enforced as collection points. The disarming of heavy weapons around [Sarajevo] should have stayed high on the political agenda.

(Y071) Integration: joint civilian and military office under one command placed under the Force Commander which could have been named administrative, construction engineering and logistics office. Procurement officers should have been placed individually within the cells: construction material maintenance [policy] good.

(Y075) Intelligence [and] gathering of information (allowed).

(Y094) UNMO's and UNCIVPOL in larger numbers as well as civil affairs officials in order to give a comprehensive liaison and monitoring at all levels.

(Y095) A clear definition of the mission and talks where the peacekeepers are involved.

(Y097) Equipes spécialisées de contrôle.
[Specialized control troops.]

(Y136) Troops and commanders who were trained and capabilities to take command in the area. Of course, this means also weapons and equipment.

(Y137) More NATO troops, armed helicopters, [and] more [armored personnel carriers].

(Y149) Reports on overflights. Satellite photography. Radar devices.

(Y151) Effective implementation of all the measures is more important than paying lip service to Security Council Resolutions/mandate controversies.

(Y159) Once again, on Croatian side UNMO's were allowed only to protest and wait until the party decided to withdraw the weapons (normally not).

Analyst's Comments:

There are important issues regarding force structure and capabilities which must be considered in peacekeeping operations. First, because political factors usually influence force composition, it is important for military leaders to stress the size, composition and capabilities of the force needed, based on the threat and the requirements of the mission. Second, other factors which characterize the environment demand careful analysis before the structure and composition of the force are finalized. These factors include: the geopolitical situation; prevailing social conditions and indigenous culture; level of conflict; number, discipline and accountability of belligerent parties; and effectiveness of the cease-fire agreements and the degree of law and order that exists. Third, with all the foregoing considered, commanders and political staff must also have a common understanding of the desired end result of the operation, and the conditions that will constitute success. This will give a further indication of the force structure and capabilities needed to complete the operation successfully.

The UN does not have a standing force to execute peacekeeping operations and therefore depends on the contributions of member states. This, however, does not imply that the UN must except every offer it receives from member states. The magnitude of problems and potential problems listed by respondents in Question 7.3 can be greatly reduced by the determination and application of screening criteria based on the factors mentioned above. Some sensitivity can be applied, however, in the composition of the different force components. Personnel who more easily adopt to other cultures and ways of doing things must be utilized. Some religious customs can also cause clashes that could be prevented if the composition of the components is considered carefully. Sensitivity on the part of the donating countries about language problems can ease the stress on a mission. If donating countries could ensure a translation capability at the different levels of deployment, or offer language-trained people for missions where they are likely to be deployed with other member states, donors could help minimize communication problems to the benefit of all concerned.

Contributions to UNPROFOR up to December 1994

Country	Police	Military (not UNMO's)	Observers
Argentina	23	854	5
Bangladesh	40	1,235	43
Belgium		1,038	6
Brazil	6		34
Canada	45	2,091	15
Colombia	12		
Czech Republic		971	37
Denmark	45	1,230	14
Egypt		427	27
Finland	10	463	12
France	41	4,493	11
Ghana			32
Indonesia	15	220	29
Ireland	20		9
Jordan	71	3,367	48
Kenya	50	967	47
Lithuania		32	
Malaysia	26	1,550	27
Nepal	49	899	5
Netherlands	10	1,803	48

New Zealand		249	9
Nigeria	48		10
Norway	31	826	39
Pakistan	19	3,017	34
Poland	29	1,109	30
Portugal	39		12
Russian Federation	36	1,464	22
Slovak Republic		582	
Spain		1,267	19
Sweden	35	1,212	19
Switzerland	6		6
Tunisia	12		
Turkey		1,464	
Ukraine	9	1,147	10
United Kingdom		3,405	19
United States		748	
Venezuela			2
TOTAL	727	38,130	680

Commanders have the responsibility for the command and control of the forces assigned to them. This relationship is established through the initial mission analysis and subsequent planning. During all military missions, continual mission analysis and revision of plans takes place. The result of this process must also be reflected in the command and control arrangements, and the commander must adjust it to the situation and rectify identified problem areas. Twenty-four percent of the respondents indicated that command and control were not adequate for executing their tasks.

VIII. OPERATIONAL PROCEDURES/RULES OF ENGAGEMENT

Q8.1   **Did you abide by national or UN rules of engagement/operational procedures during the pursuit of your mission?**

         National: 04   UN: 40

Q8.2   **Were these rules/procedures adequate for the performance of your task?**

         Yes: 35   No: 08

Q8.3   **If not, what other rules should you have had?**

         (Y002)   Les contingents, nombreux, qui ne veulent pas prendre de risque sont ceux qui critiquent le plus les règles d'engagement, dont ils n'utilisent pas toutes les possibilités dans le cadre dela légitime défense.
[The numerous contingents who do not want to take risks are those who most criticize the rules of engagement, which they do not make full use of in the realm of legitimate defense.]

         (Y009)   We had general rules. At [the] battalion level we had to clarify [them] very much in order to prevent mistakes in procedure.

         (Y013)   Military observers were unarmed and did not carry armed UN personnel in their vehicles except in special cases.

         (Y026)   [Rules of engagement] were okay [but] operational procedures were missing.

(Y075) They were realistic.

(Y097) Les règles d'engagement sont un "parapluie" pour les gens qui ne veulent pas prendre de responsabilités et leur permettant de toujours trouver un responsable en cas de "bavure".
[The rules of engagement are an "umbrella" which allow the people who do not want to take responsibility to always find someone to take the blame in case of a slip-up.]

(Y127) We should have had enough protection and properly laid down rules.

(Y147) Easier use of force. Less restrictions on freedom of movement.

(Y149) Total freedom of movement [and] authority on international borders.

(Y151) Less fear of political repercussions [or] media twistings.

(Y159) Military decisions should not be so compromised by political decisions.

(Y172) Realistic [rules of engagement], i.e. use force at the direction of the unit commander without needing to reference [a] higher authority.

Q8.4   If and when the situation changed, were your rules altered accordingly?

Yes: 17   No: 21

Q8.5   If so, summarize the relevant changes.

(Y010) When threatened with attack we were authorized to dig in [and] deploy out heavy weapons(tow/mortars/anti-tank guns.)

(Y013) It was important [that] the UNMO vehicles always be identified as carrying unarmed UN personnel.

(Y014) We were always updated by our HQ.

(Y015) The changes were minor and had no practical effect.

(Y016) Amended when cease-fire agreements [were] implemented to allow for confiscation, cordon and search [operations], and [the] establishment of [a] destruction policy. Allowed for use of force when appropriate.

(Y017) Each [rule of engagement] had different options and the Sector [Commander] or even the Battalion Commander [was] able to choose the option according to [how] the situation changed. The [rules of engagement] covered a big scope and allowed the use of arms during disarmament operations.

(Y024) [For example,] rules of engagement [were] re-drafted accordingly by the Force Commander in a clear way.

(Y026) [Rules of engagement] were relevantly changed according to the operational situation.

(Y028) The change of the location of my unit and of the area of operations.

(Y045) Not applicable.

(Y047) The patrol will change.

(Y054) Sector Commanders were authorized to change [the rules of engagement] within sectors and to delegate this authority to Battalion Commanders if time did not permit [the] Sector Commander's authorization.

(Y060) Upgrading of responses under threat, though these were entirely [under] the discretion of the subordinate commander on the spot.

(Y071) No mandate and therefore no [rules of engagement] adapted to Bosnia-Herzegovina.

(Y074) They were either more or less restrictive as required [by] changing circumstances.

(Y090) New mandate [and] new rules, but always coordinated.

(Y097) Les règles d'engagement doivent être décidées par le commandant de l'opération. Elles doivent être SIMPLES et adaptées en permanence à la situation du moment. Les règles d'engagement telles qu'elles sont envisagées par l'ONU sont un exemple "d' hypocrisie".
[The rules of engagement must be determined by the commander of the operation. They must be simple and continually adapted to the current situation. The rules of engagement that are designed by the UN are an example of hypocrisy.]

(Y130) Changes to national [rules of engagement] were made but remained within UN [rules of engagement].

IX. COERCIVE DISARMAMENT AND PREVENTIVE DISARMAMENT

Q9.1   Did you have to use force (coercive disarmament) to achieve the mission as mandated?

Yes: 11   No: 28

Q9.2   **Judging from your experience, is it possible to use coercive disarmament in these types of operations?**

Yes: 24   No: 17

Q9.3   **Do you believe that force can and should be used to enforce the disarmament components of an agreement?**

Can: Yes: 30   No: 09
Should: Yes: 25   No: 13

Q9.4   **Mention three reasons why force can/cannot and should/should not be used to enforce the disarmament component of an agreement.**

(Y002) Tout dépend de la situation sur le théâtre considéré: on n'a pas les moyens d'employer la force pour désarmer des factions en ex-Yougoslavie.
[Everything depends on the situation in the area considered. There are no means to employ the force to disarm the factions in former Yugoslavia.]

(Y009) Political agreements occasionally need to be forced to occur.

(Y010) Disarmament is the only way a secure security environment can be established. The presence of weapons ensured that isolated attacks between belligerents and against the UN would continue. Neither side will use the UN to provide security if they have the means for direct retaliation.

(Y013) Use of force may appear to put [the] UN [on] one side or another. Use of force may destroy confidence-building measures. Use of force may offer [the] only way to actually enforce disarmament but will result in casualties.

(Y014) When warring parties do not follow the agreement, sometimes it is necessary to use force, to show that you take it seriously.

(Y015) Warring sides in Bosnia understand force and respect it. Disarmament between Serbs [and] Muslims [is] not realistic.

(Y016) [Force] should be used when belligerent low-level commanders do not comply with agreements by their superiors. [Force] must be used to protect civilians under UN protection who are threatened by criminals when no police system [is] in place. [Force] should not be used when parties [are] no longer interested in peace.

(Y017) Force should be used if and [when] it is the last resort to perform the disarming of a faction, [...] to [...] absolutely accomplish the mandate: for all parties [it] is the best way to maintain a peaceful and secure environment in the region. The use of [...] force, in the right place and at the right time, is the best tool that UN troops have to obtain [...] respect and acceptance from the warring parties.

(Y025) If the forces are adequately powerful. If there is no force, disarmament does not succeed.

(Y026) If one uses force, one becomes a part of the conflict, and all parties will oppose you.

(Y028) Disarmament must be agreed [to] by all parties to the conflict. [...] the parties to the conflict must take care [...], through using [...] force, when some elements of the party do not obey the agreement.

(Y030) Negotiated agreements can be followed up with a show of power and display of decisiveness.

(Y042) Change the organization of the forces to be relatively heavy to enhance [...] capabilities of self-defense and peacekeeping [...]. The UN forces can do nothing in the event of [one] party attacking another. To have the capability to apply [...] adequate pressure against any party to fulfill the UN mission.

(Y043) Because then the UN forces will fight with the local forces.

(Y045) In order to establish a peaceful climate for the conflicting parties.

(Y047) To let the people understand what [...] peacekeeping [is].

(Y054) It will help to obtain the public perception of the UN['s] capability and will carry through the process. Some show of force is necessary to be respected. Disarmament is the foundation to achieve further success.

(Y057) If stability has not been achieved before arrival it cannot be imposed. The warring factions must agree to it otherwise [the] UN becomes the enemy and cannot effectively do its mission. Peace cannot be imposed.

(Y060) It can only be used against uncontrolled elements provided the parties to the agreement concur. Actions against one party or another change the entire content of the operation in as much as it could become a Chapter VII enforcement operation.

(Y063) The UN becomes involved as a part [of the conflict] which contradicts and jeopardizes impartiality.

(Y069) To [achieve the] UN resolution, to restore [...] peace, [and] to protect the population.

(Y074) Give the perception to both parties that we mean business. Establish credibility. Increase confidence in the UN soldiers that we have the authority to fulfill the mandate.

(Y075) Since the parties agree, force would be used on violators. That is the reason for which military forces are used in peacekeeping disarmament tasks. Risks must be assumed in order to achieve the mission (if not we should use only police forces).

(Y080) To stop the pussy-footing around. Politicians have to be [...]. New York is a long way away.

(Y088) Assist UN authority. Avoid re-arming of warring factions. Protect UN people and facilities.

(Y090) It is impossible to enforce disarmament of guerilla or insurrectional troops that live in mountain or jungle terrain. If it can be done, it shouldn't, because escalation would be the consequence.

(Y094) The use of force has the ever-present possibility of escalating out of control. Force will be used against the UN to keep the weapons so you have to be ready to take casualties. Commands should be given very unrestrictive Rules of Engagement.

(Y095) To stabilize the situation more quickly. To prevent different reactions from the warring parties. Because first we have to find a military solution to the problem and then a political solution.

(Y097) Mandat clair c'est-à-dire volonté politique affichée; forces suffisantes pour faire respecter les accords; tester la bonne volonté des parties signataires de l'accord.

[Clear mandate, that is, a showing of political will; sufficient forces to uphold the agreements; test the good will of the parties involved in the agreement.]

(Y126) The warring parties know the ground better. This will draw peacekeepers into the war. Countries may not be willing to send their forces into conflict regions where they may be drawn into war.

(Y127) The terrain is such that if force should be used the UN forces will also have a lot of casualties to personnel and equipment.

(Y129) If you have the consent of the warring parties, the UN can operate to achieve its mission.

(Y130) Can/should only be used when the tactical situation allows and you have the support of the chain of command.

(Y136) UN control in areas. UN control of the disarmed equipment. UN in charge of the area.

(Y137) The warring factions must know that failure to comply with an agreement can or will be dealt with using force if necessary. It will give the UN respect as long as no provocation by UN units [takes place] in advance of the use of force.

(Y139) If you want results in Bosnia-Herzegovina that is the language they understand.

(Y147) Free will of the conflicting parties is important. Mentality of the local population. Lack of confidence of the conflicting parties towards the UN force.

(Y149) Insufficient UN forces [...], insufficient mandate anyway, high risks for losses.

(Y151) Leads to reaction by warring factions, escalating the situation. Puts the UN troops at increased risk. Eventually becomes a self-defeating exercise.

(Y159) More effective, faster, much more credible.

(Y160) Because some people do not agree with the agreement or with their government authorities. Because some factions of the warring parties had the proper rules.

(Y174) It must be available as a last resort to show ultimately total commitment to the process.

Q9.5 **If fighting was an ongoing process, was it possible for you to continue with your disarmament tasks?**

Yes: 11 No: 26

Q9.6 **If so, describe how it was possible to continue with your disarmament tasks.**

(Y013) Monitoring TBZ, demilitarized zone or MBZ was only possible with agreement of the warring parties. This agreement could be [reached] even if fighting was ongoing.

(Y016) In [the] context of small military actions which were isolated and brought under control by negotiation or increase in UN military operations.

(Y017) First we deployed UN forces (mounted in armored personnel carriers) between the factions that were involved in the incident. [Then] we assaulted that position from the rear.

(Y026) Patience, trust, [and] persuasion.

(Y063) Yugoslavia has been an area-to-area disarmament [exercise].

(Y075) The basis of the mission is peacekeeping under an accepted agreement. Fighting is supposed [to be] over.

(Y126) Fighting was not on a large scale but involved minor skirmishes and sniper activity.

(Y130) Fighting tended to stop or reduce when UN troops were in the immediate area.

(Y136) According to your definition [disarmament involves the] control of weapons [and a] no-fly zone. These two could be [achieved] in a way.

(Y137) Different areas would have different tension levels, but in general fighting hampers disarmament tasks.

(Y149) Very low level of fighting.

(Y174) With great care.

Q9.7 **Were you involved in any preventive deployment operations (i.e., as an observer, preventive diplomacy official, etc.)?**

Yes: 24   No: 22

Q9.8 **If so, was disarmament a major concern of this deployment?**

Yes: 09   No: 16

Q9.9 **If so, were there already arms control agreements (i.e., registers of conventional weapons, MTCR, etc.) in place within the country where you were operating?**

Yes: 08   No: 06

SECTION THREE

X. INFORMATION: COLLECTION, PUBLIC AFFAIRS, AND THE MEDIA

Q10.1   **Did you receive sufficient relevant information prior to and during your disarming mission?**

Prior:	Yes:	24	No:	23
During:	Yes:	31	No:	17

(Y002) Oui. J'évoque ici le cas de l'ultimatum de l'OTAN du 9 février 1994 qui ne portait pas sur le désarmement mais sur un regroupement d'armes.

[Yes, I am refering here to the NATO ultimatum of February 9, 1994 which dealt with the collection of arms and not with disarmament.]

Q10.2   **Was information always available and reliable?**

Yes: 19   No: 29

Q10.3   **How did you receive/obtain your information prior to and during the mission? (Describe the three most important ways.)**

(Y002) Reconnaissances par le biais: de l'alliance de l'OTAN, des hélicoptères, des patrouilles au sol.

[Reconnaissance by NATO, helicopters, and ground troops.]

(Y009) Did not receive sufficient relevant information prior to the mission. Obtained information through own means, at the battalion level. Information received from the top level was poor.

(Y010) Information collection by soldiers at checkpoints [or] on patrol. Specific surveillance operations. Local services (police, civilians, UN MP's).

(Y013) From NATO sources. From previous military observer information collection. From other UN sources including non-military [ones]. From warring parties.

(Y014) Information and orders from my HQ (UNMO).

(Y015) National, UN, sought out as [...] within own resources.

(Y016) Operation orders [came] from higher headquarters in theater, from national headquarters, [and] from own unit resources.

(Y017) From HQ. Activities [were] performed by own troops [or] other UN battalions.

(Y024) In the beginning the most reliable source of information was the media, later on force HQ. Connections to home country by using UF radio [were] very important in the beginning.

(Y025) The media, HQ.

(Y026) Prior: briefs from national authorities; e.g., army command, intelligence service, representatives from universities, officers who had been in the area with the EU, etc. During: [from the] UN chain of command.

(Y030) Irregular back-stopping and guidance.

(Y043) By referring to UN reports, to UN battalions, to [the] media.

(Y044) UN battalions, UN reports, local commander.

(Y045) Through UNPROFOR media in English, [...] and the local language.

(Y046) Home country. Information sections at HQ's.

(Y047) By fax or during meetings.

(Y048) By UN battalions, by UN reports, sometimes [through] local commanders, by observation.

(Y054) Information cell was organized in sector HQ. The troops and the military observers. Force Commander HQ.

(Y057) Reports made by units in sector. ECMM [and] UNMO reports.

(Y060) Through UN troops including military observers and from the [warring] parties.

(Y069) The briefing in the UN HQ, the military information summary, the [...] UNPROFOR books.

(Y071) Prior: [through] self information (books, university memos). During the mission [through] CNN International, chiefs in the operations room, talks with locals [on] both sides.

(Y074) Briefings from our National Defense HQ and our contingent HQ in Zagreb. Briefings from the staff of HQ Sector West. Written material provided by Canadian Contingent HQ.

(Y075) I recognize [that] we tried to obtain our information but it was strictly limited. We acted [when faced with] the facts.

(Y080) Talking/negotiating with the [...] parties. Monitoring. [...].

(Y088) Civilian population. Warring factions. UN reports. Chain of command.

(Y094) Senior HQ, other UN agencies, international and local media, UNMO's.

(Y095) Press and information officer. FCDP, routine orders.

(Y097) En Bosnie, le système d'acquisition d'informations dépend entièrement des relations personnelles du commandant en chef avec certaines authorités.
[In Bosnia the information-gathering system depends entirely on the personal relations between the chief commander and certain authorities.]

(Y126) By letters from UNPROFOR HQ. By instructions from UNMO HQ. Through daily briefing at local HQ.

(Y127) Through faxes. Daily mail from UN HQ at Zagreb. Through senior military observers.

(Y129) Direct intelligence gathering by patrols of liaison officers. Visits to commanders.

(Y130) From my commander in all cases.

(Y136) Only information from your own military observers, teams.

(Y137) National sources, UN sources, news (TV/paper).

(Y138) By official briefs.

(Y139) Fc letters. Briefings from BHC.

(Y147) Briefings, reading reports.

(Y149) Briefings, reports from different UN components, intelligence.

(Y151) Prior: through official briefings. During: through PIO handouts and sit. reps.

(Y159) When visiting the sector's HQ's.

(Y160) During mission through information officer HQ, Civil Affairs, Sector Commander information officer.

(Y174) Verbal, some written reports.

Q10.4 **Was there a structured information exchange between HQ's and the units in the field?**

Yes: 43   No: 06

Q10.5 **And between the various field commanders?**

Yes: 37   No: 11

Q10.6 **Did you use sensor mechanisms for verification/information purposes?**

Yes: 16   No: 32

Q10.7 **If so, list which ones and for what purpose. (Mention not more than three.)**

(Y002) Avions de reconnaissance, hélicoptères, radars de trajectographie.
[Reconnaissance planes, helicopters, trajectographic radars.]

(Y009) Infantry radars, photo, vizco.

(Y010) TOW thermal sights. NODLR.

(Y013) NATO aerial surveillance [to] locate heavy weapons. UN radars to locate heavy weapons firing. US real time video to monitor confrontation line in aircraft.

(Y015) Satellite, thermal scan.

(Y017) Radar.

(Y026) Night vision devices of different sorts.

(Y043) Night vision to verify information.

(Y044) Night vision goggles.

(Y048) Night vision goggles only.

(Y126) Teles, radios, radars.

(Y137) RWR - to find out where anti-aircraft radar systems were based.

(Y138) NATO - by air. No-fly zone controllers.

(Y149) Only night observation devices.

(Y151) Observations.

Q10.7.1 Was the use of on-site and remote sensing an adequate tool for verifying and monitoring weapons control and disarmament operations?

Yes: 14   No: 15

(Y097) Oui dans certains cas, non en Bosnie.
        [Yes, in certain cases, but not in Bosnia.]

Q10.7.2 **In your opinion, could sensor systems (acoustic, radar, photo, video, infrared, etc.) play a useful role in monitoring the weapons control and disarmament aspects of a peacekeeping operation?**

Yes: 39   No: 02

(Y097) Non en Bosnie.
[Not in Bosnia.]

Q10.7.3 **If so, give some examples of phases of the peacekeeping process in which such sensors could be used.**

(Y009) Demobilization, disarming, control cease-fire lines.

(Y010) Monitoring the cease-fire line. Location of artillery/mortar firing points.

(Y013) To determine who fires first. To assist in weapons location particularly if freedom of movement [is] difficult. To provide coverage in areas of heavy fighting.

(Y014) To control weapon storages and overlook the area.

(Y015) Verification, violations.

(Y016) Monitoring movement and storage of weapons in approved storage sites.

(Y017) Preventive deployment. Troops deployed in separation zones. Movement control. Cease-fire monitoring.

(Y026) Throughout the operation.

(Y028) In all phases in the beginning to find all weapons and later on to monitor the situation.

(Y030) For verification.

(Y042) Surveillance day and night for a general area. Close [observation of] a specific point to confirm information. Cover the gap for a lack of forces in the area of responsibility.

(Y043) To recognize weapons [...].

(Y044) Using the night vision watching the corridor within helicopter flying.

(Y047) It is useful for studying the situation.

(Y048) After reaching [...] a cease-fire and disarmament agreement.

(Y060) They should always be available.

(Y063) Local radars to verify no-fly zone violations. MT radars to verify shelling, air surveillance to prove troop movements.

(Y069) Army withdrawal. Protection of humanitarian convoys.

(Y071) Mostly for surveillance of areas such as cease-fire lines, battery positions, barracks, assembly points.

(Y075) Since the beginning, during the withdrawal [of] forces, to monitor the contact line and limits.

(Y080) Weapon storage monitoring. Monitoring at night.

(Y090) Throughout the process, but especially at the beginning.

(Y095) During the execution and after that.

(Y129) Mortar fire locating equipment.

(Y136) Control zone of separation. Control weapon storage.

(Y137) Before deployment of major assets. Before/while aircraft corridors are in effect.

(Y138) Geographic monitoring.

(Y139) Under [cease-fire violations] and in mapping confrontation lines.

(Y147) Guarding of storage sites. Monitoring of a separation zone.

(Y149) Identification of overflights, [...] separation zone, disarmament control.

(Y151) After signing of accord between warring factions, if heavy weapons are used, the fact can be employed for registering protest or imposing sanctions.

(Y159) To monitor implementation, and to control the ongoing process.

(Y160) Night devices during night attacks, surveillance radar.

(Y174) Throughout.

Q10.7.4 **What would you suggest about the possible organizational set-up of the use of such sensor systems (i.e., UN, regional organization, national, etc.)?**

(Y002) Unités nationales de recherche du renseignements affectées sous les ordres d'un commandant de la force de l'ONU.
[National intelligence units under the control of a commander of the UN force.]

(Y009) National.

(Y010) Some at national/unit level (cease-fire line monitoring). Others at sector or UN level (artillery DF).

(Y013) Systems must tie in to UN systems.

(Y014) UN or NATO.

(Y015) UN.

(Y016) Electronic monitoring should feed to military unit HQ or UNMO HQ responsible.

(Y017) UN.

(Y026) National and regional organization.

(Y042) Regional organization.

(Y043) UN should make a contract with [a] high technology company.

(Y044) UN [and/or] ECMM.

(Y047) Training.

(Y048) UN and ECMM.

(Y060) Regional/national available on request.

(Y069) UN.

(Y080) Each on their own.

(Y095) UN.

(Y097) OTAN, organisations régionales, ou nationales (mais difficile à mettre en oeuvre) .

[NATO and regional or national organizations (but difficult to organize).]

(Y126) UN level.

(Y129) Without intelligence you cannot operate [...] any mission, especially peacekeeping.

(Y136) UN.

(Y137) NATO should have the task, reporting to UN.

(Y138) Use a lead nation.

(Y139) Create a UN air force.

(Y147) Positive.

(Y149) National set-up.

(Y151) UN or regional, both are suitable.

(Y159) National or UN service.

(Y160) Regional organization.

(Y174) UN.

Q10.8   **Do you think that normal information collection assets (i.e., intelligence) could and should be used for peacekeeping and disarming purposes?**

Yes: 48   No: 00

Q10.9   **Why? (List three reasons.)**

(Y002) Le principe de l'ONU selon lequel on ne fait pas du renseignement est complètement dépassé. L'ONU neutre, sur un théâtre, n'est pas l'ONU aveugle ou sourde. Beaucoup de morts du personnels de l'ONU viennent de cette aberration.

[The principle of the UN under which one does not gather intelligence is completely archaic. A neutral UN in an area is not a blind or deaf UN. Many deaths of UN personnel come from this absurdity.]

(Y009) To learn the intentions of the parties involved. To ensure a secure environment for the peacekeeping troops.

(Y010) Intelligence collection speeds [up] the disarmament process considerably. Safety of UN troops/civilians would be enhanced. Better evidence to prove infractions would be available.

(Y013) The more you know the more you can do. Safety of UN personnel. Warring parties use intelligence assets.

(Y014) To control agreements, find out violations, use modern military equipment.

(Y015) Reliability, accuracy, speed.

(Y016) To ensure [...] impartial application of agreements, assist investigations into allegations of violations. To obtain and present [the] true situation to UN HQ [and the] international media.

(Y017) The commander (at all levels) that will conduct or is performing [an] operation in the field (even peacekeeping operations) must know as much as possible [...] about the terrain and opposite forces (organization, strength, deployment, and operation procedures).

(Y026) There is a need to know what is in an area and where; control of disarmament; getting a "feel" of the areas.

(Y028) To get good results, to make it credible, to avoid losses.

(Y030) Provides reliable assistance in the implementation of a mandate.

(Y042) To cover gaps in the [area of responsibility].

(Y043) Because the UN forces [are] trained [to use] such equipment.

(Y044) Collect the information from the local people.

(Y046) More correct information. Could help in a dangerous situation by gathering information prior to an attack.

(Y047) It is a way to be informed of [offensive] action.

(Y048) To ensure the location and number of weapons.

(Y054) Reliable and timely information is the way to success. Information collected from the parties and the population is not trustable.

(Y057) Belligerent forces often have hidden agendas. Helps prepare for the unexpected. Less risks for all.

(Y060) Essential for conducting a mission. Safety of own force. For use in negotiation.

(Y069) Commander resolution, to prevent conflicts, security.

(Y071) To inform [the] local civilian population: on the exact role of UN, using local means (newspapers, radio), using local journalists (who should be objective and reliable).

(Y074) Verify agreements made by the belligerents. Inform UN HQ and commanders about intentions of the parties. Permits planning and deployment of troops.

(Y080)   Adequate information, timely information, accurate information.

(Y088)   Gather information about threats against UN. To know warring factions' intentions. To predict political and military future events.

(Y094)   Any military operation [must] be supported by information collection assets to have some possibility of success.

(Y095)   Because they are assets not for the execution of that type of action.

(Y127)   All information collected must be turned to [...] which could be processed for future use. If [it] will help [...] the source of certain rumors and the prove them to be true or not.

(Y130)   In order that [the] peacekeepers are aware of what is going on around them.

(Y136)   You have to use the troops you have on the ground.

(Y137)   The warring factions are in general trying to hide their capacities.

(Y138)   Correct information is very important.

(Y139)   Because in Bosnia-Herzegovina, pilots are in danger when they have no information [about] confrontation lines or surface-to-air/anti-aircraft artillery systems.

(Y147)   More accurate information. Faster.

(Y149)   Reliability, uniformity, durability.

(Y151) Plans based on incorrect [or] insufficient information are bound to fail. Warring factions manipulate the UN's authority due to ignorance.

(Y159) To prevent an action, to head the main effort in the proper way, to provide proper knowledge to command and control.

(Y160) Sector Commander has to [have] updated information [throughout] the mission. All command levels and intermediate levels too.

(Y172) Because it is accurate, and may well be the only decent information available.

(Y174) Why not?

Q10.10 Is there a need for satellite surveillance in peacekeeping/peace enforcing operations?

Yes: 44   No: 04

(Y097) J'en doute, en tout cas en Bosnie.
        [I doubt it; in any case, not in Bosnia.]

Q10.11 Did you use the local population for information collection purposes?

Yes: 41   No: 06

Q10.12 Did you implement any transparency measures to create mutual confidence between warring parties?

Yes: 35   No: 11

Q10.13 If so, did you act as an intermediary?

Yes: 32   No: 04

Q10.14   Was public affairs/media essential to the disarming mission?

Yes: 32   No: 13

Q10.15   Were communication and public relations efforts of importance during your mission?

Yes: 41   No: 05

(Y002)   Oui. Bien que le "système ONU" place la communication sous la responsabilté exclusive de la branche "affaire civile" et en exclu le Militaire, ce qui est scandaleux.
[Yes, even though the UN system places communication under the exclusive control of the civil affairs branch and excludes the military - which is scandalous.]

Q10.16   If so, give three reasons why this was so.

(Y002)   Pour une mission, avoir les moyens de dire la Vérité face au Mensonge généralisé est capital. Un bon outil de communication vient beaucoup des bataillons.
[For a mission to find a way to tell the truth in the face of the generalized lies is essential. A good means of communication comes mainly from batallions.]

(Y009)   To create confidence between parties, and to learn of their intentions in advance. UN commanders understood very well the importance of good relations with the different parties.

(Y010)   Need to ensure that national/international players understood what was happening. Need to balance local propaganda reporting.

(Y013)   To gain [the] confidence of warring parties, particularly those lower in [the] chain of command. To ensure everyone knew [the] military observer mission [was] in process. To explain [that] mutual disarmament [was] occurring [...].

(Y014)   Understanding, trust, made it easier.

(Y015)   Confidence-building, counter propaganda, truth.

(Y016)   Important to counter local propaganda against UN. Important to demonstrate [the] will and commitment of [the] UN towards achieving [its] mission. Allows key issues to be broadcasted and progress made.

(Y017)   Through the communications and mainly the public relations efforts we could convince the local authorities to provide their support to the demilitarization process, and we could transmit to the local population our message that [...] demilitarization was the first step to restore a peaceful and secure environment.

(Y025)   We worked together with [the] local population.

(Y026)   [To convey] information to locals on the UN mission and tasks, [...] to the home country; "hearts and minds" campaign.

(Y030)   Transparency was used as [a] confidence building measure. Media, radio especially, allowed [us] to explain [the] process of disarming.

(Y042)   It built the confidence of being neutral as [a] UN force. It's [a] way of convincing a warring party of your way of processing. You can solve problems in the beginning and before they expand.

(Y043)   Because you should be very close to the locals.

(Y044)   Build confidence between warring parties. [Cease-fire violations].

(Y045) Learning the local language very well. Try to get along with local people and have a good relationship. [It might] save your life [...].

(Y048) To build up trust between parties. To assist the exchange of prisoners of war. Humanitarian relief for refugees.

(Y054) Cooperation and confidence from the population is very important. It is necessary to keep everybody well-informed. To get a good image as [a] trustable, impartial and disciplined UN mission.

(Y057) Civilian population needs reassurance. Helps [the] UN explain misconceptions about [the] mission.

(Y060) Because the parties in conflict presented their own views [to] the people without objectivity. The UN forces themselves felt misunderstood. There was a need to balance the bias in the international media.

(Y069) Collected information, UN public relations with the population and political authorities.

(Y074) Let parties know of our intentions. Gain support of population, anti-propaganda.

(Y075) Because we interfered [in] the daily life of the local population. We needed them [to understand] the UN procedures in the UNPA.

(Y080) Obvious.

(Y088) Achieve civilian population's confidence. Offer locals an explanation on UN procedures and tasks.

(Y094) Transparency of intentions. Counteracting against warring parties' own [psychological operations]. Enhance the mission and its personnel.

(Y097) Explication du mandat; informer la population des activités de le FORPRONU; contrecarrer la propagande des parties en guerre.
[Explication of the mandate; informing the population about the activities of UNPROFOR; and thwarting the propoganda of the warring parties.]

(Y126) It created confidence between UN and the factions. Information was more free-flowing. It brought familiarity and therefore more friendship.

(Y127) Because it was more than a press war, and the Muslims used press propoganda for the war and to let the world know their problems.

(Y129) To advertise the UN. To shame those who broke [the] cease-fire. To maintain the morale of UN troops.

(Y136) To receive and give information. For instruction purposes. For security reasons.

(Y137) The local population must know why [the] UN is present and local military units must know what [the] UN [is equipped with].

(Y139) False accusations towards UN, opinions were affected by [incorrect information from the] government, our mandate was [neither] known nor understood by the people.

(Y147) To gain the confidence of the local [...]. To inform about the mission of the force.

(Y149) Confidence-building for both parties, security.

(Y151) As a confidence-building measure.

(Y172) To counter the continuous propaganda used by both sides in the conflict.

(Y174) The people must support the UN. Without communication nothing could happen.

Q10.17   Was there a well-funded and planned communications effort to support and explain your activities and mission to the local population?

Yes: 14   No: 35

Q10.18   If not, should there have been one?

Yes: 33   No: 01

Q10.19   Did media attention at any time hamper or benefit your disarming efforts?

Hamper: 21   Benefit: 16

Q10.20   Summarize your experience with the media.

(Y002) Ils sont souvent "écoeurés" de la "langue de bois" utilisée par les responsables civils ONU de la communication. Ils apprécient davantage ce qui leur vient du militaire, lequel, comme je l'ai dit plus haut, a du mal a s'exprimer dans le système ONU actuel.

[They are often disgusting in their use of the stereotypical information given to them by the responsible UN communication officials. They prefer what comes from the military, but as I said above, the military has difficulties expressing itself in the current UN system.]

(Y009) An Argentinean program was locally broadcast (everyday 30 minutes) in which 2-3 minutes were devoted to explaining the aims of UNPROFOR in our area of responsibility.

(Y010)   UN officials regularly went as visitors to local open line radio shows in an attempt to explain [the] operation to locals. Separation of belligerents ensured highly biased and inflammatory reporting by local media. International media seemed to have little effect on the local population.

(Y013)   World media were centered in Sarajevo and based in the Holiday Inn showing ignorance of the Bosnian Serb side and their casualties. Media were manipulated by warring parties who deliberately permitted or provided civilian casualties to obtain media coverage.

(Y014)   UN official media team was good. The rest (commercial) [were] mostly a pain in the ....

(Y015)   Belligerent [local] media [were] liars [and] distorted [news], international media were sensational and focused on Sarajevo, poorly informed.

(Y016)   Needs to be closely coordinated. UN media must be more proactive with local media. UN media or any media should not operate in military unit areas without their knowledge and consultation. Media must be escorted by military unit members, i.e., safety, location of minefields, local situations/ground.

(Y017)   We broadcasted one daily program by a local FM radio. Through this program we informed the local population about our disarmament process and we gave advice and answered the questions that the locals sent to us. It was one very important way to advertise [...] our actions.

(Y024)   The local media was very much against the force most of the time which affected the attitude of the population in a negative way.

(Y025)   The media did not like that we were there.

(Y026)   Media can both hamper and be an asset depending on the situation; great need for local public relations campaign (we set up one); media can/will misuse information and pictures.

(Y027)   Too often the media only wanted a story, not the truth. Also, Sarajevo was the consistent focus of activities but most troops are not in Sarajevo. Some media only held the Serbs as the bad side. In UNPROFOR no one was good.

(Y030)   Media is [an] important tool, but sometimes dangerous if not used smartly.

(Y042)   The media used [were]: local broadcasting from both sides and TV stations, and local press and newspapers through interviews to explain our ideas and points of view and purpose of our mission. We used the international TV stations and radios and press also through [...] personal meetings and discussions in ceremony and medal parades and conferences.

(Y045)   Not so long with media but would like to have some experience.

(Y047)   There was no contact with the media.

(Y048)   They are too pushy.

(Y054)   It is a useful tool to be used. You must be kind, firm and trustable in dealing with the media. Tell them only the truth.

(Y057)   From the UN: too little, too late. In Croatia, the media is state-controlled, and they used it for propaganda for and against UN.

(Y060) Good; but the operations were conducted, particularly in Bosnia-Herzegovina, under so much media attention that no matter what the UN forces did, it appeared inadequate.

(Y063) The media focus on drama. The presentation, therefore, is often disproportionate. Vital developments in the surroundings and more peaceful options never receive the same attention although the perspective is more wide-ranging.

(Y074) Must control or they get into trouble. Maximum cooperation with them. They did not try to negate our efforts. Mainly there to cover a certain nationality. Tell them the truth. No problem if you explain the rules to them.

(Y075) Very short because of the language.

(Y080) Poor. Too interested in themselves.

(Y088) Only minor contact.

(Y090) The media must be advised to try and avoid the non-official media that can be interested in saying untrue things.

(Y094) There is no free press in a country which is fighting a war so anything that is published has an intention against the enemy and to benefit your own operations. Inaccuracies and lies about the enemy or the UN are a daily issue.

(Y095) I have not any direct experience with the media but [they] always hampered our disarming efforts.

(Y097) Pas de problèmes avec la presse écrite. Plus difficile avec la TV: le temps "réel" est incompatible avec les situations du type Bosnie. L'influence des medias sur le déroulement des opérations est très "surestimé". Les parties en guerre se moquent des médias.

[No problems with the press, but more difficulties with the television media: real time is not compatible with situations like the one in Bosnia. The influence of the media on the progress of the operations is very overestimated. The warring parties laugh at the media.]

(Y126) The media created fear and apprehension among the civil public as to the real intention of the UN forces. Sometimes UN personnel were branded as spies.

(Y127) The media most of the time were reporting one-sided news, and the Serbs saw it as [the] UN taking sides. The Muslims used it for propaganda. We therefore had to draw the press' attention to the effects of some of their publications.

(Y129) Very good mutual respect - in contrast to the rest of UN forces! UN media relations were useless and badly run - they require major reorganization.

(Y130) Their quest for a story was often at the expense of our operations. At times, our needs were so different that they could hamper operations.

(Y136) The UN media were not able to tell/inform the civilian population about our task. The local/warring parties used their media mostly for disinformation about [the] UN - the "enemy".

(Y137) Local media is often under political control [so] if [the] UN is considered unwanted by the local government, media can bring that message out very easily.

(Y138) Very good and important.

(Y139) They were not "used" well enough by [the] UN. They were allowed to concentrate on Sarajevo only.

(Y147) This instrument was neither used enough nor appropriately.

(Y151) Majority reported events objectively. Print media more analytical than TV. Global TV networks at times project only one small aspect of an issue, thus distorting it or at times creating panic amongst the viewers.

(Y159) The local media (on both sides) were very partial. Normally both were against UN forces. Media was under political control.

(Y172) Stand near a camera and you get shot at.

(Y174) Capable of either helping or hindering according to political/social climate.

Q10.21 **Was there sufficient briefing to the general public in the conflict area on the disarming process?**

Yes: 15   No: 31

Q10.22 **If so, who organized this and who carried it out?**

<u>Organized:</u>

(Y009) Sector Commander.
(Y010) Sector HQ.
(Y017) By our battalion.
(Y026) On own initiative.
(Y030) By Sector Commander and Civil Affairs.
(Y042) UN HQ's and Battalion HQ's.
(Y045) The UN press centers in each sector.
(Y047) By HQ.
(Y069) The UN Sector HQ.

(Y074) Sector HQ.

(Y094) Press Information Office in Force HQ.

(Y097) Tous les chefs à leur niveau ont fait le maximum.
[All the chiefs at their level did the most they could.]

(Y129) Local politicians.

Carried it out:

(Y009) Sector/information officer.

(Y010) All units commanders, Civil Affairs.

(Y017) By our battalion.

(Y026) On own initiative.

(Y030) By Sector Commander and Civil Affairs.

(Y042) Battalion HQ's and sub-units.

(Y043) By UN command.

(Y044) By UN command.

(Y045) The press itself with assistance of UN troops.

(Y047) By communication and visiting the public.

(Y048) UN commanders (sectors and battalions).

(Y069) The battalions.

(Y074) Commanders/Staff Officers.

(Y094) Information officers at the sector level.

(Y129) Local radio/TV stations.

(Y138) By UN officials.

Q10.23   Was there cooperation with the local media in explaining the steps of disarmament you were carrying out?

Yes: 20   No: 21

Q10.24   Were leaflets distributed?

Yes: 13   No: 25

(Y097) Non, mais j'ai écrit ou fait écrire dans OSLOBODJENIE (Journal indépendant de Sarajevo).
[No, but I wrote or had someone write in OSLOBODJENIE (independant journal of Sarajevo).]

Analyst's Comments:

- *Nearly all respondents mentioned the need for a proper intelligence system during peace operations. The importance of this capability cannot be over emphasized.*

  • *Belligerent parties may perceive information gathering as a hostile act. Intelligence operations may therefore destroy the trust that the parties may have in the peacekeeping force. However, it is reasonable to assume that the parties will purse their divergent aims by exploiting the presence of the peacekeeping force. They may also attempt to deceive it from time to time. Circumstances may place the force under direct attack. Such attacks may come from one of the parties to the agreement or from bandit elements acting independently. These attacks pose a serious problem to force security and the delivery of humanitarian aid. Whatever the circumstances, the peacekeepers need information and must have the ability to collect it. The way in which it is collected is important, and it should as far as possible not create stones for the belligerent parties to throw back at the peacekeeping force.*

  • *Threat capabilities are usually the first consideration in determining information requirements. It is difficult for a commander to make a decision when the picture is not reasonably clear or when a total lack of information hampers his appreciation of the situation on the ground. The military is not the only component that depends on timely information to execute its task. There may also be requirements for production of economic, political, social, medical and other information. It is therefore unthinkable that an operation can be successful without proper and shared information-gathering capabilities.*

  • *The intelligence community must define intelligence requirements for supporting the military commitment as early as possible. This is crucial because the pre-deployment and planning phases of the operation require optimum support. Once deployed, a unit or formation should develop its requirements and information-gathering plan in conjunction with the operational plan and submit it along the proper channels of command for approval. Intelligence support must always focus on operational planning considerations.*

- *To ensure the safety of assigned forces and members of the different components of a mission, the commander must have the capability to disseminate critical indications and warnings to all echelons quickly. A robust theatre architecture must be in place to provide accurate and timely all-source information. This information must be formatted clearly and be at the disposal of the entire deployed mission.*

- *Mission success and the security of the force depend almost entirely on the observational skills of the personnel and leadership of the small unit and single members of other components of the mission. In the absence of other systems, human intelligence may be the primary source of timely information. It is also the first line of defense against any threat and a critical factor in determining mission success, and it must be developed to its full potential during every peacekeeping operation. Training of military and non-military personnel before a mission should therefore include observational and reporting skills.*

- *The proper and aggressive use of the media (in its broader sense) by a peacekeeping force can also contribute to the successful outcome of an operation. The successful execution of peacekeeping operations often depends on the continued cooperation of all parties concerned, the impartiality of the peacekeepers, and regional and/or world support. The correct use of the media can play an important role in facilitating this cooperation and support. It can help promote acceptance of a cease-fire and the withdrawal of troops and can influence attitudes, emotions, opinions and behavior. It can also help to counter rumors and disinformation spread by the belligerent parties to create confusion. However, one* very important *requirement is that its information should be* timely, correct and complete.

SECTION FOUR

XI. EXPERIENCES IN THE CONTROL OF WEAPONS AND IN DISARMAMENT DURING YOUR MISSION:

Q11.1 **Describe, by order of importance, your specific tasks, if any, in weapons control and disarmament during this mission.**

(Y002) J'ai été directement impliqué, comme commandant de la FORPRONU, dans une seule opération de contrôle des armes: le regroupement des armes lourdes Bosniaque et Serbes, dans le rayon des 20 km autour de Sarajevo, après l'ultimatum de l'OTAN du 9 Février 1994. J'ai vu les conséquences de 2 autres operations de désarmement entreprises avant ma prise de fonction: la Croatie (Plan Vance) et Sebrenica.

[I was directly involved as an UNPROFOR commander in only one arms control operation: the collection of Bosnian and Serbian heavy arms within a radius of 20 km around Sarajevo, after the NATO ultimatum of February 9, 1994. I saw the consequences of two other disarmament operations before I began: Croatia (Vance Plan) and Sebrenica.]

(Y009) The UN Protected Areas had to be clear of all kinds of weapons. Controlled the disarming of the Croatian Army. Population control in order to prevent the entry of weapons in the area, control of weapons already in custody.

(Y010) At checkpoints all vehicles [were] searched and weapons confiscated. When [a] "just cause" [was] determined, houses, buildings [and] institutions were searched. Control of local police forces.

(Y013) Assist in locating heavy weapons, collecting such weapons. Monitoring heavy weapons that could not be collected for [a] number of reasons. Monitoring weapon collection on sites until relieved by UN troops who then controlled. Some sites never had troops. Searching for violations. Verifying results of NATO surveillance (see below).

(Y014) Withdrawal of heavy weapons. Control of weapon storage. Monitor the [Area of Responsibility for] any violations.

(Y016) Supervision and control of heavy weapons in authorized storage sites. Removal of machine guns, [armored personnel carriers] and anti-tank weapons in direct range. Disarming personnel found to be carrying weapons in the zone. Demining. Demobilization. Effective presence throughout each phase.

(Y017) First: weapons exclusion zone control. Second: disarming of irregular groups and individuals. Third: weapons destruction. Fourth: demining.

(Y024) Not [these] kinds of orders.

(Y026) Maintain cease-fire; information collection on weapons in area; plans for withdrawal of weapons; execution; control.

(Y030) Not personally involved.

(Y042) Disarmament of weapons inside the UNPACSWJJORBAT-1. Control the cease-fire line on both sides by establishing checkpoints. Observation points, mobile patrols and observe infiltration. Control the UNPA borders from outside to observe weapons insertion. Protect humanitarian aid/convoys and economic projects inside the UNPA.

(Y045) In my opinion, the weapons control and the disarmament could be carried [out] easily if the situation [was] different from [that in] the area [in which] I served [...] during my mission [in] Croatia. [...] the problem was the distrust of [the] local people and the local authoritie' experience with the UN.

(Y047) My part was only observing [...] weapons control.

(Y054) Planning the operation. Collecting the armaments. Storing them. Securing them. Verifying the completion and fulfillment of the whole process.

(Y057) Demining. Coordinate efforts of engineer squadron. Acquire local/ UN material to support demining.

(Y060) Withdrawal of JNA from UNPA's. Disbanding of Territorial Defense Forces. Placing of heavy weaponry under joint control of UN and local authorities. Demilitarization.

(Y063) Establish and verify cease-fire. Identify weapons. Negotiate disputes. Mediate on the ground. Liaise during all phases.

(Y069) Collected information, situation reports.

(Y074) Control weapons in UN weapon depots/storage areas. Confiscate weapons in accordance with Rules of Engagement (RoE). Conduct cordon and searches with UNCIVPOL and local police. Destruction of confiscated weapons.

(Y075) Weapons withdrawal. Establishment of exclusion zones and control. Disarming of individuals (inside the UNPA and at checkpoints), storage, demining.

(Y080) Monitoring and reporting of [the cease-fire agreement/Vance Plan].

(Y088) Check number of weapons existing in concentration sites.

(Y090) Member of staff in the camp installed to collect and destroy the armaments. To coordinate and supervise the destruction.

(Y094) Detect, identify, locate, register, secure, store.

(Y095) [No] specific tasks in weapons control and disarmament during my mission.

(Y126) Monitoring weapon movements. Inspection of weapon sites. Checking state of weapons in collection sites.

(Y127) Negotiate for cease-fire. Mediate for peaceful settlement of issues. Monitoring cease-fire. Supervise disarmament. Patrolling.

(Y129) Monitoring cease-fire. Organizing cease-fire.

(Y136) My order was to control the weapons [which] were placed outside the different lines (according to type, etc.) and to control the stored weapons.

(Y147) Participation in unilateral and joint meetings. Monitoring and verification [of] the tension. Shaping of the MOU's and local agreements.

(Y149) Participation at joint control commission. Investigation of any transgression.

(Y159) According to the [cease-fire agreement], monitor (once a day) the weapons collection points and violations on the 10 and 20 km zones.

(Y160) My appointment [was] as air liaison officer (ALO) and sector commander air advisor. Specifically none.

(Y169) Separation of the warring factions. Disarmament of the warring faction. Storage of weapons.

(Y172) Monitoring weapons collection areas. Checking weapons' serial numbers.

(Y174) Demilitarize front line zones of weapons. Monitor collected weapons.

Q11.2 **Did the security situation in the mission area allow for arms control and disarmament operations?**

Yes: 26 No: 16

Q11.3 **If not, what steps were required to establish and maintain a secure environment?**

(Y013) However both parties denied military observers freedom of movement to monitor implementation of [the] Sarajevo [Total Exclusion Zone] or [the] Gorazde [Military Exclusion Zone].

(Y014) Mine-clearing; always a local [liaison officer] with us.

(Y015) Local freedom of movement.

(Y026) Establishment and maintenance of cease-fire; mutual trust; investigation of breaches of the cease-fire.

(Y042) In the beginning it was good, but step by step we started to lose control. Steps [were] taken to reinforce the UN forces [with] heavy support weapons and [to] strongly implement the agreement.

(Y045) The freedom of movement of UN troops or civilian police or any other organization [...] was not applicable during the mission.

(Y054) Negotiate an agreement. Obtain the withdrawal of both armies. Provide security to the whole UNPA. Convince both sides about your neutrality.

(Y074) Mutual respect and confidence between [both] sides. Buffer zone created on cease-fire line. Enforcement of lines of withdrawal around UNPA.

(Y088) See 7.18.

(Y127) There should have been [a] complete cease-fire to allow for disarmament.

(Y136) Agreements from all parties, and control of local military units and their commanders.

(Y139) Change the mandate.

(Y169) We needed more troops.

(Y172) None.

Q11.4   Do you think your weapons control and disarming tasks could have been handled more efficiently?

Yes: 29   No: 11

Q11.5   If so, mention three ways in which your task could have been improved.

(Y002) Ultimatum du 9 Février 1994 à Sarajevo. Disposer immédiatement de 2 à 3.000 hommes suplémentaires pour mieux contrôler les regroupements.

[The ultimatum of February 9, 1994 in Sarajevo. The immediate provision of 2 -3,000 additional men for better control of collections.]

(Y010) Uniform enforcement across the entire sector/mission area.

(Y013) Exceptions to TBZ should have been dealt with such as Bosnian Government refusal to permit verification on Mount Igman or Bosnian Serb refusal to permit verification of Hadzici workshop or Jahorina area.

(Y014) If UN put more pressure on the warring parties. The warring parties were often not serious in their efforts. Too many units from the Third World.

(Y017) The agreement with [the] Serbs was an important (the most important) hindrance. With more and reliable information. More cooperation from other battalions.

(Y027) Less direction from higher HQ. Fewer resolutions. Properly utilized media for the local populace.

(Y030) Better control mechanisms should have been developed. Troops (UNPROFOR) did not have sufficient understanding of [their] importance.

(Y042) Having a close air support on call. Having heavy weapons in our organization structure. Strongly implementing the disarmament agreement.

(Y045) If there is trust, yes. If there is a legal way. If there is a safe environment.

(Y060) With a more realistic mandate and an effective agreement between the parties.

(Y063) A continuous emphasis on establishing a well-defined weapons control policy around Sarajevo and Gorazde would have stabilized the situation and UN control would [have been] more tight.

(Y074) Common application of force between all battalions in the sector. More authority to conduct cordon and searches.

(Y075) With authorization [to] search in private and public sites (houses, buildings).

(Y080) Better [public relations] (PR). Greater diplomatic pressure.

(Y088) To forbid access of warring factions' personnel to the depots. To put out of order the weapons declared under UN supervision. To allow access to UN personnel to warring parties' inventories.

(Y095) With efficient troops, with adequate equipment, with [more specific] rules of engagement and other matters related to the mandate [...].

(Y126) If the warring factions cooperate. If the local commanders are better-educated. More protection for UN workers.

(Y127) The factions should have been schooled on the disarmament. There should have been [a] complete cease-fire.

(Y130) By having more troops.

(Y136) More activity by UN troops. UN control of all weapon storage. The UN commanders have to take charge in the area.

(Y147) Additional troops. Time frame for the disarmament agreed upon by the parties.

(Y149) Real freedom of movement guarantee for UN forces.

(Y159) More efficient mandate. Joint action with armored forces. Strong answer from the chain of command to violations.

(Y160) To keep clear the rules of engagement [from] the beginning.

(Y169) If the parties had respected it.

(Y172) Create an environment of trust with the warring sides. Have effective [command and control] arrangements.

(Y174) More resources, more commitment.

Q11.6 Were opportunities missed to take advantage of or implement weapons control and disarmament measures?

Missed: 16   Not missed: 22

Q11.7 If opportunities were missed, mention the main reasons why this happened.

(Y002) Le 9 février 1994 à Sarajevo. Le choc psychologique induit par le massacre du vieux marché aurait pu être mieux exploité, au plan politique, pour amplifier les mesures de désarmement.
[February 9, 1994 in Sarajevo. The psychological shock induced by the market massacre could have been better exploited, politically, to increase disarmament measures.]

(Y013) In the interest of having the shelling of Sarajevo stopped and due to [the] vulnerability of [the] humanitarian lifeline to Bosnian Serb pressure, the abnormalities in Hadzici/Jahorina were not resolved.

(Y016) Force policy on implementation of agreement not issued on time. Momentum lost on achieving complete compliance as specified in agreement early in implementation due to lack of clear direction and deliberate non-compliance by belligerents.

(Y017) The subsidiary disarmament agreement with [the] Serbs hindered our performance and due to this we missed some opportunities [to] implement disarmament measures.

(Y027) Lack of information, lack of time, no process to ensure there was a standard process to do the task by all units.

(Y030) No consistency in following up. Some troops more dedicated to disarming while other troops acted relaxed after some time.

(Y045) Because it was not secure.

(Y071) No rapid deployment [...] at the very moment when the warring parties were willing to stop [fighting]. No reserves within the battalions or at [the] sector levels. No action against smuggling and blackmarket (Military Police and UNCIVPOL).

(Y074) Lack of courage and conviction by commanders. Different standards between sectors.

(Y088) UN lacked either the force or the will to assert its authority. Lack of confidence between the parties to declare all existing weapons. Lack of will from the parties to stop the fighting.

(Y095) Delays, lack of training and capacity in the matter.

(Y136) See [response] in 11.5.

(Y147) No time frame, lack of interest of the superior echelons.

(Y149) No double key system for storage sites for weapons.

(Y159) Any time a [cease-fire agreement] is implemented it should be written very carefully.

Q11.8 **Did you find the national diversity of contributed troops a problem for command and control during disarmament operations?**

Yes: 28   No: 13

Q11.9 **If so, mention the three problems you considered most challenging.**

(Y002) Sarajevo - 9 février 1994. L'arrivée d'un battalion russe, mal soutenu, peu motivé a ajouté à l'inertie des Ukraniens et des Egyptiens.
[Sarajevo, February 9, 1994. The arrival of a Russian battalion which was badly equipped and little motivated added to the inertia of the Ukrainians and the Egyptians.]

(Y009) Different levels of training of the contingents involved; language was a problem.

(Y010) Language, lack of uniform enforcement of rules due to the differences in armaments/training.

(Y014) All nations are not so efficient. Some took sides - not so neutral. Some badly-trained and informed.

(Y015) Language, training deficiencies, partiality towards Serb or Muslim side.

(Y016) Varying degrees of professionalism, training, leadership, lack of equipment and proper weapons to implement agreement, i.e., mine detectors, mine rollers, [armored personnel carriers], heavy weapons.

(Y017) The most important [problem] was the different points of view about the scope of disarming [the] warring factions or individuals. Second [was] the different manner and times the battalions accomplished the sector commander's orders. Third [was] the different level of risks that each battalion wanted to assume.

(Y026) Different *modus operandi*; too wide [of a] cultural gap; different levels of discipline.

(Y027) Language, training, inability of UN to provide standard processes.

(Y045) Not applicable.

(Y054) Different quality of people. Low level of training and professionalism in some countries.

(Y057) Two of four battalions were inefficient due to poor training and discipline. Language: only officers (not all of them) spoke English. One battalion came in without equipment.

(Y060) Bias depending upon opinions in national capitals. Bias depending on perceived affiliations with parties [to] the conflict. Lack of positive political support.

(Y063) Understanding of the situation. Detailed pursuance of the aim.

(Y071) Force HQ - levels of competence and understanding too different. [...] no joint civilian and military work. Operations/logistics - lack of proper equipment and logistics personnel. No logistics support available immediately.

(Y074) Different equipment/poor equipment. Lack of moral courage by some leaders. Unwillingness to carry out difficult orders.

(Y075) Not at battalion level.

(Y080) General ignorance of the situation. General lethargy, work ethic.

(Y126) Language. Some nationals seemed interested in what happened. Some observers who did not know anything tried to push their race on others.

(Y129) Language, doctrine, [and] attitude.

(Y130) Language, capabilities, [and] commitment.

(Y137) The seriousness of threats against UN personnel/[aircraft]/vehicles.

(Y139) Language, poor equipment, poor training.

(Y147) Cooperation with the local authorities. Different procedures.

(Y149) Lack of authority, problems of coordination, lack of effectiveness.

(Y160) Different ways to do, different ways to think, different ways [of operation] of each [...] battalion.

(Y172) Inability to communicate. Large differences in skill and ability of different troops.

(Y174) Language, skill, attitude.

Q11.10   Was the disarmament process reversible (i.e., were there instances where devolution was foreseen or requested)?

Yes: 19   No: 13

Q11.11   If so, were there provisions to this effect in the mandate, mission or agreement?

Yes: 09   No: 10

Q11.12   Which types of weapons were in use, and by whom (e.g., your own unit(s), warring parties, individuals, irregular units, national officials, etc.)? (If applicable, list the five principal ones for each category.)

Weapon: Full compliment of conventional weapons.
Whom: All parties.

Other comments:

(Y002) L'ONU a accepté avec réticence que les contingents puissent se doter de blindés et d'armes lourdes. C'est une preuve supplémentaire du décalage de sa perception da la situation avec la réalité sur le terrain.
[The UN accepted with reticence that the contigents could have tanks and heavy weapons. This is extra proof of the gap between its perception of the situation and the reality on the ground.]

(Y054) There were different types.

(Y057) When disarming, [the] UN must be strong enough to inspire confidence. Canadian battalion was the key unit which gave UN the advantage in West sector.

(Y137) The ex-Yugoslav army was well equipped and Serb and Croat units basically took over the heavy weapons, while the Muslims had less sophisticated and lighter weapon systems.

(Y139) Rifle grenades widely used and impact sometimes confused with mortars [...]. Hand-held anti-tank rocket/missiles widely used and impact sometimes confused with mortars [which were] prohibited heavy weapons (over 80mm after 21 February 1994).

(Y174) All forces (warring parties) possessed full range of weapons.

Q11.13 Were you given priorities as to the type of weapons you should disarm first?

Yes: 28   No: 12

Q11.14 If so, how were priorities assigned (i.e., on what basis)? (List three reasons.)

(Y002) Sarajevo, 9 février 1995 [1994], l'ultimatum portait sur toutes les armes d'un calibre égal ou supérieur de 12,7 millimètres.
[Sarajevo, February 9, 1995 [1994], the ultimatum concerned all weapons of a caliber equal to or more than 12.7 millimeters.]

(Y009) Heavy weapons first, then the [smaller] arms.

(Y010) Tanks/Artillery units - withdrawn outside UNPA [and] stored; [armored personnel carriers] - withdrawn; small arms - highest to lowest threat as seen by belligerents.

(Y013) All heavy weapons, otherwise [they become] a NATO target.

(Y014) Heavy weapons because of their long range and effects.

(Y015) Heavy weapons.

(Y016) Heavy, long-range [weapons] such as tanks, mortars and artillery to de-escalate the war (agreement). Weapons in zone of separation (agreement-specific). Lifting of mines (agreement-specific).

(Y026) Range, lethality, mobility.

(Y027) Directions from HQ. Resolution agreements.

(Y030) Heavy weapons, long-range arms.

(Y042) Long[-range] arms inside the UNPA. To take away the military appearance. To forbid clashes and fighting. To try to go back to natural life.

(Y045) The distance of the arms, the effectiveness of the arms, the quality of the arms.

(Y054) Actually it was designed for the withdrawal on the basis of the most dangerous first. [...] the disarmament [...] was accomplished by the different units in assigned sites.

(Y060) Heavy weapons like tanks and artillery. Other weapons.

(Y074) Not sure.

(Y075) For withdrawal, from heavy to light weapons. Then any kind of weapons. The remaining were only light and portable.

(Y126) Weapons of mass destruction. Heavy artillery weapons.

(Y127) Heavy weapons. Anti-aircraft. Armor.

(Y129) Heavy weapons which could be used for offensive operations were always priority one.

(Y130) 12.7 mm and above.

(Y147) Tanks, artillery, heavy mortars, anti-aircraft guns. [Armored personnel carriers], machine guns. Small arms.

(Y149) [First priority] indirect fire, withdrawal [...] enough. [Second priority] direct fire systems (tanks).

(Y174) Heavy to small. Progressive reduction would momentarily reduce tension.

Q11.15 **At the beginning of your mission, were you able to have sufficient information on military capabilities in regard to numbers and quality of equipment used by warring parties?**

Yes: 17   No: 23

Q11.16 **Did you have the impression that there were caches of weapons in your sector or adjoining sectors?**

Yes: 35   No: 06

Q11.17 **Were illicit weapons a problem for you (illicit as in: not in your inventories)?**

Yes: 28   No: 12

Q11.18 **Was there evidence in your sector that the warring parties continued to have access to weapons through external channels of supply?**

Yes: 34   No: 07

Q11.19 **Could you control external channels of weapons supply in your sector?**

Yes: 08   No: 29

Q11.20   **How important was the control of external channels of supply for the success of the mission?**

Very Important: 25   Important: 11
Unimportant: 01

Q11.21   **In your experience, do weapons continue to flow during the conflict even after sanctions, inspections, and checks have been applied?**

Yes: 38   No: 04

Q11.22   **Were there any security zones established?**

Yes: 31   No: 10

Q11.23   **If so, were you able to control your sector effectively?**

Yes: 15   No: 17

Q11.24   **Depending on your answer to 11.23, elaborate on how you were able to control the sector or on why you were unable to control it.**

(Y002) Les Résolutions créant les zones de sécurités en Bosnie-Herzégovine (824 -836, etc.) impliqueraient le renforcement immédiat de 7.500 hommes qui n'ont été mis en place que sur une durée d'un an et incomplètement.
[The resolutions creating the zones of security in Bosnia-Herzegovina (824 - 836, etc.) would have implied the immediate reinforcement of 7,500 men, but they were only deployed for a year and incompletely.]

(Y009) [The] sector was large in comparison to the number of personnel I was in charge of. We couldn't control every meter of the sector.

(Y010) Static checkpoints, mobile checkpoints (no more than one hour). Extensive vehicle and foot patrol, night observation points, helicopter patrols.

(Y013) Warring parties decided on the UNPROFOR freedom of movement.

(Y014) Sometimes restriction of movement. Also stupid rules (agreed by UN) with 4 hours notice before inspections.

(Y015) Checkpoints, patrolling.

(Y016) See answers at 2.2 and 2.3.

(Y017) Operating checkpoints (fixed and mobile), patrolling the area (24 hours patrol), operation of hidden observation post, operation of [observation post] with radar.

(Y025) We [couldn't] fight and our force was weak and low.

(Y026) Control of all traffic into [the] sector; surveillance and spot checks; living in the area and getting a "feel" for it; good liaison with local authorities.

(Y027) Not enough troops, too many directives from higher HQ, not enough time.

(Y030) Mobile checkpoints, spotchecks of areas where weapons were kept illegally.

(Y042) I was able if we continued to confiscate weapons in the whole UNPA. I was unable because the borders on [the] Sava river were too long, covered by trees and swamps and scattered minefields here and there, and we were not authorized [later on] to confiscate weapons [except] on our checkpoints [...].

(Y045) Due to the fact that my [area of responsibility] was very wide on both sides, Serbian and Croatian, it was not possible to control the whole area because of minefields which were not exactly known to me and my crew.

(Y054) All [...] access to the sector [was] controlled [by] checkpoints. Patrolling was continuous and on a random basis.

(Y057) Checkpoints were established around perimeter of UNPA (main roads). Serb resupply had to have passed over only one bridge. Both local commanders were assigned a UN representative for liaison.

(Y074) Too many access points -- not enough troops or surveillance equipment. No conviction/determination from parties to cease bringing in weapons.

(Y075) Because of the battalion's effective capacity in relation [to] the extent of the area.

(Y088) Lack of freedom of movement.

(Y094) Very tight security in the likely crossing sites, especially along the Sava river. [Operations] were deployed along the river bank in order to detect any incoming arms.

(Y097) Pour contrôler une zone de sécurité, il faut des troupes. [Troops are necessary to control a security zone.]

(Y126) We were unable to control our sectors because of restrictions imposed on the movement of UN personnel and the constant threats of death from all the warring parties.

(Y127) Safe havens and UN controlled safe areas were established.

(Y130) I was able to exercise control, but at times it was limited in certain areas owing to the terrain and the limitations of troops available.

(Y136) Restrictions of movement. Security risk due to mines/sniping.

(Y137) Restricted freedom of movement.

(Y139) Because there was an active war going on.

(Y149) Surveillance with UN troops.

(Y151) Perforated borders were violable. UN preserve on [confrontation line] was denied. Big fish were involved in weapon smuggling.

(Y172) Lack of resources. No effective [rules of engagement]. No acceptance by warring parties of the agreement.

(Y174) In Croatian sector there [was] only a small number of unarmed observers.

Q11.25 Were you involved in any monitoring of arms embargoes/sanctions?

Yes: 04   No: 38

Q11.26 What was your experience in this respect?

(Y080) Could only report.

(Y095) No experience.

(Y126) The faction will seem to cooperate at the initial stages. Later, however, they were hostile.

(Y149) Bad.

(Y160) None.

(Y172) Monitoring sea traffic in lanes of supply. Observing weapons status of local forces for increases.

Q11.27 **Were any weapons collected for cash or land during your mission?**

Yes: 00   No: 35

Q11.28 **If so, comment on the effectiveness of this incentive.**

(Y013) Sarajevo TBZ had not reached this stage.

(Y136) The Muslims in Bihac pocket received weapons from Croatia and also from Bosnia and Krajina Serbs. Guess they paid for it.

(Y160) We never used cash to collect weapons (as far as I know).

Q11.29 **Were national police involved in the collection of arms?**

Yes: 07   No: 32

Q11.30 **Were other organizations involved in the collection of arms?**

Yes: 10   No: 30

Q11.31 **If so, which ones?**

(Y014) ECMM, UNCIVPOL, UNMO's, UNPROFOR, etc.

(Y016) UN civil force, UN military observers.

(Y027) UNCIVPOL.

(Y042) UNCIVPOL.

(Y045) The local army.

(Y080) UN.

(Y127) ECMM.

(Y137) UN in Sarajevo and occasionally the Nordic battalion.

**Q11.32   If involved in Chapter VI operations (peacekeeping), were
            military observers used in the collection of arms?**

Yes: 17   No: 18

**Q11.33   If so, what type of military observer was used (i.e., UN,
            regional, other organization, etc.)?**

(Y002) Les Nations Unies exclusivement. [The UN exclusively.]

(Y009) UNMO's.

(Y013) UN.

(Y014) UN.

(Y015) UN/ECMM.

(Y016) UN.

(Y027) UN, ECMM.

(Y054) UN.

(Y069) UN.

(Y071) UNMO's.

(Y088) UNMO's.

(Y094) To report any information relevant to the issue. They acted as a complementary information-gathering source.

(Y130) UNMO's.

(Y136) UN.

(Y149) UNMO's, ECMM, UNCIVPOL.

(Y172) UN.

(Y174) UN.

Q11.34 **Answer if applicable: was there satisfactory coordination between military observers and yourself as unit commander/chief of operation?**

Yes: 27   No: 06

Q11.35 **Were the warring factions themselves involved in the collection of arms?**

Yes: 24   No: 13

Q11.36 **Did you use opposite party liaison officers so that all factions were represented in the collection of arms and the disarming process?**

Yes: 21   No: 15

Q11.37 **If so, reflect upon your experiences in this issue.**

(Y009) It was very positive and useful.

(Y010) Liaison offices used intensively throughout the operation. Once belligerents declared all weapons out of UNPA or in storage site they no longer participated in collection efforts.

(Y013) It was needed but not done.

(Y014) It was necessary sometimes due to mine situation.

(Y015) The weapon collection was more of a gesture than effective policy.

(Y016) Collection and disarmament is only as successful as the willingness of local commanders, local police, willingness to cooperate and comply. Must be aggressive even [in the] application of [the] agreement from the outset of implementation.

(Y027) The quality of the liaison officers varied considerably from reasonable to poor. Obviously the poor ones hampered the process.

(Y030) Initially, a detailed plan was drawn up concerning the simultaneous withdrawal of weapons on both sides with participation of officers controlling the opposite sides undertaking.

(Y042) Once we observe weapons, we cordon the area, contact the liaison officer, local police and UN civil police, and then we go ahead [with] confiscating the weapons and storing [them] in the magazine. If any of the parties did not cooperate, we used to exclude [them].

(Y045) In any side and any aspect there should be [a] liaison officer with [the] UN to control the collection of arms due to the fact that it is easy and simple to manage.

(Y069) Was very important in this issue. The liaison officers work also like interpreters.

(Y074) I said yes as my predecessors informed me of this fact. I have no first-hand experience.

(Y080)   Difficult over short period of time.

(Y094)   The most important factor is to have a daily meeting with them. These meetings can be spaced weekly as the collection of arms [is] being completed.

(Y097)   Les officiers de liaison jouent un rôle essentiel dans les domaines de l'information, de la confiance mutuelle, de la présentation des incidents.
[The liaison officers play an important role in the areas of information, mutual confidence, and the presentation of incidents.]

(Y129)   Liaison officers are essential [to] peacekeeping operations.

(Y130)   It was vital to have transparency in this matter.

(Y160)   [The] UN always has to show impartiality and to guarantee [...] safe operation everywhere inside the mission area.

Q11.38   **With regard to the UN/national mission you participated in, do you believe arms can be effectively collected?**

Yes: 22   No: 19

Q11.39   **Were you involved in the disarming of individuals, private and irregular units, and/or bandits?**

Yes: 19   No: 20

Q11.40   **Was the UN police involved in these tasks?**

Yes: 17   No: 21

Q11.41   **Were local authorities involved in disarming individuals?**

Yes: 14   No: 25

Q11.42   **If so, what was their role?**

(Y002) Les autorités bosniaques de Sarajevo ont, en automne 1993, remis de l'ordre dans leurs propres forces (en particulier dissolution d'une brigade devenue incontrolable) en les désarmant et en éliminant physiquement leurs chefs.
[In the fall of 1993, the Bosnian authorities de Sarajevo re-ordered in their forces (particularly in disolving a brigade which had become uncontrollable) by disarming them and physically eliminating their chiefs.]

(Y009) Local police, under the supervision of UNCIVPOL and [peacekeeping] troops in charge of disarming individuals.

(Y016) Normally to order individuals to turn over weapons. However, local military commanders would often attempt to talk UN forces out of confiscation.

(Y026) Organizing the disarming; control of traffic under very close UN supervision; providing information.

(Y027) UNCIVPOL.

(Y042) To help in controlling the military individuals by [liaison officers] and the police to control the civilians and militias.

(Y045) Assist the UN police in collecting the arms from the local people living in [the Area of Responsibility].

(Y074) Assisted in conducting cordon and search operations.

(Y075) Cooperation of the local police.

(Y080) Removing unsolicited SA's.

(Y130) Support to my forces in dealing with their people.

(Y149) Normal police role.

(Y172) Not connected with UN; their arms control was more along the lines of ethnic cleansing.

Q11.43   Were there regulations in the mandate or peace agreement with respect to how to deal with private and irregular units?

Yes: 20   No: 20

Q11.44   If not, do you think your task would have improved if there had been such an accord?

Yes: 14   No: 05

Q11.45   Did you experience problems with snipers?

Yes: 29   No: 13

Q11.46   If so, how did you counter this?

(Y002) Problème crucial à Sarajevo mais aussi sur la ligne de front en Croatie. Utilisation d'unités de l'ONU anti-snipers qui n'existent que dans de rares contingents, dont le contingent français de Sarajevo.

[The problem was crucial in Sarajevo but also on the Croatian front line. Use of UN anti-sniper units which existed only in a few contingents, including the French contingent at Sarajevo.]

(Y010) Returning fire. Cordon and search of suspected sniper location. Use of thermal imagers to locate and isolate snipers.

(Y013) Complain to suspected warring party. Ask nearest UNPROFOR unit to take anti-sniper action. Advertise UNMO presence to warring parties so [there could be] no excuse. Deploy UNMO teams on opposite sides of confrontation line in sniper areas so as to deter by presence.

(Y015) Counter-sniper operations. Negotiations.

(Y016) Counter-sniper operations. Counter-infiltration operations to dominate problem areas in cleared security measures. Return of fire if rules of engagement were met.

(Y017) In one first phase, I made only strong protests to the local commanders and threatened them that [this] was the last time and the next time that somebody shot [at] us we [would] open fire. In a second phase, I ordered to my troops to inform [the] battalion [operations] center, fire warning shots, fire armed shots on the sniper position (battalion commander will order, if possible).

(Y025) We used helmets, flak jackets, [and armored personnel carriers].

(Y027) No real way outside of the negotiation process.

(Y030) Through negotiations directly with local commanders.

(Y054) Firing back. Calling for reinforcement. Searching the area.

(Y075) With prevention and security (not many incidents).

(Y088) Report of the local commander of the unit where the sniper fire came from.

(Y097) Organisation de la lutte anti-snipers à Sarajevo. [Organization of the anti-sniper struggle in Sarajevo.]

(Y126) Sniper problems were countered by avoiding sniper areas.

(Y127) Reports were always made to [the] unit controlling the place sniper shooting [was] coming from.

(Y129) We shot them after warnings and following UN rules of engagement.

(Y130) By negotiating with [the warring factions'] commanders. Deployment of anti-sniper operations with my [rules of engagement].

(Y136) Using flak jackets, helmets and speed when you were driving.

(Y137) Evasive maneuvers, carefully selected routes, high *en route* altitude, armed convoy escort.

(Y139) Flying helicopters.

(Y151) Passive preventive measures. Active response when RoE permitted.

(Y172) Keep moving, war protection, etc. No attempts were made to counter the problem at its source.

(Y174) Took over and reported through liaison officers.

Analyst's Comments:

There is a logical sequence to follow in demobilization operations in which disarming belligerents is one of the stages. The normal stages of a demobilization operation are securing an agreement, establishing and managing a cease-fire, withdrawing and assembling the belligerents, disarming the belligerents, and finally, dispersing and rehabilitating the belligerents. The first and foremost principle is that there can be no peace without a reasonably secure environment. Demobilization operations, representing in effect the implementation of negotiated settlements, are therefore a foundational military task in the peacekeeping context. A peacekeeping force must take actions to restore and maintain a reasonable level of peace and personal security within a given region. Disarming the belligerent parties is likely to prove the most difficult and dangerous stage of demobilization. If done prematurely, the whole theater of operations may be destabilized. Psychologically, parties to a conflict will only be prepared to disarm if they are confident that the preceding stages of the demobilization process have been securely carried out and that the resultant change in the security situation can be sustained.

- Successful disarmament in the former Yugoslavia depended on the combatants' trust of UNPROFOR, both in terms of its impartiality and its credibility. The latter depends on the combatants' perception of UNPROFOR's military capabilities and its political will to carry through the demobilization process and punish transgressors. The custody and accurate accounting of weapons and war supplies, which played such a vital role in the verification of the completion of the process, never got off the ground properly.

- It seems that there is a definite case for the use of force in certain situations. Serious thought must be given to a "use of force doctrine" within the UN operational strategy for Chapter VI operations. The use of force places great responsibilities on the mission's commander and all his subordinate commanders to maintain their impartiality and neutral profile. In the end, however, it is the outcome of the use of force that must be evaluated. If a capable force with enough firepower had been initially deployed in the former Yugoslavia to enforce the peace agreement (even merely with the presence of the forces and their potential to intervene), that *country could well have been on the way to recovery now. The use of force has certain preconditions that must be met:*

- *The military mission must be structured and equipped to use the force necessary to accomplish its objective. In other words, it must have a full range of military capabilities, with the potential to meet or exceed those of the belligerent parties.*

- *Although the preferred objective is the commitment of a capable military force to dissuade belligerents from further conflict, such forces should plan as if they will be required to use force to restore an agreement. Settlement, not victory, will be the objective of using force under these circumstances.*

- *The use of force will create problems in terms of the neutrality of the enforcing contingents. They can never be considered neutral in the same theater in which they applied force. Their replacement with a peacekeeping force which will keep the newly-generated peace must therefore be planned well in advance.*

- *The insertion of force to stop combat will only be effective in preventing the continuation of violence. It cannot in itself create lasting peace. The political plan to capitalize on this break in hostilities must also be in place long before the actual insertion of force. Political leaders must be prepared to embrace the use of force to create this opportunity to restore peace and to refrain from criticizing the military.*

- *If possible, consent to the use of force must be negotiated with the belligerent parties before the agreements are finalized. When this is the case, both parties will understand that the mission commander is serious in his intentions to hold them to their promises and that he has the capability to enforce the agreement. They will also understand the conditions which will lead to the insertion of force.*

- *Coercive disarmament measures must be seen in the same light as the use of force. An unarmed man should not be sent to coercively disarm formations of troops armed with conventional weapons. A force of equal or greater strength should be used. Different formations of the belligerent parties can be isolated by preventative deployment and disarmed one at a time. Protection measures must be in place to protect disarmed formations from attacks by armed opponents.*

SECTION FIVE

XII. DEMOBILIZATION EXPERIENCES

Q12.1   Did the disarmament component of your mission include or infer demobilization?

Yes: 25   No: 17

Q12.2   If so, what types of demobilization operations were conducted during this UN/national operation (i.e., cease-fire monitoring, weapons cantonment, etc.)?

(Y009) Cease-fire monitoring, disarmament, weapons cantonment.

(Y010) Upon cantonment in monitoring sites. Demobilization of soldiers (primarily forcing them out of uniform).

(Y016) Cease-fire implementation and storage of heavy weapons. Withdrawal of respective forces to newly agreed [...] lines [and] dcmobilization of some units including local defense companies. Decrease in number of personnel manning front line positions.

(Y017) Cease-fire monitoring, disarmament, [and] weapons cantonment.

(Y026) Same as above, and in addition, protection of civilians.

(Y027) Cease-fire monitoring, weapon collection sites, cordon and searches, destruction of weapons.

(Y030) Demobilizing of local militia.

(Y043) Patrolling areas of responsibility [and] monitoring cease-fire lines.

(Y044) Cease-fire monitoring. Weapons cantonment in the storage [area].

(Y045) Cease-fire monitoring.

(Y048) Cease-fire monitoring, weapons cantonment, [and] monitoring [the confrontation line].

(Y054) Collecting weapons in magazines. Disbanding of the troops.

(Y057) Local units disbanded or went out of UNPA. Cease-fire line monitoring by UN. Weapons storage, under UN control, [was] established. Demining controlled by UN engineers but executed by local forces.

(Y060) Cease-fire, withdrawal of JNA, disbanding of Territorial Defense Forces, collection of heavy weapons.

(Y069) Cease-fire monitoring, weapons cantonment, control to the local police (side arms), local police monitoring.

(Y074) Disbandment of units, cease-fire monitoring, cantonment, verification.

(Y080) Monitoring, upon storage and control.

(Y095) Demobilization would mean that the personnel involved would cease to wear [their] uniforms or carry any weapons, though they could continue to be paid by the local authorities.

(Y129) Cease-fire monitoring.

(Y136) Demobilization of Serbian troops in Krajina area. Cease-fire monitoring. Weapons cantonment.

(Y147) Storage of weapons. Cease-fire monitoring. Monitoring of a separation zone.

(Y151) [Cease-fire] monitoring, weapons collection points. Weapons exclusion zones.

(Y159) During [the] UN operation [...] cease-fire monitoring and weapons cantonment were conducted.

Q12.3   **Was the demobilization process accompanied by a national reintegration process involving government forces and opposing forces?**

Yes: 08   No: 20

Q12.4   **If so were sufficient means available for an effective reintegration process?**

Yes: 07   No: 08

Q12.5   **If not, elaborate on the problems you experienced with this task.**

(Y010) Serb forces could not be reintegrated since they came from locations throughout Croatia/ Bosnia. Remained as a centralized force throughout.

(Y016) Krajina Serbs retained control of captured territory.

(Y017) With Croatians I did not have problems. Serbians: during almost one month my battalion had under its responsibility one area occupied by Serbs. As they were allowed to wear uniforms and carried weapons openly, they refused to discuss [...] demobilization issues. I had to use coercive procedures frequently.

(Y030) No alternate programs for ex-combatants were offered.

(Y045) Many problems which I cannot mention in this questionnaire.

(Y048) Duplications, too much local command and most of orders issued by local commander did not reach lower level on time.

(Y054) The disbanded personnel stayed on their own side of the cease-fire line.

(Y057) Only one of four sector was demilitarized. UNPROFOR could not go ahead without having all four sectors demilitarized.

(Y060) Distrust.

(Y074) They withdrew the opposite sides of the cease-fire line.

(Y080) No will to do so on either side.

(Y136) Only for Serb/Krajina Serb unit in Krajina area, and demobilization came to a stop when Croatian army prolonged an attack on the "Krajina Serbs' Area".

Q12.6 **Which organizations assisted you in demobilizing (i.e., other services, international organizations, national organizations, or nongovernmental organizations)? List by order starting with most assistance to least assistance.**

(Y009) UNHCR.

(Y010) UNHCR, UNCIVPOL, Carritas, [and the] Red Cross.

(Y016) UNHCR, UNCIVPOL, ICRC, ECMM, local Red Cross, [and] UN Civil Affairs.

(Y017) Nobody.

(Y026) None.

(Y027) UNCIVPOL. ECMM. Other organizations to a very limited degree.

(Y030) None.

(Y043) ECMM.

(Y044) ECMM [and] civil affairs.

(Y048) UNPROFOR [and] ECMM.

(Y054) None.

(Y060) None.

(Y069) The ECMM [and] Red Cross.

(Y095) International organizations, national organizations, non-governmental organizations, other services.

(Y147) UNCIVPOL.

(Y149) UNPROFOR, UNCIVPOL, UNMO's, [and] Civil Affairs.

(Y151) UNMO's and UNCIVPOL.

Q12.7   **Was there a person or a branch responsible for plans for demobilization?**

         Yes: 15   No: 10

Q12.8   **If so, who or which branch was it?**

         (Y009)   Operations.

         (Y010)   Operations.

         (Y016)   Operations branch and civil affairs.

         (Y017)   Information got the necessary information and kept the records. Operations prepared the plans for demobilization.

         (Y030)   Sector Commander [and] troops [in] the Sector.

         (Y054)   Operations Office.

         (Y057)   Sector [Operations].

         (Y060)   The military and civil affairs including police.

         (Y069)   The Sector Commander.

         (Y074)   Operations.

         (Y136)   Operations branch.

         (Y147)   G3.

         (Y151)   The UNPROFOR military branch of operations.

XIII. DEMINING EXPERIENCES

Q13.1   Did you experience mine problems?

Yes: 38   No: 05

Q13.2   If so, what did you do to counteract them?

(Y002) Les problèmes se posent partout, en Croatie et en Bosnie-Herzégovine. Solution: mise en oeuvre d'unités de génie spécialisée qui n'existent que pour quelques contingents nationaux.
[Problems emerged everywhere, in Croatia and Bosnia-Herzegovina. Solution: implementation of specialized engineering units which existed only for several national contingents.]

(Y009) Croatian forces and UN [peacekeeping] forces made maps together in order to identify minefields.

(Y010) Build safe route traces using engineers to clear routes. Avoided uncleared areas except when [...] in [armored personnel carriers].

(Y013) Careful recognition training. Use warring party [liaison officers]. Develop local knowledge.

(Y014) Using local [liaison officer] or sometimes avoid the area.

(Y015) Training, experience, physical control of movement.

(Y016) Designated coordinated plan to supervise lifting program. Supervising belligerent engineers lifting mines. Providing routes using UN resources/own resources. Destroying mines/booby traps. Let both sides know, obtained their minefield records, training own soldiers.

(Y017) Adopted preventive procedures. Mine/demining training. Reconnaissance of roads, paths or field used frequently by our troops.

(Y025) We tried to avoid these areas. We used only the roads; we did not go into the forests and fields.

(Y026) Close control with all movements, mine search, information from local authorities.

(Y027) Training, demining operations by qualified engineers or warring parties, leave the area alone.

(Y028) Mine awareness training.

(Y030) Minefield identification.

(Y042) Coordinate with engineering units and their counterparts from both sides to clear the mines under our supervision.

(Y043) Accompany a guide or liaison officer of the local forces.

(Y044) Using UN units, local commanders.

(Y045) Getting some maps from the local army about the areas which are mined according to the good relationship which I had with the local army liaison officers.

(Y054) Detailed orders were issued.

(Y057) Demining [operations] took place under control of UN engineers.

(Y060) Carried out mine clearance when feasible.

(Y074) Coordinated mine removal by the belligerents themselves; lifted mines by UN engineers (Canadian).

(Y075) Our mission included only supervision of the demining carried out by Croatian military engineers.

(Y080) Called in UN/local forces.

(Y088) Requesting assistance of the UN engineer units.

(Y094) Demining the areas, warning personnel-military and local population, help from the warring parties.

(Y097) Equipes de démineurs particulièrement compétents. [Teams of particularly competent deminers.]

(Y127) Patrols were done on tracks. Mined areas were marked by warring factions and Canadians.

(Y129) Disarmed where we could. Otherwise avoided.

(Y130) Improved on mine information [and] training. Operated with a great deal of care.

(Y136) Abandon some areas, roads. When driving/movements in dangerous areas, you should use flak jackets/helmets.

(Y137) Personnel instructed to stay on hard surface. Mine clearing units cleared vital areas.

(Y139) Started to take them up.

(Y147) Demining by the conflicting parties under supervision of UN forces.

(Y151) Mine awareness training. Mine clearing operations.

Q13.3　Was there an exchange of maps of minefields at the outset when the agreements were signed?

Yes:　19　　　　　No:　19

Q13.4   If not, was it feasible to have such maps?

        Yes: 13   No: 12

Q13.5   If so, do you think there should have been an agreement for the exchange of maps at the outset as part of the agreements signed?

        Yes: 28   No: 01

Q13.6   If no maps were available and it was not feasible to chart the location of minefields, did you consider yourself adequately prepared to deal with the demining of haphazard minefields?

        Yes: 10   No: 22

Q13.7   Did your unit play a role in the demining process?

        Yes: 22   No: 16

Q13.8   Was the UN involved in demining?

        Yes: 38   No: 03

Q13.9   Was the UN interested in becoming involved in demining?

        Yes: 34   No: 06

Q13.10   Was the host nation involved in demining or interested in becoming involved in demining?

        Yes: 30   No: 10

Q13.11   Were local groups/militias involved in demining?

        Yes: 24   No: 19

Q13.12 **Do you think local groups and militias should be encouraged to undertake demining tasks?**

Yes: 38 No: 04

Q13.13 **Why?**

(Y009) Sometimes local groups knew where minefields were located because, for most of the time, the militias worked together with the army.

(Y010) Mines make it virtually impossible to restore normal economic activity.

(Y013) To encourage demilitarization.

(Y014) It is their minefield, their country, and they know the area best.

(Y015) Less risk to UN soldiers, accountability, local knowledge.

(Y016) Most mines are laid by local engineers. They have best knowledge of types, numbers and locations.

(Y017) They will try to get the necessary information and they have better contacts than UN troops. They have to take the main risks. They have to assume that [risk] because the demining is [of] benefit [to] their compatriots.

(Y025) There are thousands of mines in the field and roads and these [require] demining.

(Y026) They know best their techniques and mines. It is help to self-help. [There is] no waste of UN lives.

(Y027) They placed the bulk of them in location and would probably have some records.

(Y028) To mine-clear the areas where they have been laying the mines.

(Y030) Joint interest should be created. Confidence-building element.

(Y042) They know the exact minefields locations and booby traps.

(Y043) Because they know the terrain very well.

(Y044) Because they know the area.

(Y045) To enhance and [keep] safe and assist the local army due to the ability of demining areas and the availability of equipment.

(Y048) From experience; [a] number of militias were killed by mines and they should be informed.

(Y054) The armies are aware of the locations of mines. Should be combat engineers. Every party has to take care of demining its own side.

(Y057) Safety: they know their mines and tactics. It is a sign that they are ready for peace. UN can supervise large amount of sites and do more faster.

(Y060) So that the dangers [to] their population are eliminated.

(Y069) Because [it] is a troops' problem (special engineer task).

(Y074) Sometimes they laid them. Local knowledge. They will benefit from the removal of the mines.

(Y075) When they have participated in the laying down of the mines.

(Y080) Stop the dying.

(Y088) They know exactly the location of the mines, etc., and they should be more interested in demining than UN forces as a means to clean [up] and get back to normal life in certain areas.

(Y094) They might have information on them.

(Y095) Because they are not considered as soldiers and they are not professionals to do that kind of job.

(Y097) Ces groupes ne savent pas où sont les mines.
[These groups do not know where the mines are.]

(Y126) The mining in most cases were done by them. The locals were at more risk of mine accidents.

(Y127) Because they know the way out of their mines and could retrieve them.

(Y129) Those that laid mines must remove them.

(Y130) Because they have the relevant information.

(Y136) Familiar with the area, the minefields, the different mine types.

(Y137) They would benefit from that after a peace agreement.

(Y139) It is their land and they know where mines are.

(Y147) No appropriate means.

(Y149) Experience. Those who lay the mines know best how to demine.

(Y151) General lack of know-how by militias. Inadequate aids/equipment held for demining.

(Y174) Preserves UN resources. Gives responsibility to these who should bear it.

Q13.14   Were humanitarian organizations or private firms involved in demining?

Humanitarian Organizations: Yes: 01   No: 41
Private Firms: Yes: 02   No: 40

Q13.15   In your opinion, who should undertake demining processes and why?

(Y002) Unités de génie spécialisée. Dans le contexte de l'ex-Yougoslavie, où la guerre sévit encore, ce sont les seules qui peuvent faire cela.
[Specialized engineering units. In the context of former Yugoslavia where there is still war, they are the only ones who can do it.]

(Y009) UN and opposing forces.

(Y010) The belligerents should lift mines under UN supervision. The knowledge that this will be [done] will improve marking, mapping and reporting of minefields.

(Y013) Warring parties, if possible, as a confidence-building measure.

(Y014) See above, 13.13. Local authorities.

(Y015) The military experience. Minefields were along active front lines.

(Y016) Competent, well-equipped, well-trained military engineers supervising belligerent force engineers. This should be supported by mine rollers and dog teams capable of finding buried mines. This type of organization would have best chance of success, minimize injuries to UN personnel and others. Obtain copy of UNPROFOR directives regarding demining procedures.

(Y017) Local armed forces or paramilitary and militias. UN troops can provide technical assistance and maybe some special devices (mine detectors). But the local forces must perform the demining processes. Because the demining is in benefit of the local population and local activities restitution.

(Y025) Humanitarian organizations, private firms, local groups (army).

(Y026) See 13.13.

(Y027) Local military under UN supervision or if possible a fully-trained civilian firm.

(Y028) The parties which have been laying the mines on the area where they have control. On other areas local troops assisted by UN organizations.

(Y030) National mine clearance authority with regional and local affiliates. Equipment and training to be provided by international community.

(Y042) Local [and] national engineering units and UN supervision to avoid likely casualties.

(Y043) An engineer unit of UN together with engineer unit of local forces.

(Y044) UN forces (engineer units).

(Y045) The local army with their special engineers, who have the maps and the experience to do this task.

(Y048) UN forces [and] local troops. Reason: to safeguard the area where UN forces should monitor [the cease-fire] and to help UNPROFOR in case of withdrawal.

(Y054) It depends on the situation.

(Y057) Local forces must do this demining. If we demine and they do not agree, they will remine the area and nothing will have been achieved. They must want to demine. UN should only facilitate.

(Y060) Military units.

(Y069) See 13.13.

(Y071) Force combat engineers and combat engineers of the warring parties.

(Y074) The units which laid them. They know where the mines are and how they were laid.

(Y075) The warring parties.

(Y080) Those trained to do so.

(Y088) Warring factions assisted by UN experts and engineers' units. Same reasons as in paragraph 13.13.

(Y094) The warring parties under supervision of the UN. Because it is a military practice that minefields should be cleared by the one who planted them if it is possible.

(Y095) The warring parties because they have the maps, they know the field, they know how to undertake their own mines.

(Y097) Unités militaires - leur entraînement est complet et
"intensif".
[Military units because their training is complete and
intensive.]

(Y126) The UN and the local government. First the UN has the
facilities and the local governments could show specific
mine areas.

(Y127) UN in conjunction with the locals. For safety of UN and
the locals.

(Y129) Those that laid the mines - only they know where they
are.

(Y130) The warring factions. The UN should only be involved if
our operations are being hindered and there is no other
way of dealing with the mines.

(Y136) Host nation - see 13.13.

(Y137) UN and serious organizations - if they can do it at a
reasonable cost.

(Y139) UN together with [the warring factions].

(Y147) The conflicting parties.

(Y149) Warring parties - confidence-building measure.

(Y151) Military component of the UN, situation permitting
private firms may also be tasked.

(Y174) Local groups. Danger of ownership.

SECTION SIX

XIV. TRAINING

Q14.1   **Prior to deployment, did your units undertake specific training programs related to disarmament operations?**

Yes: 18   No: 29

Q14.2   **If so, were these training programs based on guidance from the UN forces already in the field, from the UN in general, or from your national authorities?**

UN forces in field: 08   UN in general: 06
National authorities: 14   Other: 01

Q14.3   **Were your units trained specifically for the collection of arms and cantonment of factions?**

Yes: 10   No: 33

Q14.4   **Were you and/or your units trained in on-sight inspection and observation techniques?**

Yes: 24   No: 21

Q14.5   **Have you been trained in verification technologies nationally?**

Yes: 12   No: 31

Q14.6   **Were you trained and prepared to conduct specific weapons control and disarmament operations (i.e., weapons searches, inventories, elimination, etc.)?**

Yes: 22   No: 23

Q14.7   Were you trained and prepared to conduct specific demobilization operations?

Yes: 12   No: 33

Q14.8   Were you trained and prepared to conduct specific demining operations?

Yes: 19   No: 25

Q14.9   On the whole, did you consider yourself technically and tactically prepared for the accomplishment of your mission?

Technically: Yes: 30   No: 10
Tactically: Yes: 38   No: 02

Q14.10   Was there anything done at the end of the mission to gather lessons learned?

Yes: 32   No: 07

Q14.11   Back in your own country, were you debriefed?

Yes: 29   No: 12

SECTION SEVEN

XV. INTERACTIONS

Given that there are three common elements to a UN mission -- the military, the humanitarian agencies, and the political branch:

Q15.1   Would you consider the relationship between humanitarian elements/organizations and the military personnel during the mission to have been very good, adequate, or inadequate?

Very good: 09   Adequate: 21
Inadequate: 11

Q15.2   If you think it could have been improved, specify three ways in which this could have been achieved.

(Y002) C'est tout le problème "philosophique" de la compatibilité de l'action militaire et de l'action humanitaire. Les organisations humanitaires, dont le HCR, ont beaucoup de réticence à côtoyer les militaires et collaborer avec eux. Ils y viennent par nécessité !
[This is the philosophical problem of the compatibility of the humanitarian and military actions. Humanitarian organizations, such as the HCR, were very reluctant to work next to or with the military. But necessity forced them to!]

(Y009) There was no coordination between the military and the agencies. In practice, there were two chains of command, the military on the one hand, and the humanitarian and political branch on the other.

(Y014) More information on each task. Too much red tape. Sometimes you feel that there is a wall between different organizations.

(Y017) The peacekeeping operation must be conceived as a whole, and the sector commander must conduct the operation. The humanitarian organizations and other agencies must prepare their plans and perform their duties according to the commander's plan, otherwise they will be a hindrance to the military effort.

(Y024) To have a sort of seminar training at least for the chiefs (commanders) of [each] sector at the beginning of the mission.

(Y025) Cooperation.

(Y026) Better coordination, mutual trust and goodwill, information exchange.

(Y027) Better training for all but especially humanitarian organizations. Better directives from UN NY. Better personnel selection process, too. Many humanitarian personnel have a distrust of the military due to their age and training (lack).

(Y028) Giving more information on the tasks of other organizations. Having more meetings on all levels of [the] organizations.

(Y030) More understanding about the work of the others is necessary. Important to work closely and as a team.

(Y042) Employ more employees. Attach employees with the unit/units. More coordination at the higher and lower levels.

(Y044) Visiting between the units, meeting commanders.

(Y048) Exchange of ideas and visits. Be at the same HQ's. Briefing and debriefing.

(Y054) With coordination at the highest level. Informing commanders in the field about all movements and convoys. Asking for security in advance.

(Y060) Some institutionalized arrangements for getting to know one another. Understanding one another's sphere of activity and responsibility. Better briefing.

(Y069) Equal salary, rank respect.

(Y071) Task of the Special Representative of the Secretary-General (we did not have at that time and asked for). Should be the very head of the mission and direct chief of the elements named above and not only coordination.

(Y075) I did not see that relationship working because I served in the mission during the first five months. But I remember we could not get help from humanitarian organizations (Red Cross, etc.) during weekends.

(Y080) Not for me to comment.

(Y088) Establishing joint commissions. Liaison officer's job should be more in contact with UNMO's and UN units.

(Y090) More dialogue, more coordination, only one command.

(Y094) A solid policy at the highest level as a guideline for all concerned. Clear regulations for type and amount of support provided by military units to humanitarian agencies. Balance of basic resources to be given to humanitarian organizations such as food, water and accommodation. Humanitarian organizations should be self-sufficient in manpower and resources.

(Y095) More liaison between elements which would include meetings, information, etc. Coordination and cooperation between elements, commanders and branches inside the military components. Coordination and cooperation among the civilian staff and between military and civilian staff.

(Y097) Entraînement systématiquement organisé en temps de paix entre militaires et organisations humanitaires. Etablissement de structures de coopération. Limiter le nombre d'organisations humanitaires participant à une opération.

[Systematic training which is organized between military and humanitarian organizations during times of peace. Establishment of structures of cooperation. Limitation of the number of humanitarian organizations participating in an operation.]

(Y129) A better-organized system of regular meetings at all levels.

(Y130) By a top-down process of training. Mutual understanding. Exchange of information/assistance.

(Y136) More communication between UN troops/agencies. Remove the fight between UN troops and agencies. Better training for agency personnel.

(Y137) More careful selection of leaders that are capable of establishing good cooperation. More information and more specific guidelines describing the mission of each organization.

(Y147) Joint briefings-meetings. Exchange of operational plans, joint planning committee.

(Y149) Regular coordination between both organizations, common procedures, coordination of headquarters.

(Y151) Decentralized working/powers within civil UN branch. Military command structure with UN civil branches should be more balanced in power and strength. Civil branches/HQ's are far too out of touch with actual ground environment.

(Y172) Liaison officers from the military working continuously for the humanitarian organizations.

(Y174) Greater communication and central control.

Q15.3 How was the overall cooperation of the three elements of the UN components achieved during your mission? Summarize.

(Y002) La collaboration entre le Militaire et les responsables des Affaires Civiles, telle que je l'ai vécue et pour des raisons d'incompatibilités de personnes, a été très mauvaise. Le responsable des Affaires Civiles est jaloux de ses prérogatives, particulièrement dans le domaine de la communication, et est porté à marginaliser le militaire. [The collaboration between the military and those responsible for civil affairs, like those that I lived with and because of incompatible personalities, was very bad. The responsible civil affairs officers are jealous of their prerogatives, particularly in the realm of communications, and are inclined to marginalize the military.]

(Y009) Good, but not as [good] as it should [have been]. Reasons are mentioned in point 15.2.

(Y014) As long as you work with modern people from countries with western standards - no problems. Field service, civil affairs is sometimes a big obstacle.

(Y017) I did not receive cooperation from the humanitarian agencies or from the political branch, when I asked for their assistance in serious problems that I had (settlement of refugees - humanitarian relief needs) [or in] discussions with local authorities.

(Y024) Some frustrating arguing between the field commanders and the HQ civilians which even got worse [from] time to time. Both should realize the importance of the other. Nobody can run the operation alone!

(Y026) Hard to give overall [assessment as] we worked locally. Main lesson: it is dependent on [the] persons.

(Y027) Primarily the personal approach. Continual conference and planning sessions. Showing humanitarian agencies that the military really know something about humanitarian tasks.

(Y028) In the beginning of the operation the cooperation was very poor but after a few months it came to an adequate level.

(Y030) Joint meetings improved [the] situation and understanding. There are, however, attitudes that need to change. The components are equally important but the military emphasis should be weakened and military should be involved more in civilian tasks of rebuilding.

(Y042) It was not going well at the beginning. Our unit was playing most of the roles, then coordination started to improve although it was not sufficient.

(Y043) There should be very good coordination meetings between the three. Exchange of information.

(Y044) Good cooperation between the three elements, through information, meetings.

(Y047) UN was very good.

(Y048) By visiting the UN components in the field and discussing the situation and exchanging information with such agencies as the UNHCR, UNCIVPOL, civil affairs and NGO's.

(Y054) Actually the humanitarian agencies were not part of the mission. Within the mission the three components are the military, the civil affairs or political branch and the UN civil police. You'd better consider the administrative branch, too. Coordination was too lose and cooperation depended on the people in charge.

(Y057) Success in Western sector came because of excellent cooperation. All was coordinated centrally so that refugees and convoys could be controlled and protected by the UN. Plans were discussed by all three and one option was chosen by all and implemented.

(Y060) By periodic meetings at the higher levels and perseverance by all elements.

(Y071) Not [in the] mandate [of] UNPROFOR. [The existence of four] separate chains of command from New York hampered the mission. The negative action of some national contingent commanders [should also] be mentioned.

(Y074) We met regularly -- they were invited to our morning briefings. We cooperated on all issues. Open/free exchange of information. We mixed socially.

(Y088) In general was based on personal relations and not on established procedures.

(Y090) Adequate, but should be improved by the methods suggested in 15.2.

(Y094) It was good in general terms but there [was] some complication regarding the parallel chains of command. This issue is paramount during crises, which have to be solved in very close cooperation.

(Y095) [From] my personal point of view, I saw they tried to do their best, but they have to improve themselves as I said [throughout the] questionnaire.

(Y097) Cette coopération a été de plus en plus positive et efficace. Dépend essentiellement de la bonne volonté des chefs.
[This cooperation was more and more positive and effective. Depends on the good will of the chiefs.]

(Y127) UN troops [...] seemingly for political branch. Political branch assisted or supported UN observers and troops in their negotiations and mediations.

(Y129) Good cooperation but almost entirely dependent on personal relations.

(Y130) By my acting as a focus for their work. At the end of the day, this matter is personality-driven and depends on mutual respect and support.

(Y136) See 15.2.

(Y137) Political agencies seemed unable to be firm enough toward the warring factions. Military units distrusted the responsiveness of political agencies when in distress. Political agencies involved units not suited for their mission into the area. Humanitarian organizations demanded action from military units that was stretching their capacities to the limit.

(Y147) Informal contacts [and] joint meetings.

(Y149) Inadequate with IRC (Red Cross). Civil affairs could be better. UNCIVPOL [was] good. UNMO's [were] inefficient (too many different nations). UNHCR [was] sometimes good.

(Y151) Not known.

(Y169) There was always communication [...] available.

(Y172) The only reasonable co-operation came from a few individuals who took it upon themselves to do so.

(Y174) Largely left to local elements to arrange own cooperation.

Q15.4   Did cooperation exist between the UN military, private and irregular elements, and existing police forces (UN or local)?

Yes: 29   No: 08

Q15.5   If so, describe which components cooperated with whom and the level of their cooperation.

(Y009) At the battalion level: local political leaders, chiefs of police, irregular leaders, commanders of the armies.

(Y014) On local level, sometimes very good. As an UNMO you have to cooperate with all sorts of authorities.

(Y017) Croatian side: UNCIVPOL; the relationship with UNCIVPOL was good but we had some problems due to the behavior of some of its members. And also in situations when we asked for cooperation. Local police: we received very good cooperation. [Croatian] army: we received an excellent level of cooperation. Serbian side: we did not receive any kind of cooperation. UN military forces: the relationship and the cooperation between the sector HQ and battalions were outstanding.

(Y025) Construction with locals: water pipes, electricity wire, communication, telephone, roads.

(Y026) Regular meetings and conferences, local authorities were in charge of police, local structures were [functioning].

(Y027) All elements cooperated with like organizations, i.e., UNCIVPOL - local CIVPOL. At HQ level we worked with all components, be [they] military, civilian, political, police or whatever.

(Y030) Joint patrols, UN military, UN police and local police.

(Y042) The military units used to cooperate with both the local police and the UN police and the militias. There was also cooperation between the UN and local police elements.

(Y043) UNCIVPOL cooperates with local police. UN troops cooperate with local troops.

(Y044) Local units, military police, UNCIVPOL, ECMM, UNHCR, [and] liaison officers.

(Y048) There was cooperation on all levels between the UN and UNHCR, NGO's, local liaison officers, Civil Affairs and UN battalions.

(Y054) The military had to deal with everybody in the area; then, they tried to obtain cooperation and got a good level.

(Y057) It was limited in some circumstances. At all times, lines of communications were kept open and this allowed eventually [the resolution of] most issues. It was established that local and UN police (similar for military) would resolve problems amongst themselves first.

(Y074) UNCIVPOL with local police -- [high level of cooperation]. Civil affairs with local political authorities -- good. UN military with local police, military and humanitarian agencies -- good. UN humanitarian agencies with local agencies -- excellent.

(Y075) UNCIVPOL [and] local police. Both at the level of Battalion Commanding Officer.

(Y088) Cooperation was done through UNMO's at all levels.

(Y090) Local military, UN military, police, [and] local government.

(Y097) Essentiellement par officiers de liaison, observateurs des NU, ou de la communauté Européenne.
[Essentially by liaison officers and observers from the UN or the European Community.]

(Y127) UN observers cooperated with UNCIVPOL and UN peacekeepers (units) in negotiations and mediations for cease-fire.

(Y129) Some cooperation but only when it suited local police.

(Y130) UN police with local police - daily meetings, joint patrols, joint checkpoints.

(Y137) UNHCR cooperated with local contractors. UN hospital cooperated with local hospital.

(Y149) Local police with UNCIVPOL. Local military authorities with UN military component. Civil affairs with regional Red Cross, local authorities.

(Y151) UN military and UN [military police] - adequate cooperation. UN military and local police - adequate cooperation. UN military and irregular elements - inadequate cooperation.

(Y174) UN with existing police forces. Good.

Analyst's Comments:

The need for a joint doctrine/procedure within the UN system to unite the civilian and military missions, aims, and objectives is evident in the analysis of this section of the questionnaires. The levels of liaison between the UN military and civilian components and NGO's also need some sort of formalization if successful operations of this kind are to be executed in the future. During

UNPROFOR there was a common goal by force of circumstances shared by the NGO's and the military. As can be seen from the responses to Q15.2 and Q15.3, the interaction between the various actors in the operation was stressed. This is very much a symptom of the lack of defined structures and procedures for directing and coordinating field operations towards one common goal.

The need for the timely preparation of an integrated strategy for the mission as a whole cannot be over emphasized. Success can only be achieved when all components of a mission pursue the same goal along the same route and with the same set of rules. The relationship between the different components of the mission must be determined before deployment, and formal liaison forums must be established on the different levels of command. Joint procedures for planning, liaison, intelligence sharing and support must exist to ensure that the mission as a whole achieves its goal.

XVI. PERSONAL REFLECTIONS

On reflection,

Q16.1 **What was the overall importance of the disarmament task for the overall success of the mission?**

Very important: 03 Important: 10
Not important: 04

Q16.2 **What were the three major lessons you learned from your field experience?**

(Y002) L'autorité militaire de l'ONU (à New York et sur le terrain) incapable (ou ne veut pas) donner des directives précises au chef militaire. Il n'y a pas d'unité d'action au sein d'une mission entre les affaires civiles, l'administration, le militaire, l'humanitaire. L'ONU est un monde de fonctionnaires que le militaire dérange.
[The military authorities of the UN (in New York and in the field) are incapable of giving (or do not want to give) precise orders to the military chief. There is no unity of action within a mission between civil affairs, the

administration, the military, and the humanitarian organizations. The UN is a world of civil servants which the military disturbs.]

(Y009) Level of training should be UN standardized for those contingencies deployed [in] a UN peacekeeping operation. Command and control should include [non-governmental and governmental] agencies.

(Y010) Multinational forces under a strong central command can and must disarm belligerents. Certain nations need considerably more training and equipment before undertaking aggressive UN duties.

(Y014) Corruption, lies, sorrow for the people.

(Y015) Pre-mission training is invaluable; [rules of engagement] must be clear. Impartiality is paramount.

(Y016) Develop quick interpretation of agreement and implement aggressively and rapidly. Civic operations [must be] developed and implemented in concert with cease-fire agreement implementation. Military units must be well-equipped mechanized forces who are professionally trained and competently lead.

(Y017) First, the complete ignorance of UNPROFOR's doctrine about the fulfillment of the mandate by the majority of the key persons that were participating in this [peacekeeping operation] (even UN officials). Second, the necessity of one clear "chain of command" with only one head (Force Commander or Sector Commander or the sectors), and everybody (UN and military personnel) must accept this rule. Because the worse hindrance for the commander is that each key person in his [area of responsibility] would have his own "specific" chain of command. Third, all personnel must be convinced that they are [in] the service of [the] UN, not that they are there only to get some benefits.

(Y024) If the UN force is not able to carry out the task as agreed it is better to withdraw. If a mandate is given by [the] UN Security Council, the resources should be given simultaneously. Ignorant troops should not be used in any of the operations.

(Y025) Do not take unnecessary risks.

(Y026) You need a will for peace if a UN operation [is to] succeed; UN troops and officials must be viewed by the locals as completely impartial; create an air of transparency and mutual trust.

(Y027) The need for a standard direction by the UN for training and equipping units -- and adherence to it. Less direction from higher HQ, more listening, better cooperation between all members of the three components.

(Y028) UN is using too many troops who are not capable of peacekeeping [...]. There is too much bureaucracy.

(Y030) Disarmament [is the] centerpiece of [the] mission. Without fulfilling this objective, all other objectives cannot be carried out. Hence [the] stalemate. Disarmament must be linked to the provision of civilian programs.

(Y042) UN members (military and civilian) should be neutral in dealing with the warring parties -- you can achieve main success. Never give up when dealing with a problem even if you thought that you reached a dead-end for a solution. Be flexible to the acceptable point, then show your way of insisting to achieve your aim.

(Y043) How [...] to work with other nations to achieve one task. It is very important for countries to conduct training on unfamiliar terrain. Learn new lessons on how to deal with locals.

(Y044) Cooperation, impartiality, good experience.

(Y045) UN missions in such conflict areas might lead to the loss of life. Cooperation between UN organizations could be very good.

(Y047) Self-confidence, helping people, relationship with the UN.

(Y048) Trust and cooperation, impartiality (neutrality), experience in dealing with different nationalities.

(Y054) Demilitarization and disarmament are the center-pieces for the success of a mission. Impartiality and neutrality are the most important weapons in any UN mission. Unity of command is absolutely necessary.

(Y057) Local confidence must be gained first; if not, forget achieving anything. UN leadership is most important (the best man for the job. Forget national representation). Strong UN presence to back up our engagement. Limit number of participating countries to limit the associated chaos.

(Y060) The mandate must be framed on firm written agreements. Political backing of the international community is vital. Deployment must be undertaken speedily once a decision is taken after due deliberation.

(Y069) The consequences of the war, the cooperation between different troops, the UN peacekeeping organization.

(Y071) Cooperation between the chains [of command] is not enough: a clear mandate, one command, a proper budget adapted to the mandate.

(Y074) Must have negotiating skills. Encourage maximum cooperation. Recognize differences in various participating nations and use them to best advantage. Do not trust belligerents.

(Y075) Peacekeeping cannot succeed when the warring parties do not give up their objectives [and] do not act honestly because of the lack of trust. Peacekeeping forces have restrictions [on the fulfillment of] their mission.

(Y080) The difficulties [....] if neither side is interested, lack of injury, ethic, work ethic of some.

(Y088) UN should have complete authority to control, monitor and even destroy all weapons. That authority should include free access to real inventories and stores and units in [the] field.

(Y090) Possibility of accomplishing a very difficult mission.

(Y094) Weapons should be out of the protected area with no exceptions -- no magazines. Real time intelligence from overhead platforms, equal treatment to both warring parties, high tech sensors and communications, full-strength units, self-sufficient and minimum UN support (civilian).

(Y095) I have no experience in [the] field, but I suppose it would be the treatment between the warring parties, the training the soldiers need to carry out their duties and the information updates you need to clarify the current situation daily.

(Y097)   L'ONU est incapable de gérer une crise comme celle de Bosnie. Les moyens militaires doivent être cohérents (en ex-Yougoslavie, nous avons eu un ensemble hétéroclite d'unités). Il faut que les politiques aient un objectif. En Bosnie personne ne sait quel est le but *réel* poursuivit. [The UN is incapable of managing a crisis like the one in Bosnia. The military means should be coherent (in ex-Yugoslavia we had a heterogeneous assembly of units). It is necessary that politics have an objective. In Bosnia no one knows what is really being pursued.]

(Y127)   It is peacekeeping and peacemaking that can solve conflicts. Negotiations and mediations play [a] more important role in peacekeeping. The command of the mediating force should be premium.

(Y129)   Accept the situation as it is. Gain and maintain consent. Liaison officers are essential.

(Y130)   Without consent, the UN is helpless. Consent is earned by peacekeepers. Every situation is different.

(Y136)   UN troops [and] commanders were trained/prepared for the task they were given. The lack of commanders who were able to take charge in the area. The UN bureaucracy and the Field Service can sometimes almost stop a mission.

(Y137)   The local population must feel [that the] UN is doing something to help their situation get better both in the short term and [the] long term. Firm but fair treatment of the warring factions is essential. Disarmament must be followed up, otherwise [the] UN will have a very difficult if not impossible task. To succeed in border control, sufficient troops and a firm policy must be exercised.

(Y139)   Everybody must know and understand the mandate.

(Y147) Most important, clear mandate. Sufficient soldiers in the field. To show your willingness towards the parties.

(Y149) UN organization is too heavy, too complex, [has] too many different nations, [and is] too expensive. Extremely complicated situation and coordination of four warring factions; too many (50) humanitarian aid organizations without coordination, common procedures or objectives.

(Y151) Disarmament should always be part of initial mandate and proceed simultaneously with other tasks. UN should be able to enforce agreement/[Security Council Resolutions] either through sanctions or force. Otherwise it loses its credibility. All activities including those of senior members must be transparent to all [warring factions].

(Y159) It's difficult to achieve peace without cooperation of warring parties. It's necessary to confront the violations by giving the parties a strong answer. In general the professional experience was not very important.

(Y169) UN has no experience in dealing with the kind of conflict present in Yugoslavia - especially the one in Bosnia-Herzegovina.

(Y172) Must have a mandate that has political support from UN/NATO/national levels and from the warring factions. Must have realistic [rules of engagement].

(Y174) There must be adequate resources applied to solve the problem. There must ultimately be military power available to demonstrate commitment. There must be professional and well-trained UN forces.

Q16.3   **What other question should we have asked here and how would you have answered it?**

Questions:

(Y015) Were the warring sides at peace or war? Nature of the conflict? Were the belligerents willing to be disarmed?

(Y027) What areas require improvements?

(Y030) Work ethics of UN personnel? Could more have been achieved if more perseverance of personnel has been displayed?

(Y042) Is there a full determination by [the] UN to achieve the main purpose ?

(Y043) Were you successful in completing your mission?

(Y044) Did UNPROFOR achieve its goals?

(Y045) Do you think that you would like to join any other mission (UN)?

(Y048) What was the final achievement of the UN mission?

(Y060) What is the responsibility of the Security Council towards the force it deploys?

(Y069) At this time is peace possible between Croatia and Serbia?

(Y071) [What is the] importance of administration (mostly finance and logistics) to the mission?

(Y094) Should the local police force continue operating in UN-controlled areas?

(Y095) Which [...] of the elements carry out the most important duty in a UN mission?

(Y129) What are the greatest weaknesses of the UN?

(Y130) What was the key ingredient missing in resolving the situation?

(Y169) Do you think that the Security Council has been impartial in dealing with the problems in the former Yugoslavia?

Answers:

(Y027) Will depend upon the mission. However, should concentrate on organization, command and control or training aspects. The mandates could also be considered to ensure they are better written for the problem. UN accountability in decision-making, budgeting and so on.

(Y030) You may give an answer yourself.

(Y042) Little determination.

(Y043) Yes.

(Y044) Yes: [cease-fire] between the parties and collection [of] weapons, convoys for humanitarian aid did help people, demilitarized zone, exchange [of] prisoners and bodies, utility mission, transportation.

(Y045) [...] I [would] join [a] mission trying to achieve peace. Why not? As long as I am going to return back home safely. Nevertheless, what benefits might I get from such [a] mission? [I would go] as long as I am going to represent my country as an ambassador of peace.

(Y048) Did not achieve [or] reach a final resolution and peace agreement between the parties. Helped in settling down the war temporarily. Helping in the exchange of POW's, distributing aid to refugees.

(Y060) Framing a realistic and achievable mandate.

(Y069) No. Because there are too many years of historic, religious and political problems between Croatia and Serbia and the UN [has not found] the answer.

(Y071) Immediate support [and] careful preparation (6 months before). No contracts with the best states [or] within the mission territory. To avoid purchases of arms. War economy rising. Joint military and civilian administrative office.

(Y094) No. Police forces should act as liaisons integrated in an all-UN police organization. If you leave the local police in control, inside the area, then you are not controlling the area in a comprehensive way. The local police forces start being a problem for UN forces because they are part of the warring parties and keep on acting in support of any action.

(Y095) The soldiers, so the UN staff here should take care of them [by] encouraging their own mission and tasks in such a way [that] they can do their best.

(Y129) Poor media relations. Corruption. Waste of money.

(Y130) A coherent and accepted political campaign plan.

(Y169) No.

To be answered only by those who participated in completed UN/national peacekeeping missions:

Q16.4 **Do you think that the disarmament-related tasks which you undertook had an impact on the national reconstruction processes which followed the end of the mission?**

Yes: 03   No: 01

Q16.5 **If so, briefly explain how and why:**

(Y043) Because when civilians are liberated from the influence of arms then they feel that they have the spirit to work.

(Y090) They support the arrival of peace.

Analyst's Comments: Summary of Lessons Learned

1. *Demilitarization and disarmament are the cornerstones of a successful operation (Y094). Without disarmament, there is no chance of success and the other intentions of the mission cannot be achieved (Y030). The protection of the population in particular depends heavily on the ability to ensure a reasonably secure environment. The suffering can be reduced by properly-executed disarmament operations, and the necessary ability to follow-up and sustain the process.*

2. *Disarmament and demobilization can only take place with the full consent of both parties. If this is unobtainable, coercive measures are the only other viable option. The forces that are designated to execute the operation must have the firepower, resources and will to enforce the agreement on the party not complying with the intentions thereof (Y094, Y010).*

3. *Where disarmament operations have had effect, weapons, equipment and personnel were kept at different locations. These locations must be properly secured to prevent any faction from re-arming itself.*

4.   *Where pre-determined disarmament objectives are vital to the successful outcome of a whole mission, they must not be abandoned in preference for time or political favor.*

5.   *The UN needs to develop a screening mechanism to ensure that it only receives and accepts personnel with training and experience suited for specific operations.*

6.   *Proper interaction between the civilian and military components of a mission is vital to the success of the mission. The levels of liaisoning between the UN military and civilian components and the NGO's also must be formalized. The need for the timely preparation of an integrated strategy for the mission as a whole cannot be over emphasized. Success can only be achieved when all components of a mission pursue the same goal in a uniform and coherent way. The relationship between the different components of the mission must be determined before deployment, and formal liaison forums must be established at the different levels of command. Joint procedures for planning, liaison, intelligence-sharing and support must exist to ensure that the mission as a whole achieves its common goal.*

7.   *The situation in the former Yugoslavia is testimony to the ability of conflict to re-ignite and keep going without strong united and sustained international support and resolve.*

8.   *Once an agreement is reached on disarmament and the role it plays in the whole process, the process becomes subject to the successful execution of the disarmament. In the case of the former Yugoslavia, successful resolve was not possible without containing the military force of the warring parties.*

9.   *The strategist must find the "center of gravity" for an operation, i.e., the single most important event or condition that will stabilize the situation or reverse the destruction and strife. The organization must then direct all effort and resources towards that one identified center. The center of gravity for UNPROFOR should have been effective disarmament and demobilization before any other operations were mounted within the area.*

10. *The collection, interpretation and distribution of information is essential for the success of any military operation. Disarmament operations must be pro-active to be successful and not reactive or dependent on what others want the force to believe. The timely collection of information is thus essential to the efficient execution of this type of operation.*

11. *All public information-dissemination means at the disposal of the Mission HQ's (civilian and military) must be deployed to keep the people and the belligerents informed of the progress, problems and successes of the operation. Such dissemination can also help to counter rumors and disinformation spread by the belligerent parties to create confusion. One* very important *requirement is that this information be* timely, correct *and* complete.

12. The planning and contingency planning for the demobilization operation was not conducted according to acceptable principles. This is evident in the inexact method through which such planning was carried out. Management measures like "checks and balances" and "rewards and punishments" were absent and thus made the process ineffective.

13. The goodwill of belligerent parties, their word of mouth and the information they release to monitoring missions is simply not enough to base a disarmament operation on. The monitoring mission must follow the rules for disarmament, irrespective of what the belligerent parties want them to do. Arms, ammunition and war supplies must be separated from combatants and must be well-secured. Other arrangements, like preventive deployment, secure zones, technological surveillance, etc., can be used to address the security fears of the belligerent parties.

UNIDIR Publications

The *Research Reports* produced by UNIDIR are intended for publication and wide dissemination through free distribution to diplomatic missions, as well as research institutes, experts, academics and sales through the United Nations Sales Section and other outlets. In addition to research reports, UNIDIR publishes *Research Papers* written by researchers within the UNIDIR programme of work or in association with UNIDIR. They are disributed in the same manner as the research reports. UNIDIR also publishes a quarterly bilingual *UNIDIR Newsletter/Lettre de l'UNIDIR*.

Research Reports / Rapports de recherche

La guerre des satellites: enjeux pour la communauté internationale, par Pierre Lellouche (éd.) (IFRI), 1987, 42p., publication des Nations Unies, numéro de vente: GV.F.87.0.1.
* Also available in English: *Satellite Warfare: A Challenge for the International Community*, by Pierre Lellouche (ed.) (IFRI), 1987, 39p., United Nations publication, Sales No. GV.E.87.0.1.

The International Non-Proliferation Régime 1987, by David A.V. Fischer, 1987, 81p., United Nations publication, Sales No. GV.E.87.0.2.

La question de la vérification dans les négociations sur le désarmement aux Nations Unies, par Ellis Morris, 1987, 230p., publication des Nations Unies, numéro de vente: GV.F.87.0.4.
* Also available in English: *The Verification Issue in United Nations Disarmament Negotiations*, by Ellis Morris, 1987, 230p., United Nations publication, Sales No. GV.E.87.0.4.

Confidence-Building Measures in Africa, by Augustine P. Mahiga and Fidelis Nji, 1987, 16p., United Nations publication, Sales No. GV.E.87.0.5.

Disarmament: Problems Related to Outer Space, UNIDIR, 1987, 190p., United Nations publication, Sales No. GV.E.87.0.7.
* Existe également en français: *Désarmement: problèmes relatifs à l'espace extra-atmosphérique*, UNIDIR, 1987, 200p., publication des Nations Unies, numéro de vente: GV.F.87.0.7.

Interrelationship of Bilateral and Multilateral Disarmament Negotiations / Les relations entre les négociations bilatérales et multilatérales sur le désarmement, Proceedings of the Baku Conference, 2-4 June 1987 / Actes de la Conférence de Bakou, 2-4 juin 1987, 1988, 258p., United Nations publication, Sales No. GV.E/F.88.0.1, publication des Nations Unies, numéro de vente: GV.E/F.88.0.1.

Disarmament Research: Agenda for the 1990's / La recherche sur le désarmement: programme pour les années 90, Proceedings of the Sochi Conference, 22-24 March 1988 / Actes de la Conférence de Sotchi, 22-24 mars 1988, Geneva, 1988, 165p., United Nations publication, Sales No. GV.E./F.88.0.3, publication des Nations Unies: GV.E./F.88.0.3.

Conventional Disarmament in Europe, by André Brie (IIB), Andrzej Karkoszka (PISM), Manfred Müller (IIB), Helga Schirmeister (IIB), 1988, 66p., United Nations publication, Sales No. GV.E.88.0.6.

* Existe également en français: *Le désarmement classique en Europe*, par André Brie (IIB), Andrzej Karkoszka (PISM), Manfred Müller (IIB), Helga Schirmeister (IIB), 1989, 90p., publication des Nations Unies, numéro de vente: GV.E.89.0.6.

Arms Transfers and Dependence, by Christian Catrina, 1988, 409p., published for UNIDIR by Taylor & Francis (New York, London).

Les forces classiques en Europe et la maîtrise des armements, par Pierre Lellouche et Jérôme Paolini (éd.) (IFRI), 1989, 88p., publication des Nations Unies, numéro de vente: GV.F.89.0.6.

* Also available in English: *Conventional Forces and Arms Limitation in Europe*, by Pierre Lellouche and Jérôme Paolini (eds) (IFRI), 1989, 88p., United Nations publication: GV.E.89.0.6.

National Security Concepts of States: New Zealand, by Kennedy Graham, 1989, 180p., published for UNIDIR by Taylor & Francis (New York, London).

Problems and Perspectives of Conventional Disarmament in Europe, Proceedings of the Geneva Conference 23-25 January 1989, 1989, 140p., published for UNIDIR by Taylor & Francis (New York, London).

* Existe également en français: *Désarmement classique en Europe: problèmes et perspectives*, 1990, 226p., publié pour l'UNIDIR par Masson (Paris).

The Projected Chemical Weapons Convention: A Guide to the Negotiations in the Conference on Disarmament, by Thomas Bernauer, 1990, 328p., United Nations publication, Sales No. GV.E.90.0.3.

Verification: The Soviet Stance, its Past, Present and Future, by Mikhail Kokeev and Andrei Androsov, 1990, 131p., United Nations publication, Sales No. GV.E.90.0.6.

* Existe également en français: *Vérification: la position soviétique - Passé, présent et avenir*, 1990, 145p., publication des Nations Unies, numéro de vente: GV.F.90.0.6.

UNIDIR Repertory of Disarmament Research: 1990, by Chantal de Jonge Oudraat and Péricles Gasparini Alves (eds), 1990, 402p., United Nations publication, Sales No. GV.E.90.0.10.

Nonoffensive Defense: A Global Perspective, 1990, 194p., published for UNIDIR by Taylor & Francis (New York, London).

Aerial Reconnaissance for Verification of Arms Limitation Agreements - An Introduction, by Allan V. Banner, Keith W. Hall and Andrew J. Young, D.C.L., 1990, 166p., United Nations publication, Sales No. GV.E.90.0.11.

Africa, Disarmament and Security / Afrique, désarmement et sécurité, Proceedings of the Conference of African Research Institutes, 24-25 March 1990 / Actes de la Conférence des Instituts de recherche africains, 24-25 mars 1990, United Nations publication, Sales No. GV.E/F.91.0.1, publication des Nations Unies, numéro de vente: GV.E/F.91.0.1.

Peaceful and Non-Peaceful Uses of Space: Problems of Definition for the Prevention of an Arms Race, by Bhupendra Jasani (ed.), 1991, 179p., published for UNIDIR by Taylor & Francis (New York, London).

In Pursuit of a Nuclear Test Ban Treaty: A Guide to the Debate in the Conference on Disarmament, by Thomas Schmalberger, 1991, 132p., United Nations publication, Sales No. GV.E.91.0.4.

Confidence-Building Measures and International Security: The Political and Military Aspect - A Soviet Approach, by Igor Scherbak, 1991, 179p., United Nations publication, Sales No. GV.E.91.0.7.

Verification of Current Disarmament and Arms Limitation Agreements: Ways, Means and Practices, by Serge Sur (ed.), 1991, 396p., published for UNIDIR by Dartmouth (Aldershot).

* Existe également en français: *La vérification des accords sur le désarmement et la limitation des armements: moyens, méthodes et pratiques*, 1991, 406p., publication des Nations Unies, numéro de vente: GV.F.91.0.9.

The United Nations, Disarmament and Security: Evolution and Prospects, by Jayantha Dhanapala (ed.), 1991, 156p., United Nations publication, Sales No. GV.E.91.0.13.

Disarmament Agreements and Negotiations: The Economic Dimension, by Serge Sur (ed.), 1991, 228p., published for UNIDIR by Dartmouth (Aldershot).

* Existe également en français: *Dimensions économiques des négociations et accords sur le désarmement*, par Serge Sur (éd.), 1991, 211p., publication des Nations Unies, numéro de vente: GV.F.91.0.18.

Prevention of an Arms Race in Outer Space: A Guide to the Discussions in the Conference on Disarmament, by Péricles Gasparini Alves, 1991, 221p., United Nations publication, Sales No. GV.E.91.0.17.

Nuclear Issues on the Agenda of the Conference on Disarmament, by Thomas Bernauer, 1991, 108p., United Nations publication, Sales No. GV.E.91.0.16.

Economic Adjustment after the Cold War: Strategies for Conversion, by Michael Renner, 1991, 262p., published for UNIDIR by Dartmouth (Aldershot).

Verification of Disarmament or Limitation of Armaments: Instruments, Negotiations, Proposals, by Serge Sur (ed.), 1992, 267p., United Nations publication, Sales No. GV.E.92.0.10.

* Existe également en français: *Vérification du désarmement ou de la limitation des armements: instruments, négociations, propositions*, par Serge Sur (éd.), 1994, 246p., publication des Nations Unies, numéro de vente: GV.F.92.0.10.

National Security Concepts of States: Argentina, by Julio C. Carasales, 1992, 131p., United Nations publication, Sales No. GV.E.92.0.9.

* Existe également en français: *Conceptions et politiques de la République argentine en matière de sécurité*, par Julio C. Carasales, 1992, 136p., publication des Nations Unies, numéro de vente: GV.F.92.0.9.

National Security Concepts of States: Sri Lanka, by Vernon L. B. Mendis, 1992, 205p., United Nations publication, Sales No. GV.E.92.0.12.

Military Industrialization and Economic Development. Theory and Historical Case Studies, by Raimo Väyrynen, 1992, 121p., published for UNIDIR by Dartmouth (Aldershot).

European Security in the 1990s: Problems of South-East Europe, Proceedings of the Rhodes (Greece) Conference, 6-7 September 1991, by Chantal de Jonge Oudraat (ed.) / *La sécurité européenne dans les années 90: Problèmes de l'Europe du Sud-Est*, Actes de la Conférence de Rhodes (Grèce), 6-7 septembre 1991, sous la direction de Chantal de Jonge Oudraat, 1992, 219p., United Nations publication, Sales No. GV.E/F.92.0.14, publication des Nations Unies, numéro de vente: GV.E/F.92.0.14.

Disarmament and Limitation of Armaments: Unilateral Measures and Policies, Proceedings of the Paris Conference, 24 January 1992, by Serge Sur (ed.), 1992, 94p., United Nations publication, Sales No. GV.E.92.0.23

* Existe également en français: *Désarmement et limitation des armements: mesures et attitudes unilatérales*, Actes de la Conférence de Paris, 24 janvier 1992, sous la direction de Serge Sur, 1992, 103p., publication des Nations Unies, numéro de vente: GV.F.92.0.23.

Conference of Research Institutes in Asia and the Pacific, Proceedings of the Beijing (China) Conference, 23-25 March 1992, 1992, United Nations publication, Sales No. GV.E.92.0.29.

Maritime Security: The Building of Confidence, by Jozef Goldblat (ed.), 1992, 163p., United Nations publication, Sales No. GV.E.92.0.31.

Towards 1995: The Prospects for Ending the Proliferation of Nuclear Weapons, by David Fischer, 1992, 292p., published for UNIDIR by Dartmouth (Aldershot).

From Versailles to Baghdad: Post-War Armament Control of Defeated States, by Fred Tanner (ed.), 1992, 264p., United Nations publication, Sales No. GV.E.92.0.26.

Security of Third World Countries, by Jasjit Singh and Thomas Bernauer (eds), 1993, 168p., published for UNIDIR by Dartmouth (Aldershot).

Regional Approaches to Disarmament, Security and Stability, by Jayantha Dhanapala (ed.), 1993, 282p., published for UNIDIR by Dartmouth (Aldershot).

Economic Aspects of Disarmament: Disarmament as an Investment Process, by Keith Hartley, 1993, 91p., United Nations publication, Sales No. GV.E.93.0.3.

* Existe également en français: *Aspects économiques du désarmement: le désarmement en tant qu'investissement*, par Keith Hartley, 1993, 104p., publication des Nations Unies, numéro de vente: GV.F.93.0.3.

Nonmilitary Aspects of Security - A Systems Approach, by Dietrich Fischer, 1993, 222p., published for UNIDIR by Dartmouth (Aldershot).

Conference of Latin American and Caribbean Research Institutes, Proceedings of the São Paulo Conference, 2-3 December 1991, by Péricles Gasparini Alves (ed.), 1993, 202p., United Nations publication, Sales No. GV.E.93.0.8.

The Chemistry of Regime Formation: Explaining International Cooperation for a Comprehensive Ban on Chemical Weapons, by Thomas Bernauer, 1993, 480p., published for UNIDIR by Dartmouth (Aldershot).

Civil Space Systems: Implications for International Security, by Stephen Doyle, 1994, 271p., published for UNIDIR by Dartmouth (Aldershot).

Nuclear Deterrence: Problems and Perspectives in the 1990's, by Serge Sur (ed.), 1993, 173p., United Nations publication, Sales No. GV.E.93.0.16.

Conference of Research Institutes in the Middle East, Proceedings of the Cairo Conference, 18-19 April 1993, by Chantal de Jonge Oudraat (ed.), 1994, 132p., United Nations publication, Sales No. GV.E.94.0.13.

Disarmament and Arms Limitation Obligations: Problems of Compliance and Enforcement, by Serge Sur (ed.), 1994, 296p., published for UNIDIR by Dartmouth (Aldershot)

  * Existe également en français: *Obligations en matière de désarmement et de limitation des armements: problèmes de respect et mesures d'imposition*, sous la direction de Serge Sur, 1995, 430p., publication des Nations Unies, numéro de vente: GV.F.95.0.27.

European Security in the 1990s: Challenges and Perspectives, by Victor-Yves Ghebali and Brigitte Sauerwein, Avant Propos by Serge Sur, 1995, 230p., United Nations publication, Sales No. GV.E.94.0.28.

Arms and Technology Transfers: Security and Economic Considerations Among Importing and Exporting States, Proceedings of the Geneva (Switzerland) Conference, 14-15 February 1994, by Sverre Lodgaard and Robert L. Pfaltzgraff (eds), 1995, 287p., United Nations publication, Sales No. GV.E.95.0.10.

Nuclear Policies in Northeast Asia, Proceedings of the Seoul (South Korea) Conference, 25-27 May 1994, by Andrew Mack (ed.), 1995, 263p., United Nations publication, Sales No. GV.E.95.0.8.

Building Confidence in Outer Space Activities: CSBMs and Earth-to-Space Monitoring, by Péricles Gasparini Alves (ed.), 1995, 357p., published for UNIDIR by Dartmouth (Aldershot)

Disarmament and Conflict Resolution Project - Managing Arms in Peace Processes: Somalia, by Clement Adibe, 1995, 242p., United Nations publication, Sales No. GV.E.95.0.20.

Disarmament and Conflict Resolution Project - Managing Arms in Peace Processes: Rhodesia/Zimbabwe, by Jeremy Ginifer, 1995, 127p., United Nations publication, Sales No. GV.E.95.0.28.

Research Papers / Travaux de recherche

No. 1 -   *Une approche juridique de la vérification en matière de désarmement ou de limitation des armements*, par Serge Sur, septembre 1988, 70p., publication des Nations Unies, numéro de vente: GV.F.88.0.5.

   * Also available in English: *A Legal Approach to Verification in Disarmament or Arms Limitation*, 1988, 72p., United Nations publication, Sales No. GV.E.88.0.5.

No. 2 -   *Problèmes de vérification du Traité de Washington du 8 décembre 1987 sur l'élimination des missiles à portée intermédiaire*, par Serge Sur, octobre 1988, 64p., publication des Nations Unies, numéro de vente: GV.F.88.0.7.

   * Also available in English: *Verification Problems of the Washington Treaty on the Elimination of Intermediate-Range Missiles*, by Serge Sur, October 1988, 62p., United Nations publication, Sales No. GV.E.88.0.7.

No. 3 -   *Mesures de confiance de la CSCE: documents et commentaires*, par Victor-Yves Ghebali, mars 1989, 112p., publication des Nations Unies, numéro de vente: GV.F.89.0.5.

   * Also available in English: *Confidence-Building Measures within the CSCE Process: Paragraph-by-Paragraph Analysis of the Helsinki and Stockholm Régimes*, by Victor-Yves Ghebali, March 1989, 110p., United Nations publication, Sales No. GV.E.89.0.5.

No. 4 -   *The Prevention of the Geographical Proliferation of Nuclear Weapons: Nuclear-Free Zones and Zones of Peace in the Southern Hemisphere*, by Edmundo Fujita, April 1989, 52p., United Nations publication, Sales No. GV.E. 89.0.8.

   * Existe également en français: *La prévention de la prolifération géographique des armes nucléaires: zones exemptes d'armes nucléaires et zones de paix dans l'hémisphère Sud*, par Edmundo Fujita, avril 1989, 61p., publication des Nations Unies, numéro de vente: GV.F.89.0.8.

No. 5 -   *The Future Chemical Weapons Convention and its Organization: The Executive Council*, by Thomas Bernauer, May 1989, 34p., United Nations publication, Sales No. GV.E.89.0.7.

   * Existe également en français: *La future convention sur les armes chimiques et son organisation: le Conseil exécutif*, par Thomas Bernauer, mai 1989, 42p., publication des Nations Unies, numéro de vente: GV.F.89.0.7.

No. 6 -   *Bibliographical Survey of Secondary Literature on Military Expenditures*, November 1989, 39p. United Nations publication, Sales No. GV.E.89.0.14.

No. 7 -   *Science and Technology: Between Civilian and Military Research and Development - Armaments and development at variance*, by Marek Thee, November 1990, 23p., United Nations publication, Sales No. GV.E.90.0.14.

No. 8 -   *Esquisse pour un nouveau paysage européen*, par Eric Remacle, octobre 1990, 178p., publication des Nations Unies, numéro de vente: GV.F.91.0.2.

No. 9 -   *The Third Review of the Biological Weapons Convention: Issues and Proposals*, by Jozef Goldblat and Thomas Bernauer, April 1991, 78p., United Nations publication, Sales No. GV.E.91.0.5.

No. 10 -   *Disarmament, Environment, and Development and their Relevance to the Least Developed Countries*, by Arthur H. Westing, October 1991, 108p., United Nations publication, Sales No. GV.E.91.0.19.

No. 11 -   *The Implications of IAEA Inspections under Security Council Resolution 687*, by Eric Chauvistré, February 1992, 72p., United Nations publication, Sales No. GV.E.92.0.6.

No. 12 -   *La Résolution 687 (3 avril 1991) du Conseil de sécurité dans l'affaire du Golfe: problèmes de rétablissement et de garantie de la paix*, par Serge Sur, 1992, 65p., publication des Nations Unies, numéro de vente: GV.F.92.0.8.

             * Also available in English: *Security Council Resolution 687 of 3 April 1991 in the Gulf Affair: Problems of Restoring and Safeguarding Peace*, by Serge Sur, 1992, 65p., United Nations publication, Sales No. GV.E.92.0.8.

No. 13 -   *The Non-Proliferation Treaty: How to Remove the Residual Threats*, by Jozef Goldblat, 1992, 36p., United Nations publication, Sales No. GV.E.92.0.25.

             * Existe également en français: *Le Traité sur la non-prolifération: comment parer les menaces*, par Jozef Goldblat, 1993, 40p., publication des Nations Unies, numéro de vente: GV.F.92.0.25.

No. 14 -   *Ukraine's Non-Nuclear Option*, by Victor Batiouk, 1992, 34p., United Nations publication, Sales No. GV.E.92.0.28.

No. 15 -   *Access to Outer Space Technologies: Implications for International Security*, by Péricles Gasparini Alves, 1992, 160p., United Nations publication, Sales No. GV.E.92.0.30.

No. 16 -   *Regional Security and Confidence-Building Processes: The Case of Southern Africa in the 1990s*, by Solomon M. Nkiwane, 1993, United Nations publication, Sales No. GV.E.93.0.6.

No. 17 -   *Technical Problems in the Verification of a Ban on Space Weapons*, by Stanislav Rodionov, 1993, 104p., United Nations publication, Sales No. GV.E.93.0.12.

No. 18 -   *Index to the Chemical Weapons Convention*, by A. Walter Dorn, 1993, 59p., United Nations publication, Sales No. GV.E.93.0.13.

No. 19 -   *Migration and Population Change in Europe*, by John Salt, 1993, 86p., United Nations publication, Sales No. GV.E.93.0.14.

No. 20 -   *La sécurité européenne dans les années 90, défis et perspectives. La dimension écologique*, par Jean-Daniel Clavel, 1993, 40p., publication des Nations Unies, numéro de vente: GV.F.93.0.15.

No. 21 -   *Les minorités nationales et le défi de la sécurité en Europe*, par Dominique Rosenberg, 1993, 45p., publication des Nations Unies, numéro de vente: GV.F.93.0.21.

No. 22 - *Crisis in the Balkans*, by Ali L. Karaosmanoglu, 1993, 22p., United Nations publication, Sales No. GV.E.93.0.22.

No. 23 - *La transition vers l'économie de marché des pays "ex de l'Est"*, par Louis Pilandon, 1994, 90p., publication des Nations Unies, numéro de vente: GV.F.94.0.3.

No. 24 - *Le désarmement et la conversion de l'industrie militaire en Russie*, par Sonia Ben Ouagrham, 1993, 110p., publication des Nations Unies, numéro de vente: GV.F.94.0.4.

No. 25 - *Development of Russian National Security Policies: Military Reform*, by Andrei Raevsky, 1994, 48p., United Nations publication, Sales No. GV.E.94.0.5.

No. 26 - *National Security and Defence Policy of the Lithuanian State*, by Gintaras Tamulaitis, 1994, 66p., United Nations publication, Sales No. GV.E.94.0.11.

No. 27 - *Le défi de la sécurité régionale en Afrique après la guerre froide: vers la diplomatie préventive et la sécurité collective*, par Anatole N. Ayissi, 1994, 138p., publication des Nations Unies, numéro de vente: GV.F.94.0.17.

No. 28 - *Russian Approaches to Peacekeeping Operations*, by A. Raevsky and I.N. Vorob'ev, 1994, 182p., United Nations publication, Sales No. GV.E.94.0.18.

No. 29 - *Une approche coopérative de la non-prolifération nucléaire: l'exemple de l'Argentine et du Brésil*, par Thierry Riga, 1994, 100p., publication des Nations Unies, numéro de vente: GV.F.94.0.22.

No. 30 - *The CTBT and Beyond*, by Herbert F. York, 1994, 21p., United Nations publication, Sales No. GV.E.94.0.27.

No. 31 - *Halting the Production of Fissile Material for Nuclear Weapons*, by Thérèse Delpech, Lewis A. Dunn, David Fischer and Rakesh Sood, 1994, 70p., United Nations publication, Sales No. GV.E.94.0.29.

No. 32 - *Verification of a Comprehensive Test Ban Treaty from Space - A Preliminary Study*, by Bhupendra Jasani, 1994, 58p., United Nations publication, Sales No. GV.E.94.0.30.

No. 33 - *Nuclear Disarmament and Non-Proliferation in Northeast Asia*, by Yong-Sup Han, 1995, 83p., United Nations publication, Sales No. GV.E.95.0.3.

No. 34 - *Small Arms and Intra-State Conflicts*, by Swadesh Rana, 1995, 52p., United Nations publication, Sales No. GV.E.95.0.7.

No. 35 - *The Missing Link? Nuclear Proliferation and the International Mobility of Russian Nuclear Experts*, by Dorothy S. Zinberg, 1995, 45p., United Nations publication, Sales No. GV.E.95.0.18.

No. 36 - *Guardian Soldier: On the Future Role and Use of Armed Forces*, by Gustav Däniker, 1995, 141p., United Nations publication, Sales No. GV.E.95.0.19.

No. 37 - *National Threat Perceptions in the Middle East*, by James Leonard, Shmuel Limone, Abdel Monem Said Aly, Yezid Sayigh, the Center for Strategic Studies (University of Jordan), Abdulhay Sayed and Saleh Al-Mani, 1995, 109p., United Nations publication, Sales No. GV.E.95.0.24.

UNIDIR Newsletter / Lettre de l'UNIDIR
(quarterly / trimestrielle)

Vol. 1, No. 1, March/Mars 1988, *Disarmament-Development/Désarmement-Développement*, 16p.

No. 2, June/Juin 1988, *Research in Africa/La recherche en Afrique*, 28p.

No. 3, September/Septembre 1988, *Conventional Armaments Limitation and CBMs in Europe/Limitation des armements classiques et mesures de confiance en Europe*, 32p.

No. 4, December/Décembre 1988, *Research in Asia and the Pacific/La recherche en Asie et dans le Pacifique*, 40p.

Vol. 2, No. 1, March/Mars 1989, *Chemical Weapons: Research Projects and Publications/Armes chimiques: projets de recherche et publications*, 24p.

No. 2, June/Juin 1989, *Research in Latin America and the Caribbean/La recherche en Amérique latine et dans les Caraïbes*, 32p.

No. 3, September/Septembre 1989, *Outer Space/L'espace extra-atmosphérique*, 32p.

No. 4, December/Décembre 1989, *Research in Eastern Europe/La recherche en Europe de l'Est*, 48p.

Vol. 3, No. 1, March/Mars 1990, *Verification of Disarmament Agreements/La vérification des accords sur le désarmement*, 48p.

No. 2, June/Juin 1990, *Research in North America/La recherche en Amérique du Nord*, 72p.

No. 3, September/Septembre 1990, *Nuclear Non-Proliferation/La non-prolifération nucléaire*, 43p.

No. 4, December/Décembre 1990, *Research in Western and Northern Europe (I)/ La recherche en Europe de l'Ouest et en Europe du Nord (I)*, 72p.

Vol. 4, No. 1, March/Mars 1991, *Research in Western and Northern Europe (II)/La recherche en Europe de l'Ouest et en Europe du Nord (II)*, 72p.

No. 2, June/Juin 1991, *Biological Weapons/Armes biologiques*, 40p.

No. 3, September/Septembre 1991, *Naval and Maritime Issues/Questions navales et maritimes*, 54p.

No. 4, December/Décembre 1991, *Bilateral (US-USSR) Agreements and Negotiations/Accords et négociations bilatéraux (EU-URSS)*, 52p.

Vol. 5, No. 1, April/Avril 1992, *Conference on Disarmament/La Conférence du désarmement*, 63p.

No. 18, June/Juin 1992, *Disarmament - Environment - Security/Désarmement - Environnement - Sécurité*, 52p.

No. 19, September/Septembre 1992, *Economic Aspects of Disarmament/Aspects économiques du désarmement*, 66p.

No. 20, December/Décembre 1992, *The Chemical Weapons Convention/La Convention sur les armes chimiques*, 100p.

Vol. 6, No. 21, March/Mars 1993, *Research in the Middle East/La recherche au Moyen et Proche Orient*, 70p.

No. 22-23, June-September/Juin-septembre 1993, *START and Nuclear Disarmament: Problems of Implementation/START et le désarmement nucléaire: problèmes d'exécution*, 101p.

No. 24, December/Décembre 1993, *Peace-Keeping, Peace-Making and Peace Enforcement/Maintien, construction et imposition de la paix*, 88p.

Vol. 7, No. 25, March-April/Mars-avril 1994, *Research in Eastern Europe and in the Newly Independent States/Recherche en Europe de l'Est et dans les nouveaux Etats indépendants*, 70p.

No. 26/27, June-September/Juin-septembre 1994, *Non-Proliferation/Non-prolifération*, 91p.

Vol. 8, No. 28/29, December 1994-May 1995/Décembre 1994-mai 1995, *Land Mines and the CCW Review Conference/Les mines terrestres et la Conférence d'examen de la Convention sur certaines armes classiques*

No. 30/95, June 1995-September 1995, *Information Technology and International Security*

No. 31/95, October 1995-December 1995, *Nuclear Disarmament: What is Next?*

How to Obtain UNIDIR Publications

1. *UNIDIR publications followed by a United Nations Sales Number (GV.E... or GV.F...) can be obtained from UNIDIR or from bookstores and distributors throughout the world. Consult your bookstore or write to United Nations, Sales Section, Palais des Nations, CH-1211 Geneva 10, Switzerland, Phone (41.22) 917.26.12, Fax (41.22) 740.09.31, or United Nations, Sales Section, UN Headquarters, New York, New York 10017, USA. The UNIDIR Newsletter is available at a voluntary subscription price of US $ 25 a year.*

2. *UNIDIR publications published by Dartmouth can be obtained through Dartmouth Publishing Company Limited, Gower House, Croft Road, Aldershot, Hampshire, GU11 3HR, England, Phone (01252) 33.15.51, Fax (01252) 34.44.05.*

3. *UNIDIR publications published by Taylor and Francis can be obtained through Taylor and Francis Ltd, Rankine Road, Basingstoke, Hants RG24 8PR, England, Phone (01256) 84.03.66, Fax (01256) 47.94.38.*